Introduction to Logic and Critical Thinking

Second Edition

Introduction to Logic and Critical Thinking

Second Edition

Merrilee H. Salmon
University of Pittsburgh

Under the general editorship of
Robert J. Fogelin
Dartmouth College

HBJ

Harcourt Brace Jovanovich, Publishers

San Diego   New York   Chicago   Austin   Washington, D.C.
London   Sydney   Tokyo   Toronto

Requests for permission to make copies of any part of the work should be mailed to: Permissions, Harcourt Brace Jovanovich, Publishers, Orlando, Florida 32887.

ISBN: 0-15-543062-9

Library of Congress Catalog Card Number: 88-82147

Printed in the United States of America.

Preface to the First Edition

This book is designed to help students who are beginning college to acquire a deeper understanding of the relationships between logic and language and to increase their skills in critical thinking. Students must be equipped with these skills if they are to be able to recognize situations in which unsupported assertions require justification, to analyze and assess the arguments they encounter in everyday life, and to formulate and present cogent arguments of their own.

Motivation for achieving these goals is provided by means of a variety of examples and exercises that show the usefulness of critical-thinking skills in everyday life. Students are asked to analyze exactly what claims are being made in various contexts and to determine whether reasons are given or should be given to support the claims they are asked to accept. Once assertions that require support have been distinguished from arguments (in which reasons are given for claims), three categories of argument types are distinguished: deductive arguments, inductive arguments, and fallacies. Standards for evaluating various types of arguments are presented. Many examples and exercises focus on the reconstruction of arguments in ordinary language.

A special feature of this text is the careful analysis of inductive reasoning prior to the treatment of deductive arguments. Several reasons can be given for this reversal of what has become the standard order in introductory texts.

- Inductive reasoning based on samples, arguments from analogy, statistical syllogisms, and arguments that attempt to establish causal connections have already been encountered frequently by students in their roles as consumers, citizens, and problem-solvers. Interesting real-life examples can be used to illustrate and explain the standards for evaluating these pervasive forms of argument.
- In their examination of familiar types of inductive reasoning, students gradually gain sensitivity to the structural features of arguments and to such important logical distinctions as the difference between universal and statistical generalizations. They are thus better able to appreciate the value of the more formal treatment of deductive reasoning that follows the analysis of inductive arguments.
- When inductive arguments are presented in this way, students are less likely to be left with the impression that only deductive arguments are really effective and that inductive reasoning is an inferior alternative to be relied on when nothing better is available.

After 16 years of teaching introductory logic courses to small groups of students and to large lecture groups with the assistance of teaching fellows, I am convinced of the value of treating induction before deduction. However, the text is designed so that it can be used by instructors who prefer the more usual order. Chapters 1, 2, 6, 8 (followed by Appendix 1), 9, and 10 may be followed by Chapters 3, 4, 5, 7, and 11.

Another unusual feature of this text is its treatment of fallacies. After a brief general account of fallacies is presented in Chapter 2, particular types of fallacies are addressed throughout the text within the context of analyzing the correct forms of inductive and deductive arguments that various fallacies resemble. In addition, some theoretical background is supplied to show that fallacious reasoning frequently involves systematic types of error. One example is the belief that causes must somehow *resemble* their effects; another is the common tendency to overlook solid statistical data when presented with some particularly vivid information that conflicts with the data. Such errors are not the result of carelessness, individual psychological quirks, or an intent to deceive. This approach to fallacies fosters a deeper understanding of correct as well as incorrect forms of reasoning.

The language used in the text is as simple and direct as possible. Technical vocabulary is introduced only when it is required and is redefined in Review sections at the end of each chapter. Formal methods are employed when they are useful for clarification, and even those students who begin the course with an aversion to formalization ("math anxiety") can usually master these methods with little difficulty. Instructors who wish to minimize attention to formal methods can omit the material on probabilities (Chapter 5 and Section VI of Chapter 7), the formal proof method in Appendix 1 and Section VII on logic and computers in Chapter 8 without loss of continuity.

All of the material in the text can be covered comfortably in a semester course that meets four times a week. If the course is fast-paced, most of the material can be covered in a semester course that meets three times a week. Fewer hours of class time may require more selective coverage, but the chapters and sections are designed so that this can be done easily. For example, Chapter 5, Section VI of Chapter 7, Section VII of Chapter 8, and the Appendix may be omitted. If time is short, Section IV on Venn diagrams in Chapter 9 may also be omitted, inasmuch as an alternative set of rules is presented for evaluating syllogistic arguments.

Over the years of teaching logic and thinking about how it should be taught, I have received much help from those who were my teachers, teaching assistants, and students. Although they cannot all be named, it is a pleasure to acknowledge their contributions. Special thanks go to Robert Fogelin at Dartmouth College, and to the reviewers, who offered valuable criticisms of a draft of this text: Donald Anderson, Los Angeles Pierce College; Paul Bassen, California State University, Hayward; Leslie Burkholder, Carnegie–Mellon University; Charles Chastain, University of Illinois at Chicago Circle; Allan S. Gnagy, University of Kansas; Russell Kahl, San Francisco State University; Walter H. O'Briant, University of Georgia; Ric Otte, University of California at Santa Cruz; Elliott R. Sober, University of Wisconsin; Eric Stiffler, Western Illinois University; and Robert Wengert, University of Illinois at Champaign-Urbana. Bill McLane of Harcourt Brace Jovanovich provided expert advice and editorial assistance for which I am most grateful.

Finally, my deepest thanks go to my husband, Wesley C. Salmon, for his logical expertise, generous advice, and staunch support.

Merrilee H. Salmon

Preface to the Second Edition

This edition has been revised and expanded in a number of ways. It contains many more examples and exercises than did the first edition. Solutions to about 20 percent of the exercises are included in a section at the end of the book so that students can check their own work. Appendix 2 is new. It lists the fallacies treated in the book, along with brief definitions and page references to the discussion of each fallacy. This makes it easier for instructors who do not cover the entire text to include discussion of any fallacy they deem important.

In Chapter 3, the discussion of arguments based on samples now follows the treatment of analogical arguments and statistical syllogisms to provide a more natural transition to the treatment of causal arguments in Chapter 4. In addition, some nontechnical material on sample size and margin of error has been added to Chapter 3.

The overall approach of treating inductive arguments before deductive arguments has not been altered in this edition. Special care has been taken, however, to see that the materials in the book are suitable for those instructors who prefer to start with deductive reasoning. After beginning with the first two chapters, courses may proceed with the materials on inductive logic (Chapters 3 through 7). In this sequence, Chapter 6, which introduces deductive conditional arguments, prepares students for the hypothetico-deductive reasoning encountered in Chapter 7. Alternatively, the materials on deductive logic (Chapters 6, 8, 9, and 10) can be introduced immediately after Chapter 2. Chapter 11, on definitions and the language of arguments, can be taken up immediately after Chapter 2, instead of at the end of the course, without loss of continuity.

Many changes have been made in the Second Edition which should improve its accuracy and clarity. For the suggestions that prodded me to make these changes, I am very grateful to generous readers. I especially want to acknowledge the help received from Jarret Leplin, University of North Carolina at Greensboro; Bruce Paternoster, University of Evansville; Charles Kielkopf, The Ohio State University; Martin Curd, Purdue University; Gale Justin, California State University, Sacramento; Spencer Wertz, Texas Christian University; Richard B. Angell, Wayne State University; Wayne Davis, Georgetown University; and Saul Traiger, Occidental College. Charlotte Ashby Broome deserves special thanks for preparing the Index to the Second Edition.

Merrilee H. Salmon

Contents

C H A P T E R   1

Introduction to Arguments

I. INTRODUCTION
II. ARGUMENTS
III. RECOGNIZING ARGUMENTS
IV. EXTENDED ARGUMENTS
V. RECONSTRUCTING ARGUMENTS
    1. Incompletely Stated Arguments
    2. Extracting the Essentials of an Argument from Its Surrounding Context
VI. REVIEW
VII. EXERCISES

C H A P T E R   2

Deductive Arguments, Inductive Arguments, and Fallacies

I. INTRODUCTION
II. DEDUCTIVE ARGUMENTS
III. INDUCTIVE ARGUMENTS
IV. FALLACIES
V. REVIEW
VI. EXERCISES

C H A P T E R   3

A Closer Look at Inductive Arguments

I. INTRODUCTION
II. STATISTICAL SYLLOGISMS
    1. Forms of Statistical Syllogisms
    2. Standards for the Strength of Statistical Syllogisms

C H A P T E R   4

Causal Arguments

C H A P T E R   5

Probabilities and Inductive Logic 145

C H A P T E R   6

Deductive Reasoning: Conditional Arguments 175

C H A P T E R 11

Paying Special Attention to the Language of Arguments: Definitions

323

A P P E N D I X 1

Proof Method for Truth-Functional Logic

342

A P P E N D I X   2

Index of Fallacies   354

Introduction to Arguments

CHAPTER 1

I. INTRODUCTION

"Don't believe everything you hear!" is advice that you have probably received, and given to others, more than once. That advice is not just a warning against liars. Even when we don't doubt people's honesty, sometimes it makes sense to question what they say. Suppose, for example, you want to buy a stylus for your record player. The only store in town that sells them is far away. Your friend says that the store always stocks the stylus. But you don't want to go there and not find it, so you call to check. After the salesclerk looks over the stock, he tells you that they have it.

When you make that phone call, you are seeking *evidence* for your friend's *assertion* that the store has the stylus. When the clerk says that there are some on the shelf, he supports your friend's assertion with *verbal evidence*. Verbal evidence consists of sentences which, if true, are reasons for believing some other sentence. The clerk's assertion that the store has the stylus is, in turn, supported by *physical evidence*. He sees it on the shelf. In this situation, though not always, verbal evidence is a description of some physical evidence.

Suppose, to take another example, that you want to go to a rock concert on the Fourth of July, and plan to take a bus to the arena. Your father, who works near the arena, rides a bus to work regularly, and tells you that the buses run every ten minutes. Because you would hate to miss any of the concert, you find a bus schedule with the exact times the bus stops near your house. You learn the buses run only once an hour on holidays. Here again, you have obtained verbal evidence (written, in this case, rather than spoken), but this time the evidence fails to support the assertion made by your father. He wasn't lying—he did not intend to deceive you—he just forgot that the holiday bus schedule is different from the daily schedule.

Gathering evidence and determining whether it supports or undermines assertions are two aspects of *critical thinking*.

Critical thinking also involves paying careful attention to what we hear and read so that we can understand and respond appropriately. We use language primarily to communicate with one another, and communication takes many forms. We engage in small talk just to "stay in touch" with others. We express our feelings of joy, sorrow, sympathy, anger, hope, and fear in language. We ask questions, make requests, and issue commands. We also use language to convey information. Normally, we convey information by asserting declarative sentences, such as "Thirty students are enrolled in the critical thinking class," or "The college volleyball team has nine scheduled games this year, but only three of them are home games."

We should seek evidence when it is important to know whether information is correct. In general, we prefer to be well informed instead of mistaken. But it should be clear that more is at stake than a desire to be well informed. We *act* on the basis of our beliefs, and what we do can have important consequences.

Knowing when to seek evidence requires sensitivity to the context in which words are spoken or written. In some contexts, it is silly to ask for evidence. A complaint about the weather, for example, usually just opens a conversation; asking for evidence in such circumstances could be done jokingly, but not seriously.

When your friend tells you that her head hurts or that chocolate ice cream is wonderful, she is expressing how she feels, and a request for evidence is not appropriate. In another context, however, say a survey conducted by a company selling pain killers or ice cream, seeking evidence to support what people say about their pains and preferences makes sense.

Questions, requests, directives, and commands do not usually require evidence. When someone at the dinner table asks for the salt, information may be conveyed (perhaps the food needs salt), but the person who requests salt does not *assert* that the food needs salt, and it would be odd to ask for evidence.

Responding to songs or poetry by seeking evidence is not, in most contexts, suitable. When we read an epic poem, such as Homer's *Iliad,* we normally do so to savor the poem's language, to commiserate with heroic characters' trials, and to admire their triumphs. That is to say, we are concerned with the expressive content of the poem rather than the information it presents about what might have happened in the eastern reaches of the Mediterranean some 3,300 years ago. We respond aesthetically without raising the question of whether Helen of Troy really was kidnapped (or even whether Helen existed) and whether this caused a war between the Greeks and Trojans. The *Iliad* is a work of art, and as such, can be enjoyed and appraised on those terms without raising questions of factual accuracy.

We *can,* of course, also ask whether or not the events described in Homer's *Iliad* actually occurred, but then we are reading the *Iliad* as a (possible) historical document, rather than responding to it as epic poetry. In fact, many expeditions have been sent forth to try to find evidence for the Trojan War, using Homer's work as a guide. Scholars have found some physical evidence. They have also deciphered a form of writing, Linear B, that may eventually yield verbal evidence for the Trojan war. In the meantime, scholars continue to debate whether and to what extent the *Iliad* was based on actual historical events, and to use the poem as a set of clues to guide their research. These scholars are focusing on the information contained in the poem, rather than on its expressive features. In this sense, they are no longer reading it as poetry, but as history, and if the *Iliad* is treated as a historical document, it is reasonable to ask for evidence.

As these examples show, whether or not it is appropriate to seek evidence depends on context—either the situation in which something is said, or the context of the (later) assessment of what has been said. Context also influences the amount and type of evidence that is required. If a stranger tells me there is a fire in the office building where I'm working, I won't bother to acquire much evidence; I will get out as soon as possible. If that same stranger tells me a building where I used to work burned today, I might turn on my radio, buy a newspaper, or go to see the building before I accept what I have been told. Gathering evidence takes time and sometimes money. Frequently, there are other costs as well, such as offending people by questioning their accuracy or invading their privacy. Before we decide how much to spend on the collection of evidence, we have to balance those costs against the cost of being wrong.

Besides the abilities already mentioned—figuring out what language means in various contexts, determining when evidence is required to support assertions, and marshalling evidence when it is required—critical thinking also involves other abilities: being able to think coherently, to comprehend instructions and advice, to formulate problems and solve them, to judge whether or not bits of information are relevant to an issue, to survey possible outcomes of decisions and plans, and to decide how to make the best choices from those available. In this text, we will be especially concerned with understanding the relationship between assertions and verbal evidence for those assertions, but we will also be concerned with improving the other critical thinking skills mentioned here.

Although you probably have not studied critical thinking in a class before, you have surely engaged in critical thinking. At one time or another, for example, you have probably thought critically about advertising claims that promise quick and easy weight loss or that guarantee to teach techniques that will make you irresistible to members of the opposite sex. If you are like most people, you distrust politicians' assertions about what they can accomplish if they are elected. You probably wouldn't take the word of a used-car salesman, without additional evidence, that the car you are interested in buying was owned by a little old lady who drove it only on Sundays.

Critical thinking comes easily in the cases just mentioned, but we are less concerned with evidence when information comes from friends and various "authorities," such as teachers, television newscasters, and newspaper reporters. Trustworthiness of the source inclines us to accept what it says. A trusted source, however, does not always override the need for further evidence, as the examples earlier about the bus schedule and the search for a stylus showed. We should insist on evidence when we plan to act on the basis of the information and when our actions have important—and possibly harmful—consequences. If a trusted friend tells you that a powdered substance produces a feeling of euphoria and well-being when inhaled, with no unpleasant side effects, you—knowing the risks—will be wise to seek further evidence before trying the substance yourself. The amount of evidence you require before you act depends in part on the type of consequences for you, or others, if the assertion turns out to be false.

To be critical thinkers, we must also understand the difference between *evidence* and other devices that people sometimes use to make us believe what they say. Advertisers are notorious for convincing people that what they say about their products is true. Some present physical evidence, such as washing dirty sweatsocks in different detergents and showing the results on television. Other advertisers describe tests performed by "independent laboratories." These descriptions constitute verbal evidence for the value of the product. Or, advertisers may present another type of verbal evidence in the form of testimonials from satisfied customers.

Many advertisements, however, contain no evidence. Instead, an ad may show beautiful, athletic, fashionably dressed people cheerfully smoking the advertised cigarettes, or drinking the advertised brand of gin. These ads use psychological pressure in place of evidence to persuade us that their product is superior to others.

Threats, which can be either subtle or blunt, are another nonevidential way of getting people to believe things. Political campaigns often play on the fears of voters by showing scenes of violence and proclaiming that the candidate will reduce crime in the streets. This tactic exhibits the candidate's concern with crime. Pictures or descriptions of violent crime, however, are obviously not *evidence* that the candidate can do anything about crime. Nevertheless, people are often convinced by such techniques that the candidate will stamp out crime.

It is not always wrong to use means other than evidence to persuade people. It may not be improper, for example, to appeal to people's sense of compassion to persuade them to aid victims of poverty or oppression. But it is not appropriate to believe, on the basis of such compassion alone, that a particular group is responsible for the oppression, for example, or that a particular type of aid is more appropriate than some other type, or that the democratic government of the impoverished people will collapse if the aid is withheld. It is a serious intellectual mistake to fail to distinguish between nonevidential persuasion and evidence that supports an assertion. This mistake is called *committing a fallacy.* Avoiding fallacies is another aspect of critical thinking.

The expression *critical thinking* thus refers to many different abilities and activities. Because this is so, it is hard to define the term precisely. Nevertheless, we can begin to understand what it means when we realize that thinking critically involves analyzing what is said, assessing it carefully, seeking evidence if this is appropriate, putting various pieces of information together in a coherent way, attempting to avoid mistakes in thinking, questioning things that do not make sense, and making decisions and plans in the light of the best available information.

Sometimes, just being aware of the pitfalls of not thinking critically is enough to spur us to more careful thought. As in many other areas of life, however, practice and exercise are the best way to improve critical thinking skills.

Exercises

1. Suppose a friend tells you there is a special unadvertised sale of tapes and records at a nearby store. She says that you can pick up some incredible bargains if you go quickly. You are not busy, you have a few dollars, and you share your friend's taste in music. Should you try to get evidence in support of your friend's assertion before shopping? Why or why not? *No – good friends and you can't check up on an unadvertised sale*

2. You read the following in a nonfiction travel book, *Prospero's Cell,* about the Greek island Corcyra (Corfu):

> Climb to Vigla in the time of cherries and look down. You will see that the island lies against the mainland roughly in the form of a sickle. On the landward side you have a great bay, noble and serene, and almost completely landlocked. Northward the tip of the sickle almost touches Albania and here the troubled blue of the Ionian is sucked harshly between ribs of limestone and spits of sand. Kalamai fronts the Albanian foothills, and into it the water races as into a swimming pool; a milky ferocious green when the north wind curdles. it.
>
> —L. Durrell

Durrell says that from a given vantage point (Vigla) in summer (the time of cherries), you can see the sickle shape of the island. He describes (makes further assertions about) Corcyra's location with respect to surrounding geographical features, states, and towns. His language is expressive (for example, "the troubled blue . . . is sucked harshly between ribs of limestone") and is designed to convey the feelings of both serenity and untamed beauty that the island has inspired.

    a. Does the author offer any evidence for the assertions he makes? *no*

    b. Suppose you are reading this book to acquire some information about the island because you hope to visit it as a tourist someday. Should you gather evidence to support the accuracy of Durrell's descriptions? *yes*

    c. Suppose you are a military commander who plans an invasion of the island. Should you seek evidence for the truth of Durrell's descriptions? *yes*

3. You read the following account of *Amanita verna,* a type of wild mushroom, in *The Mushroom Hunter's Field Guide,* by Professor A. H. Smith, a recognized expert on mushrooms. He describes its appearance, which is similar to mushrooms you buy at the grocery; it is pure white (when fresh) and very beautiful. Then he says:

> "Edibility: Deadly poisonous. The symptoms are delayed, making applications of first aid almost useless. Never eat a white *Amanita*."

    a. What assertions does Dr. Smith make in the quoted passage? *deadly*

    b. Is "Never eat a white *Amanita*," an assertion? *no*

    c. Would you seek further evidence before following Dr. Smith's advice? *no*

4. Taken from "Make Your Soil Smile," *Organic Gardening,* March, 1987. The method of shallow cultivation is offered as an alternative to the use of poisonous herbicides to control weeds.

> Shallow cultivation is an effective way to control weeds. Experiments have shown that hoeing or tilling only the top 2–4 inches of soil *before seed sprouts can set* eventually exhausts most of the vast supply of weed seeds that lie dormant in the soil.
>
>   —P. H. Johnson

    a. What assertions does the author make? *There's a way to control weeds*

    b. Is any evidence (physical or verbal) presented?

    c. If you are a backyard gardener who is trying to save money and avoid poisons, would you seek further evidence before using shallow cultivation instead of herbicides to control weeds? *yes*

    d. If you are a truck farmer whose only income depends on the success of your crops, would you seek further evidence that shallow cultivation is an effective means of weed control? *yes*

5. Taken from an ad for a management consultant firm:

> Whatever your problem, I'll solve it. Over two thousand men and women, doctors, lawyers, executives, have invested the time, money and effort to create a breakthrough in business, career, social life.

a. What assertions are made here? *He can solve your problems*

b. Is any evidence offered? Should you seek any before you invest your time, money, and effort in a consultation with this firm? Can you suggest how to acquire evidence? *no, yes, call Better Business Bureau*

6. Taken from a story in a college newspaper, the *Arizona Daily Wildcat:*

> A comparison of annual rates of four major insurance companies reveals that [the costs of] identical automobile insurance policies for college students vary by as much as $200. [The comparison, described later in the same story, consisted of telephone interviews with insurance agents from the four companies. The reporter inquired about rates for a 20-year-old male college student, who had no history of automobile accidents; she specified the automobile make, model, and year in each case.] So it pays to shop around and research the various types of coverage in order to get the best deal.
>
> —Beverly Medlyn

What evidence supports the author's assertion that it pays to shop for the best deal in auto insurance? *says that it varies by $200*

7. Taken from a newspaper report:

> Proponents of legalizing [marijuana] are apparently growing in number. They argue that it is less dangerous than alcohol, which kills thousands of Americans each year. No one becomes physically addicted to pot, they say, and it doesn't kill anyone under its influence. Marijuana, they assert, is safer than smoking regular cigarettes.
>
> —Alton Blakeslee, Associated Press Science Writer

a. Describe what evidence, if any, is offered for the assertion that marijuana is less dangerous than alcohol. *no one becomes addicted; doesn't kill*

b. Describe what evidence, if any, is offered for the assertion that marijuana is safer than smoking regular cigarettes. *none*

c. If marijuana really is no more dangerous than alcohol or cigarettes, is that a good enough reason to believe that marijuana should be legalized? Why or why not? *no, might not be a market for it*

8. Taken from "*Don't* teach your children to read," *Carnegie Magazine,* May–June, 1987:

> The Commission on Reading recently reviewed decades of reading research and concluded that: "The single most important activity for building the knowledge required for eventual success in reading is reading aloud to children." The experts also noted that this simple activity works as well or better than formal teaching of letters, sound, and words. Parents who want to do right by their children will be glad to know that they can throw away those baby flashcards and preschool workbooks in favor of engaging storybooks, books which quickly endear themselves to both child and adult.
>
> —E. Segal and J. B. Friedberg

a. Do you think that the title "*Don't* teach your children to read" accurately reflects the message in the article? (Isn't reading aloud a form of teaching?) *no, yes*

b. What evidence is cited for the assertion that reading aloud to children is most important for eventual success in reading? *none*

9. Taken from a *Chicago Daily News* story about the alleged decline of the institution of marriage:

> It is false to say that the institution of marriage is falling apart; it is true, I think, that people are demanding more of their marriage partners than they used to—which, in the long run, is a step forward despite the chaos it creates for our age. If marriage were *really* falling apart, divorced persons wouldn't be as eager as they are to find another partner as speedily as possible.

Here, the author says that divorced persons are eager to marry again as soon as possible, and regards this as evidence against the assertion that the institution of marriage is falling apart. Could someone admit that divorced persons are eager to remarry but still believe that a high divorce rate is evidence that the institution of marriage is falling apart? (Hint: Are there several different possible meanings for the sentence: "The institution of marriage is falling apart"?) *Yes - marriage is already screwed up in divorce*

10. In a television commercial for a particular brand of travelers' checks, a young American couple is on vacation in the Orient. The woman, who looks worried, tells the man that she has lost her purse, which holds all their money, checks, and identification. Together they hurry to the tour director. After the tour director learns that their checks are the advertised brand, he assures them there is no need to worry, because they can get help at a nearby office.

a. What method is used to persuade the viewer that this brand of travelers' checks should be purchased? *creating visual scenario*

b. Is any evidence presented here that this brand of travelers' checks is superior to any other? *no*

11. Taken from a newspaper column, "Let's Explore Your Mind":

> *Why does it cost Dad more these days to send Daughter to college?*
> Changes in styles are responsible. When Matthew Vassar founded Vassar College in 1861, three nails were provided for each girl's clothing—one each for nightgown, day dress and Sunday frock. Nowadays, when a girl unpacks her trunks at college, she has far more feminine contraptions than a family of 10 daughters had 100 years ago. Poor Dad!
>
> —A. E. Wiggam

a. Suppose that it is true that women today go to college with far more clothes than women took to school 100 years ago. Is this a good reason to believe that changes in style are responsible for the great increase in the cost of a college education for women? *no - tuition*

b. Can you think of any evidence against Wiggam's assertion that changes in style are responsible? *transportation*

12. In the last act of Shakespeare's *King Lear,* the lifeless body of Lear's daughter Cordelia is placed into his arms. He says:

> She's gone for ever.
> I know when one is dead and when one lives;
> She's dead as earth. Lend me a looking glass;
> If that her breath will mist or stain the stone,
> Why then she lives.

The grief-stricken Lear first admits Cordelia is dead, and then hopes in vain that she is still alive. What evidence does he call for to settle the matter?

looking glass

13. Taken from a newspaper letter to the editor, regarding the Supreme Court decision disallowing school prayer:

> Communism has won its greatest victory. Communists do not pray in school. Americans will not pray in school.... Without the sincere planting of the seeds of prayer in all of our children, Catholic, Protestant, and Jewish, we are finished. Communism has won. It's just a matter of time.

What does the author regard as evidence that the decision prohibiting school prayer is a victory for Communism?   *Communists dont pray*

14. Lead poisoning is a serious illness. It causes mental and physical decay, and often leads to death. Taken from *The Population Bomb:*

> It is a sobering thought that overexposure to lead was probably a factor in the decline of the Roman Empire.... Romans lined their bronze cooking, eating, and wine storage vessels with lead. They thus avoided the obvious and unpleasant taste and symptoms of copper poisoning. They traded them for the pleasant flavor and more subtle poisoning associated with lead. Lead was also common in Roman life in the form of paints, and lead pipes were often used to carry water. Examination of the bones of upper-class Romans of the classical period shows high concentrations of lead—possibly one cause of the famous decadence of Roman leadership. The lower classes lived more simply, drank less wine from lead-lined containers, and thus may have picked up far less lead.
>
> —Dr. Paul R. Ehrlich

The picture painted here is of a decadent upper class, suffering from lead-poisoning, leading Rome to ruin. However, the author does not say that any bodies of lower-class Romans have been examined for levels of lead.
   a. Assume it is true that the lower classes lived more simply and drank less wine from lead-lined containers. Does this persuade you that they picked up far less lead than the upper classes? Why or why not?   *no other pots & pans*
   b. What evidence might support the assertion that the lower classes were exposed to just as much lead? (Hint: Who was doing most of the work with lead paints, lead pipes, and so on?)   *lower class*

15. Taken from a United Press International newspaper story quoting Dr. L. Nelson Bell, a moderator of the Presbyterian Church in the United States:

> "To deny the existence of Satan and the reality of evil spirits is to be more foolish than a soldier reconnoitering enemy territory without admitting that there is an enemy out there to do him harm."
>
> Acknowledging that the "unseen power" of evil spirits is a difficult concept for the modern mind, Dr. Bell added, "Electricity is also mysterious, but we do not question its existence or its power."
>
> "We can be sure electricity is real, because we can see and feel the things it accomplishes, such as lighting and cooling homes.
>
> "But if pain, hatred, war, suspicion, racism and other evils are manifestations of the devil's work, who is to say there is any lack of evidence in the modern world for his reality?"

    a. Dr. Bell compares the devil with electricity in the following way: both are "unseen powers" whose presence is detected by their observed effects.

    b. Do we have any evidence that lighting and cooling of houses are effects of electricity? (Could you demonstrate this to someone who doubts it?)

    c. Do we have any evidence that pain, hatred, war, and racism are the effects of the devil's work? (Could you give a similar sort of demonstration, or provide other evidence?)

16. On a recent sports news show on television, a football player comments on whether college football players should be paid for playing ball:

> Football players should be paid because they work five or six hours a day, and have to play—work again—on Saturdays. It is just like a real job.

    a. The player asserts that playing college football is just like a real job. Does he give any evidence for this?

    b. Can you think of any important differences between playing college football and working at a real job? (To answer this you may have to clarify the meaning of "real job.")

    c. Is it obvious that anyone who works five or six hours a day and again on Saturdays should be paid for that work?

II. ARGUMENTS

Evidence, as we noted earlier, can be either verbal or physical. When you return damaged goods to a store to prove their condition before you collect a refund, you are presenting physical evidence to support your claim that the goods are damaged. Some situations—like requests for refunds—customarily require physical evidence. Remember all those detective stories which say that without a body there is no evidence a murder was committed?

In this text, we will be more concerned with verbal evidence than with physical evidence. Verbal evidence may be oral or written, and can include descriptions of physical evidence, since descriptions are formulated in words. A set of sentences consisting of an assertion to be supported and the verbal evidence for that assertion is called an *argument*. When we support sentences by offering verbal evidence for them, we are *arguing* for those sentences.

The terms "argument" and "arguing" are frequently used in a different way: "argument" to refer to a dispute or disagreement and "arguing" to refer to the activity of engaging in verbal disagreement. The two ways of using the terms, while different, are not entirely unrelated. For when we are involved in a disagreement or dispute, we often try to show that our position is correct by stating evidence to support it. In dealing with problems of critical thinking, however, the word "argument" most commonly refers to a set of sentences related in such a way that some of the sentences purport to provide evidence for one of the sentences, without any suggestion of dispute or disagreement.

Logic is the field of study concerned with analyzing arguments and appraising their correctness or incorrectness. The logician is interested in discovering and stating general principles by which to decide whether the alleged evidence in an argument would, if it were true, support some assertion. Thus, logic is an important part of critical thinking.

In our study of arguments, it will be helpful to use special terms to refer to the separate parts of an argument. The sentences that assert the evidence are called *premisses;* and the sentence that is being argued for is called the *conclusion.* An argument can have any number of premisses, but (by definition) it can have only one conclusion. The following argument, for example, has just one premiss:

> Mary has a twin sister.
> Therefore, Mary is not an only child.

The next argument has two premisses:

> Abortion is the same as murder.
> Murder is wrong.
> Therefore, abortion is wrong.

Many arguments have more than two premisses. Darwin once said that his entire book, *The Origin of Species,* was just one long argument for a single conclusion: the truth of evolution.

A sentence acquires status as a premiss or a conclusion according to the role it plays in a given argument. The sentence "Abortion is the same as murder," which is a premiss in the above argument, might be the conclusion of a different argument in which someone tried to establish *its* truth, as in, for example:

> Human fetuses are persons.
> Any deliberate killing of a person is murder.
> Abortion is the deliberate killing of a human fetus.
> Therefore, abortion is murder.

Of course, we might want to develop other arguments with new premises to support any of the sentences that are the premises of this argument, particularly if their truth is challenged.

Although it is always possible to question the premises of an argument—and to ask for other arguments to support those premises—this process stops in actual discussion when premises that can be agreed on as a starting point are reached. Sometimes this happens quite quickly, especially when premises state what easily can be observed as true. But when the arguments concern important issues, such as the morality of abortion and the legalization of marijuana, it may be hard to agree on premises any less controversial than the proposed conclusions. Sometimes, disagreements are so deep that it is not possible for opponents to find any acceptable premises they can share.

Normally, the point of an argument is to establish the truth of its conclusion, which requires that (1) the premises in the argument must themselves be true,* and (2) the premises must provide the right type of support for the conclusion. Logic is concerned chiefly with the second point, namely, the relationship between the premises and the conclusion. When we examine an argument in order to determine its *logical* strength, the question of whether the premises are actually true is set aside in favor of answering whether the premises *would* support the conclusion *if* they were true.

Critical thinking is thus broader in scope than logic, for in the former we always must be concerned with whether the premises are true, and perhaps with the possibility of finding further arguments to support any questionable premises. However, even when we are concerned with the truth of premises, it is advisable to treat that question separately from whether the premises, *if* true, would support the conclusion of a given argument.

Premises and conclusions of arguments are usually stated in *declarative sentences*. These sentences are most commonly used in English for presenting information and making assertions and—in contrast to questions and commands—it is appropriate to ask whether they are true or false.

Consider the following argument given by opponents of the legalization of marijuana:

> Marijuana should not be legalized because it is potentially dangerous and not enough is known about its long-term effects, and because use of marijuana leads to use of hard drugs.

Even though this argument is stated in a single sentence, we can divide that sentence into parts that are themselves sentences, and that stand in the relationship of premises and conclusion. The conclusion of this argument is the declarative sentence: "Marijuana should not be legalized." The three assertions, conjoined in a compound declarative sentence, that serve as premises are: "it is potentially dangerous," "not enough is known about its long-term effects," and "use of marijuana leads to use of hard drugs." Each of these component sentences

---

*An exception to this requirement for true premises occurs in a form of reasoning called *indirect argument,* which we will discuss in Chapter 2.

is an assertion, the truth of which can be questioned. For this argument to establish the truth of its conclusion, all of these premises must be true *and* together they must provide reasons for accepting the conclusion.

Although premises and conclusions of arguments are usually declarative sentences, occasionally other types occur. The following argument, taken from *Our Mutual Friend,* by Charles Dickens, is presented by Gaffer, a river boatman, to a friend who has just helped him empty the pockets in clothing taken from a body they found floating in the Thames. Gaffer tries to convince his friend that this was not a robbery.

> And what if I had been accused of robbing a dead man, Gaffer?
> You COULDN'T do it.
> Couldn't you, Gaffer?
> No. Has a dead man any use for money? Is it possible for a dead man to have money? What world does a dead man belong to? T'other world. What world does money belong to? This world. How can money be a corpse's? Can a corpse own it, want it, spend it, claim it, miss it? Don't try to go confounding the rights and wrongs of things in that way.

The premisses supporting the assertion that dead men cannot be robbed are stated here in a series of questions. But these are not ordinary questions. They are called *rhetorical questions* because it is assumed that only one answer can be given to them. Thus, these questions are similar to sentences that say that something is so (they "state the facts"), and are unlike ordinary questions. Sometimes rhetorical questions are used to assert the premisses or the conclusion of an argument in a dramatic fashion. If Gaffer had flatly said, "Money cannot be owned, wanted, spent, claimed, or missed by a corpse," the information conveyed would have been the same, but the interest and color displayed in his speech would have been quite different, and his argument may have seemed less persuasive.

III. RECOGNIZING ARGUMENTS

Before we can begin our detailed study of different types of arguments, we have to be able to recognize arguments as they occur in ordinary speech and writing. That is to say, we want to distinguish cases in which a sentence is merely being asserted from those in which the sentence is supported by other sentences. It makes no sense to accuse someone of presenting a poor argument for a case if no argument at all is offered. The most we can reasonably do in such circumstances is to say that an argument *should* be given to support the assertion.

When we are looking for an argument, the first question to ask ourselves is what point the author or speaker is trying to make. When we have identified the sentence that makes the point (the conclusion, if it is an argument), then we can ask what assertions, if any, are intended as support or evidence for that point (the premisses).

Recognizing arguments is sometimes relatively easy because certain words in English, called *indicator words,* frequently signal the presence of either premisses or conclusions of arguments. In several of the arguments presented already, the word "therefore" served to introduce conclusions. This is such a common use of the term in English that whenever "therefore" occurs, we should look for an argument. Other terms that often introduce conclusions of arguments are "thus," "and so," "consequently," "necessarily," "hence," "it follows that," and "for that reason." Words that frequently indicate premisses are "because," "since," "for," and "for the reason that."

In the following arguments, the *indicator words* are italicized:

1. Taken from an ad paid for by the Mobil Corporation:

   Since private business is the most effective instrument of economic change, the government should utilize the resources of private business in its economic planning and decision making.

   The main point here is stated in the sentence that follows the comma: "the government should utilize the resources of private business in its economic planning and decision making." The premiss that is offered in support of this conclusion is signaled by the indicator word *since*: "business is the most effective instrument of economic change."

2. Taken from a newspaper story:

   Women office workers work just as hard as men office workers, and are just as productive. *Therefore* women office workers should receive the same pay as men in comparable positions.

   In this argument for equalizing pay between men and women office workers, the indicator word *therefore* introduces the conclusion of the argument. The premisses are stated before the conclusion.

3. From a book, *The Vietnam War and the Right of Resistance:*

   Those who opposed the war by resistance to Selective Service may not fairly be charged with violating their moral obligation to obey the law of the land. *For* a condition of that obligation has been violated by government, and in so doing, government has forfeited its moral right to call upon citizens for obedience in this area.

   —J. G. Murphy

   Murphy states the conclusion first and follows it with two supporting premisses, introduced by *for*.

   Although these indicator words often signal the premisses or conclusions of arguments, they have other uses as well. Thus, when we see these words, we should not take it for granted that we have identified an argument. "Since," for example, is sometimes used to indicate passage of time, as in "Since Harry has been away at college he has been receiving his hometown paper in the mail."

   "Because" is frequently used to express a causal connection between two events, rather than to offer evidence that one of those events occurred.

An example of this use of "because" occurs in the sentence "Richard Nixon resigned the presidency because a scandal resulted from the Watergate break-in and subsequent investigations." Here, no attempt is made to prove that Nixon resigned. Presumably, that needs no support. The sentence asserts, but does not argue, that a specific set of events caused him to resign.

If we want to *argue* that Watergate was the cause of Nixon's resignation, we would present evidence that the Watergate events were *causally related* to the resignation. For example, in our premises we might say that it was not merely coincidental that the burglary occurred before the resignation, that the motive of the burglary was political, not economic, that Nixon knew about such clandestine activities authorized by his staff, that he believed the investigation ensuing from the burglary might result in his impeachment, and so on. Or the argument might try to show that other possible causes, such as Nixon's concern for national harmony, were not causally related to the resignation. Although sentences that assert a causal connection between two events are not themselves arguments, they can be premises or conclusions of arguments.

Sometimes, particularly when the subject matter is unfamiliar, it is difficult to tell whether a causal assertion or an argument is being presented. If, for example, someone were to tell me that the National Collegiate Athletic Association will soon rule that football players can be paid by colleges for playing ball *because* there has been so much pressure in favor of this move, I would not know whether he was presenting evidence for the assertion that the rule would be changed or whether he was presenting an assertion about why the rule would be changed. Since I don't keep up with football news, I don't know what rulings have been made or are being contemplated.

It is an argument if I am being told that pressure for paying players is a *reason to believe* that the ruling will change. It is a causal assertion if I am being told that the new rule that is going into effect is a result of pressure that was exerted. In many cases, we must ask questions, examine the context for clues, or make "educated guesses" about the intent of the person before we can decide whether a cause is asserted or an argument is presented.

In addition to "because," the terms "for," "since," "thus," and "therefore" can also state a causal connection: "He was invited to the wedding, since he's my mother's favorite cousin." "My dog ran away; therefore, I am putting up this sign to ask for help in finding him." "She sets high goals for herself; thus, she is disappointed sometimes."

Another use of "thus" and "therefore" is to introduce an example or instance of some important point, as in "Not all mammals give birth to live young. *Thus* the platypus is an egg-laying mammal." Closely related to this meaning of "thus" is its use as a synonym for "in this way": "Every day during the last school term, I read over what I had written the previous day, crossed out the rough parts, and rewrote bits of it. Thus I learned to write a decent essay."

Because "therefore," "since," and the other "indicator words" have other uses, they don't always indicate arguments. Another problem in recognizing arguments is that some arguments lack any indicator words. In these cases, we depend on the context as well as the meanings of the sentences to determine whether someone is presenting an argument or merely a series of assertions, none of which support any of the others.

Here is an argument, taken from a decision by the United States District Court of Appeals (District of Columbia; Bazelon, *Washington v. United States*), that has no indicator words:

A judgment of acquittal by reason of insanity is appropriate only when a jury verdict of guilty would violate the law or the facts. We cannot say that this was the situation in Washington's case. The district court did not err in its refusal to enter a judgment of acquittal by reason of insanity.

The context (a decision by a court of appeals) is helpful in determining that this is an argument, because court rulings are supposed to be supported by reasons. The last sentence of the passage asserts that the district court's judgment was not in error, and the reasons for this (the premises) are given in the first two sentences. When in doubt whether an argument is present, we should ask ourselves (1) "What point is being made?", and (2) "What evidence is offered to support it?" In this case, we can spot the conclusion if we know that it is the business of district courts of appeals to decide whether lower court rulings are correct. Without background knowledge, however, it is sometimes difficult to decide whether a given sentence is intended to be a premiss or conclusion.

When no indicator words are present, it may be helpful to insert them (premiss indicators before suspected premisses, and conclusion indicators before conclusions) to see whether or not the passage makes sense when it is reconstructed in this way. This method will not always work, because if we are very unclear about the context, we may be unable to see whether one way of constructing the passage makes more sense than another way. Assuming that the district court of appeals was ruling on whether the lower court was correct or not, if we insert indicator words in the previous example, it reads like this:

Since a judgment of acquittal by reason of insanity is appropriate only when a jury verdict of guilty would violate the law or the facts and *since* we cannot say that this was the situation in Washington's case, *therefore* the district court did not err in its refusal to enter a judgment of acquittal by reason of insanity.

The meaning of the original passage is not changed when the indicator words are inserted; this supports our view that an argument is presented, and that we have identified its premises and conclusion correctly.

When we insert indicator words to mark the premises and conclusion of an argument, we must be sensitive to stylistic variations in the way arguments are presented in ordinary language. Frequently, for emphasis, the conclusion of an argument is stated before the premises, but it is stylistically awkward to begin an argument with "therefore." If we want to insert indicator words and at the same time to have the passage retain correct English style, we sometimes have to reorder the sentences, putting the conclusion sentence last.

In summary, it is helpful, when trying to decide whether an argument is present, to consider the context carefully and to ask:

  (i) What point is the speaker or writer trying to make?
 (ii) Is the speaker or writer presenting evidence to support the truth of some assertion?
(iii) Is the speaker or writer trying to explain why something happened when the fact that it did happen is not in question?
 (iv) Is an example or illustration—rather than an argument—being presented?

Exercises

A. In each of the following arguments, use the indicator words to help identify the premises and the conclusion. Enclose the conclusion in parentheses, then underline and number each premiss, as in the following example:

(The earth is spherical in shape.) For the night sky looks different in the northern and southern parts of the earth,[1] and this would be so if the earth were spherical in shape.[2]

—Aristotle

1. In England under the blasphemy laws it is illegal to express disbelief in the Christian religion. It is also illegal to teach what Christ taught on the subject of non-resistance. Therefore, whoever wishes to avoid being a criminal must profess to agree with Christ's teachings but must avoid saying what that teaching was.

—Bertrand Russell, *Skeptical Essays*

2. A coin has been tossed twelve times and has shown a "head" each time. Thus it is very likely that the next time this coin is tossed it will also show a "head."

3. All 70 students who ate dinner at the fraternity house on Friday became ill during the night. None of the students who live at the house but who didn't dine there that night became ill, so the illness must have been food poisoning caused by something served for dinner at the house on Friday.

4. Since the exercise, training and development of our powers of discriminating among works of art are plainly aesthetic activities, the aesthetic properties of a picture plainly include not only those found by looking at it but also those that determine how it is to be looked at.

—Nelson Goodman, "Art and Authenticity"

5. We can suspect that the inventor [of eyeglasses] was not an academic, for professors delight in boasting of their inventions, and before the thirteenth century we have no record by any such self-styled inventor.

—D. J. Boorstin, *The Discoverers*

6. "Over a period of two years now, I have tested my instrument [the newly invented telescope] (or rather dozens of my instruments) by hundreds and thousands of experiments involving thousands and thousands of objects, near and far, large and small, bright and dark; hence I do not see how it can enter the mind of anyone that I have simplemindedly remained deceived in my observation."

—Galileo, quoted by Boorstin in *The Discoverers*

7. Since creationism can be discussed effectively as a scientific model, and since evolutionism is fundamentally a religious philosophy rather than a science, it is clearly unsound educational practice and even unconstitutional for evolution to be taught and promoted in the public schools to the exclusion or detriment of special creation.

—H. Morris, *Introducing Creationism in the Public Schools*

8. Evolutionary theory merits a place among the sciences for . . . [i]t offers a unified set of problem-solving strategies that can be applied, by means of independently testable assumptions, to answer a myriad of questions about the characteristics of organisms, their interrelationships, and their distributions.

—Philip Kitcher, *Abusing Science*

9. The integrated effect [of the Chernobyl nuclear power-plant accident] on the health of the world's population can be described by adding up all the calculated cancers, leading to a prediction of many thousand cancer deaths. But the effect is probably less than that caused by burning fossil fuels for 1 year in the Soviet Union. If, therefore, the average public health is the sole objective, and a Chernobyl accident happens less than once a year, the RBMK reactors in the Soviet Union can be considered less hazardous than coal-fired plants of similar size.

—R. Wilson, "A visit to Chernobyl," *Science* 236 (1987): 1636

10. I say [Mr. Glass is] 'old' with intention, though not with certainty . . . my reason for it might seem a little far-fetched. The hair of human beings falls out in very varying degrees, but almost always falls out slightly, and with the [magnifying] lens I should see the tiny hairs in a hat recently worn. It has none, which leads me to guess that Mr. Glass is bald. Now when this is taken with the high-pitched and querulous voice which Miss MacNab described so vividly, when we take the hairless head together with the tone common in senile anger, I should think we may deduce some advance in years.

—G. K. Chesterton, "The Absence of Mr. Glass"

B. In each of the following arguments, enclose the conclusion in parentheses and underline the premises, as in the exercises above. Use the technique of inserting appropriate indicator words before sentences suspected of being premises or conclusions, and see whether the passage makes sense.

1. Women tend to do better on essay tests than on timed, multiple-choice tests. Men tend to do better on timed, multiple-choice tests than on essay tests. SAT tests are timed, multiple-choice tests. SAT tests are biased in favor of men.

2. The human mind is not the same thing as the human brain. The human body, including the brain, is a material thing. The human mind is a spiritual thing. Nothing is both a material thing and a spiritual thing.

—Keith Campbell, *Body and Mind*

3. [E]ven if there is a non-negligible probability of a [nuclear] reactor accident, still that is acceptable, being of no greater order than the risks of accidents that are already socially acceptable.

—R. and V. Routley, "Nuclear Power"

4. The year 1859 is perhaps the most important one in the history of biology to date. In that year Charles Darwin published his theory of evolution by natural selection, which has deeply affected not only biology, but other branches of human thought as well.

—L. C. Dunn and T. H. Dobshansky, *Heredity, Race and Society*

5. In spite of the general's years, he evidently is a little vain of his person, and ambitious of conquests. I have observed him on Sunday in church eyeing the country girls most suspiciously; and have seen him leer upon them with a downright amorous look, even when he has been gallanting Lady Lilycraft with great ceremony through the churchyard.

—Washington Irving, *Bracebridge Hall*

6. With no legal, regulated disposal facilities available, illegal dumping becomes more attractive. Far more damage will be done to the environment from illegal dumping than from regulated, legal disposal. Hazardous-waste disposal facilities are essential to the protection of Pennsylvania's environment.

—Frank Kury, *Pittsburgh Post-Gazette*

7. After so much lying, even for purposes [Lt. Col. Oliver] North considered patriotic, his protestations that now he only wants to tell the truth aren't worth much. Why should he be considered believable, even under oath, when he testified under oath that he had so often considered other values more important than truth?

—Tom Wicker, *New York Times*

8. As protectress of wild animals, [Artemis] was also the patron goddess of hunters. This is not so contradictory as it sounds. The huntsman never regards himself as the enemy of the creatures he hunts. The fox is supposed to enjoy the chase, the owner of estates speaks of "preserving" game and lives to visit with heavy penalties those who disturb it at the wrong time or in the wrong way.

—W. K. C. Guthrie, *The Greeks and their Gods*

C. In each of the following, try to determine whether an argument is offered or whether the "indicator words" have some other meaning.

1. In some parts of the country parents have objected to students in high school reading *Romeo and Juliet* because it portrays teen lust, drug use, and suicide.

2. It is not fair of course to judge a book by whether its title is apt or not. All the more so, because often it is the publisher who decides the matter.

—A. Margalit, "The Birth of a Tragedy," *New York Review of Books* 33:16

3. Since the 1967 war the right wing in Israel has been speaking of the "Greater Israel," and the Labor party of the "demographic problem," the former in the name of the pleasure principle, the latter in the name of the reality principle.

—"The Birth of a Tragedy," *New York Review of Books* 33:16

4. You're perfect, Raleigh. You're so perfect, you're going to lend me this money because rotten as I am, I'm still your brother and you've got to come through for me. That's what it's going to cost you to keep on being good old perfect old Raleigh.

—M. Malone, *Handling Sin*

5. This promotion of colleges to universities is consistent with the long-honored American custom of "raising" a thing by adding to the number of syllables used to describe it. For example, *rain* is raised to *precipitation. College* has only two syllables, and even *seminary* only four. But *university,* with five syllables, adds distinction. Thus: University of Montevallo, Alabama . . . Upper Iowa University . . . Midwestern University, Texas.

—P. Fussell, *Class*

6. Rock [music], Bloom says, "ruins the imagination," so it is difficult for students to have a relationship with the art and thought that are the substance of liberal education.

—"Insight," *The Washington Times*

7. Tipperary, made large by its fame and my imagination, is but one main street with a few stores and houses. This eerie scene repeated itself again and again during my visit to this most beautiful of European lands. For Ireland, contrary to the trend of most other countries, is a depopulated nation.

—S. Gould, *The Flamingo's Smile*

8. Most professors are specialists, concerned only with their own fields, interested in the advancement of those fields in their own terms, or in their own personal advancement in a world where all the rewards are on the side of professional distinction. They have been entirely emancipated from the old structure of the university, which at least helped to indicate that they are incomplete, only parts of an unexamined and undiscovered whole. So the student must navigate among a collection of carnival barkers, each trying to lure him into a particular sideshow.

—A. Bloom, *The Closing of the American Mind*

9. Describing how a process works is valuable for two reasons. First it forces you to make sure that *you* know how it works. Then it forces you to make sure that the reader will understand it as clearly as you do.

—W. Zinsser, *On Writing Well*

10. Taken from an interview with Benazir Bhutto, Pakistani opposition leader, in which she talked about her agreement to marry a man chosen by her family:

> I did meet him, and because I felt he's nice and had a sense of humor and he seemed to be a tolerant person in that he could handle having a wife who had an independent career of her own, I thought it was wise to accept the proposal.

—H. Raines, *The New York Times*

IV. EXTENDED ARGUMENTS

Thus far, we have looked at arguments that offer one or more premisses in support of a single conclusion. Frequently, however, in real life, we meet not only arguments like this but also series of interrelated arguments—sometimes in a single paragraph or even a single sentence. We call these *extended arguments*. Some extended arguments attempt to establish a conclusion by stating premisses and, in addition, by producing evidence for those premisses. Thus the premisses of the main argument are conclusions of the subsidiary arguments. Other extended arguments present several different arguments in support of the same conclusion. Still others argue for several closely related conclusions. The techniques for analyzing these more complicated extended arguments, that is, for identifying premisses and conclusions, are just the same as for simpler arguments, with slight "bookkeeping" modifications.

First of all, as before, it is helpful to try to discover the main point the speaker or writer is trying to make, and to enclose that conclusion in parentheses. Since, however, in a series of arguments, there will be more than one conclusion, the parentheses should be marked with letters to keep track of which premisses go with which conclusions. After locating the main conclusion and marking it, underline the premisses that support it, marking them with numbers and the index letter that goes with the conclusion.

Next, look at those premisses and consider whether any evidence is offered to support them. If so, bracket them as conclusions (with a new index letter) and underline and index the premisses that support these conclusions. This sounds complicated, and can be a bit messy. But our goal is to understand complicated arguments by reducing them to simpler subarguments.

In this example, a number of arguments, each with a single premiss, are provided for related conclusions:

> (The Prince needed ... a designer for his court festivals),[a] for they were to emulate those of the Medici;[1a] (a court portrait painter),[b] for the Prince must be presented both at home and abroad as a man-at-arms and the perfect cortigiano;[1b] (an expert on hydraulics),[c] for his gardens must outshine Pratolino;[1c] ... and (even an engraver),[d] for the visual arts of his court must be taken to the people through the art of mass reproduction.[1d]
>
> —R. Strong, *Henry Prince of Wales, and England's Lost Renaissance*

For stylistic reasons, the expression "the Prince needed ..." is not repeated in the statement of each conclusion, though it is understood.

Example

> Since there can be no talk of an independent ideology formulated by the working masses themselves in the process of their movement,[1b] (the *only* choice is either bourgeois or socialist ideology).[b] There is no middle course....[b-1a] Hence (to belittle the socialist ideology *in any way, to turn*

aside from it in the slightest degree means to strengthen the bourgeois ideology).[a]

—V. I. Lenin, What Is to Be Done?

In this extended argument, the main conclusion is stated last, following the conclusion indicator word "hence." The premiss that supports this conclusion immediately precedes it. This premiss in turn is supported by the sentence following the premiss indicator word "since." In this example, as in many extended arguments, after a conclusion of a preliminary argument has been stated, it is restated when it is used as the premiss of the next argument.

Exercises

Isolate the component arguments in each of the following passages, and identify their premisses and conclusions.

1. Because publishers are aiming at a national market, the number-one criterion for any textbook is avoidance of controversy. Since they must respond to a variety of specific criteria from their buyers, this has resulted in what has been called the "dumbing down" of textbooks.

—C. Holden, "Textbook controversy intensifies
nationwide" Science 235 (1987): 19

2. Cycads can, therefore, justifiably claim our interest if only because of their rarity and uncertain future. A further and possibly more important consideration is their value to students of plant evolution, for they appear but little changed from ancestors that flourished along with dinosaurs and our own insectivorous antecedents. They are, in a true sense, living fossils.

—K. Norstog, "Cycads and the Origin of Insect
Pollination" American Scientist (May–June 1987):75

3. Through analytic techniques of diverse kinds, through group therapies and encounter groups, by means of hypnosis, drug therapy, and brain stimulation, self-disclosure [the revealing of personal secrets] is aided and interpreted. But the therapeutic value of any one of these techniques is far from established; and the need for caution in choosing persons best qualified to listen to personal revelation is increasingly clear.
    The caution is well founded. One cannot trust all who listen to confessions to be either discreet or especially capable of bringing solace or help. In addition, the act of confessing can in itself increase the vulnerability of persons who expose their secrets, especially in institutionalized practices. Studies have shown that when self-revelation flows in one direction only, it increases the authority of the listener while decreasing that of the speaker. In ordinary practices of confiding, the flow of personal information is reciprocal, as the revelations of one person call forth those of another; but in institutionalized practices, there is no such reciprocity. On the contrary, therapists and others who receive personal confidences are often taught to restrain their natural impulse to respond in kind.

—S. Bok, Secrets

4. The grouping of these drugs [LSD, DOM, DMT, psilocybin, mescaline, and their congeners as hallucinogenic] is not arbitrary or simply for the sake of convenience. They can be considered members of the same drug class for two important reasons. First, they elicit a common set of effects: sensory perceptual (distorted time sense;

altered sensations of colors, sounds, and shapes, ultimately developing into complex, often multimodal hallucinations; and synesthesia, or mixing of the senses); psychic (dreamlike feelings; depersonalization; and rapid and often profound alternations of affect such as depression or elation); and somatic (dizziness, tingling skin, weakness, tremor, nausea, and increased reflexes). Second, and perhaps more important, these drugs display cross-tolerance—that is, a decreased efficacy of one drug taken shortly after another drug. Thus, if a person has a full-blown hallucinatory experience following ingestion of LSD, the normal hallucinatory response to mescaline or DOM taken the next day will be dramatically blunted or abolished. Therefore, even though it may be argued, and perhaps correctly so, that drugs such as marijuana and PCP should also be classified as hallucinogenic, they do not belong to the class of LSD-like drugs since they show no evidence of cross-tolerance with them.

—B. L. Jacobs, "How hallucinogenic drugs work,"
American Scientist 75 (July–August 1987):386

5. Background information: Victims of Guam disease (Guam ALS/P-D) exhibit symptoms of ALS (Lou Gehrig's disease), Parkinson's disease, and dementia. The study discussed here provides new evidence that all of these diseases could be triggered by some environmental factor.

Scientists fed monkeys moderate amounts of [an amino acid, beta-methylamino-L-alanine] and found that the animals developed severe nerve disorders similar to those in ALS. The severity of the disease and the time it took for symptoms to develop depended on the amount the animals ate.

The chemical is found in the seeds of a cycad, the "false sago palm." During the wartime occupation of Guam by the Japanese, the seeds were used as nourishment and even medicine.

After the war an unusual number of cases involving nerve degeneration began to appear among Guam's native inhabitants. . . . At the height of the outbreak in the early 1950s, it accounted for one death in five among natives over the age of 25.

In more recent years, the Guam ALS has become much less common, indicating that the source of nerve damage is no longer present and suggesting to scientists that a slow-acting environmental cause was previously at work. Furthermore, the age at which patients developed symptoms has risen steadily, another strong indication of a causative factor that was present years ago but has since disappeared. After World War II, use of the cycad seed dwindled as other sources of food and medicine were made available.

—H. M. Schmeck, *The New York Times*

V. RECONSTRUCTING ARGUMENTS

We have already considered the problem of identifying premises and conclusions when there are no indicator words to help us recognize the parts of the argument. In addition to this problem, many arguments in English are incompletely stated, which is to say some premises, or even the conclusion, of an argument may, for various reasons, be omitted. Reconstruction of some arguments is further complicated when they occur in a context that includes language that is inessential to the argument itself. Once we recognize the presence of an argument, we frequently have to reconstruct it, either by supplying missing parts and/or eliminating extraneous remarks, before we can evaluate its strength. We will consider the question of missing parts first.

1. Incompletely stated arguments

In ordinary language, arguments are often stated incompletely to avoid boring the listener or reader with information that is presumably obvious to all concerned.

Consider a context in which you are wondering whether your friend John, who was worried about paying a tuition bill, settled his account. Another friend says to you, "John must have come up with the money to pay his overdue tuition bill, since his application to graduate on Sunday has been approved." The approval of John's application to graduate persuades you that his bills have all been paid, because you and your friend both know that no one with an unpaid tuition bill can be graduated. Even though your friend did not *say* "No one with an unpaid bill can be graduated," this unstated premiss is an essential part of the argument that supports the conclusion that John paid his tuition bill, for otherwise it would not be at all clear what the fact that John is graduating has to do with his having paid his bills. Since you and your friend are both well aware of the relevance and the truth of this premiss, there was no need to be tedious and say it.

Sentences, like the unstated premisses in this argument, that say that *all* or *no* members of one class are members of another class are called *universal generalizations.* Universal generalizations that are premisses of arguments are frequently unstated when they are the sorts of things that "everyone knows."

"The Jones are wealthy, since they drive a new Cadillac" is another example of an argument with a missing—but presumably obvious—premiss: "Most families who drive new Cadillacs are wealthy." Sentences, like this premiss, which state that some proportion of members of one class are members of another class, are called *statistical generalizations*. In this argument, the universal generalization "*All* families who drive new Cadillacs are wealthy," might be considered as a candidate for the missing premiss, but since driving an expensive automobile is not an infallible mark of wealth, "most" is more likely to yield a true premiss than "all." When we supply a missing premiss we want it to be true. We assume, unless there is evidence to the contrary, that the proponent of the argument is truthful, and is leaving a premiss unsaid because it is obviously true.

Statistical generalization can sometimes be stated numerically, as in "60 percent of eligible voters voted in the last presidential election," or "1 percent of the world's people are redheads." A generalization is statistical if the percentage is greater than 0 percent and less than 100 percent; otherwise the generalization is universal.

Missing premisses, like the two just supplied in the arguments above, are frequently either statistical or universal generalizations. In the contexts in which arguments that require these premisses are presented, the generalizations are presumed to be well known. The required generalizations say that two types of things are always or usually connected, or—in negative cases—that the two types are never or seldom connected. The generalizations that serve as premisses in arguments like the ones above connect the particular facts mentioned in the stated premisses ("John's application for graduation was approved" and "the Joneses drive a Cadillac") with the conclusion.

Ordinarily, when a missing premiss is an obviously true generalization, there is nothing wrong with omitting it. However, if we are particularly concerned with checking the correctness of an argument, we should see that the argument is stated as completely as possible. This means that we must occasionally spell out even what is obvious to everyone.

Another reason for searching out the intended or assumed, but unstated, premisses in an argument is that some hidden premisses turn out, when exposed, not to be obviously acceptable. When this is the case, the argument may be weaker than at first we might have supposed. Consider the following two arguments, each of which depends on a general claim that is somewhat more questionable than those in the two examples just presented.

The first argument is taken from *Crime and the Criminal Law,* by Barbara Wootton, who served as a magistrate in Great Britain and was also one of the first women members of Parliament.

> To punish people merely for what they have done would be unjust, for the forbidden act might have been an accident for which the person who did it cannot be held to blame.

The conclusion of Wootton's argument is that it would be unjust to punish people merely for what they have done (without taking into account their intentions as well as their actions). The reason she offers for this conclusion is that the forbidden act may have been a blameless accident. The unstated premiss, required to connect actions for which persons are not to blame with actions for which they should not be punished, is a generalization: No one should be punished for acts for which they do not deserve to be blamed.

Is this general principle correct? Certainly in the British system of law, and in our own, actions committed with an evil intent or a "guilty mind" (*mens rea*) are distinguished from accidental actions. Most of us would agree that people should be *blamed* only for acts they intended to do, or at least were negligent in preventing. But both the American and British legal systems sometimes do punish people for "accidental" acts, even when no blame is warranted.

For example, if you are caught in an elevator between floors in an office building for an hour, and as a result find an expired parking meter (and a ticket) when you return to your car, you are not to blame for overparking. Nevertheless, you will still be punished (you will have to pay the fine) because the law treats this as a case of "strict liability," or, in other words, the law recognizes no excuses. Many considerations can be offered to justify strict liability laws. In the case of parking fines, strict liability is justified by appealing to the good use the city makes of the money collected from this source, the minor nuisance of paying a small fine even when the violator is not to blame, and the excessive court costs of allowing defenses for parking violations.

If we accept the principle of strict liability for some kinds of action, we cannot accept the general principle that connects punishment with blame in an unqualified way. The apparent conflict between strict liability and the principle that conduct should be punished only if it is blameworthy can be resolved by restricting the application of strict liability to *noncriminal* cases. Wootton's book, *Crime and the Criminal Law*, is clearly concerned with criminal justice, and her remarks can be taken to apply to this context. The principle connecting punishment with blameworthiness is well established in Anglo-American criminal law.

The second example is taken from *A Treatise of Human Nature* by David Hume:

> Since reason alone can never *produce* any action or give rise to volition [desire], I infer that the same faculty [that is, reason] is incapable of *preventing* volition or of disputing the preference with any passion or emotion.

Hume, writing in the eighteenth century, was concerned with the nonrational aspect of human life—the area of feelings and emotion. One of his famous sayings is "Reason is and ought only to be the slave of the passions." Hume's words are less startling when we realize that "passions" in those days referred in a general way to human feelings, not specifically to sexual passion. Hume believed that human mortality must be founded on the sort of goodness that human beings—with all their biological limitations, natural feelings, and sympathies—are able to achieve, rather than on some intellectual view of an ideal form of goodness.

In this argument for "natural morality," Hume's conclusion is "reason is incapable of preventing volition or of disputing the preference with any passion or emotion." The words "I infer that" indicate a conclusion is being drawn. Hume offers as evidence the claim that "reason" (the human intellect) cannot by itself produce or cause our desires and wishes. The hidden premiss in this argument seems to be the claim that a general connection exists between the lack of power to cause something and the lack of power to prevent that same thing:

> Nothing that is powerless to cause an activity or event of a certain sort is powerful enough to prevent that activity or event.

Does this premiss seem obviously true to you? A wall can stop a rolling ball, but it cannot set the ball in motion. Sometimes it seems to me that I can just look the wrong way at machines and *prevent* them from operating properly, but I certainly have no power to cause those same machines to work the way they should. I can prevent my watch from operating by dropping it into dishwater, but I am powerless to build a new watch or to repair a damaged one.

Perhaps we could restate or qualify Hume's missing premiss so that it appears more plausible. If, for example, Hume was referring not to individual human capacities but to what humans in general can do, the example concerning my watch is no longer applicable, because human beings can both produce and destroy watches. Can you think of a case in which humans in general have no power to cause or produce something but do have the power to prevent its operation?

When we are reconstructing arguments, as when we are determining whether an argument is being offered, careful attention to context—written, spoken, or implied—is crucial. If we intend to deal seriously with Hume's or Wootton's arguments, we must consider them in the larger context of these authors' works, and use whatever information we can gather to supply missing premisses. When we are engaged in a discussion with another person who presents an argument, we should ask questions to clarify any unstated premisses. When we are presenting arguments of our own, we should be sure they do not contain any hidden premisses that, if stated explicitly, would undermine our arguments.

When we are reconstructing arguments in situations that provide inadequate contextual information, we should supply the missing premisses that are the most plausible under the circumstances. This means that the missing premisses should have "the ring of truth." They should be premisses that, although they may not actually *be* true, at least are not known to be false or are not wildly unbelievable. The missing premisses should also be sentences we could reasonably expect the proponent of the argument to accept.

Missing premisses of arguments are not always generalizations like those discussed in this section. However, we will postpone looking at other kinds of missing premisses until we examine specific types of arguments in a more detailed way.

Exercises

A. Identify each of the following sentences as a universal generalization or a statistical generalization. In some of the exercises you must depend on common sense or general background knowledge to interpret the sentence as a universal or statistical generalization.

1. Fifty-five percent of students on the Dean's List are women. *S*
2. Most football players are missing at least one tooth. *S*
3. Zero percent of the ingredients of Brand X breakfast cereal are toxic. *U*
4. Whales are mammals. *U*
5. Politicians are honest. *S*
6. No babies are Olympic swimmers. *U*
7. Soldiers are brave. *S*
8. Few computer programs are free of all bugs. *S*

B. In each of the following examples, an unstated generalization is required to complete the premisses of the argument. Enclose the conclusion of each argument in parentheses, and underline the stated premisses, as in the previous exercises. Try to supply a plausible generalization to complete each argument. If no generalization seems plausible, explain why.

1. Women office workers work just as hard as men office workers and are just as productive. Therefore, (women office workers should receive the same pay as men in comparable positions.)
2. (Marijuana should not be legalized) because it is potentially dangerous with respect to its long-term effects.
3. (Marijuana should be legalized) because it is no more dangerous than alcohol, which is already legal.

4. Marijuana should be legalized because the laws against it are not respected, and this breeds contempt for law in general.

5. Marijuana should not be legalized because it leads to the use of harder drugs, such as heroin.

6. Tomatoes will be expensive in late winter, since growers in Florida were hit by a hard freeze in December. *Tomatoes will always be expensive if growers in Florida are hit by a hard freeze*

7. The boy who sits next to me in class doesn't have a home telephone, for he isn't listed in the telephone directory.

8. The governor doesn't have a private telephone, for there is no listing for her private phone in the telephone directory.

9. Prices are bound to drop soon, since they have been rising for a long time now.

10. You will pass the final exam in math, since you have passed all the earlier exams in the course.

11. Your tires should hold out for the coast-to-coast drive, since they have made it six times before without any trouble. *If tires have made it 6 times coast to coast then they will make it another time*

12. A heads will show on the next toss of the coin, for the past six tosses have been heads. *If heads shows up on six previous tosses, then it will show up on the next toss (not plausible)* *without trouble (bad)*

2. Extracting the essentials of an argument from its surrounding context

We will return to the problem of missing premises in later chapters, after we have had more to say about evaluating arguments. Now we will turn to the question of sorting out the parts of an argument in contexts that contain sentences that are neither premises nor the conclusion of the argument.

Sometimes the additional material is background information inserted to tell us something about the quality of the evidence, how it was gathered, or why it is relevant to the conclusion. Consider the following passage, taken from *Sexual Politics* by Kate Millett:

> A witty experiment by Philip Goldbert proves what everyone knows, that having internalized the disesteem in which they are held, women despise both themselves and each other. This simple test consisted of asking women undergraduates to respond to the scholarship in an essay signed alternately by one John McKay and one Joan McKay. In making their assessments, the students generally agreed that John was a remarkable thinker, Joan an unimpressive mind. Yet the articles were identical; the reaction was dependent on the sex of the supposed author.

Our first clue that this passage contains an argument is the assertion in the opening sentence that something is being proved. To *prove* something is to produce evidence that shows it is true. The conclusion of the argument (the sentence that is proved) is "having internalized the disesteem in which they are held, women despise both themselves and each other." The evidence for this conclusion is contained in the premiss: "the reaction [to the essays that were identical except for the sex of the supposed author] was dependent on the sex of the supposed author." Millett's premiss is in turn supported by (is a conclusion drawn from) the outcome of Goldberg's experiment:

> Women undergraduates evaluated identical essays, which differed only in the sexually distinctive names of the supposed authors, as being the work of a remarkable thinker when the supposed author was male, and an ordinary thinker when the supposed author was female.

Additional background information provided in Millett's passage assures us that the conclusion was something already widely known and that the experiment was witty. We are also told that the experiment was a simple test. None of this information is evidence to support the truth of the conclusion, but it does tell us something about the *quality* of the evidence presented and helps us to understand the author's point of view.

Here is another argument stated in a context that contains additional information. This example is taken from a newspaper column entitled "How to Spot Rich People" by social commentator Andy Rooney:

> Another way to tell a rich person from a poor person is one I learned years ago when I worked for a morning news broadcast. We often had important people on it as guests and I began to notice one thing that the rich men had in common. They never wore overcoats.
>
> Nelson Rockefeller must have been on the show five times on different winter days and he never wore an overcoat or carried one. It was a long while before I realized he was so rich he didn't need one. He was never out in the cold because all he did was walk the 10 feet from his chauffeur-driven limousine to the building and anyone can stand that much cold. For all I know Rockefeller didn't even own a raincoat or an umbrella. Most of the restaurants a rich person like him would eat in have canopies extended to the street.

The conclusion of Rooney's argument is "Rich men never wear overcoats." His premisses state that the sample of rich men he observed never wore overcoats. This evidence is strengthened by his suggestion concerning why rich men don't need overcoats. The rest of the passage contains information about how Rooney gathered his sample and humorous speculation about rich men's ability to dispense with raingear as well as overcoats.

Sometimes the context of an argument provides information that indicates something is true, while the argument itself attempts to establish that the situation is a good one or a bad one. In the following argument, philosopher Bertrand Russell, after telling us that rats behave a certain way toward food, argues that rats are sensible to do so.

> Rats will eat food that contains rat poison. But if, before eating, they were to subject their food to scientific analysis, they would die of hunger meanwhile, and so they are well advised to take the risk.

Frequently, examples that illustrate a point occur in the context of arguments. Such *illustrations* are not part of the argument, but they clarify points and aid understanding by making general ideas concrete. Patrick Devlin does this in the following passage from *The Enforcement of Morals:*

> *No society can do without intolerance, indignation, and disgust;* they are the forces behind the moral law, and indeed it can be argued that if they or something like them are not present, the feelings of society cannot be weighty enough to deprive the individual of freedom of choice. I suppose that there is hardly anyone nowadays who would not be disgusted by the thought of cruelty to animals.

Devlin supports his conclusion, which is italicized, with the premisses that succeed it in the complex sentence. (His argument also depends on a premiss that Devlin does not state here, but tries to establish elsewhere in his book: No society can live without morals.) Devlin's concrete example of disgust is provided in the last sentence of the quoted passage.

In addition to background information and examples that serve to illustrate and clarify points, arguments often contain remarks that are intended to put the reader or listener in a *properly receptive frame of mind* to accept their conclusions. Such additional material might convey an atmosphere of humor, fear, seriousness, or any number of other moods. Millett does this, in the argument quoted earlier, when she tells us that Goldberg's experiment proves "what everyone knows." Such a remark may intimidate a reader who feels inclined to disagree with Millett, because it suggests that anyone who does not agree with her conclusion is disputing common wisdom. This tends to distract the reader from a critical examination of Millett's particular argument for that claim.

When we examine the support that the evidence provides for a conclusion, we should separate carefully any additional material from the actual evidence. The extra material may appeal to our emotions and discourage us from taking a close critical look at the central issue: Does the alleged evidence support the conclusion?

Sometimes arguments repeat, in slightly different words, points that already have been made in a premiss or in the conclusion of the argument. This is done for a variety of reasons. For example, when a conclusion is stated at the beginning of a passage, and then the reasons for accepting that conclusion are presented, the conclusion may be restated for emphasis. Restating points when arguments are long and complicated can clarify a presentation by keeping track of where the argument has been and where it is leading. Repetition is designed to ensure that the reader or listener does not fail to get the point.

Less savory motives, however, also inspire repetition. As advertisers have taught us, repeated exposure to an assertion can convince people that it is true, even when only flimsy evidence, or no evidence at all, has been offered. Thus an advertising campaign for Brand X soap might call for billboard signs, newspaper and magazine ads, television and radio spots, all flooding the market with the message "Brand X is the best soap." Moreover, the use of repetition is not confined to advertisers. Consider the following passage, taken from *The Odd Woman,* a novel by George Gissing, and try to decide what use is served by repeating the conclusion at the end of the argument after stating it initially:

It is the duty of every man, who has sufficient means, to maintain a wife. The life of an unmarried woman is a wretched one; every man who is able ought to save one of them from that fate.

Exercises

Each of the following passages contains at least one argument. For each argument, enclose the conclusion in parentheses, and underline the premises as in previous exercises. Discuss the role of any additional material in the passages.

1. Dear Readers: Here is the second part of Dr. George Ryan's testimony at a Senate Judiciary Subcommittee hearing on the human-life bill. [The bill would make abortion, the Pill, and the intrauterine contraceptive device illegal.]
Question: What economic effect would this bill have on those women?
Answer: Paradoxical. The president has promised to get government off our backs. This bill would not only LEAVE government on our backs, it would put government in our bedrooms. If this bill is passed and abortions are made illegal, it means at least another 700,000 babies will be born next year. A substantial percentage will be born to the poor and the very young—about two-thirds of whom will collect welfare.
    Instead of a single cost of $125 for an abortion, we will pay $1,000 to $1,500 for a delivery, and at least $100,000 to support these welfare children until they reach maturity. This is a commitment of about 40 billion dollars each year.
Question: How did you come up with those figures?
Answer: Simple mathematics. I took the 1.4 million abortions [now being performed] a year—let's be conservative and say only half those women actually have babies. The other half would probably get illegal abortions or go out of the country to get one. But the remaining half are stuck—and probably poor. If two-thirds are on welfare, we are talking about 400,000 babies a year.

—Ann Landers Column

2. In the past there has been much argument whether, in the strategy of inflation control, one should seek to come to grips with the level of demand or whether one should seek to deal with the wage-price spiral. . . . The proper answer is that both are important. Inflation could be controlled by a sufficiently heavy reduction in the level of demand. It could also be controlled with a less drastic reduction if something could be done to arrest the interreactions of wages and prices, or, to speak more precisely, of wages, profits, and prices.

—John Kenneth Galbraith, *The Affluent Society*

3. Discrimination—refusing to admit someone to a public place or business on grounds of race, sex, or religion—is against federal law. However, the law also respects the rights of people to associate privately with whomever they wish.

Last year [the national organization of Jaycees] voted to kick out the women members they had previously recruited. They even voted to kick out the chapters who wouldn't kick out the women they had previously invited. (Who says that chauvinists are chivalrous?)
    But in Minnesota, the courts ruled that the Jaycees were actually operating as a public business. They were soliciting memberships, and open to anyone so long as that anyone was a male. So, this duly designated public business was forbidden to discriminate.

—Ellen Goodman's newspaper column

4. "I could tell you things about Renaissance Popes that would make your hair stand on end," [said Leonie].

"I'm beginning to think there's something to be said for being a Protestant after all," said Clare.

"Oh, no, Clare," Nanda assured her, horrified at seeing the prospective convert wavering. "Don't you see it's just another proof that the Church really is divine and inspired? Any other institution would have been done for centuries ago with so much corruption in individual members. There really is something that keeps it going in spite of all that, and the gates of hell don't prevail in spite of all the horrors."

—*Frost in May,* Antonia White

5. "Most people wear some sign and don't know what it's saying. Choose your sign according to your audience," Malloy said. . . . "A good dark suit, white shirt and conservative tie are a young man's best wardrobe friends, if he's applying for a white collar job in a big range of business and professional categories. They're authority symbols. It's that simple," he said.

—"Fashion," *Chicago Daily News*

6. An apparently progressive [evolutionary] advance may turn out ultimately to be a limitation. For instance, the insects successfully conquered the land by developing a method for breathing with the aid of fine air-tubes penetrating every tissue of the body. This constitutes an admirable mechanism so long as the creature remains small, but makes large size impossible. An insect as big as a rat just won't work properly; actually no insect is bigger than a mouse. This limitation of total size naturally sets a limit to the size of the brain, and so to the number of cells in the brain, which in turn sets a low limit to the degree of intelligence and the flexibility of behavior. That is why insects are never very intelligent, but have to depend mainly on the marvelous but always rigid and limited behavior-mechanisms we call instincts. This limitation of insect size is very lucky for us, because without it, man assuredly could never have evolved.

—Julian Huxley, *New Bottles for Old Wine*

7. "Of course—Mrs. Fairford gives the smartest little dinners in town. There was an account of one she gave last week in this morning's *Town Talk;* I guess it's right here among my clippings." Mrs. Heeny, swooping down on her bag, drew from it a handful of newspaper cuttings, which she spread on her ample lap and proceeded to sort with a moistened forefinger. "Here," she said, holding one of the slips at arm's length; and throwing back her head she read, in a slow unpunctuated chant: "'Mrs. Henley Fairford gave another of her natty little dinners last Wednesday as usual it was smart small and exclusive and there was much gnashing of teeth among the left-outs as Madame Olga Loukowska gave some of her new steppe dances after dinner'—that's the French for new dance steps," Mrs. Heeny concluded, thrusting the documents back into her bag.

—Edith Wharton, *The Custom of the Country*

8. "A woman knows very well that all the talk about elevated subjects is just talk, but that what a man wants is her body and all that presents it in the most deceptive but alluring light; and she acts accordingly. If we only throw aside our familiarity with this indecency, which has become second nature to us, and look at the life of our upper classes as it is, in all its shamelessness—why it is simply a brothel. . . . You don't agree? Allow me, I'll prove it," he said, interrupting me. "You say that the women of our society have other interests in life than prostitutes have, but I say no, and will prove it. If people differ in the aims of their lives, by the inner context of their lives, this difference will necessarily be reflected in externals and their externals will be different. But look at those unfortunate despised women and the highest society ladies: the same

costumes, the same fashions, the same perfumes, the same exposure of arms, shoulders, and breasts, the same tight skirts over prominent bustles, the same passion for little stones, for costly glittering objects, the same amusements, dances, music, and singing. As the former employ all means to allure, so do these others."

—Leo Tolstoy, "The Kreutzer Sonata"

9. Other physicists, notably Arthur Holly Compton at the University of Chicago, contended that the cosmic rays were particles. There was a way to investigate the question. If they were charged particles, they should be deflected by the earth's magnetic field as they approached the earth from outer space. Compton studied the measurements of cosmic radiation at various latitudes and found that it did indeed curve with the magnetic field; it was weakest near the magnetic equator and strongest near the poles, where the magnetic lines of force dipped down to the earth.

—Isaac Asimov, *The Intelligent Man's Guide to the Physical Sciences*

VI. REVIEW

The purpose of this chapter was to introduce you to the subject matter of *logic* and *critical thinking*. We have identified a number of skills that contribute to critical thinking:

1. Sensitivity to different uses of language;
2. The ability to recognize when evidence is required to support an assertion;
3. Awareness of the distinction between the truth of sentences and the support they would provide for some other sentence *if* they were true;
4. The ability to recognize arguments, to identify their parts, to supply missing premises that are unstated, and to separate the essential parts of an argument from the context in which it is stated;
5. The logical skill of evaluating an argument in terms of how well the premises support the conclusion.

All of these critical-thinking skills are useful and important in our everyday lives. Our language reflects what is important in human culture, and, as with other vitally interesting aspects of human life, a special vocabulary has been developed for discussing issues in logic and critical thinking. Since some of this vocabulary may be new to you, it will be helpful to review the definitions of the most important terms:

Argument: A set of sentences related in such a way that some of the sentences are presented as evidence for another sentence in the set.

Conclusion: The sentence in an argument that is supposedly supported by the evidence.

Committing a Fallacy: Making the mistake of supposing evidence has been presented in support of an assertion—or pretending that it has been—when some form of nonevidential persuasion has been used instead.

Declarative Sentence: Declarative sentences—as opposed to questions, commands, requests, and exclamations—assert that something is the case.

Evidence: Evidence is support that is offered for some assertion. It may be physical evidence, as when damaged goods are presented to support the claim that they are defective; or it may be verbal, in which case some sentences are offered to support the truth of another sentence.

Indicator Words: English words commonly used to signal premises or conclusions of arguments. Examples of premiss indicator words are "for," "since," "because," and "for the reason that." Examples of conclusion indicator words are "hence," "thus," "therefore," "and so," "it follows that," and "for that reason."

Logic: The study devoted to analyzing and evaluating arguments.

Premiss: A sentence that is offered as evidence in an argument.

Statistical Generalization: A sentence that states that some proportion of the members of one class are members of another class. Common forms of these sentences are: "Most . . . are _____" and "Most . . . are not _____." Statistical generalizations may also be expressed numerically, as in "x percent of . . . are _____."

Universal Generalization: A sentence that states that all or none of the members of one class are members of another class. Common forms of these sentences are: "All . . . are _____" and "No . . . are _____."

These terms are the most important ones introduced in Chapter 1. We will be using them throughout our discussion. Two other terms that are a part of the standard vocabulary of logic and critical thinking are so often *misused* that they should be mentioned here.

Infer: To infer is to conclude from something known or assumed. This is a mental activity that may be—but need not be—expressed in language.

For example, on the basis of the dark circles under my eyes, you may infer that I didn't get enough sleep last night, but you may be too considerate to mention that to me or to anyone else. However, if you *argue* that I didn't get enough sleep, you *state* the evidence (cite the dark circles) and the conclusion. Arguing, unlike inferring, is an activity that requires the use of language. When you state your reasons for drawing an inference—when you express in language the premises and the conclusion—you transform the inference into an argument.

Imply: To imply is to provide a basis from which an inference may be drawn. Words, actions, looks, appearances may all "have implications"—that is, they may provide a basis for someone to infer something from them. It is also appropriate to speak of a person's implying something, through words, silence, looks, or some other feature. "Imply" also has another special meaning, in the context of deductive logic, which will be discussed later. "Infer" is sometimes confused with "imply," as in "Your scowls infer that you disapprove of Mary Ann." As Fowler, in his *Dictionary of Modern English Usage,* says of "imply" and "infer:" "Each word has its own job to do, one at the giving end and one at the receiving."

The best way to review this type of subject matter is to work more exercises. If you can complete the exercises in the following section successfully, you will know that you have mastered the material covered in Chapter 1. Some of these exercises are rather difficult, so do not be discouraged if they seem to require a lot of effort. Moreover, since these arguments are stated in ordinary language—which is not always as precise as we would like it to be—and since the selected passages are all taken out of broader contexts, different interpretations of a given passage are quite possible. In a given case, for example, it may not be entirely clear whether the author is providing an argument or a causal explanation or whether the author is providing just one argument or several. If a premiss seems to be missing, the most plausible missing premiss to supply may not be clearly identifiable. Whenever you think that more than one interpretation is plausible, mention this and give your reasons for each interpretation. If the skills of logic and critical thinking you are developing in this course are to be useful to you in the ordinary situations you encounter in everyday life, you must practice with examples taken from such contexts.

VII. EXERCISES

For each of the following passages:

(1) Indicate whether or not the passage contains an argument (or several arguments). Enclose conclusions in parentheses; underline and number the premisses.
(2) Reconstruct the arguments: Write each premiss and conclusion as a separate sentence, and indicate which sentences are premisses and which sentences are conclusions.
(3) If the argument depends on a missing generalization as an implicit premiss, supply the generalization.
(4) Discuss any cases in which nonevidence, such as a threat, might be mistaken for evidential support.
(5) Indicate what role any additional material that is not part of the premisses or the conclusion plays in the passage.

1. Adam was led to sin by Eve and not Eve by Adam. Therefore it is just and right that woman accept as lord and master him whom she led to sin.

—Saint Ambrose

2. Men were thinking, writing, and creating, because women were pouring their energy into those men; women are not creating culture because they are preoccupied with love.

—Shulamith Firestone, *The Dialectic of Sex*

3. [Pennsylvania] could lose about $91 million in federal highway construction aid because lawmakers have blocked the start of an emission-inspection program for autos in Pittsburgh and Philadelphia.

   Senator Eugene Scanlon, D–Allegheny, a leading emission-program critic, said last month he thought the $91 million was worth it as a matter of principle.

   He and his colleagues have maintained the federal government has no right to force a State Legislature to spend money for anything.

—*Pittsburgh Post-Gazette*

4. Pennsylvania may still have an out, if proposed clean-air-law revisions are enacted. [However, the Environmental Protection Agency] "feels the Clean Air Act as now writ-

ten must be enforced because it is the rule of the land," Wassersug [EPA regional direc-
tor] said.

—*Pittsburgh Post-Gazette;* same story as in Exercise 3

5. Hair analysis has been found to be a good test in screening large groups of people
for exposure to toxic trace metals. It is not as widely used as blood analysis, but studies
have shown that concentrations of lead, cadmium, arsenic, and mercury in hair provide
a good record of exposure.

Also, since the metal grows out with the hair, lengthwise sections of hair can show
the approximate time when a short, intense exposure occurred. . . .

Chromium is essential for the hormone insulin to work properly. Thus, in time, it
may be that measurements of chromium in hair will be useful in identifying people
with diabetes and in monitoring the course of the disease.

—Newspaper column "Food for Thought" by Dr. Jean
Mayer and Jeanne Goldberg, R.D.

6. My suggestion for a wine to accompany chocolate desserts is different [from wines
made from the muscat grape]. I prefer a rich, slightly sweet red wine. Indeed, it was a
chocolate dessert that led me to change my mind about late-harvest zinfandels.

The proper use for those alcoholic, full-fruited wines with considerable residual
sugar is with chocolate. The very strength of the wine cuts through the rich heaviness
of the chocolate.

—Newspaper column "Wine" by Peter Machamer,
Pittsburgh Post-Gazette

7. Dear Ann: I am boiling over with the statement that the Air Force spends $12.6
million per year for private pet service by veterinarians. What nonsense!

Having put in 23 years in the armed forces, I happen to know that every base with a
mess hall, in all branches of the Department of Defense, requires that all meat be
inspected by veterinarians at the supply points. The meat is then distributed to the
various units of the military. This is where the taxpayers' dollars go, and I'm sure you
will agree it is a legitimate expenditure.

All services performed on privately owned animals must be paid for by the owners.

—Ann Landers' column

8. The thought tends to wrap itself in a joke because in this way it recommends itself
to our attention and can seem more significant and more valuable, but above all
because this wrapping bribes our powers of criticism and confuses them. We are
inclined to give the *thought* the benefit of what has pleased us in the form of the joke;
and we are no longer inclined to find anything wrong that has given us enjoyment and
so spoil the source of the pleasure.

—Sigmund Freud, *Jokes and Their Relation to the*
Unconscious

9. It is incontestable that sense perception plays a crucial role in the natural sciences.
It serves as the sole means through which we can gather information about the world
around us. Knowledge of general laws is posterior, in the empirical sciences, to knowledge of particular instances, and for the latter the evidence of the sense is required.

—Robert Swartz, *Perceiving, Sensing and Knowing*

10. If a person is known to lie occasionally, it is not reasonable to accept something
simply on the ground that he testifies to it. Similarly, once the senses have been discovered to be capable of deception, it is not reasonable to regard a belief as solid or per-

manent *merely* because it is based on sensory evidence. For it may turn out that the occasion on which the senses provided the evidence for the belief was one on which the senses were deceptive; and then, of course, the belief would have to be abandoned. Despite this, however, it may still be reasonable to regard some sensory beliefs as permanent and indubitable, if occasions on which the senses are absolutely reliable can be distinguished from those on which they are likely to deceive.

—H. Frankfurt, *Demons, Dreamers, and Madmen*

11. Noting the diversity of Paraguayan languages, Dobrizhoffer comments: "Truly admirable is their varied structure, of which no rational person can suppose these stupid savages to have been the architects and inventors. Led by this consideration I have often affirmed that the variety and artful construction of languages should be reckoned among the other arguments to prove the existence of an eternal and omniscient God."

—Marvin Harris, *The Rise of Anthropological Theory*

12. If great art is a product of a great soul only a critic of spiritual stature can hope to recognize and appreciate artistic greatness when he sees it. To the trivial all things are trivial. A critic with limited powers of observation, a weak imagination, and a restricted scale of values must remain blind to artistic greatness and incapable of distinguishing artistic profundity from artistic triviality.

—T. M. Greene, *The Arts and the Art of Criticism*

13. Rules and regulations of the Securities and Exchange Commission compel the prospectus to dwell on all the problems and all the shortcomings the company faces in its competitive battle for survival and success. This is true, and since this is undoubtedly the first and last public occasion on which a company will stress the negative aspects of its situation, and since this is the point of entry for many new stockholders, the value (for investors) of reading the prospectus is enormous.

—J. Diamond, *The Fine Art of Making Money in the Stock Market*

14. Poetry, indeed, cannot be translated, and therefore it is the poets who preserve languages; for we would not be at the trouble to learn a language when we can have all that is written in it just as well in translation. But, as we cannot have the beauties of poetry but in its original language, we learn it.

—Samuel Johnson

15. Encouragement of contempt for laws is more dangerous to society than occasional use of marijuana. Severe laws against marijuana do not discourage use of marijuana, but rather breed this contempt not only for drug laws, but for laws in general. Therefore severe laws against marijuana are more dangerous to society than the activity which they are designed to prevent.

—A. Blakeslee, "Should Marijuana Be Legalized?", *Associated Press*

16. At this moment the King, who had been for some time busily writing in his notebook, called out "Silence!" and read out from his book, "Rule forty-two. All persons over one mile high to leave the courtroom."
"... that's not a regular rule; you inserted it just now."
"It's the oldest rule in the book," said the King.
"Then it ought to be number one," said Alice.

—Lewis Carroll, *Alice in Wonderland*

[Here, what is Alice's argument?]

17. Referring to the island of Corsica, note the rhetorical question:

> What can be found so bare, what so rugged all around as this rock? What more barren of provisions? What more rude as to its inhabitants? What in the very situation of the place more horrible? What in climate more intemperate? Yet there are more foreigners than natives here. So far then, is a change of place from being disagreeable, that even this place hath brought some people away from their country.

—Seneca, *Ad Helviam de Consolatione,* quoted in
James Boswell, *Boswell on the Grand Tour*

18. Referring to a debate about whether humans have free will:

> We were eating cold fruit-soup. The soup was served in a huge tureen. It was a beautiful piece of china, and Maria was particularly fond of it. She hated things being broken, even a Woolworth tumbler. The veranda was surrounded by large polished panels of glass. I got up, by now trembling with anger, and lifted the tureen up from the table. I said:
> "Look, Maria, let us settle this problem in an empirical way, once and for all. If you continue to assert that I have a Free Will, you will thereby enrage me to the point when I cannot help smashing this tureen against the windowpane, for my actions are determined by your words. If you recognize that there is no such thing as a Free Will, the tureen will automatically be safe. But what is a tureen compared to the problem we are trying to settle?"
> "It is *my* tureen," Maria said, watching my hands with anguish.
> "I give you ten seconds to decide." I started counting—one-two-three, in a cold rage.... At the count of nine, Maria said:
> "All right, you win, put it down."
> "You admit that I have no Free Will?" I asked, to make quite sure.
> "*You* certainly haven't."

—Arthur Koestler, *The Invisible Writing*

19. [B]ecause the ... rules are designed to benefit all and because the punishments prescribed for their violation are publicized and the defenses respected, there is some plausibility in the exaggerated claim that in choosing to do an act violative of the rules an individual has chosen to be punished.

—Herbert Morris, "Persons and Punishment"

20. And although it is utterly true that God's existence is to be believed in because it is taught in the Holy Scriptures and, on the other hand, that the Holy Scriptures are to be believed because they have God as their source (because, since faith is a gift from God, the very same one who gives the grace that is necessary for believing the rest can also give us the grace to believe that he exists); nonetheless, this cannot be proposed to unbelievers because they would judge it to be a circle.

—René Descartes, "Letter to the Dean and Doctors of
the Faculty of Sacred Theology of Paris"

Deductive Arguments, Inductive Arguments, and Fallacies

CHAPTER 2

I. INTRODUCTION

In any argument, the truth of the premisses is intended to provide reasons for accepting the conclusion. A natural first question to ask when confronting an argument is whether its premisses are true. To answer this, we need factual knowledge, often of a specialized sort. Another question we can raise about arguments is whether their premisses *if true* would support their conclusions. To answer this we need to know something about the structure of arguments, a subject that can be studied in a general way, without reference to specialized factual knowledge. In this chapter, we will focus on the structural question, that is to say, we will look at how premisses, *if* true, can provide support for conclusions. We can do this to a large extent without knowing, or even considering, whether premisses and conclusions of arguments are actually true.

Arguments can be classified in terms of whether their premisses (if true) would provide (1) conclusive support, (2) partial support, or (3) only the appearance of support (that is, little or no support at all). When we say that the premisses provide *conclusive support* for the conclusion, we mean that *if* the premisses of the argument were all true, then the conclusion would also be true. Arguments that have this characteristic are called (correct or *valid*) *deductive arguments*. When we say that the premisses of an argument provide *partial support* for the conclusion, we mean that *if* the premisses were true, they would give us good reasons—but not conclusive reasons—to accept the conclusion. That is to say, if the premisses were all true, the conclusion would probably be true but just might be false. Arguments of this type are called (correct) *inductive arguments*.

Into the third category fall those arguments that are neither correct inductive arguments nor valid deductive arguments. These fallacies, or fallacious arguments, often superficially resemble correct deductive or inductive arguments. In a fallacious argument, some sentences are presented in support of a conclusion, but, in fact, the alleged evidence is either very weak or is irrelevant to the conclusion. The premisses of fallacious arguments, even if true, fail to guarantee or even make it probable that the conclusion is true. The conclusion of a fallacious argument may actually be true, but the premisses of the argument are not good reasons to believe that this is so.

Arguments (either deductive or inductive) that provide the proper kind of support for their conclusions and in addition also have *all true premisses* are called *sound arguments*. Obviously, if we want to establish the truth of a conclusion, a sound argument is required, for if some of the premisses are false, then even though the argument may be logically impeccable, the *truth* of the conclusion is not supported by false premisses.

In this chapter, we will look at examples of inductive and deductive arguments and learn to tell the difference between them. Recognizing each type is important because we apply different standards for evaluating inductive and deductive arguments.

We will also discuss some general characteristics of fallacious arguments, but will postpone a detailed examination of fallacies until we are more familiar with the specific types of correct arguments that various fallacies resemble.

II. DEDUCTIVE ARGUMENTS

In a valid deductive argument, if all the premises are true, the conclusion must be true as well. This guarantee that true premises will yield true conclusions is the outstanding characteristic of deductive arguments, and it is obviously a valuable feature. How is the truth preserved? The answer points to a limitation on the powers of deductive reasoning. For while the conclusion of a deductive argument can restate or recombine information from the premises, and thus can make explicit what was formerly only implicit, the conclusion of a deductive argument provides no new information that was not already present, at least implicitly, in the premises. Deductive arguments are *truth-preserving*, but they cannot extend factual knowledge.

To understand the truth-preserving character of valid deductive arguments, we must examine what "new information" means, and how premises of an argument can "implicitly" contain information. It will be convenient to discuss these issues by looking at some examples of deductive arguments.

To simplify matters, we will often write arguments in a *standard form*. Each premiss will be listed on a separate line, and the conclusion, also listed on a line by itself, will be separated from the premises by a solid line. When we use this device we do not have to indicate verbally which sentences are the premises and which sentence is the conclusion of each argument.

The first argument that we will examine is as old as the first text in logic—about 2,300 years old! It is so commonly used in logic classes that you can hardly escape it, so you might as well be exposed to it now.

> All men are mortal.
> Socrates is a man.
> _____
> Socrates is mortal.

The first premiss is a universal generalization. It contains the information that *all* members of one class, or type of thing (the class of men) are also members of another class (the class of mortals). The second premiss provides the information that the individual whose name is Socrates is a member of the class of men.

The conclusion of the argument combines the information contained separately in the two premises but does not introduce any additional information. It is fairly obvious in this example that, strictly speaking, the conclusion contains no "new" information, not already present in the premises. Neither premiss says explicitly (in just those words) what is said in the conclusion, but the information in the conclusion is there in the premises *implicitly*. Moreover, this is true not only for the simple argument in our example but also for every argument in which the conclusion follows deductively from its premises.

If deductive arguments cannot give us any new information that was not already present in the premises, what purpose do they serve? Why should you bother to state a conclusion if all of the information you need is already provided in the premises? If all arguments were as simple as the above example there would be little reason to state conclusions. The mere mention of both of these premises together would be sufficient for most people to "get the point" or "to put two and two together." Sometimes people do present such simple arguments without bothering to state the conclusion. For the same reason that premises can be omitted, conclusions can also be unstated. It is boring and occasionally condescending to dwell on the obvious.

Not all deductive arguments are simple, however. Sometimes the chain of reasoning that connects the premises to the conclusion is long and complex. When this is so, even though the conclusion contains no new information (in the sense that it only selectively *recombines* information stated in the premises), the conclusion may seem "new" to us because we had not put together the information in the premises in just that way. Even the person constructing the argument might be surprised to see where the premises lead. Thus, we can say that although the conclusion of a correct deductive argument can contain no new information, it can put information together in ways that might not have occurred to anyone before. Thus we can reach conclusions that are "new" from a psychological standpoint. Even when the conclusions of deductive arguments are novel, surprising, or startling in this sense, however, they can only draw out what was already there in the premises.

The following deductive argument reaches a conclusion that is apt to be psychologically new and surprising, even though its conclusion contains no new information. Smith presents the argument to his neighbor, Jones, who commutes from his suburban home to a job in the city, to convince Jones that he is spending three weeks of every year riding a commuter train.

> *Jones:*   Three weeks a year—that's ridiculous!
> *Smith:*   No, it's a simple matter of logic. You ride the train to and from work, one hour each way, five days a week, for a total of forty-nine weeks a year, allowing for your vacation and holidays. Using simple arithmetic, that comes to a total of 490 hours per year on the train. There are 24 hours in a day, and if you divide 490 by 24, you get 20 and 10/24 days. That's almost 21 days, or three weeks a year you spend on the train.
> *Jones:*   Ouch.

The reasoning in this argument depends on the use of mathematics. Mathematical arguments are almost exclusively deductive in character. It is especially in our use of mathematics, including simple arithmetic calculations, that deductive arguments pervade our everyday lives. Balancing checkbooks, counting change, and setting up a budget all require deductive reasoning. Although you probably do not use geometry much in your everyday life now, if you studied it in high school, you were intensely involved in constructing and evaluating deductive arguments. You began the course in geometry with a set of first principles—axioms, postulates, and definitions—and then proceeded to derive theorems (conclusions!) on the basis of those first principles. This was an exercise in deductive reasoning, and some parts of it were quite subtle. Even though you had all of the necessary premises in hand, it was not at all obvious in many cases how these premises could be combined to deduce the theorem you were supposed to prove.

All other areas of mathematics, including those that, unlike geometry, are not formulated as axiomatic systems, essentially depend on deductive arguments. All mathematical *proofs* are deductive arguments. Furthermore, we can regard mathematical proofs as the purest form of deductive reasoning, because even the premisses contain no information about what the real world is like. The mathematical principles that form the basis for mathematical proofs are themselves not now usually considered to contain factual information but rather to be true by definitions of the terms involved or to be true claims about abstract constructions of the human mind, such as numbers or geometric figures. This is what Bertrand Russell was referring to when he said "I fear that, to a mind of sufficient intellectual power, the whole of mathematics would appear trivial, as trivial as the statement that a four-footed animal is an animal" (*My Philosophical Development*).

Russell does not mean to say that all mathematics is trivial to *our* minds, for our intellectual powers are limited. When we *apply* mathematical reasoning to factual claims, as we did in the preceding example, in which the premisses included the information that Jones spent two hours on the train each working day, the results may seem surprising—just as the results of a complicated mathematical proof may seem surprising. The point is that the use of mathematical calculations in an argument does not introduce any new *information* that goes beyond what is already stated in the premisses.

Most arguments concerning ethics—in which the proponent attempts to show that an action is right or wrong or that a moral principle is acceptable or unacceptable—are deductive arguments. A standard way to establish that some kind of action is right (or wrong) is to show that all actions of that type are right (or wrong) because they fall into a broader class of right (or wrong) actions. The following argument provides an example:

All deliberate killing of helpless persons is wrong.
Euthanasia (mercy killing) is a deliberate killing of a helpless person.

Euthanasia is wrong.

In this argument, as in all correct, or valid, deductive arguments, *if* the premisses are true, the conclusion must be true as well. The question of whether the premisses *are* true (or acceptable, if one objects to regarding moral claims as true) is an important and interesting question, but the deductive character of the argument is independent of the answer to that question.

Other arguments commonly employed in ethics attempt to show that some moral principle is not acceptable because it would condone or permit actions that we consider to be immoral. This pattern of argument is somewhat more complicated than the last one, for it really contains an argument within a larger argument. The following example is an argument of this type:

(*First part*)

Whatever is done as an expression of love is morally acceptable.
Mrs. X, who believed her infant child's soul was possessed by demons that

could be driven out only by beating, beat her infant child severely because she loved him.

Mrs. X did something morally acceptable when she beat the child.

(*Second part*)

The conclusion of the argument in the first part is obviously false.
But that argument is deductive (if all its premisses are true, then its conclusion must be true as well).
The second premiss states a fact about Mrs. X's behavior, and its truth is not in question.

The first premiss is false. (It is not true that whatever is done as an expression of love is morally acceptable.)

This method of proving that a sentence is false—taking it as a premiss, and showing that it, alone or in combination with other premisses whose truth is not in doubt, leads deductively to an obviously false conclusion—is fairly common, not only in ethical arguments, but in mathematics and many other fields as well. It may seem odd to begin an argument with a premiss that is believed to be false. Nevertheless, this often happens in dialogues, when one person makes a statement and the other person tries to show that it is false, as in the following example:

> He: You don't love me anymore.
> She: Don't be silly. Suppose that I don't love you. If a woman doesn't love a man, she doesn't care what happens to him, she doesn't want to spend time with him, and she doesn't give him presents. But I do care what happens to you, I do want to spend time with you, and I do give you presents. So you see, I do love you.

This way of arguing is called *indirect proof*. We will look more carefully at the logical structure of this useful form of deductive argument in later chapters.

One other feature of many arguments in ethics is worth mentioning here. It might seem that because there are exceptions to general principles of morality these principles are statistical generalizations rather than universal generalizations. If moral principles were statistical generalizations then the arguments in which they were premisses would be inductive rather than deductive. When we understand how exceptions are treated, however, we can see that moral principles are regarded as universal generalizations, and that ethical arguments employing them are intended to be deductive.

For example, although the deliberate taking of human life is morally unacceptable in general, exceptions are recognized. If Jones deliberately kills Smith in self-defense, this act is not necessarily considered wrong. Such actions are permissible according to the general principle that allows killing in self-defense. The important point about such exceptions is that they too are governed by universally general principles, although these principles may be somewhat more limited in their application. Thus, to show that a particular killing was not a wrongful act even though it was deliberate, we might show that the circumstances surrounding the act make it a case of "killing in self-defense" rather than another sort of killing. Then according to the principle that killing in self-defense is morally justifiable, the act would not be considered morally wrong. When an apparent exception to some accepted moral principle is encountered, another deductive argument, based on a different acceptable general principle, will usually be employed to handle the exception.

Because in a valid deductive argument if the premisses are true the conclusion *must* be true as well, certain words and phrases are often used in ordinary language to mark or note the strong support provided in these arguments. Words and phrases such as "must," "it must be the case that," "necessarily," "inevitably," "certainly," "it can be deduced that," are frequently used to indicate that an argument is deductive. The terms "entail" and "imply," when used to refer to the connection between the premisses and the conclusion of an argument, frequently indicate a deductive connection.

These terms are sometimes used, however, when a conclusion is very strongly supported by evidence, but the argument is *not* deductive. To test whether or not an argument is deductively correct, ask the question: Do the premisses provide *conclusive* support for the conclusion of the argument? To answer this question for any except the simplest arguments, however, we need to know how to judge whether or not support is conclusive. We will concentrate on this point in later chapters. In the meantime, the clues provided here regarding the contexts in which deductive arguments are normally used and the special words used to indicate the presence of a deductive argument will provide some guidance. If the proponent of an argument intends it to be truth-preserving (here again we may need to grasp the context to see this), we can judge the argument by the standards for correct deductive arguments.

Our task can be complicated when arguments in ordinary language are stated incompletely. Then it is especially difficult to tell whether or not the missing premisses are universal or statistical generalizations. Contextual clues for judging whether or not arguments are deductively valid are particularly useful at this stage, because they help us to supply the appropriate type of missing premiss. If a missing premiss is to provide any real support for the conclusion, however, it should be no less plausible than the conclusion itself. If we ignore this caution about plausibility, we could transform *any* argument into a deductive argument with the addition of some premiss. (For example, the conclusion itself added to the premisses would make the argument deductive!)

Occasionally, people use terms like "necessarily" to bolster an argument—to make it look as if more support is present—when the support is considerably less than conclusive. This may be so in the following argument, taken from an advertisement paid for by a large oil corporation:

> Because it is keyed so closely to the marketplace and so responsive to it, private business is *necessarily* the most effective instrument of [economic] change.

It is fairly easy to see that although the fact that private business is so closely tied to what people buy and sell may provide a *good* reason to believe that private business is the most effective instrument of economic change, it is hardly a *conclusive* reason to believe this. It is clearly possible that government, with all its powers (including the power to control the money supply, interest rates, taxes, import duties, and other aspects of the economy) may be a far more effective instrument of economic change than private business, even though private business is more closely tied to the marketplace. Many large, private corporations, however, like the one that paid for this ad, would prefer that government refrain from using those powers and let a free market determine the state of the economy.

Another context in which arguments are presented as deductive although the evidence is less than conclusive should be noted: the stories about the master detective, Sherlock Holmes. We can recognize and admire the impressive logical powers of Holmes in these stories, but we should realize that most of his so-called "deductions" are really inductive arguments. Consider the following passage from "A Scandal in Bohemia," in which Dr. Watson visits Holmes after a long absence. Although Watson hasn't told him so, Holmes figures out that Watson has returned to the practice of medicine.

> "And in practice again, I observe. You did not tell me that you intended to go into harness."
>
> "Then, how do you know?"
>
> "I see it, I deduce it. How do I know that you have been getting yourself very wet lately, and that you have a most clumsy and careless servant girl?"
>
> "My dear Holmes," said I, "this is too much. You would certainly have been burned [as a witch] had you lived a few centuries ago. It is true that I had a country walk on Thursday and came home in a dreadful mess; but, as I have changed my clothes, I can't imagine how you deduce it. As to Mary Jane, she is incorrigible, and my wife has given her notice; but there again I fail to see how you work it out."
>
> He chuckled to himself and rubbed his long nervous hands together.
>
> "It is simplicity itself," said he; "my eyes tell me that on the inside of your left shoe, just where the firelight strikes it, the leather is scored by six almost parallel cuts. Obviously they have been caused by someone who has very carelessly scraped round the edges of the sole in order to remove crusted mud from it. Hence, you see, my double deduction that you had been out in vile weather, and that you had a particularly malignant boot-slitting specimen of the London slavery. As to your practice, if a gentleman walks into my rooms smelling of iodoform, with a black mark of nitrate of silver upon his right forefinger, and a bulge in the side of his top hat to show where he has secreted his stethoscope, I must be dull indeed if I do not pronounce him to be an active member of the medical profession."

The fiendishly clever Holmes is right on all counts, as usual, *but* it is just *possible* that Watson cleaned his own boots and that the signs of medical practice were the results of Watson helping out in an emergency rather than setting up his own practice. It may be possible to analyze arguments such as the ones Holmes gives here as *intended* deductive arguments in which a universally general premiss has been left unstated. Here, however, such an approach is unlikely to work, because the required premises, such as "Every pair of boots scored by cuts was cleaned by a clumsy servant," are no more plausible than the conclusion. Holmes's conclusion goes beyond the information he states in his premisses, and so his argument, although ingenious, is not a truth-preserving deductive argument.

Before turning to inductive arguments, it should be noted that the term "deductive argument" is often used when we mean *correct* or *valid* deductive arguments, that is, arguments in which if the premisses were true, it would necessitate the truth of the conclusion.

Sometimes, an argument's proponent intends it to be deductive, but the premisses, even if true, fail to guarantee the truth of the conclusion. An argument may *purport* to be deductive, for example, by using terms that indicate that the conclusion follows necessarily from the premisses, and fail to be so. Some authors define deductive arguments as arguments in which the premisses *purport* to provide conclusive support for the conclusion, or in which the proponent *intends* the argument to be deductive. Others define deductive arguments as those in which the premisses (including implicit premisses) actually provide conclusive support. Each way of defining the term "deductive argument" has its advantages and disadvantages. The disadvantage of defining "deductive argument" as "an argument in which the premisses, if true, provide conclusive support for the conclusion" is that the usual way of referring to fallacies that mimic deductive arguments as "invalid deductive arguments" is awkward since, by the definition, any argument that is deductive is automatically valid. An advantage of this definition is that it does not suggest that all inductive arguments are invalid deductive arguments solely because their premisses do not provide conclusive support for their conclusions. The structure and perspective of this textbook reflects the belief that it is better to recognize inductive augments as a separate type of argument with a special role and value instead of viewing them as deductive arguments that don't quite succeed. Students, nevertheless, should be aware of the two ways of defining deductive arguments. In this text, we will specify "correct" or "valid" deductive argument if the context does not make this clear. When we talk about fallacies that superficially resemble correct (valid) deductive arguments, we will adopt the usual practice and call them "deductive fallacies" or "invalid deductive arguments."

Exercises

1. Find an example of a deductive argument—one that does not depend on any unstated premisses—in a source other than a logic textbook (a newspaper, book, magazine, and so on). Identify the premisses and the conclusion of the argument.

2. If we define a deductive argument as one in which it is impossible for the conclusion to be false if all the premisses are true, which of the following sentences are true?
   a. A deductive argument can have a false premiss.
   b. A deductive argument can have a false conclusion.
   c. A deductive argument can have all false premisses and a false conclusion.
   d. A deductive argument can have all false premisses and a true conclusion.
   e. A deductive argument can have all true premisses and a false conclusion.

3. Which of the following arguments is deductive? Do any of the arguments require the addition of an obviously true, but unstated premiss?

   a. John is Mary's brother. Therefore, Mary has a brother.

   b. Mary is Michael's sister. Therefore, Michael is Mary's brother.

   c. In Australia there are black swans. Therefore, not all swans are white.

   d. Every student admitted to this college has the ability to perform well in college classes. You have been admitted to this college. Thus, you have the ability to perform well in college classes.

   e. Every senior can register for this class. Sally is not a senior. Sally cannot register for this class.

   f. Every senior can register for this class. Carlos cannot register for this class. Carlos is not a senior.

   g. If the Americans pursue their present policies in the Persian Gulf, they will antagonize the leaders of Iran. If the leaders of Iran are antagonized, they will start a war. So, if the Americans pursue their present policies in the Persian Gulf, the leaders of Iran will start a war.

   h. Every political survey has indicated that the next governor of the state will be a Republican. Therefore, the Republican candidate will win the governor's seat in the next election.

   i. Every graduating senior receives four tickets to graduation. There are 150 graduating seniors. So 600 graduation tickets are reserved for seniors.

   j. In the past, every time I have studied hard for an exam, I have done well, and I certainly studied hard for my logic exam, so I will do well on it.

III. INDUCTIVE ARGUMENTS

Arguments in which the premisses provide some support, but not conclusive support, for their conclusions are called *inductive arguments*. Thus, all of the premisses of an inductive argument can be true, and can support the conclusion, but the conclusion can still be false. Inductive arguments lack the definitive and the most valuable feature of deductive arguments—the ability to guarantee the preservation of truth. However, this apparent shortcoming is more than offset by a feature of inductive arguments that is lacking in deductive arguments. Inductive arguments can extend our factual knowledge. Their conclusions contain new information that is not present, even implicitly, in the premisses of the arguments. Although the field of mathematics is well suited to the sole use of deductive reasoning, in all other fields of human endeavor—natural science, the social sciences, history, literary criticism, and the practical knowledge of everyday affairs—inductive inferences and arguments are indispensable.

Holmes's arguments that so impressed Dr. Watson in Section II, established the existence of a *causal connection* between two types of things or events, such as the connection between the bulge in Dr. Watson's top hat and his hiding a stethoscope in the hat. The following argument, which is the opening passage in Charles Darwin's *The Origin of Species,* is also causal.

> When we compare the individuals of the same variety or sub-variety of our older cultivated plants and animals, one of the first points which strikes us

is, that they generally differ more from each other than do the individuals of any one species or variety in a state of nature. And if we reflect on the vast diversity of the plants and animals which have been cultivated, and which have varied during all ages under the most different climates and treatment, we are driven to conclude that this great variability is due to our domestic productions having been raised under conditions of life not so uniform as, and somewhat different from, those to which the parent species had been exposed under nature.

Darwin argues that great differences among individuals of the same species of domestic plants or animals (for example, think of the variety of dogs from miniature poodles to Great Danes)—which are much more noticeable than in wild species (for example, elephants)—are the result of humans breeding these plants and animals under a much greater variety of conditions than the conditions to which wild species are exposed. Humans have bred dogs for centuries in almost every part of the world—for sport, show, work, and a variety of other purposes. Elephants flourish in highly specialized environments in only two or three specific places, and there are only a couple of varieties of elephants.

Causal arguments are among the most frequently presented inductive arguments. We will have more to say about them in later chapters.

Other common types of inductive arguments are:

1. Arguments in which we conclude something about the future on the basis of what has happened in the past.

> That a stone will fall, that fire will burn, that the earth has solidity, we have observed a thousand and a thousand times; and when any new instance of this nature is presented, we draw without hesitation the accustomed inference.
>
> —David Hume, *Dialogues Concerning Natural Religion*

Philo, the speaker in this passage of the dialogue, does not actually state the obvious conclusion—that in the future stones will continue to fall; fire to burn; the earth to be solid—but his meaning is clear.

2. Arguments in which we conclude something about the past on the basis of present evidence.

> Pollen grains, though microscopic, are preserved in peat bogs in a remarkable manner for hundreds and even thousands of years. Since the pollen of every plant has its own special form, it is possible with the microscope to establish what plants were growing at different points in time. The distinct layers in peat-bogs thus become, as it were, the pages of a great picture book illustrating the changing flora of the land through the ages.
>
> —P. V. Glob, *The Bog People*

Here, the pollen, which is observed in the present, provides the basis for reconstructing the types of vegetation that grew in prehistoric times. Historians, geologists, archaeologists—all who are concerned with knowledge of the past—use inductive reasoning in this way.

3. Arguments in which we generalize on the basis of a sample of observations or experiments.

This is the type of inductive reasoning that is used by persons who conduct public opinion polls to determine who is a favorite political candidate or to learn about the public's attitude toward a particular piece of legislation. You have seen or heard such arguments, particularly in election years. Here is a different example of this form of reasoning, taken from a newspaper report about some recent research:

> Los Angeles—Equal property splits in divorces make men richer and women substantially poorer, a California study has found, buttressing nationwide efforts to include a husband's earning potential in settlements.
>
> The study of 3,000 divorces by a Stanford University researcher shows men improved their standard of living an average 42 percent in the first year after a divorce, while the living standard for women and children dropped 73 percent when income was compared to need.
>
> —Jay Matthews, *The Washington Post*

In this passage, the reporter not only provides the conclusion and the evidence on which it is based but also includes additional information about the effect the conclusion may have on future financial calculations for divorce settlements. Generalizing on the basis of samples is one of the most useful ways in which we extend our knowledge through inductive reasoning.

4. Arguments that conclude something about a particular case on the basis of what happens usually, or frequently, but not always.

The following passage, taken from Mark Twain's *Notebook,* is an amusing example of this common form of inductive argument:

> At bottom I did not believe I had touched that man. The law of probabilities decreed me guiltless of his blood, for in all my small experience with guns I had never hit anything I had tried to hit. And I knew I had done my best to hit him.

5. Arguments that conclude that a particular kind of similarity holds on the basis of other known similarities between two types of things.

You often use this form of reasoning when you make the decision to buy a particular brand of merchandise on the basis of good performance by other items of the same brand. Similarities in materials, methods of manufacturing, and other product qualities provide evidence to support some further, as yet unobserved similarity (such as durability). This kind of reasoning also provides the focus for much of our medical research. Investigators observe the effects of various substances on experimental animals, which are similar to humans in certain respects, and conclude that those substances will affect humans in similar ways. Here is an example, taken from a newspaper article:

> Marian C. Diamond, professor of anatomy at the University of California at Berkeley, warned recently that birth control pills may inhibit development of the brain.

Dr. Diamond said that research reveals that female sex hormones contained in birth control pills limit growth of the cerebral cortex, a part of the brain which regulates intelligence.

Dr. Diamond has been working with female rats into which she has injected a hormone equivalent to a birth control pill. Such rats showed less growth of the cerebral cortex than rats not injected with the hormone.

—*Parade Magazine*

Recognizing contexts in which inductive arguments are appropriate will help us to determine whether a given argument is inductive or deductive, although, of course, the real test of a correct inductive argument is to ask: Do its premises provide some support, but not conclusive support, for the conclusion? For an argument to be inductive, the truth of the premises should make it *probable* or *likely* that the conclusion is true as well. As in deductive arguments, special terms point to the nature of the inductive link between the premises and the conclusion in an inductive argument. These terms include "probably," "usually," "tends to support," "likely," "very likely," "almost always." When Mark Twain said "The law of *probabilities* decreed me guiltless," he indicated that his argument was inductive. The terms "may" or "might" are sometimes used to point to the tentative nature of an inductively drawn conclusion, as in Dr. Diamond's claim that "birth-control pills *may* inhibit development of the brain."

Another important difference between deductive and inductive arguments is that whereas deductive support is an all-or-nothing affair (either the premises conclusively support the conclusion or they do not), support in inductive arguments may vary from very strong to not-so-strong. The terms used to indicate that an argument is inductive frequently provide information about the degree of strength of the argument as well. For example, "may," "might," and "possibly" indicate rather weak or moderate support; whereas "almost always," "highly probable," and "highly likely" indicate strong support. The expressions "with practical certainty" or "with moral certainty" indicate a very high degree of inductive support. They are used when the evidence is overwhelmingly strong. Nevertheless, this support still falls short of the *logical*, or *truth-preserving*, certainty demanded in deductive arguments. The phrase "beyond all reasonable doubt" is often used to indicate a strong inductive argument, but it is sometimes used to signal a deductive argument as well.

Still another difference between inductive and deductive arguments concerns the effect of additional information on the strength of the argument. Suppose you have received $1,000 from the estate of a distant relative. You want to invest it in a mutual fund, and your main objective is preservation of capital with reasonable income from your investment. You select a fund that has paid a dividend every quarter for forty years, and has shown moderate growth. Your argument looks like this:

Fund X has a forty-year record of paying regular dividends while maintaining a slow growth of capital.
My investment objectives are regular income and preservation of capital.

Fund X is a suitable investment for me.

Suppose you later learn that Fund X has just undergone a reorganization, and that the new managers have a reputation for picking speculative stocks with aggressive growth potential. With the addition of this new information to your original argument, the support for the conclusion is considerably weaker.

Alternatively, additional information can strengthen an inductive argument. Consider some recent research conducted to study the role of heredity in alcoholism. On the basis of a ten-year study of 202 alcoholic men, Dr. T. Reich, at the Alcohol Research Center at Washington University, learned that 38 percent had alcoholic fathers, 21 percent had alcoholic mothers, 57 percent had alcoholic brothers, 15 percent had alcoholic sisters, 32 percent had alcoholic sons, and 19 percent had alcoholic daughters. When we realize that in the general population, alcoholism will eventually develop in only 3 percent of women and 8 to 10 percent of men, this information supports the conclusion that hereditary factors are important in the development of alcoholism. Additional information from Swedish studies of adopted children, which clearly showed that the children of alcoholics are four times more likely than other children to become alcoholics even if the children are adopted early in life by people who do not abuse alcohol, makes the argument in support of the hereditary character of alcoholism even stronger.

Thus, as these examples show, additional information can either strengthen or weaken an inductive argument. In contrast, if a deductive argument is valid, then the addition of premises cannot either strengthen the argument (its premisses already provide conclusive support) or weaken it in the sense of making it invalid. Since if the premises in the original argument were true, then the conclusion would be true as well, adding anything to the premises cannot change that. As we have said before, an argument that purports to be deductive is either valid or invalid; there are no degrees of validity. Premises of inductive arguments, however, can offer a range of support—from very strong to moderate to weak—for their conclusions. So additional premises can make an argument either stronger or weaker. If the support in an inductive argument is extremely weak, but the argument superficially resembles a correct inductive argument, the argument is called an inductive fallacy.

Some arguments, particularly those used in science, combine inductive and deductive elements. For example, even before Louis Pasteur, the famous French scientist, applied his method of pasteurization to destroy harmful organisms in fresh milk, he suggested the process of gentle heating as a solution to the problem of wine souring during the aging process. Yeast cells, which are living organisms, are responsible for the fermentation necessary to make wine. Pasteur, however, noted with the aid of a microscope that there were several types of yeast, and he believed that some of them were responsible for souring in wine during the aging process. He reasoned that if all yeast cells in the wine were destroyed by gentle heating after the fermentation was completed, the wine could age without souring. His method worked and earned him the enthusiastic thanks of the wine industry in France.

The deductive part of Pasteur's argument is

> Yeast cells are the cause of souring in wine.
> Gentle heating destroys yeast cells.
> _____
> Gently heated wine does not sour.

Based on the success of Pasteur's experiment (heated wine did not sour), Pasteur *inductively* concluded that his belief about yeast causing the wine to sour was correct. This conclusion follows inductively, rather than deductively; although the yeast cells were killed by heating, it is *possible* that some agent that also could be destroyed by heating was the causal factor in wine spoilage. Even though there is a deductive component to arguments of this type, their overall structure is inductive, because the conclusion about the cause does not follow with certainty from the premisses concerning the success of the experiment. Arguments of this type, which are fundamental to scientific reasoning, will be examined more closely in Chapter 7.

Exercises

1. Find an example of an inductive argument in a newspaper, magazine, or other contemporary source. Reconstruct the argument in standard form (see p. 41), and tell whether it falls into any of the categories described in this section.

2. Identify the premisses and the conclusion of each of the following arguments. Classify each argument (as it is stated) as deductive or inductive. If you believe that an argument *purports* to be deductive but fails to be (perhaps because it lacks some obvious universal generalization), discuss why you think the missing premiss is any more plausible than the conclusion of the argument.

    a. The introduction of cooperative marketing into Europe greatly increased the prosperity of the farmers, so we may be confident that a similar system in the United States will greatly increase the prosperity of our farmers.

    b. Workers should vote for a program that will see that they get their fair share of the products of industry. Whenever taxes go up, prices go up; whenever prices go up, profits go up; and whenever profits go up, the workers get less than their fair share of the products of industry. So workers should vote for lower taxes.

    c. The last four presidents of the United States have supported equality of races and civil liberties. But we do not have equality of races, and the erosion of our civil liberties continues. Therefore, Congress or some other force must be preventing our presidents from bringing about the reforms they want.

    d. The *Farmers' Almanac,* which has an excellent record on such matters, predicts that we are in for a hard winter this year. So there is going to be a tough winter ahead.

e. Arguments (e) and (f) are concerned with astrology.

[handwritten: purports to be deductive, but it's error is that Pliny says that men born under the same star should have same fortune. However, It is not everyone's destiny is the same]

If a man's destiny is caused by the star under which he is born, then all men born under that star should have the same fortune. But masters and slaves and kings and beggars [whose fortunes differ greatly] are born under the same star at the same time. Thus, astrology—which claims that a man's destiny is caused by the star under which he is born—is surely false. —Pliny the Elder, *Natural History*

f. There are events which are foreknown by persons who have applied their observation to that end. Of this kind are tempests and gales of wind, produced by certain aspects of the Moon, or the fixed stars, towards the Sun, according to their several courses, and the approach of which is usually foreseen by mariners....

Since it is thus clearly practicable, by an accurate knowledge of the points above enumerated, to make predictions concerning the proper quality of the seasons, there also seems no impediment to the formation of similar prognostication concerning the destiny and disposition of every human being. For by the constitution of the Heavens, at the time of any individual's primary conformation, the general quality of that individual's temperament may be perceived ... [and] an event dependent on one disposition of the Heavens will be advantageous to a particular temperament, and that resulting from another unfavorable and injurious. From these circumstances, and others of similar import, the possibility of foreknowledge is certainly evident.

—Ptolemy's *Tetrabiblos,* quoted in Patrick Suppes, *A Probabilistic Theory of Causality*

g. Skin hue is neither a necessary nor a sufficient condition for being classified as black in our culture. That looking black is not in our culture a necessary condition for being black can be seen from the phenomenon of passing.* That it is not a sufficient condition can be seen from the book *Black Like Me,* by John Howard Griffin, where "looking black" is easily understood by the reader to be different from being black.

—R. A. Wasserstrom, "Racism, Sexism, and Preferential Treatment," in *UCLA Law Journal* 3(1977):581

h. The real justification (perhaps a cynical one) for progressive taxation is that the wealthier receive more benefits from government and, therefore ought to pay more. This may not be true in a strict accounting sense; the middle and upper classes don't use food stamps. But in this country, the essence of government is to preserve the social order. The well-off benefit from this far more than do the poor.

—Robert Samuelson, "Economic Focus," *Pittsburgh Post-Gazette*

i. When the elaborate methods of preparation of some of the plants used to break down the monotony of life are studied, it becomes quite evident that

---

*Passing is the phenomenon in which a person who in some sense knows himself or herself to be black "passes" as white because he or she looks white.

primitive man must have possessed something other than chance to reveal to him the properties of food and drug plants. He must have been a keen observer of accidents to discover fermentation, the effects and localization of alkaloids and toxin resins, and the arts of roasting and burning a product to gain from it the desired narcotization or pleasing aromas (coffee).

—Oakes Aimes, quoted in *Technics and Human Development,* by Lewis Mumford

j. It is clear that our *Iliad, Odyssey, Erga,* and *Theogony* are not the first [embodiments of the saga]. These ostensibly primitive poems show a length and complexity of composition which can only be the result of many generations of artistic effort. They speak a language out of all relation to common speech, full of forgotten meanings and echoes of past states of society; a poet's language, demonstrably built up and conditioned at every turn by the needs of the hexameter metre. There must therefore have been hexameter poems before our *Iliad.*

—Gilbert Murray, *The Literature of Ancient Greece*

k. Every state is a community of some kind, and every community is established with a view to some good; . . . But, if all communities aim at some good, the state or political community, which is the highest of all, and which embraces all the rest, aims at good in a greater degree than any other, and at the highest good.

—Aristotle, *Politics*

l. *Note:* The long-lost bowerbird was found in the Foja Mountains of west New Guinea, and its bower and display were discovered. The bower is a stick tower on a rimmed moss platform, adorned with separate piles of fruit of three different colors. The displaying male extends toward the female a blue fruit set against his golden crest.

> In many other kinds of birds, males court females and stimulate them to ovulate by constructing real or mock nests and by ritualized offering of food (courtship feeding). If bower building developed as an exaggerated form of such courtship behavior the bower may represent a gigantic courtship nest. The decoration of bowers by colored objects has been viewed as derived from courtship feeding, since males of all species for which the display is known pick up a decoration and hold it in the bill toward the female, and since these objects are sometimes edible (fruit).
>
> —J. M. Diamond, "Rediscovery of the Yellow-Fronted Gardener Bowerbird," *Science* 216 (1982):431

m. The economy will soon be in good shape. A pair of government reports pointed yesterday to an improving economy. The Commerce Department reported that construction spending rose 1.4 percent in December, the second straight monthly gain, and orders to U.S. factories for new manufactured goods rose a strong 4.8 percent.

—Newspaper report

n. [The Assistant Secretary for Health of the Department of Health and Human Services] released the results of the National Household Survey on Drug

Abuse, which examined a national sample of Americans over age 12, and the High School Senior Survey.

The surveys showed that one out of three Americans over age 12 has tried some kind of illicit substance.

—Newspaper report

IV. FALLACIES

Fallacies or fallacious arguments can appear to provide support for conclusions. As we know, however, appearances can deceive.

Committing a *logical fallacy* is different from simply making a *factual error.* Although in ordinary language, the term "fallacy" is sometimes used to refer to false beliefs (particularly ones that are believable because they are attractive to us), we will use the term only to refer to certain mistakes in reasoning. False beliefs are not fallacies in and of themselves in this sense, and merely being in error about something should not be regarded as committing a fallacy. To believe, for example, that Thomas Jefferson did not own slaves is erroneous but not fallacious. The person who doesn't believe that Jefferson owned slaves is ignorant of certain facts, but that person's logical ability to draw conclusions on the basis of evidence may not be at fault. To commit a fallacy, we must offer or accept nonevidence as evidence for a claim. A fallacy may appear to offer sufficient evidence to support the conclusion of an argument without actually doing so.

Fallacies can mislead us for many reasons. Sometimes a conclusion is so attractive that we are ready to accept almost anything that is offered as evidence in support. Swindlers and "confidence men" present preposterous "evidence" for the reliability of their money-making schemes, but they count on the desire for money to cloud the judgment of their victims. Alternatively, an assertion may be so repugnant that we will accept almost any statement as evidence against it. Critical thinking requires us to separate the psychological desire to believe or deny a claim from considerations of how well supported that claim is.

In other cases, we may be moved by a strong like or dislike, or respect or disapproval, for the *person* making a claim, which may blind us to such a degree that we fail to consider the nature of the evidence. Fond parents are notorious for their willingness to accept a child's word as sufficient evidence for fantastic claims. Critical thinking requires that we be on guard in this respect as well.

When a fallacy is presented in the context of a threat or an enticement, we may not notice that no evidence is being offered. An "argument" that substitutes a threat of force for evidence has, like many fallacies, a special name. It is called "appeal to force," or (in Latin) "*ad baculum.*" This fallacy appeals to our emotions (fear) rather than our reasoning ability.

Another fallacy that makes an emotional appeal is called "appeal to pity" or "*ad misericordium.*" This occurs when we confuse feeling sorry for someone with evidence for the truth of an assertion. A well-known scientist who is dying of cancer made an appeal to pity when he said in response to recent challenges of his pet theory: "I can say these things . . . because this is my last hurrah, and I have to tell the truth."

Instead of playing on our emotions, a fallacy can deceive us by mimicking some aspect of a correct form of argument. We will be better able to understand this property of fallacies after we have studied correct forms of argument in some detail, but a few examples here will make this point somewhat clearer.

Things that are causally connected occur together with some regularity, and the premisses of causal arguments cite such regular connections. But to argue that there is a causal connection *merely* on the basis of the fact that things have occurred together occasionally in the past is to argue fallaciously, because the joint occurrence could be mere coincidence. All sorts of things can happen together without any causal connection existing between them. Suppose that you have received good news on Mondays on several occasions in the past. It would be fallacious, solely on this basis, to argue that the day of the week was the cause of the good news.

An example of a fallacy that mimics a correct deductive argument occurs in Woody Allen's "Love and Death," a film that pokes some fun at philosophy. The hero offers this argument to demonstrate his skill in logic:

A $\supset$ B C $\supset$ B

All men are mortal. Socrates is mortal. Therefore, all men are Socrates.

The way in which this fallacious argument parodies the classic example of this deductive form of argument is transparent enough to make it amusing rather than deceptive. Life would be simpler if all fallacies were so easy to detect.

Sometimes fallacies are committed because relevant evidence is ignored. This can happen as a result of thinking in terms of *stereotypes*—fixed, rigid, or conventional mental patterns that leave little room for noting individual variations in information received or for classifying new information appropriately. A blatant example of this kind of fallacy would be to argue that a person was intelligent on the basis of the fact that he or she was a member of some racial or ethnic group. This argument ignores the well-known fact that individual members of any ethnic or racial group vary considerably in intelligence. Prejudicial judgments of this type are a particularly invidious form of thinking in terms of stereotypes.

Stereotypic thinking is not always this obvious (or obnoxious). Psychologists have demonstrated the pervasiveness of fallacious reasoning involving stereotypic thinking in the absence of any racial or ethnic prejudice. Two psychologists presented the following problem to several student groups and professional colleagues (Amos Tversky and Daniel Kahneman, "Judgments Under Uncertainty," *Science* 185 [1974]:1124). Persons to whom the problem was presented were told that a description had been drawn at random from a sample containing descriptions of 30 lawyers and 70 engineers. This is the description:

> John is a 39-year-old man. He is married and has two children. He is active in local politics. His favorite hobby is the collecting of rare books. He is competitive, argumentative, and articulate.

The problem is to tell whether John is an engineer or a lawyer.

A large majority of these people answered "lawyer," even though the number of descriptions of engineers outnumbered the number of descriptions of lawyers by more than two to one! It is thus much more likely that a description drawn at random from such a collection would be a description of an engineer, but almost everyone simply ignored this bit of evidence. On the basis of the results of this test and similar tests, these psychologists concluded that people are the captives of certain stereotypes pertaining to lawyers and engineers. Presumably, the general stereotype of a lawyer is formed by media (primarily newspaper and television) exposure to high-powered trial lawyers, who are competitive, argumentative, and articulate. Collecting rare books can be an expensive hobby, and many lawyers earn large incomes. In addition, many high-level political offices are held by men and women trained in the law. None of the information presented in the description is incompatible with the engineering profession, however, and a large number of lawyers lead less glamorous lives than those lawyers who exemplify the stereotype. If the information that the engineers in the sample far outnumbered the lawyers is simply ignored, then the judgment that a lawyer (not an engineer) is being described is based on a stereotype while some solid information is simply not considered.

V. REVIEW

In this chapter, we have learned to distinguish deductive arguments from inductive arguments and to understand the general nature of fallacies. In Chapter 3, we will examine some specific types of arguments so that we can develop standards for evaluating them. But before we can do this, we must make certain preliminary distinctions. Once it becomes apparent that an argument is being presented, the pertinent questions to ask and to answer are:

1. What is the conclusion?
2. What evidence is offered in support of the conclusion?
3. Is the evidence conclusive or partial? Is it very weak, or does the conclusion fail to take account of some important evidence?
4. If the answer to the third question is unclear, look at the context in which the argument is offered.

   Is it a mathematical argument, or some other argument in which the conclusion simply combines or restates information already stated in the premises? Arguments of this type are probably deductive.

   Is it an argument that tries to establish something about the future or the past on the basis of present evidence? Is it an argument designed to show that something is the cause of something else (a causal argument)? Is the argument based on a sample study, or on what happens most of the time, or on similarities? These arguments are probably inductive. Remember, too, to look for words such as "probably" and "necessarily," because they often indicate which type of argument is being presented.

The most important new terms introduced in this chapter are defined below.

Deductive Argument: An argument in which the premisses provide (or purport to provide) conclusive support for the conclusion.

Factual Information: Information about what the real world is like, in contrast to what is true merely by definition of the terms involved or what is mathematically true.

Fallacy (*Fallacious argument*): An argument in which the premisses provide only very weak support, or no real support, for the conclusion.

Indirect Proof: When we argue for a claim by indirect proof, we show that a contradiction or obviously false sentence follows deductively from the assumption that the claim is false. Since a deductive argument with a false conclusion must have at least one false premiss, we use this method to show that the assumption that the claim is false is itself false, or, in other words, that the claim is true.

Inductive Argument: An argument in which the premisses provide some support, but less than conclusive support, for the conclusion.

Sound Argument: A correct inductive or deductive argument in which all the premisses are true.

Standard Form: A way of writing arguments in which the premisses are listed on separate lines and separated from the conclusion by a solid line.

Truth-preserving: The property of correct deductive arguments that guarantees that if their premisses are all true, their conclusions will also be true.

Valid argument: A correct deductive argument, that is, an argument in which the premisses, if true, guarantee the truth of the conclusion.

VI. EXERCISES

Reconstruct all of the arguments in the following passages. Write them in standard form, and then categorize them as inductive or deductive. Try to identify and supply any missing premisses. If you use any clues from the context of the argument to identify the type of argument and/or any missing premisses, describe them.

1. Fluorescent light is good for houseplants. In an experiment in a commercial nursery, a group of houseplants was exposed to four hours of flourescent light in addition to normal daylight. These plants grew much more quickly than others that were not exposed to the additional lighting. They were also generally greener and healthier looking.

—Newspaper article, *Arizona Daily Star*

2. Of course, the human brain [which weighs about 1,500 grams] is not the largest in the animal kingdom. The elephant's brain weighs 2,500 grams (some five and a half pounds), and the brains of the biggest whales are twice that size.

—Isaac Asimov, *The Intelligent Man's Guide to the Biological Sciences*

3. If we ask precisely wherein consists the greatest good of all, which ought to be the aim of every system of legislation, we shall find that it is summed up in two principal objects, *liberty* and *equality*. Liberty, because any individual dependence is so much force denied to the body of the State; equality because liberty cannot subsist without it.

—Jean-Jacques Rousseau, *The Social Contract*

4. We are bound in duty to pay due respect, not only to what is truly the right of another, but to what, through ignorance or mistake, we believe to be his right. Thus, if my neighbor is possessed of a horse which he stole and to which he has no right, while I believe the horse to be really his and am ignorant of the theft, it is my duty to pay the same respect to this conceived right as if it were real.

—Thomas Reid, *Essays on the Active Power of Man*

5. From an account of Joseph Lister's search for an antiseptic chemical to prevent deaths that followed surgery.

> At the end of 18 months, Lister had used the carbolic acid treatment on 13 cases of compound fracture, with results that could be tabulated as follows:
> Deaths 2
> Hospital gangrene. 2
> (amputation and recovery. . . . . .1)
> (recovery without amputation . . . . .1)
> Recovery without complications 9
> These were not enough cases to prove conclusively that carbolic acid was the weapon which Lister sought to fight hospital diseases, but they represented a mortality of only 15 percent as against the usual record of more than twice that figure.
>
> —Agatha Young, *The Men Who Made Surgery*

6. The vandals mutilated five sacred statues, destroyed a sacred book, smeared black paint around, and scribbled obscenities and racial remarks on walls.

Temple leaders said the attack seemed to be planned. They note that the vandals had to bring the paint with them.

—Report about the desecration of a Hindu temple in suburban Pennsylvania, *Pittsburgh Post-Gazette*

7. An *association* between two or more elements within a geological deposit in no way implies a systematic, behavioral, or dynamic relationship between the components. All that is implied is a roughly coincidental contextual relationship for the events of which the elements were derivatives. For instance, the finding of a whale bone and a tuna vertebrate in a geological deposit in no way implies that whales ate tuna or for that matter that tuna ate whales! Nevertheless, the depositional context of an aquatic environment may be indicated.

—Lewis Binford, *Bones*

8. I recommend that you close the sales tax loopholes which currently exempt cigarettes, alcoholic beverages sold in bars and restaurants, arcade games, cable television, confection products, paper and cleaning products, and non-prescription drugs—most of which are taxed, in fact, in a majority of our states today.

Surely we must question a system that taxes furniture while exempting cigarettes, or taxes the radio while exempting the arcade game, or taxes the prime rib in a restaurant while exempting the martini from the bar of that same restaurant.

—Pennsylvania Governor Richard Thornburgh's Budget Address, *Pittsburgh Post-Gazette*

9. From a report of an excavation of a Mesolithic site in Ireland, inhabited approximately 9,000 years ago.

> At what times of year were the Mount Sandel huts occupied? Could the site have served as a year-round settlement? Our excavations have uncovered much evidence with seasonal connotations. For example, the salmon bones are evidence of summer occupation. Today the main salmon run up the Bann is in mid-summer: June, July, and August. In Mesolithic times there may also have been an earlier run, say in April or May. Although the lower water temperatures [at that time] make it unlikely that the salmon run would continue beyond the fall, eels do run downstream in the fall: September, October and November are the best months of the eel run. Hence the eel bones at the site are evidence of fall residence. So is the presence of hazelnuts, which are ready for picking by mid-fall, and of water-lily seeds, which are best collected in September.
>
> —P. C. Woodman, "A Mesolithic Camp in Ireland,"
> *Scientific American* 2(1981):126

10. [Approximately 10 million people are living or will live in western Russia outside the 30-kilometer zone around Chernobyl during the next 70 years.] "Outside the 30-kilometer zone, radiation exposure [from the nuclear accident at Chernobyl] was of course much lower, but because millions of people were affected, the anticipated number of excess cancers could be very large. As a rough estimate, the report calculates that exposure to relatively short-lived radionuclides from the Chernobyl accident will increase cancer mortality by about 0.05% in western Russia. [Thus there would be] some 5000 additional deaths over 70 years."

—*Science* 233(1986):1031

deductive but figures are estimated

11. "Is it possible that he was conscious all that time?" asked Peter Ivanovich.

"Yes," she whispered. "To the last moment. He took leave of us a quarter of an hour before he died, and asked us to take Voloyda away."

The thought of the sufferings of this man he had known so intimately, first as a merry little boy, then as a school-mate, and later as a grown-up colleague, suddenly struck Peter Ivanovich with horror, despite an unpleasant consciousness of his own and this woman's dissimulation. He again saw that brow and that nose pressing down on the lip, and felt afraid for himself.

"Three days of frightful suffering and then death! Why that might suddenly, at any time, happen to me," he thought, and for a moment felt terrified.

—Leo Tolstoy, *The Death of Ivan Ilych*

12. Doctors in Texas have reported finding a virus in patients with multiple sclerosis, a discovery that could help explain the origin of the disease and possibly lead to a way to prevent it.

"What's exciting is that the virus has been found at the time people have the disease," Dr. Melnick said.

Melnick and his colleague, Edward Seidel, analyzed spinal fluid taken from 12 patients with nerve diseases and 27 others without such illnesses.

The virus was found in four of the 12 patients with the diseases; it was not found in any of the patients without nerve ailments.

The scientists bolstered their case by also finding antibodies to the virus in the blood serum of the four patients with the virus. That provides additional evidence that the virus was not a contaminant picked up accidentally in the laboratory.

—Associated Press newspaper story

13. [E]verything would seem to be heading up for the beer business. Per capita consumption of the golden brew in the United States last year reached an all-time high, currently equaling about a six-pack a week for every American 18 and over. Beer sales for the past several years have been going up 4 percent to 5 percent annually; so far the rise this year is running around 2 percent—not bad for a recession year.

inductive –

—*Time Magazine*

14. A lawyer offers the following argument in a burglary case to prove the defendant's innocence:

> Assume that the defendant was burglarizing the store at 7:30 PM, on Friday the 13th of October. This is the time that the burglar alarm sounded. No fewer than six of his co-workers can testify that he was at his job from 4 PM until midnight on that day. In order to break into the store, he would have had to have been in two places at the same time.

15. The question of nutrition is closely related to that of locality and climate. None of us can live anywhere; and he who has great tasks to perform, which demand all his energy, has, in this respect, a very limited choice. The influence of climate upon the bodily functions, affecting their retardation or acceleration, is so great, that a blunder in the choice of locality or climate may not merely alienate a man from his duty, but may withhold it from him altogether, so that he never comes face to face with it. . . . Enumerate the places in which men of great intellect have been and are still found; where wit, subtlety, and malice are a part of happiness; where genius is almost necessarily at home: all of them have an unusually dry atmosphere. Paris, Provence, Florence, Jerusalem, Athens—these names prove this: that genius is dependent on dry air, on clear skies—in other words, on rapid organic functions, on the possibility of continuously securing for one's self great and even enormous quantities of energy.

—Friedrich Nietzsche, *Ecce Homo*

16. A layman seldom sets out the premises from which he is arguing, so it is generally impossible to tell whether some false conclusion is the result of thinking illogically about true premises, or the result of thinking logically about false premises. Or both!

—G. A. Miller, citing John Stuart Mill, "Is Scientific Thinking Different?" *Bulletin of The American Academy of Arts and Sciences,* February, 1983.

17. An important element in the analyses used to justify the counterforce [nuclear weapons designed to destroy the nuclear weapons of the adversary] race is the idea that it might be possible to fight a nuclear counterforce war in a carefully controlled manner. However, because the means of command and control are inevitably vulnerable to nuclear destruction, it is extremely doubtful that a nuclear war could be limited and prevented from escalating into an all-out civilization-shattering exchange. Moreover, even if a nuclear exchange could be strictly limited to military targets, a strategically significant counterforce attack would probably cause tens of millions of civilian deaths.

—H. Feiveson and F. von Hippel, "The Nuclear Freeze—Pro and Con," *Physics Today* (1983):40

18. Paleolithic inhabitants who decorated the [Lascaux] cave were predominantly right-handed. Not only do the majority of the animals face right (an orientation generally preferred by right-hand draftsmen) but also the "fossilized" rope depicted . . . was obviously the work of a right-handed individual. Since the natural twisting motion

involves the overhand rotation of the thumb away from the body, the twist in this case must have been imparted by the right hand.

—Letter from T. A. Reisner, *Scientific American* 4(1982):7

19. Although incest taboos do possess social functions, these cannot account for their origins, because it is impossible to believe that early men who instituted these rules could have known their possible social advantages.

—Annemarie de W. Maalfjit, *Images of Man*

20. Yes, and if oxen and horses and lions had hands, and could paint with their hands, and provide works of art, as men do, horses would paint the forms of gods like horses, and oxen like oxen, and make their bodies in the image of their several kinds.
    The Ethiopians make their gods black and mule-nosed; the Thracians say theirs have blue eyes and red hair.

—Xenophanes, *Fragments*

21. To be able to read the classics you have to know "from where" you are reading them, otherwise both the book and the reader will be lost in a timeless cloud. This, then, is the reason why the greatest "yield" from reading the classics will be obtained by someone who knows how to alternate them with the proper dose of current affairs.

—Italo Calvino, trans. by P. Creagh, "Why Read the Classics?"

A Closer Look at Inductive Arguments

CHAPTER 3

I. INTRODUCTION

In this chapter, we will take a closer look at some specific types of inductive arguments. The aim of any inductive argument is to establish its conclusion. This cannot be done with absolute certainty, because, by definition, inductive arguments present less than conclusive evidence to support the truth of their conclusions. But an inductive argument should provide *some* assurance that the conclusion will be true if the premises are all true. The very least we can expect is that an inductive argument will give us some measure of how likely we are to be correct if we draw a conclusion on the basis of the evidence presented.

Our task of studying inductive arguments will be made somewhat simpler if we classify them according to *form*. The concept of form is very important in logic. The term *form of an argument* refers to the structure of the argument, without regard to its subject matter or content. Although you may not have thought about forms of argument before, the term "form" in the sense used here is not new to you. You have undoubtedly been concerned with structures in many real-life situations.

For example, most high-school students are required to take a civics course in which various forms of government are discussed. In the United States, we have a democratic constitutional form of federal government composed of three main branches—executive, judiciary, and legislative. The powers and responsibilities of each of these branches are outlined in our Constitution.

The British form of government, in contrast, is a constitutional monarchy composed of a legislative branch (Parliament), a judiciary branch, and a crowned king or queen, who—except in cases of abdication—holds his or her office for life. The head of government is the prime minister, but unlike our president, the prime minister is not the head of state. The powers and responsibilities of the various branches of the British government are, like our own, outlined in a constitution.

There are many other forms of government in addition to constitutional democracies and constitutional monarchies. The Soviet Union has an entirely different form of government. The point is that it is possible to study these various forms of government in a rather *abstract* way, without taking particular notice of the individuals who fill the positions determined by the form of government at any given time. When we study forms of government in this way, we learn something about their parts and how these parts are related to one another. Similarly, when we study forms of arguments, we will learn something about their parts and how they relate to one another.

In the sections that follow, we will identify several forms of inductive argument and establish standards for determining how well the premises in the various argument forms support the conclusions. The correctness of an inductive argument is not determined, however, merely by its form. Other considerations are important as well, and these too will be discussed.

II. STATISTICAL SYLLOGISMS

The word "syllogism" is derived from the Greek and literally means "a putting together of ideas." The use of the term in logic is related to this meaning.

Syllogisms are arguments with two premisses, and a conclusion that "puts together" information presented in the premisses. The argument

> All men are mortal.
> Socrates is a man.
> _____
> Socrates is mortal.

is an example of a syllogism. This particular syllogism is deductive, but there is an inductive form that closely resembles the deductive form. In the inductive form of syllogism, the first premiss is a statistical generalization, rather than a universal generalization, and this form is therefore referred to as a "statistical syllogism." The argument

> 90 percent of freshmen at State University are residents of the state.
> Elena is a freshman at State University.
> _____
> Elena is a resident of the state.

is an example of a statistical syllogism.

The statistical syllogism is the form of argument we use when we argue that what is generally true (or false) is also true (or false) for a particular case. The first premiss, which is a statistical generalization, is not always stated numerically. "Almost all," "most," "very often," "almost never," and similar expressions may be used to form statistical generalizations. Here is an example:

> Hardly any freshmen had a philosophy course in high school.
> Oscar is a freshman.
> _____
> Oscar didn't have a philosophy course in high school.

Reasoning in this form pervades many everyday life occurrences. We don't plan outdoor picnics in Chicago in January because the weather usually won't be favorable. If we are fortunate enough to travel in the south of France, we expect to find good food at the country inns because that's usually the case. A summons for an audit of our tax return is dreaded because most audits of tax returns are costly and unpleasant.

1. Form of Statistical Syllogisms

With the preceding examples in mind, we are ready to look at the abstract form of statistical syllogisms:

> X percent of all F's are G's.
> a is an F.
> _____
> a is a G.

In this form of argument, *F* and *G* represent classes of individuals or properties that are possessed by members of a class. The lower-case letter *a* represents an individual person, place, or thing. The class denoted by *F* is called the *reference class* (the class that the individual mentioned in the second premiss is referred to or belongs to.) The class denoted by *G* is called the *attribute class*. (Members of the attribute class have the property *attributed to* the individual in the conclusion.)

Notice that this form of inductive argument proceeds from a generalization in the premiss to a claim about a particular individual in the conclusion. Statistical syllogisms are exceptions to the often-offered (but incorrect) characterization of inductive arguments as arguments that go from particular premisses to a general conclusion.

Since arguments of this form are inductive arguments, their conclusions may be false even though their premisses are true. However, as is true of other inductive forms of argument, there are both strong and weak statistical syllogisms. We will now examine some criteria for appraising statistical syllogisms.

2. Standards for the Strength of Statistical Syllogisms

The most obvious standard for judging the strength of a statistical syllogism is the closeness to 100 percent (or 0 percent in the negative case) of the statistical premiss. It is readily apparent that if the premiss in the preceding sample argument had stated that 99 percent instead of 90 percent of the freshmen at State University were state residents, a stronger case would have been presented for the conclusion that "Elena is a state resident." Similarly, the argument would have been weaker if only 85 percent rather than 90 percent of all the freshmen were state residents. If only 51 percent of all freshmen were state residents, the argument would be so weak that we would call it fallacious.

Another standard for strong statistical syllogisms is just as important—perhaps even more important—but is less obvious. This standard requires us to use all available relevant evidence when we select the *reference class* to which the individual is assigned. The problem is that any individual belongs to an *indefinite number* of classes. Let us assume that we have the following information about Elena, for example. She belongs not only to the class of freshmen at State University, but also to the class of women, the class of brown-haired persons, the class of supporters of equal rights for women, the class of 18-year-olds, the class of part-time office workers and the class of members of the Foreign Students' Club. In constructing an argument with the conclusion "Elena is a state resident," we must take into account *any* class that Elena belongs to that might affect the probability that she is a state resident. Suppose, for example, we know that only 2 percent of the members of the Foreign Students' Club are state residents. If we assign Elena to this reference class, ignoring all the other information, we have the following argument:

2 percent of all members of the Foreign Students' Club are state residents.
Elena is a member of the Foreign Students' Club.

Elena is *NOT* a state resident

Both this argument and the original argument have true premises, and their statistical premises are very close to 100 percent and 0 percent. So, if we were to use only the standard that requires a strong statistical generalization, both arguments would appear to be strong ones. Yet their conclusions contradict one another. The requirement that we use all available relevant evidence when choosing the reference class—called the requirement of *total evidence*—can prevent this unfortunate result. The statistical premiss must contain the percentage (although this need not be expressed numerically) of freshmen who are members of the Foreign Students' Club and who are also members of any other class Elena belongs to that is relevant to state residency.

Let us assume that the only classes for which information relevant to state residency is available are the class of freshmen and the class of Foreign Students' Club members. A check of school records for past years shows us that generally only 3 percent of freshmen who are state residents join the Foreign Students' Club. We are now in a position to construct the proper statistical syllogism that embodies all available relevant evidence:

3 percent of all freshmen at State University who are members of the Foreign Students' Club are state residents.
Elena is a freshman member of the Foreign Students' Club.

Elena is *NOT* a state resident.

In many arguments, the statistical premiss is not stated when it is a generalization that forms part of our common background knowledge. The argument

The student who sits next to me in logic class doesn't have a home telephone, for he isn't listed in the telephone directory.

is an example of a statistical syllogism with the implicit premiss, "Almost all phone-owners are listed in the telephone directory." As always, when we are concerned with evaluating arguments, we should try to state any implicit premisses. Sometimes when implicit premisses are exposed, we find that they are somewhat questionable, or that they fail to represent all available relevant evidence. When the implicit premiss in this argument is exposed, we may realize that the student belongs to a class of persons who usually do not have their home phone numbers listed (for example, the class of persons who have changed residences recently), and that a different reference class is required to state the statistical premiss properly.

Exercises

1. In each of the following statistical syllogisms, which are not stated in standard form, identify the reference class and the attribute class and assess the strength of the argument, using the criteria discussed in this section.

 a. About 95 percent of all professional hair dyes and a considerable portion of home dyes now contain paraphenylenediamine or related chemicals (also called peroxide dyes). My hair was dyed at the hairdresser's. Therefore, peroxide dye was used on my hair.

b. Most Pittsburgh winters include at least one heavy snowfall, so they will almost certainly have one heavy snow this winter in Pittsburgh.
c. Of all the students who registered this term, 75 percent favor the university's requiring students to pay an activity fee to be used by the student government. Since Ellen is registered this term, she undoubtedly is in favor of the fee.
d. Very few people dislike chocolate, so Jill will be pleased with the chocolate dessert you made.
e. Since most German shepherds are easy to train, your German shepherd puppy should do well in dog-training school.
f. Stocks typically outperform bonds in the first recovery year after a recession. Since this is such a year, stocks should outperform bonds.
g. Only about 3 percent of cigarette smokers actually die from lung cancer, so my smoking won't result in death from lung cancer.

2. Each of the following passages gives advice that is based on a statistical syllogism. In each case, reconstruct the argument and explicitly state the statistical premiss, the premiss that refers to a particular individual, and the conclusion.

a. Always remember that the odds in this hobby [mushroom collecting] are heavily against the collector. He is gambling the price of a mess of mushrooms against the doctor and hospital bills. With such odds in mind it is up to the collector to be critical of what he collects.
—A. H. Smith, *The Mushroom Hunter's Field Guide*

b. Dear Dr. Molnar: I am 56 and considering an operation. Would you advise against it? I've had a loss of hearing since about age 12. On a recent checkup my doctor said two bones have grown together in the middle ear. He thinks there is an 85 percent chance of improvement to 'very good;' 10 percent chance of no improvement; 5 percent chance of further damage.
Answer: Why should I advise against the operation? Only one chance in 20 of being worse off; 17 chances in 20 of being better off. There are few if any operations in which 100 percent success can be guaranteed. If I were the patient in such a case, I'd take the 17 to 1 odds.
—"Doctor Molnar," syndicated newspaper column

c. At a Democratic committee meeting the incumbent prosecuting attorney loses his party's endorsement. He considers running as an Independent, but his advisers tell him not to because hardly any Independents could receive enough votes to win an election in that city.
d. Take your umbrella when you go out today because there is a 70 percent chance of rain in your area.

3. The Fallacy of Incomplete Evidence

Arguments in the form of statistical syllogisms that fail to take into account all available relevant evidence when choosing the reference class (the class denoted by F in "X percent of all F's are G's") are fallacious. Any evidence that might influence the probability that the individual (a) has the property attributed to it in the conclusion (G) is relevant evidence. Although we can say what "relevant" means is this context, we require background knowledge to determine whether or not any particular evidence is relevant. Without appropriate background knowledge, deciding just what evidence is relevant may be difficult or impossible.

It is also difficult to say in a general way what "available" means in this context. How much research is required to be sure that we have accounted for all available relevant evidence? Obviously, we are seldom in a position to spend years of our lives—or even hours—acquiring evidence that is "available" in the sense that it is part of the storehouse of human knowledge. Often, we must make judgments and/or take actions (such as agreeing to an operation) in the absence of evidence that may be "available" but that we are unable to obtain because we lack time or money. The requirement of total evidence is not intended to place unrealistic restrictions on reasoning. What it demands is that we make a reasonable effort to find appropriate reference classes, that we do not simply ignore—through carelessness, prejudice, or laziness—evidence that is within our reach, and that we do not suppress evidence that is known to be relevant. Consider the following example of a fallacious statistical syllogism:

> 90 percent of all medical-school faculty are men.
> Dr. Shirley Jones is a medical-school faculty member.
> ———————————————————————————————
> Dr. Shirley Jones is a man.

This argument appears to be a strong one only if we ignore the well-known fact that "Shirley" is almost always a female name and is rarely given to a man. If we accept the argument as it stands, we will be more likely to accept a false conclusion than a true one, for the probability that a faculty member named Shirley is male is surely very low. Even though we do not have exact figures to assign a probability to the proper reference class (male medical-school faculty member named Shirley), we can see that this additional evidence is relevant and that it undermines the original argument.

The argument

> The governor of this state doesn't have a private home telephone, for there is no listing for this in the telephone directory.

is also fallacious, for it fails to take into account the well-known information that many government officials have private phones with unlisted numbers. Similarly, it would be a violation of the requirement of total evidence to infer that your bus for work, which is normally on time, will be on time when the city streets are covered with ice.

In statistical syllogisms, the requirement of total evidence is designed to ensure that we choose the right reference class. The requirement of total evidence actually applies to all other forms of inductive argument as well. In other forms of argument, there may not be a reference class, but the requirement of total evidence demands that we take account of all available relevant evidence that could affect the truth of the conclusion of the argument. The rules of critical thinking do not permit us to construct arguments in which we selectively choose evidence that supports our conclusions while we ignore available evidence that would undermine them.

Exercises

Each of the following arguments commits the fallacy of incomplete evidence. In each case, discuss what relevant evidence is ignored.

1. Most Russians don't speak English, so the newly appointed Russian ambassador to the United Nations probably doesn't speak any English.

2. Most movie actors aren't politicians, so Ronald Reagan, a former movie actor, is not a politician.

3. Most Americans earn less than $100,000 a year, so the president of General Motors earns less than $100,000 a year.

4. Only about 2 percent of college football players ever play professional ball after college, so the Heisman trophy winner probably won't play pro ball after he is out of college.

4. Special Types of Statistical Syllogism

A number of special uses of statistical syllogism are so common that they have been given standard names. The names are also applied to the fallacious forms of argument that superficially resemble the correct forms.

i. Arguments from Authority

All of us depend to some extent on the counsel and advice of those who know more than we do. Sometimes when we present arguments, we appeal to what experts have said on the matter instead of presenting any direct evidence to support the claim we are making. Such reliance on experts is not opposed to critical thinking, for—under certain restrictions—it may be justified as a type of strong statistical syllogism. After all, experts or authorities are almost always, or usually, correct when they make statements about the subject in which they are experts. Their talent, training, and experience combine to place them in a position to understand and evaluate evidence in areas that are not easily accessible to everyone else.

When the following conditions are met:

> (i) The authority invoked is an expert in the area of knowledge under consideration;
> (ii) There is agreement among experts in the area of knowledge under consideration; and
> (iii) The statement made by the authority concerns his or her area of expertise;

then it is reasonable to take the authority's word on the matter. When these conditions are fulfilled, the form of argument from authority can be stated thus:

Most of what authority *a* has to say on subject matter *S* is correct.
a says *p* about *S*.

---

p is correct.

This form of argument is obviously a version of statistical syllogism. The first premiss is a statistical generalization; the second premiss is a statement about a particular assertion (a member of the reference class); and the conclusion attributes the property of being correct to that assertion.

Actually, arguments from authority are rarely presented in just this form. Usually the authority is merely cited or quoted in support of some conclusion. For example, a point in advanced physics might be settled by quoting Albert Einstein's views on the matter; a claim concerning the best way to bake a successful soufflé might be supported by citing the method recommended by Julia Child. Sometimes, not just one authority but a whole group of authorities is cited: "All the leading physicists agree that the earth is older than 16,000 years." Regardless of the way in which these arguments are stated in English, they are acceptable only when they meet criteria (i)–(iii).

It is always *possible* for the conclusion of an argument from authority to be false even when these three criteria are satisfied. In any inductive argument, the truth of the conclusion is not guaranteed by the truth of the premisses and the correctness of the form of argument. The history of science offers many examples of expert authorities who were mistaken in their beliefs and were proved wrong in the light of new evidence. It often takes time for new evidence to be assimilated and for experts in a field to recognize the significance of the evidence and to change their opinions. Nevertheless, arguments from authority do have an important place in both scientific and everyday reasoning.

ii. Fallacious Appeals to Authority

Arguments that mimic correct arguments from authority but that fail to meet one or more of criteria (i)—(iii) are fallacious appeals to authority. Such arguments can deceive us in several ways. First, some persons set themselves up as authorities—or their followers set them up—when they actually lack the expertise of a genuine authority. Knowledge of advanced areas of modern science, for example, is achieved only after years of training and study. Yet there always seem to be some people who claim to have achieved such knowledge through quite different means (self-study of obscure texts, visions, inspirations, hunches, and so on). They claim to have found cures for diseases that have eluded standard medical research or to be able to explain major cosmic events in ways that defy the truth of well-accepted scientific theories. People who make such claims, called "cranks" by all but their followers, are not reliable authorities in the subject area in which they profess expertise. Thus, arguments that appeal to their authority are fallacious.

Second, in certain areas of some fields of knowledge (psychiatry and economics are two important examples) there is still widespread disagreement among those who have all the academic and professional credentials possessed by experts in a field. In criminal cases that invoke an insanity defense, for example, it is common to find "expert" psychiatric witnesses for both the defendant and the plaintiff—one willing to testify, in complete sincerity, to the insanity of the defendant; the other, no less sincere, willing to testify to the sanity of the defendant. When this kind of disagreement occurs among experts in a field, an appeal to the authority of one side or the other is fallacious. There can be no legitimate appeal to authority in such a case, although, of course, the *evidence* presented by the experts may be evaluated on its own merits. When such evidence is considered, however, the form of argument is not an argument from authority but some other type of argument related to the nature of the evidence.

Finally, when someone is a genuine expert in a particular field of knowledge or has achieved success in a difficult and highly competitive enterprise, that person is properly entitled to prestige and recognition for his or her accomplishments. Such people are often asked to express their views on a wide variety of issues, many of which lie completely outside their field of expertise. Famous physicists are asked their opinions on moral questions; a football hero testifies to the virtues of one brand of panty hose. Their statements cannot carry the weight of a legitimate appeal to authority, for they are obviously speaking about subjects not within their area of expertise. We must be careful not to accept arguments that rely on the glamour or prestige of an authority in one field to support truth of claims in another, unrelated area of knowledge.

iii. Arguments Against the Person (*Argumentum Ad Hominem*)

Closely related to arguments from authority are *arguments against the person*, or, in Latin, *argumentum ad hominem*. In these arguments, the conclusion states that a particular claim is *false* because it is made by a certain individual. Such arguments are legitimate only when there is reason to believe that most of the claims made by the individual concerning a particular aspect of that subject matter are false. Arguments against the person are often made in legal cases when lawyers wish to attack the credibility of witnesses on the opposing side. If a lawyer can show that a witness has committed perjury when questioned about the subject at issue and, in addition, that a lie would benefit the witness in the case under consideration, the argument may be strong. Like arguments from authority, correct arguments against the person can be construed as statistical syllogisms:

Most of what individual a says about a particular subject matter S is false.
a says p about S.

_____

p is false.

Although the two forms of argument are similar, few of us are ever in a position to claim that most of what an individual says about a subject is false. There are many expert authorities in various fields; there are probably many fewer individuals who lie regularly or who are almost always wrong about a subject. Truth-telling, rather than lying, is the normal mode of human communication. Usually—there are exceptions, of course—people do not go around making pronouncements in subject areas in which they are more often wrong than right. For this reason special care should be exercised when arguments against the person are evaluated.

With this caution in mind, we can mention other circumstances (in addition to the courtroom situation already mentioned) in which legitimate arguments against the person can occur. One concerns pronouncements of scientific cranks whose views are in opposition to the collected wisdom of scientists; in the area of their weird theories, scientific cranks are more apt to be wrong than right. Similarly, exaggerated claims about products sold by high-pressure salespeople are probably more often false than true, especially when these people work for organizations that have bad records with the local chamber of commerce. The performance records of some stockbrokers are so poor that their clients would be advised to hold off when those brokers say "Buy."

iv. Fallacious Arguments Against the Person

Arguments that a claim is false on the grounds that it was made by a particular individual are *fallacious arguments against the person* unless most claims made by the individual on that subject are false. We may commit this fallacy for several reasons. We may dislike the person who is making the claim, or we may disapprove of the person's looks, clothing, views, habits, religion, ethnic origin, or some other personal characteristic or association. Obviously, such prejudices should not be allowed to intrude on our critical judgments of the evidence for truth or falsity of claims.

A second reason why we sometimes are misled by fallacious arguments against the person is our desire to believe that the claim made in the conclusion is false. When we disagree with a claim someone makes, we may, in the absence of any evidence against that person's claim, try to discredit it by attacking the character or qualifications—however irrelevant they may be to the issue—of the individual who is making the claim. Samuel Johnson actually defends this fallacious use of the argument against the person!

> "When there is a controversy concerning a passage in a classic, or concerning a question in antiquities, or some such subject, one may treat an antagonist with politeness and respect. But where the controversy is concerning the government or religion of my country, it is of such vast importance to have the better, that the *person* of the opponent is not to be spared. If a man firmly believes that religion is a great treasure, he will consider a writer who endeavors to deprive mankind of it as a robber; he will look on him as *odious* even though the infidel may think himself in the right. . . ."
>
> Dr. Johnson said that when a man voluntarily engages in an important controversy, he is to do all he can to lessen his antagonist, because authority from personal respect has much weight and often more than the reasonings. "If," said he, "my antagonist writes bad language, though that may not be essential to the question, I will attack him for his bad language."
>
> —James Boswell, *The Ominous Years*

Johnson is probably correct in saying that people are more often moved by their respect (or lack of respect) for a person than by the strength of argument. It is an unfortunate fact that people usually pay less attention to reasons than to the person providing them. Nevertheless, we, as critical thinkers, do not want to be deceived by such ploys!

When an argument against the person (or *ad hominem* argument) attacks the character of an individual, the argument is called an "abusive *ad hominem.*" When the attack is not against the person *per se,* but is rather an attack on the circumstances of the person (such as the person's religion, nationality, or membership in a political party), the argument is called a "circumstantial *ad hominem.*"

Another variant of *ad hominem* arguments is called "*tu quoque,*" which can be translated "you too." This occurs when someone attacks the truth of a conclusion, by accusing the person who offers the argument of holding a position that is similar to the one being criticized. These arguments are almost always fallacious.

Regrettably, fallacious arguments against the person of all these types occur in an interchange among very distinguished scientists, reported recently in the *New York Times.* The focus of the discussion is the contention by Dr. Luis W. Alvarez, a Nobel-prize winner in physics for work on nuclear particles, and his son, Dr. Walter Alvarez, a geologist, that the impact of a large comet 65 million years ago (evidenced by a layer of metallic iridium found in sedimentary rock all over the world) was responsible for the extinction of the dinosaurs. Although there is some evidence for this position, it is not conclusive, and most paleontologists (scientists who specialize in fossil evidence for extinct life forms) reject the Alvarezes' theory that a single catastrophe caused the extinction, which (they interpret the fossils as showing) took place over a very long period. This situation has all of the features that promote the use of fallacious arguments from authority and fallacious arguments against the person: a distinguished expert in one field (L. Alvarez, a nuclear physicist) speaking in an area outside his expertise (paleontology) and disagreement among expert paleontologists about the nature of the fossil evidence.

In the quoted portions of the *Times* report below, fallacies are identified in square brackets.

> Dr. Luis Alvarez also criticizes three earth-sciences professors at Dartmouth College, Charles B. Officer, and his colleague Charles L. Drake as well as Robert Jastrow, who all reject the cometary impact hypothesis. "It is now clear," Dr. Jastrow said in an interview, "that a catastrophe of extraterrestrial origin had no discernible impact on the history of life as measured over a period of millions of years."
>
> Dr. Alvarez responded: "There isn't any debate. There's not a single member of the National Academy of Sciences who shares Jastrow's point of view." (Dr. Alvarez is himself a member of the Academy). [Fallacious appeal to authority; members of the academy are scientists distinguished in many different fields but do not constitute a legitimate authority in paleontology.]
>
> He added: "Jastrow, of course, has gotten into the defense of Star Wars, which for me personally indicates he's not a very good scientist. In my opinion, Star Wars doesn't stand a chance." [Circumstantial *ad hominem;* Jastrow's conclusion about the comet is rejected because Jastrow has aligned himself with supporters of the government's Strategic Defense Initiative.]
>
> In rejoinder, Dr. Jastrow noted that Dr. Alvarez had personally flown on the nuclear raid that destroyed Hiroshima, and that in 1954, Dr. Alvarez had been one of only five physicists willing to appear before the Atomic Energy

Commission to denounce J. Robert Oppenheimer as a security risk. . . . [*Tu quoque*: In response to Alvarez's accusation that Jastrow is aligned with questionable government science policy, Jastrow points out Alvarez's own connection with other questionable government science-related activities.]

In his public barbs at Dr. Officer, Dr. Alvarez asserted that the Dartmouth geologist was laughed to scorn at a 1985 meeting of the American Geophysical Union and that the incident had shorn Dr. Officer of scientific credibility. [Abusive *ad hominem*] . . . Dr. Officer responded: "This is a misstatement. There was no outburst of laughter following Walter's (Alvarez's) brief comment, and no direct or implied derision of me as a scientist by the audience. . . .

Closer to home, Dr. Alvarez has harsh words for some of his colleagues at Berkeley. Among them is Dr. William A. Clemens, a paleontologist who recently reported in *Science* that he had found abundant dinosaur fossils along Alaska's North Slope. The dinosaurs would not have faced the danger of freezing since temperatures were much milder then, but at such high latitudes, total darkness must have persisted for several months every winter, thereby halting the growth of plants and curtailing food supplies.

That the dinosaurs nevertheless survived such conditions, Dr. Clemens contends, undermines the comet theory because a cometary impact would not have blocked sunlight for nearly as long as the polar winter.

Dr. Alvarez responds by saying that he considers Dr. Clemens inept at interpreting sedimentary rock strata and that his criticisms can be dismissed on grounds of general incompetence [abusive *ad hominem*], a charge Dr. Clemens rejects.

—*The New York Times*

v. Arguments from Consensus

In an *argument from consensus* some assertion is held to be correct (or incorrect) on the grounds that most people, or a great number of people, believe (or reject) the assertion. An automobile advertisement arguing that one brand of car is the best states that "50 million Americans can't be wrong!" It is not at all unusual—particularly in advertising campaigns—to try to win acceptance for some claim by saying that "everyone" accepts it. Such arguments, when they are correct, can be cast in the following form of statistical syllogism:

When most people agree on a claim about subject matter *S*, the claim is true. *p* is a claim most people make about *S*.

---

p is true.

When the form of the argument is exposed in this way, we can see that it may be very difficult to construct arguments in which the first premiss is plausible. In arguments from authority, the authority has acquired expert knowledge that entitles us to accept his or her claims in some subject area. The primary question in arguments from consensus is whether or not majority opinion entitles us to judge an assertion to be true. In most cases, when the opinion of the majority is correct, better forms of evidence that would constitute support for the claim are available to almost anyone. Thus, we regard arguments from consensus as weak even when they are correct and as fallacious in most cases. When matters of importance hang on the conclusion of such an argument, consensus usually carries only supplementary weight and the conclusion would have to be supported by other evidence as well.

An apparent exception to these remarks about argument from consensus occurs when majority opinion validates the truth of a claim *by definition*. One example is the recent judicial ruling that a movie is pornographic if it violates local standards of decency (if most people in that community would consider it pornographic). Under these circumstances, the following argument would be correct:

A movie is legally pornographic if most people consider it pornographic.
Most people consider movie *M* pornographic.

Movie *M* is legally pornographic.

However, careful examination of this argument reveals that it is not of the same form as an argument from consensus. The first premiss is *not* a statistical premiss; instead the first premiss states something that is true as a result of a definition (in this case, the legal definition of "pornographic"). The second premiss, although it is a statistical generalization, states that the circumstances for the application of the definition have been fulfilled for the movie in question; the conclusion states that the movie belongs to the class of pornography thus defined. If the premisses of this argument are true, then the conclusion must be true as well. It is not an inductive argument, but a deductive one. It is a correct argument, but it is not an argument from consensus.

5. An Incorrect Form of Inductive Argument

The following argument is a correct deductive syllogism:

All humans are mammals.
All mammals are animals.

All humans are animals.

Letting upper-case letters represent class terms, we can exhibit the form of this argument as follows:

All *F*'s are *G*'s.
All *G*'s are *H*'s.

All *F*'s are *H*'s.

When we replace "all" with "most" in the syllogistic form just shown, we change a deductive form of argument to an inductive form:

Most *F*'s are *G*'s.
Most *G*'s are *H*'s.

Most *F*'s are *H*'s.

However, unlike the statistical syllogism, this is *NOT* a good inductive form of argument, because even when we are careful about taking account of all available relevant evidence, this form of argument is not likely in general to lead us from true premisses to true conclusions. Consider the following argument which contains all true premisses:

> Most physicists are men.
> Most men are non-physicists.
> _____
> Most physicists are non-physicists.

Exercise

Construct another example of an argument in this inductive form with obviously true premisses and an obviously false conclusion. *Hint*: Choose classes in such a way that F is a much smaller class than G, so that it is possible for most F's to be G's and most G's to be H's, while most or even *NO* F's are H's, since the H's could simply be just all things that are not F's.

6. Missing Premisses in Statistical Syllogisms

Once the form of an argument is identified, the task of providing any missing premisses becomes somewhat easier. We have already noted that the statistical premiss in statistical syllogisms is frequently suppressed, particularly when it represents a claim that is widely known. In arguments from authority, arguments against the person, and arguments from consensus, the statistical premiss is almost always suppressed. However, we need to supply this premiss to evaluate these arguments, because their correctness depends on whether or not most of what an authority says is right, or whether or not most of what a person says about a subject is false, or whether or not majority opinion on a subject is reliable. We can often prevent the acceptance of fallacious arguments by making suppressed premisses explicit.

Exercises

Reconstruct each of the following arguments. Identify the form of each argument, and note any that are fallacious. Discuss whether or not additional background knowledge is required to evaluate the argument.

1. Charles Colson, a former White House aide and a convicted perjurer, charged that the CIA knew about the Watergate break in in advance. Referring to Colson's charge, William Colby, former CIA Director, said, "His lack of credibility should cause the charge to fall of its own weight." (Reconstruct Colby's argument.)

2. My favorite fashion model, Cheryl Teigs, says that Cover Girl cosmetics are safest for delicate skins. Therefore Cover Girl is the safest brand for sensitive skins.

3. Many prisoners have complained that conditions in the county jail are unsanitary. However, these persons are outlaws, so we can safely deny the truth of their charges.

4. Both the American Medical Association and the American Dental Association have formally endorsed fluoridation of drinking water. Therefore, fluoridation promotes dental welfare and is not generally harmful to people's health.

5. Most people believe that smoking marijuana is dangerous to one's health. Therefore, smoking marijuana is dangerous to one's health.

6. During both the Ford and the Carter administrations, economic advisors to the president agreed that the best way to encourage the United States to conserve oil would be to impose a tariff of three dollars a barrel on imported oil. Therefore, such a tariff would be the best conservation measure.

7. Congresswoman Sanders has argued that failure to restructure our foreign policy in the Mideast will result in an outbreak of war. She's a woman, however, and we all know that feminine logic is not reliable when it comes to affairs of state.

8. You are in no position to challenge my argument that my school's team will defeat yours in the big match, for you are just as biased in favor of your school as I am in favor of mine.

9. The following argument supports the use of folk medicines or natural remedies:

> I know they have been well reported of and many wise persons have tried remedies providentially discovered by those who are not regular physicians, and have found a blessing in the use of them. I may mention the eminent Mr. Wesley [the founder of Methodism], who, though I hold not altogether with his Arminian doctrine, nor with the usages of his institution, was nevertheless a man of God.
>
> —George Eliot, *Felix Holt*

10. Now you are better equipped to analyze this argument that appeared in Chapter 1:

> After so much lying, even for purposes North considers patriotic, his protestations that now he only wants to tell the truth aren't worth much. Why should he be considered believable, even under oath, when he testified under oath that he had so often considered other values more important than truth?
>
> —Tom Wicker, *New York Times*

III. ARGUMENTS FROM ANALOGY

When we draw an *analogy* between two things or two types of things, we point out an observed similarity between them. We often notice and comment about similarities in everyday life. Analogies—particularly unusual and surprising ones—are the stuff of which literature, especially poetry, is made. Thus, Boswell (*In Search of a Wife*) draws an analogy between his character and a kind of fabric: "I am a weaker man than can well be imagined. My brilliant qualities are like embroidery on gauze." Lawrence Durrell (*Reflections on a Marine Venus*) compares the close of days in Rhodes to falling fruit: "In Rhodes the days drop softly as fruit from trees." Open almost any page of Shakespeare and you will find beautiful analogies, which in literature are called "similes" and "metaphors":

> How far that little candle throws his beams!
> So shines a good deed in a naughty world.
>
> —*Merchant of Venice*

When, on the basis of analogies, we conclude that items that are similar in observed ways are also similar in some further, as yet unobserved, respect, we employ an *argument from analogy.* In an example in Chapter 2, analogical reasoning from the observed effects of the birth-control hormone on rats (which are physiologically similar to humans) was used to conclude that birth-control pills may affect human brain development.

Not every use of analogy is an *argument* from analogy. For an argument to be present, a conclusion must be drawn on the basis of the noted analogy. The examples from Boswell, Durrell, and Shakespeare are not arguments from analogy, for the analogies that are stated there are not used to support some further unobserved similarity; instead these analogies encourage us to see the world a bit differently by directing our attention to an interesting similarity.

1. Form of Arguments from Analogy

Although arguments from analogy are stated in a variety of ways, they can be reconstructed to exhibit the following basic form:

Objects of type X have properties F, G, H, etc.
Objects of type Y have properties F, G, H, etc.,
and also an additional property Z.

Objects of type X have property Z as well.

The premisses of these arguments mention the respects (F, G, H, and so on) in which the two types of objects have been observed to be similar. The second premiss also mentions a property (Z) that has been observed in one type of object. The conclusion states that the other type of object has that property as well.

In the argument that concludes that birth-control pills may affect human brain development, the properties F, G, H, and so on—although unspecified in the premisses—are the physiological properties that humans (objects of type X) and rats (objects of type Y) have been observed to share. It is because rats possess these properties that they are used in medical experiments. The further property Z of brain development being affected by the birth-control hormone has been observed for rats and is inferred to hold for humans as well.

Testing drugs and other potentially harmful substances on experimental animals and—in the absence of sufficient information about the effects of these substances on humans—concluding that humans will be similarly affected is well understood not only by scientists but also by the general public. In view of this widespread familiarity with the role of experimental animals, the similarities between these animals and humans are rarely stated explicitly in the premises of the analogical arguments that depend on such similarities.

When we reconstruct analogical arguments to judge their strength, we should try to state explicitly any *implicit* points of analogy contained in the premises. Sometimes special knowledge is needed to state the implicit similarities. For example, most of us do not know enough physiology to be able to state precisely the important similarities between experimental animals and humans. We must then rely on experts' claims that the similarities are present, but we should at least be aware that the nature of these similarities is crucial to the argument.

2. Standards for the Strength of Analogical Arguments

The strength of an argument from analogy, or an *analogical argument,* depends heavily on the *relevance* of the similarities mentioned in the premises to the similarity stated in the conclusion. One feature is relevant to another if the presence of the first increases (is positively relevant to) or decreases (is negatively relevant to) the probability that the second feature will also be present.

In the argument we have been discussing, the conclusion states that a certain substance will produce a physiological effect in humans similar to the physiological effect it produces in rats. The implicit premise asserts the existence of physiological similarities between rats and humans. The similarities employed in the implicit premise are relevant to the similarity drawn in the conclusion, because similar physiological features are relevant to whether or not the same substance will produce a similar physiological effect. Of course, the physiological features of rats are not exactly similar to those of human. Rats are much smaller, their brains are less complex, and there are undoubtedly other important (relevant) differences between rats and humans. Such dissimilarities between rats and humans account in part for the tentative nature of the conclusion of this argument, which is indicated by the use of the term "may."

The *number* of relevant similarities in the premises and the number of relevant dissimilarities between the two types of objects are also important in judging the strength of analogical arguments. Obviously, the more relevant similarities the two types of objects share, the stronger the argument that the feature mentioned in the conclusion will also be shared. By the same token, the greater the number of relevant dissimilarities, the weaker the argument is.

Consumer decision-making frequently employs arguments from analogy. You may, for example, decide to buy another American car made by the manufacturer of the old car you now own because your own car has been so reliable. If your conclusion that the new car will be reliable is based on a suitable number of relevant analogies between the old car and the new one, and if there are few relevant dissimilarities, your argument will be strong.

Some features that we believe to be relevant to automotive reliability are incorporated in the type of engine, the braking system, the transmission, and the suspension systems. If these features in the new car and the old car are similar, the conclusion that the new car will be reliable may be strongly supported. If, however, the new car has many innovations (perhaps a new fuel-injection system and a new computer-controlled starter) or if your old car is a family sedan and the new car is a sports model with radically new design features, your argument from analogy will be weakened by these relevant dissimilarities. Of course, not every feature of a car is relevant to reliable performance. The color of the car and the style of upholstery, for example, probably make no difference at all.

Other criteria for determining the strength of analogical arguments are the number and the variety of instances mentioned in the premises, or in other words, the size and diversity of the sample from which the analogy is drawn. The special value of a larger and more varied set of instances is that this facilitates recognition of just which similarities *are* relevant. If the similar properties mentioned in the premises and the similarity stated in the conclusion go together in a variety of otherwise dissimilar circumstances, we have reason to believe that their connection with one another is not accidental—that a causal connection or some other real connection exists between the properties mentioned in the premises and the property mentioned in the conclusion.

Suppose, for instance, that you had owned not just one reliable car made by the same manufacturer but had owned and driven six of this manufacturer's cars, in various models and styles. Your argument that another car made by this manufacturer will be reliable will be strengthened, because the additional evidence would tend to show that the manufacturer produces a variety of reliable cars and that you were not just exceptionally lucky when you purchased your last car.

Similarly, if experiments had shown that birth-control hormones had an adverse effect on brain development not only in rats but also in monkeys and other experimental animals, then the conclusion that birth-control hormones have an adverse effect on humans would have been strengthened. The additional evidence would tend to show that there is not something special about the reaction of rats that makes them relevantly dissimilar to other mammals (and possibly to humans) in their response to the hormone.

The principle that a variety of cases strengthens an analogical argument may seem to conflict with the principle that says relevant dissimilarities between instances in the premises and the instance in the conclusion weaken an analogical argument. There is no real conflict between these two principles, however. The instances mentioned in the premises can have properties that differ in *nonrelevant* ways, but must also be similar in ways which are relevant to the property inferred in the conclusion.

3. Fallacies Associated with Analogical Arguments

Arguments that fail to meet the standards for strong analogical arguments but that somehow resemble correct arguments from analogy are fallacious. Arguments that attempt to establish a conclusion on the basis of irrelevant analogies are defective in this way. In *A System of Logic* (first published 1843), John Stuart Mill named this fallacy the *"fallacy of false analogy."* To argue that Joan is probably lazy because her brother John is lazy is an example of this fallacy, for the similarities between Joan and John that are implicit in the premiss (whatever similarities siblings typically share) are not particularly relevant to the property of laziness. Many families have both lazy and industrious children.

One of Mill's own examples of this fallacy is the argument that a paternalistic form of government is superior to other forms of government, on the basis of the similarities between families and states, and the benefits of a paternalistic system of governance in families. Mill points out that the relevant qualities for the successful paternalistic governance of a family—affection of the parents for the children and parental superiority in wisdom and experience—are conspicuously absent in most paternalistic forms of state government. States and families are therefore relevantly dissimilar to one another with respect to how they should best be governed.

Many examples of false analogy are found in early anthropological studies of primitive cultures. Because scholars falsely assumed that certain aspects of these cultures were similar to our own, they viewed the behavior of individuals in primitive societies as perverse or bizarre. For example, early observers of some tribal cultures noted that in these societies the words for "mother" and "father" refer to several persons—not only to the biological parent, but also to the parent's sisters and/or brothers. Since the observers believed that in our own society this could only occur when a child was confused about the identity of the biological parents, they concluded that the same was true in these societies, and that the usage of the terms meant that at some time in the past there had been a system of group marriage in which the terms that mean "mother" and "father" were applied to a variety of persons because the child could not know which members of the group were actually the biological parents. Later, and more detailed, anthropological studies—notably those of A. R. Radcliffe-Brown—showed that the kinship terminologies used in our society and in tribal societies are relevantly dissimilar but equally systematic ("logical") and useful in their own contexts. It is no more mysterious for a child in a tribal society with a different kinship terminology to call his or her mother's sister "mother" than it is for a person in our own society to call father's sister, mother's sister, father's brother's wife, and mother's brother's wife all "aunt," despite the difference between the relationships.

4. Analogy in Archaeology and in Legal and Moral Reasoning

We have already discussed the use of analogy in medical research. Archaeology is another science that depends heavily on arguments from analogy. Archaeologists study prehistoric peoples by examining the material remains of their implements, artifacts, and buildings. Since the people who made these objects are no longer alive, archaeologists cannot directly observe how these things were used by their makers. In many cases, moreover, the peoples studied by archaeologists lived before the invention of writing, left only fragmentary records, or wrote in languages that we do not yet understand.

Archaeologists note, however, that other people, who are living now or whose lives are historically documented, use or once used items *similar in form* to those found in archaeological excavations. On the basis of these observed similarities, archaeologists infer by analogy that the prehistoric items were *used for similar purposes*. Thus, when archaeologists working in caves in Oaxaca, Mexico, found awl-like objects made from sharpened deer bones that were analogous in virtually every relevant respect (including patterns of wear) to bone tools used by contemporary Oaxacan farmers to scrape kernels from corn, these archaeologists—who found remains of corn in the caves as well—unhesitatingly attributed the same function to the prehistoric objects.

Judges rule on the legality of actions and cases brought before them in trials. In a civil court, for example, a trial might be held to determine whether a proposed merger between two companies involves a violation of the antitrust laws. To rule on such actions, judges must be aware of any laws that are applicable to the particular case being tried before them. However, in addition to being guided by laws—which are usually stated rather broadly and are sometimes difficult to apply to complex cases—judges are guided in their rulings by *precedent*. Legal precedents are previous judicial rulings (interpretations of the law for particular cases). Analogical reasoning plays an important role in the legal process, particularly with regard to the use of precedents.

For example, lawyers who are arguing that a merger should be declared illegal will examine previous rulings on mergers. Frequently, they will find an especially important decision, called a "controlling case." If the controlling case is unfavorable to a merger, they will try to present relevant similarities between the case they are arguing and the controlling case in which the merger was denied. Lawyers who are arguing in favor of a merger will try to point out the absence of analogy (relevant dissimilarities) between the controlling case and the case in question.

If there is no controlling case, lawyers on both sides will search through reports of court decisions on mergers and argue relevant similarities between their case and those decisions that are favorable to their position as well as point out relevant dissimilarities between their case and those decisions that are unfavorable to their position. The judge, after hearing the arguments, decides whether the case in question should be regarded as relevantly similar to the mergers that were denied or permitted in the past.

When we make moral judgments about whether or not a given act deserves blame, we frequently use analogical arguments to show that the act is relevantly similar to other actions that are classified as blameworthy or not. If we conclude that the act is relevantly similar to other blameworthy acts, then we use the ethical principle that like acts should be treated similarly to argue deductively that the act in question deserves blame. It might be argued analogically, for example, that a particular case of promise-breaking is relevantly similar to other cases in which ignorance was an important factor. Then a further deductive (nonanalogical) argument would conclude that this case of promise breaking should be excused, since it occurred under conditions of ignorance that generally make promise-breaking excusable.

Analogical reasoning is also used to attribute various characteristics, motives, desires, and feelings to other people. This is another way in which analogy is often involved in our moral judgments of others. For example, we might judge a politician to be too weak to be able to handle the stresses of high office because he behaved irresponsibly in situations of similar, but less severe, stress on other occasions. We often make the following sort of judgment:

> Mary must not be herself today, for she had all four wisdom teeth pulled yesterday, and I know how I felt the day after mine were pulled. I couldn't help being cross.

We infer that other persons, who are similar to us in many observable respects, share similar hopes, fears, and feelings when confronted with situations that would inspire those hopes, fears, or feelings in ourselves.

Exercises

Reconstruct the analogical arguments explicitly or implicitly offered in each of the following passages. Identify the points of analogy in the premisses—including any unstated premisses—and the analogies argued for in the conclusions. Assess the strength of the arguments on the basis of the criteria presented in this section. Discuss any cases in which further background knowledge is required to determine relevance.

1. Tar (extracted from cigarette smoke) when smeared on the skin of mice in laboratories causes skin cancers. Therefore, cigarette smoking causes lung cancer in humans.

2. My last pair of Brand X running shoes were comfortable, gave excellent support to my feet and ankles, and lasted a long time. I expect my new pair of Brand X running shoes, which have the same design, to give the same kind of service as my old pair.

3. A perfect thought can only come from someone who is perfect. After all, you can't get heat from something cold.

4. In field trials where the soil was a moderately heavy clay and natural rainfall the only source of water, the roses offered in this catalogue bloomed heavily and were untroubled by disease. Therefore, they will perform well in your own garden.

5. Technology was once thought to be a uniquely human attribute, but the discovery of tool use in apes, otters, birds, and even wasps has scotched [all] that. Nevertheless,

the extent and nature of tool use among apes remains a subject of considerable importance in relation to the development of technology among the earliest members of the human family, the hominids. William McGrew of Stirling University, Scotland, therefore decided to survey what has been observed among our simian cousins. . . . "For most of my career I've worked with chimpanzees," he said, "and I have tended to generalize from chimps to the other apes. Great apes [gorillas, orangutans, gibbons] have usually been considered to be of similar intelligence, and I expected similarities in tool use to what I had known about chimps."

—*Science* 236(1987):776

6. Wives, be subject to your husbands as to the Lord, for the husband is head of the wife as Christ also is the head of the church; as the church is subject to Christ, so wives are to be subject to their husbands in every respect.

—St. Paul, Ephesians, 5,22

7. The force that binds planets to the sun (gravity) obeys the same general form of law as the electrical force that binds electrons to the nucleus of an atom. (Both gravity and electricity decrease in strength with the square of the distance between the bodies or particles.) Therefore the electron particles, which have negative charges, when attracted by the positive electricity of the nucleus, should move around it in the same way that the planets move around the sun.

Note: This was British physicist Ernest Rutherford's argument in favor of the arrangement of parts of the atom offered in opposition to a "plum pudding" model that held that the electrons were arranged randomly throughout the atom like raisins in a pudding.

8. From an editorial written in response to a rejection by voters of a measure that would have provided money for additional officers of the court:

> Anyone who has bought a cheap used car knows that paying less for repairs now may prove to be more expensive later. This basic truth is often forgotten by people who call for reduced federal spending. The tendency to let tomorrow take care of itself is exemplified in America's approach to the administration and enhancement of justice. . . .
>
> The path to justice is never easy. Those truly committed to the promotion of justice must be willing to pay the price—a price that must take into account future costs of present inaction. We must not forget principles of preventive medicine when undertaking to remedy social ills. If the public truly desires to ensure the nation's long-term health, it must be willing to pay the doctor's bill for the cures.
>
> —Judge Irving Kaufman, *The New York Times*

9. *Background information:* In the case of *Langridge v. Levy* (1837), the court allowed recovery to the plaintiff, who said that the defendant sold his father a defective gun. The gun had blown up in the plaintiff's hand, and the court ruled that the seller had falsely declared the gun safe when he knew it was defective.

> In *George v. Skivington* (1869), a chemist who compounded a secret hair wash was liable to the wife of the purchaser for injuries caused by the wash. . . . [The court] thought that the imperfect hair wash was like the imperfect gun in the *Langridge* case. It chose to ignore the emphasis in the *Langridge* case on the purported fact that the seller knew the gun was de-

fective and lied. It said, "substitute the word "negligence" for "fraud," and the analogy between *Langridge v. Levy* and this case is complete.

—E. H. Levi, *An Introduction to Legal Reasoning*

10. *Note:* Remains of early man—pre-Neanderthal—were found at Choukoutien, China. All the human skulls there had been carefully opened through the base, presumably to extract the brain. This was regarded as evidence for cannibilism.

> We tend to think of cannibalism as a bestial and inhuman practice, but in fact nothing better demonstrates the humanity of the Choukoutien people. Among living peoples, cannibalism is never a matter of nutrition; no animal, human or nonhuman, eats its dead for food. Rather, it is a solemn ritual act, sometimes to express family piety toward the deceased or magically to impart the deceased's spirit and qualities to the living. We may be confident that the atmosphere of Choukoutien during the cannibal meal was closer to Mass than to McDonalds.
>
> —C. Jolly and F. Plog, *Physical Anthropology and Archaeology*

11. Johnson told me that he went up thither without mentioning it to his servant when he wanted to study, secure from interruption; for he would not allow his servant to say he was not at home when he really was. "A servant's strict regard for the truth (said he) would be weakened by such a practice. A philosopher may know that it is merely a *form* of denial [that is, a "little white lie"], but few servants are such nice distinguishers. If I accustom a servant to tell a lie for *me,* have I not reason to apprehend that he will tell many lies for *himself?*"

—James Boswell, *Life of Johnson*

Reconstruct the argument that Johnson believes his servants would use if he allowed them to lie for him.

12. In the following passage, an analogy is drawn between shade trees and knowledge, or the habit of intellectual activity. The analogy is used to argue for the importance of educating persons during their youth. Discuss whether you think the similarities are relevant.

> Knowledge is a comfortable and necessary retreat and shelter for us in an advanced age; and if we do not plant it while young, it will give us no shade when we grow old.
>
> —Lord Chesterfield, *Letters*

13. 'Tis education forms the common mind;
    Just as the twig is bent, the tree's inclined.

—Alexander Pope

14. It seems that the Latin races are far more deeply attached to their Catholicism than we Northerners are to Christianity generally, and that consequently unbelief in Catholic countries means something quite different from what it does among Protestants.

—Friedrich Nietzsche, *Beyond Good and Evil*

15. Now, pro-life folk need to understand that just as it can be said that some highly civilized folk believed that slavery was a normal human institution (St. Paul, John C.

Calhoun) so some people feel that way about abortion. And as long as people feel that way, they are perplexed, indignant and outraged at condemnations of their behavior, let alone efforts to restrict it.

It is for this reason that one should be no more tempted to scorn a woman who terminates a pregnancy by abortion than one would have been to associate with Thomas Jefferson, a slaveowner.

—William F. Buckley, Jr., Syndicated newspaper column

16. Find an example of an analogical argument in a magazine or newspaper. Assess its strength according to the criteria discussed in this section.

IV. ARGUMENTS BASED ON SAMPLES

Arguments based on samples share a common form that is called, alternatively, simple induction, induction by enumeration, statistical generalization, and inductive generalization. In this text, we will refer to this argument form as *inductive generalization.*

You may have heard inductive arguments defined, somewhat inaccurately, as "arguments from the particular to the general." This definition is misleading, because not all inductive arguments go from particular premises to general conclusions. Statistical syllogisms, for example, draw particular conclusions from general premises. Inductive generalizations, however, are arguments from the particular to the general. Their premises state what happens in particular cases (the cases that make up the sample), and their conclusions state what happens in the population. Moreover, inductive generalization is such a common form of inductive argument that those who define induction as arguing from the particular to the general perhaps may be excused for focusing on this one important type.

Inductive generalization is the form of inductive argument political pollsters use to forecast election results. Before an election, polltakers interview a sample of the population of registered voters who plan to vote in the election and, on the basis of what members of the sample say about their voting preferences, the pollsters say how the population will vote. The information contained in the premises (called "the statistics") is extended in the conclusion to apply to the entire population. Such an argument might look like this:

1,200 (60 percent) of the 2,000 voters polled plan to vote for the incumbent.

---

60 percent of all voters plan to vote for the incumbent.

Although the pollsters are sometimes mistaken in their predictions, their overall record of success is very impressive. Such success motivates us to understand how this powerful type of argument works.

Inductive generalization is also the form of inductive argument used in quality-control studies. Suppose that a manufacturer wants to know what proportion of his products are defective. He can employ an inspector to examine a certain percentage of the items as they come off the assembly line. If, for example, during a one-year period, the plant produces approximately 5,000 stereo receivers (the population) and 100 receivers are inspected (the sample), the argument can be constructed:

98 out of 100 receivers that were examined were without defects.

---

98 percent of the receivers produced at the plant are without defects.

Inductive generalizations are used in many types of scientific studies. New drugs are administered to selected individuals to test their effects, and if these individuals suffer no ill effects, the drugs are deemed safe for the general public. The functions of various features of animals, such as their distinctive patterns of coloration, are studied by interfering with one of these features in a sample group and noting how the behavior of the animals is affected. The findings are then generalized to apply to all animals of that type. Investigators recently used this form of reasoning when they applied a harmless black paint to high-contrast wing stripes on tropical butterflies and noted that masking the stripes did not affect survival or wing damage in the sample group.

You have probably noticed that inductive generalizations are similar in some ways to arguments from analogy. Indeed, strong inductive generalizations may be viewed as arguments that are strong by virtue of the high degree of relevant analogy between the sample and the population it represents. Although we can distinguish between the *forms* of the two types of arguments (in inductive generalizations, a general claim is based on what happens in a sample; in analogical arguments, a conclusion about an unobserved similarity is based on similarities that have been observed), ordinary language arguments are often incompletely stated and so could be classified as examples of either form of argument. Reasonable people can disagree about how an argument that is stated in ordinary language (rather than in one of the explicit forms outlined in this chapter) can best be reconstructed.

Generalizations that are the conclusions of inductive generalizations can be either universal or statistical. *Universal generalizations* state that *all* (100 percent) or *none* (0 percent) of the members of a class have a certain property. *Statistical generalizations* state that some percentage equal to less than 100 percent, but more than 0 percent, of members of a class have the property. Alternatively, statistical generalizations can be stated nonnumerically, by using such terms as "most," "almost all," and "very few." The conclusions in the two examples just presented were statistical generalizations, stated numerically. Whether the conclusion of an inductive generalization should be statistical or universal depends on the information contained in the premises. If *all* members of the sample exhibit the property in question, then the conclusion that all members of the population exhibit that property *may*—provided certain other conditions are satisfied—be appropriate.

1. Preliminary Account of the Form of Arguments Based on Samples

We are now ready to present a preliminary version of the abstract form of inductive generalizations:

$$X \text{ percent of observed F's are G's.}$$
$$\overline{X \text{ percent of all F's are G's.}}$$

The letters F and G in this form represent such terms as "voters," "voters for the incumbent," "receivers," and "items without any defects," which refer to classes of individuals or to properties possessed by all members of a class. The conclusion of such an argument states that the percentage in the *population* of F's that are G's is the same as the percentage in the *observed sample*. (Remember that the percentage need not be expressed numerically.)

2. Standards for Making Correct Inductive Generalizations

When are arguments in this form that have true premisses likely to lead to true conclusions? The crucial feature that determines the strength of such arguments is the representativeness of the sample. When samples are representative of the populations from which they are taken, the conclusions based on the samples are strongly supported. This is so because to say that a sample is representative is to say that the features of the population that concern us in an argument (for example, voter preferences) are reflected in features of the sample. When this is the case, what is true of the sample will probably be true of the population as well. It is, of course, not always easy to tell whether or not a sample is representative, but two criteria are important to note:

1. The sample must be large enough.
2. The sample must contain sufficient variety.

To determine whether a sample is large enough, we must know something about the subject matter of the argument. Sometimes, a very small sample can support a strong generalization; in others, a very large sample is required. It is quite obvious that a sample of only five voters, all of whom said they would vote for the incumbent, would be too small to use as a basis for predicting a landslide vote for the incumbent in a national election. Such a sample is so small that it is almost worthless. However, if an argument is concerned with the election of the chairman of the board of directors in a small company, the opinions of five voters might constitute a sufficiently large sample for an accurate forecast. The population of voters in such an election may be so small that a sample of five is significant.

A very small sample may be sufficient even when it must represent a very large population *provided* there is a great deal of uniformity in the population.

If a cook in a kitchen on top of a mountain is testing samples to determine the boiling point of water at that altitude, one sample—or perhaps two (to check the reading)—would be sufficient, because the population of pans of water is quite uniform with respect to the property of boiling point.

The real question is whether the sample is large enough to capture, or represent, the variety present in the population. This brings us to the second criterion for satisfactory, or *representative,* samples: Is the sample varied enough? The questions of size and variety are not the same, for a very large sample might not represent the variety present in the population. A sample consisting of 10,000 voters in a national election would not be varied properly if all members of the sample were wealthy business executives. The question of the size of a sample is somewhat less crucial than whether the sample is sufficiently varied to represent the population. Sufficient size may be viewed as an important (and sometimes the most important) aid to achieving appropriate variety in samples. A sample that is too small automatically fails to provide the required variety.

A sample that is taken haphazardly from a population may, through luck, be a representative sample. However, arguments based on samples that are gathered without attention to sufficient size and variety do not form a basis for strong arguments.

In the study of logic, it is important to keep separate the *truth* of a conclusion from the *strength* of an argument. Bad or weak arguments may turn out to have true conclusions, and good or strong arguments may turn out to have false conclusions. In inductive logic, the standards for strong arguments are designed to make it *probable* that if the premisses of the argument are true, the conclusion will be true as well. If we adhere to these standards, conclusions that are based on true premisses will usually, but not always, be true.

Several methods are used to obtain representative samples. These methods do not *guarantee* that a sample will be representative but their use increases the probability that it will be so.

When a population is known to be varied but there is little information about just how it varies, a sampling method called *random sampling* is often used. In random sampling, each member of the population has an equal chance of being chosen as a member of the sample.

The value of larger samples can be shown by an example of taking random samples from an ordinary deck of playing cards. We know that half of the cards in the deck (the population) are red. But suppose we did not know that, and that we wanted to sample the deck randomly to determine the proportion of red cards. Keeping the cards face down, we shuffle the deck so that each card has an equal chance of being selected for the sample. Then we select a sample of two cards, replacing the card drawn and shuffling after each draw. There are four possible outcomes of such a selection (or trial): The first card is red and the second is black; the first card is black and the second is red; both cards are red; or both cards are black (RB, or BR, or RR or BB). In just two of the four possible outcomes (half the time) do we get a sample that is truly representative of the population.

Now suppose that we start again, only this time our sample consists of four trials. Then there are sixteen possibilities: RRRR; RRRB; RRBR; RRBB; RBRR; RBRB;

RBBR; RBBB; BRRR; BRRB; BRBR; BRBB; BBRR; BBRB; BBBR; or BBBB. In only six of the sixteen possible outcomes (three-eighths of the time), there are exactly half red cards. HOWEVER, in all but two outcomes (seven-eighths of the time), we get a mixture of between one-fourth and three-fourths red cards, and in only one-eighth of the outcomes (as opposed to one-half in the smaller sample) would we be misled into thinking the deck contained cards of only one color. So when our sample is four cards instead of two cards, we are more likely to get an answer that is *close to* half red cards, and less likely to get an answer that the deck is all red or all black. In general, as our sample size increases, we are much more likely to get a proportion of red cards that is *closer* to the true proportion in the deck. This is so, even though as the sample size increases, our chances of getting exactly the true proportion ($\frac{1}{2}$) gets smaller. (When the sample size is two, half the possible outcomes were exactly half red; when the sample size is four, three-eighths of the possible outcomes are half red; in a sample size of ten, one-fourth of the possible outcomes are exactly half red—but in about two-thirds of the possible outcomes of sample size ten, there are between 40 percent and 60 percent red cards.) Thus, as sample sizes increase, we can be more and more confident that our random samples will closely represent the population from which they are drawn.

Another sampling technique that is used to reduce bias when information about the nature of variation in a population is available is called "matching the sample to the population" (or "stratified random sampling"). When we know something about how segments of the population would be apt to differ with respect to some property that interests us, and when we also know the proportion of the population each segment constitutes, we can construct stratified samples. We know, for example, that voting preferences are often shared by persons of similar social class, occupation, and religious or ethnic background. If we also know the proportion of each of these groups in the population of voters, we can sample randomly *within* the groups to construct a sample that "matches" those proportions. With such a technique we can be somewhat confident that even rather small samples represent the population. This method of sampling is used by professional pollsters, such as the Gallup Poll and the Harris Poll. These polls are very reliable even though their samples usually consist of fewer than 2,000 persons and the population they represent consists of millions of American voters. The predictions of these polls are not always correct, but the arguments on which the predictions are based are strong inductive generalizations.

From what we have said thus far, we can see that background knowledge plays a large role when we try to assess the strength of an inductive generalization. We not only have to examine the premises of the argument; we also have to consider whether the sample is representative, and this requires information that is not contained in the premises. When we cannot tell whether a sample is large enough or varied enough, we cannot tell whether or not an inductive generalization is strong. This dependence on background knowledge—on information that is not a part of the premises—is a feature of all inductive arguments. Success at critical thinking does not demand that we acquire the background knowledge to judge every case. It demands instead that we are aware that certain questions must be raised and that, if these questions cannot be answered, we recognize that the strength of an argument is in doubt.

3. Fallacies Associated with Inductive Generalizations

We are now ready to consider some fallacies that are associated with inductive generalizations. One fallacy arises from failing to meet the requirement of obtaining a large enough sample. This fallacy has a number of common names: the *fallacy of insufficient statistics, hasty generalization,* and *leaping to a conclusion.*

If a friend snaps at you when you ask a question, you commit the fallacy of hasty generalization if you argue that this one instance of unfriendly behavior showed that he was no longer your friend. If you conclude that no one likes turnips because none of your friends do, this too would be a hasty generalization. The psychological reasons for leaping to a conclusion are fairly obvious in these cases. In the first, hurt feelings may color your judgment; in the second, personal interest in opinions of friends may obscure the fact that they are only a small part of the population. To avoid making hasty generalizations, we should dispassionately consider the size of the sample before we draw any conclusion from it. If feelings are not clouding our judgment, but we lack the appropriate background information on which to decide whether a sample is large enough, we should try to acquire the information. If this is not possible, it is better to suspend judgment than to jump to a conclusion.

The second fallacy associated with inductive generalizations is the *fallacy of biased statistics.* To say that statistics are biased means that the sample lacks proper variety. Biased samples are not representative; they fail to capture, or represent, the variety present in the population from which the sample is taken. Again, background information is required to judge whether a sample is sufficiently varied. Knowing, as we do, that business executives are apt to think alike on political matters, the set of statistics generated by a sample of voters that is comprised only of business executives (no matter how large the sample is), would be considered biased if these statistics were being used to infer the outcome of a national election.

A recent example of biased statistics, taken from a newspaper, reported a study in which the investigator tried to show that usually when a person is falling in love with someone, the other person is likely to reciprocate the affection. But the investigator's sample was biased, for the group he questioned consisted entirely of couples who had recently become engaged!

In another newspaper story, the reporter surveyed residents of a large city to see whether they would object to having a streetcar line out of service for several months while a new subway was being built. Every person questioned objected to the plan, but all the persons surveyed were riding that streetcar line during the hours when most riders are going to work or returning from their jobs. Riders who depend on the streetcar for getting to and from work do not constitute a representative sample of city residents.

Still another fallacy associated with inductive generalization consists of rejecting a generalization that is strongly supported by premisses citing sufficient and unbiased statistics. This sometimes happens when we acquire new information that apparently conflicts with the statistics. The following case provides an example.

Someone is planning to buy a new car, and carefully collects all the appropriate statistical information. The statistics include comparisons of thousands of automobiles, in terms of performance, safety, repair bills, and other important features. On the basis of these statistics, the person concludes that a certain brand of automobile is the best buy. Before the purchase is made, however, the person announces the decision to a friend at a party and is informed that the friend's brother bought the same model of car, which turned out to be a real lemon. The friend describes all the things that went wrong with the car in vivid detail. If the person then rejects the conclusion that the chosen brand is the best buy, a fallacy is committed. Can you see why?

It is not that new information should be ignored. Additional information—either in the premises themselves or in the form of new background information—can strengthen or weaken inductive arguments. But this new information concerns only one case, and one new case cannot outweigh all the statistical information that has been carefully collected. The statistics do not fail to take account of defective automobiles. The information that some cars of the chosen brand are lemons is already known, but presumably fewer cars of this brand, in general, are lemons. This is what the statistics say, and no reason has been given to doubt their reliability.

Psychologists Richard Nisbett and Lee Ross (*Human Inference*) have recently studied instances of this fallacy, which David Hume had already noticed and commented on in the eighteenth century. The psychologists agree with Hume's explanation of why the fallacy occurs. The problem, they say, is that new information received about a car from a friend at a party is more *vivid* than an impersonal collection of statistics. When you actually know someone (or someone who knows someone) to whom the lemon belongs, the information seems more startling and impressive than a "mere statistic." The vividness of the new information about a single car psychologically cancels out the far more complete, but less vivid, information about thousands of cars. The expense and inconvenience of owning a lemon is brought home to the prospective buyer in an alarming way that tends to override the better information. It is a fallacy to allow a single vivid case to outweigh strong statistical data. This mistake in reasoning can be called the "*fallacy of misleading vividness.*"

4. The Revised Form of Inductive Generalization

Thus far, we have discussed two criteria for evaluating inductive generalizations (size of sample and variety in the sample), the fallacies resulting from the failure to meet these criteria, as well as the fallacy of rejecting a strongly supported conclusion when faced with a small amount of vivid information. A further criterion for evaluating the strength of inductive generalizations applies to all other forms of inductive reasoning as well. This criterion is concerned with the strength of the conclusion relative to the strength of the premises in the argument. Remember that an argument is a whole that is composed of parts (the premisses and the conclusion). The strength of the whole is determined by considering how much support the premisses provide for the conclusion. Thus, an argument can be strengthened by providing better premisses (a larger or less biased sample) to support the original conclusion, but an argument can also be strengthened by *weakening the conclusion,* and leaving the premisses unchanged. A statement is weakened when it is qualified or guarded in such a way that it presents less information, or less specific information, than the original statement.

Some examples will help to clarify this point. Suppose a poll is taken to determine the outcome of a student-body election. An attempt is made to interview students from various classes, and members of fraternities and sororities, as well as unaffiliated students and students in other organizations who might have different preferences. Approximately 2,000 students are expected to vote in the election, and the size of the sample is 100. Of those interviewed, 40 (40 percent) say they will vote for the Student Conservative Party, and 60 (60 percent) say they will vote for the Student Liberals. The following argument could be constructed:

> 60 percent of those interviewed said they would vote for the Liberals.
> ———————————————————————————————————
> 60 percent of the students plan to vote for the Liberals.

Even though there is some assurance that the sample is representative, we know from our discussion of samples from a deck of cards that it is unlikely that the percentage of Liberal voters in the population of students will be *exactly* the same as the percentage in the sample. To account for this, it is common to build into the conclusion a departure—a little less or a little more—from the percentage in the sample. This departure is called a "margin of error," and is an example of "weakening" the conclusion relative to the premisses. The altered argument might look like this:

> 60 percent of those interviewed plan to vote for the Liberals.
> ———————————————————————————————————
> Between 50 percent and 70 percent of the students will vote Liberal.

In this example, the margin of error chosen is a plus or minus 10 percent. Since the sample size was 100 students (and since we can make certain reasonable assumptions about the nature of voting behavior) this plus or minus 10 percent margin of error would make it very probable (about 95 percent probable) that our conclusion was correct.

If 500 students were sampled, then we could choose a smaller margin of error, about plus or minus 5 percent and be just as confident (with 95 percent probability) that our conclusion was correct. Alternatively, if our sample was very small, say only about 30 students, then to achieve the same confidence level, we would have to increase the margin of error to about a plus or minus 20 percent.

Statisticians have calculated the margins of error associated with various sample sizes for estimating percentages in populations with various probabilities of being correct (confidence levels). Their calculations are based on random sampling and some reasonable assumptions about how properties are distributed in a population. While some of the arithmetic can be complicated, the basic idea is just the rather simple one that was presented in our example with the playing cards in Section 2: The larger the sample size the more likely it is that what is true of the sample will also be more or less true of the population. The confidence level is a measure of how *likely* it is that the conclusion will be correct. The margin of error is a measure of how much (*more or less*) the sample resembles the population.

Margin of error, confidence level, and sample size are all related to one another. Obviously, the appropriate margin of error to adopt in an inductive generalization is connected with the desired confidence level that can be attached to the conclusion. If you want to be almost certain of being correct, you are better off with a wider margin of error. You pay for the extra certainty, however, with a loss of precision. If you are willing to accept a lower confidence level (that is, a greater chance of being wrong), then you can adopt a smaller margin of error for a comparable sample size. So for example, we might, using the sample of 100 students in the example above, have concluded that between 55 percent and 65 percent of the students would vote Liberal, but then our confidence level in the conclusion would only be about 70 percent rather than 95 percent. This means that in ten arguments similar to this one, we would draw a true conclusion about seven times. If we want to retain the higher confidence level (95 percent) *and* reduce our margin of error to a plus or minus 5 percent, then we must increase our sample size to about 500.

Confidence levels and margins of error are sometimes stated in nonnumerical form. For example, if all members of a large sample have some property, the conclusion might be *almost* all the members of the population will have this property, and the confidence level might be expressed by some other phrase such as "It is very likely that . . .". Or, if half the members of the small sample have the property, the conclusion might state that *roughly* half the members of the population have the property, and the confidence level could be "It is probable that . . .".

Because samples, no matter how carefully they are taken, infrequently present an *exact* picture of the population, the conclusion of an inductive generalization should include some allowance for a margin of error. In light of this ever-present possibility of *sampling error,* we will represent the form of inductive generalization in the following way:

X percent of observed F's are G's.

X plus or minus z percent of all F's are G's.

In this form, z represents the degree of departure in either direction from the observed percentage in the sample. It is possible to measure precisely the margin of error in some carefully conducted statistical studies, and margins of error are sometimes stated in reports of political surveys and other polls. You should be aware, however, that these quantities need not be expressed numerically in every inductive generalization.

Exercises

Decide whether each of the following arguments is an acceptable inductive generalization or a fallacy. Identify the premises and the conclusion of each argument. In the case of a fallacy, explain what is wrong. Discuss what sort of additional background information is required, if any is needed.

1. A chemistry student is told to determine the boiling point of copper. The student tests two very pure samples of copper and finds that each sample has a boiling point of 2,567° Celsius. The student concludes that this is the boiling point for copper.

2. A nationwide poll of a random sample of thousands of homeowners revealed that 70 percent of them are opposed to increases in welfare payments. Therefore, roughly 70 percent of the adult population opposes such increases.

3. An investigator studied several thousand heroin users and learned that 70 percent of them had used marijuana before they tried heroin. He concludes that roughly 70 percent of all marijuana users will go on to try heroin.

4. It has rained during the last two home football games at our school. Therefore, it will probably rain at all the home games this year.

5. Pueblo sites (prehistoric Indian "apartment villages") are located in many places in Arizona, New Mexico, and Colorado. To determine the number of rooms in pueblo sites that were located by surface surveys but were not excavated, archaeologists examined the relationship between the size of the surface rubble mound prior to excavation and the number of rooms that were ultimately uncovered in each of six sites excavated in the Upper Little Colorado River region. The number of rooms in each excavated site was equal to (.10 × Area of rubble mound in square meters) + 4.

6. In 1977 at the University of Pennsylvania, psychiatrists conducted a study to determine the social factors that affect the well-being of coronary patients. There were 93 patients in the study; slightly more than 50 percent of them had pets of some kind (dogs, cats, fish, and one iguana). At the end of a year, one-third of the patients who did not own pets had died but only three animal owners had succumbed. The psychiatrists concluded that pet ownership may have a positive effect on the health of humans.

7. There is no overestimating the importance of pets to people it seems. Katcher [the psychiatrist in charge of the study mentioned in Exercise 6] reported that in one ques-

tionnaire, on which people were given the opportunity to indicate whether they thought their pet was an animal or a human member of the family 48 percent responded that the animal was a human family member.

—"Human-Animal Relationship under Scrutiny," *Science*
214(1981):418

8. Jonathan has to travel to a distant city. He wants to take the safest mode of transport, so he compares statistics over the past ten years on accidents involving buses, trains, automobiles, and planes that occurred between his city and the one he will visit. Jonathan determines that the safety record of buses is far better in terms of lives lost than any of the other forms of travel. As he is about to purchase his ticket, however, he sees a newspaper story about a bus accident in which six people died. Jonathan decides not to buy the bus ticket and to drive instead.

9. When all his sophisticated electronic equipment fails to help him move his boat as fast as he would like, Conny van Rietschoten resorts to more primitive methods. He tosses coins into the sea, "for luck, to bring wind." Who's to say if such tribute influences the gods? But it can be reported from personal observation that during last June's Annapolis-Newport tuneup race, when van Rietschoten tossed several Dutch guilders into a flat sea on two different occasions, the wind subsequently picked up.

—*New York Times*

10. Find an example in a newspaper or magazine of an inductive generalization. Use the criteria discussed in this chapter to assess the strength of the argument.

V. EXTENDED INDUCTIVE ARGUMENTS

In our discussion, we have treated separately the various forms of inductive arguments. In real life, they frequently occur in combination with one another. Several different forms of argument can be presented to support the same conclusion. No inductive argument provides conclusive support, and no combination of inductive arguments can provide conclusive support either. A conclusion can be more strongly supported, however, when several types of favorable arguments can be mustered for it. Arguments against the person, arguments from authority, and arguments from consensus are often presented in combination with other arguments.

The conclusion of an inductive generalization is sometimes used as the premiss of a statistical syllogism. For example, a person might read a report citing statistics about the dangers of off-the-road bikes, and conclude off-the-road bikes are unsafe. Then, using that generalization as a premiss, the person might conclude that the off-the-road bike that he or she owns is unsafe, even though it has not given any trouble so far. No new special techniques are needed for evaluating these extended arguments. We just have to sort out the different arguments and apply the appropriate standards to them.

VI. PRO AND CON ARGUMENTS

Frequently we find ourselves confronted with not just one argument, or an extended argument, to support a single conclusion, but rather with a situation in which arguments are presented both for some conclusion (pro arguments) and against the same conclusion (con arguments). Sometimes this happens when participants in a debate disagree about the truth of premises. It is not so surprising that different sets of premises can lead to different conclusions. Other times, however, different (and conflicting) conclusions can be drawn because of different views about how evidence should be interpreted.

Consider, for example, the pro and con arguments centering on the career of Casanova. He was an eighteenth-century libertine whose twelve volumes of *Memoirs* present detailed accounts of his seduction of hundreds of women from all walks of life—noblewomen to servants and nuns to prostitutes. From the first publication of *Memoirs* (nearly a quarter of a century after Casanova's death), historians questioned the veracity of the work, pointing out many inconsistencies as well as the use of many pseudonyms. Recently, however, a former American diplomat, J. R. Childs, has published a book in which he argues that Casanova was telling the truth. He tries to show that the pseudonyms can be matched to real people, that the apparent inconsistencies in time and place can all be explained, and that the *Memoirs* provide us with a valuable piece of social history. He also says that if Casanova were not telling the truth that he never would have presented himself in such an unflattering light.

In a review of Childs's book, however, Angeline Goreau (*The New York Times*) contends that in order for Childs to identify real persons with the pseudonyms, we must assume that Casanova was telling the truth in the first place—but this is just what is denied by his critics. Goreau points out that over and over again in the *Memoirs,* the author himself proclaims his powers of deceit and his ability to deceive "without the slightest qualm of conscience." Goreau also says that even if Casanova is not trying to dupe us in his autobiography, we must place his *Memoirs* in the context of the times in which works of this sort were written. She says that such documents are dubious as social history because they were designed rather to make some religious or philosophical point (Casanova was preaching the philosophy of moral relativism), or to justify the author in the eyes of posterity.

Neither side in this dispute denies the basic premises: inconsistencies and pseudonyms abound in the *Memoirs,* and Casanova presents himself as a deceiver. However, these premises are used in different ways. On both sides the arguments employed are inductive. Childs uses inductive generalization when he tries to go from individual instances of Casanova's truthtelling (supported by identifications of pseudonymous characters) to a general claim that Casanova was telling the truth. Statistical syllogism is probably used when he argues that most persons who lie do not present themselves in an unflattering light, but Casanova does present the worst side of himself, so he is not a liar. Goreau uses analogical reasoning when she argues that Casanova's *Memoirs* are similar to other autobiographies of his time in the propensity to promote some religious, philosophical, or justificatory theme; these other autobiographical works are not reliable guides to social history, so Casanova's work is not a reliable guide either. She also accuses Childs of committing the fallacy of *circular reasoning,* because he assumes as a premise just what his book is supposed to prove as a conclusion, namely that Casanova was telling the truth.

Circular arguments are actually deductively valid, for their conclusions cannot be false if all their premises are true. A circular argument, however, cannot prove that its conclusion is *true,* for to do so, all the premisses must be true, and the premiss from which it begins is just as dubious as the conclusion.

In trying to decide which conclusion about Casanova to accept, readers can only try to assess the evidence for both sides in the best way that they can, and try to keep an open mind when there is some doubt about the correctness of either the evidence on which the conclusion is based or the conclusion itself. Sometimes, further evidence is needed to resolve an issue. When additional evidence can be uncovered this may help, but there is no guarantee that every dispute can be settled.

VII. REVIEW

In Chapter 3, we have looked closely at three important and commonly used forms of inductive argument:

1. Statistical syllogisms
2. Arguments from analogy
3. Inductive generalizations (arguments based on samples)

In evaluating arguments in these forms, a number of criteria have been suggested. Some of these criteria apply only to particular forms; others apply to all forms of inductive reasoning.

The strength of *inductive generalizations* depends on whether the sample in the premiss is representative of the population. Two factors are important here: the size of the sample, and the degree of variety in the sample. *Random sampling,* in which each member of the population is equally likely to be a member of the sample, and *stratified random sampling,* in which relevant variety in the population is proportionately matched in the sample, are two methods frequently used to obtain representative samples.

The strength of *arguments from analogy,* or *analogical arguments,* depends crucially on whether the similarities mentioned in the premisses are *positively relevant* to the similarity inferred in the conclusion. A similarity mentioned in the premisses is *positively relevant* to the similarity in the conclusion if the similarity mentioned in the premiss increases the probability that the similarity in the conclusion will obtain. Whether or not analogies are relevant depends on background information that is not usually contained in the premisses of the argument. The *number* of relevant similarities and relevant dissimilarities, as well as the *variety* in the instances cited in the premisses, are also important determinants of the strength of these arguments.

Statistical syllogisms are judged on the basis of the strength of their statistical premisses and also on whether or not they meet the requirement of *total evidence.* In statistical syllogisms, the requirement of total evidence demands that we choose the appropriate *reference class* in the premisses of the argument.

A number of special cases of statistical syllogism—*argument from authority, argument against the person (argumentum ad hominem)* in its various forms: abusive *ad hominem,* circumstantial *ad hominem,* and *tu quoque,* as well as *argument from consensus*—have also been discussed. In their correct form, these arguments contain a statistical premiss that states that in most cases dealing with the subject matter under consideration, the person who makes the claim speaks truthfully (authority), or the person who makes the claim speaks falsely (against the person), or the majority opinion is correct (consensus).

When we evaluate any inductive argument, we must consider the strength of the premisses relative to the strength of the conclusion. In general, an argument can be strengthened by bolstering its premisses with additional evidence. This might involve providing a larger or more varied sample for an inductive generalization, more relevant analogies in the premisses of an argument from analogy, a stronger statistical premiss, or a more appropriate reference class in a statistical syllogism. Arguments can also be strengthened by *weakening their conclusions.* Since the strength of an argument is determined by how well the premisses support the conclusion, if the conclusion is qualified, as when the conclusion of an inductive generalization allows for a margin of error in moving from the percentage in the observed sample to the percentage attributed to the population, a stronger argument results.

All inductive arguments, not only statistical syllogisms, are subject to the requirement of total evidence. In statistical syllogisms, the requirement of total evidence forces us to choose the reference class that embodies all available relevant evidence about the individual mentioned in the conclusion. When we construct inductive generalizations, the requirement of total evidence forbids us to ignore or disregard any evidence that, for example, would reduce bias in our sample. In an argument from analogy, we cannot ignore any relevant dissimilarities that may hold between types of objects mentioned in the argument.

A number of fallacies are associated with these correct forms of argument. In each case, a fallacy occurs when some standard is violated. Not every fallacy has a special name, but many do. A list of named fallacies follows:

Fallacy of Hasty Generalization: (also called *insufficient statistics,* or *leaping to a conclusion*) Occurs when the sample in an inductive generalization is too small.

Fallacy of Biased Statistics: Occurs when the sample is not sufficiently varied to represent the population.

Fallacy of False Analogy: Occurs when the types of objects in the premisses of an analogical argument are relevantly dissimilar.

Fallacy of Incomplete Evidence: Occurs when the requirement of taking account of all relevant available evidence is violated.

Fallacy of Misleading Vividness: Occurs when a small amount of particularly vivid information is allowed to outweigh a substantial amount of statistical support for a conclusion.

Fallacious Argument from Authority: Occurs when the authority cited is not a genuine expert in the field of concern, or when the authority is speaking outside his or her field of expertise, or when experts in the area of concern disagree among themselves.

Fallacious Argument Against the Person: Occurs when there are not good grounds to believe that a claim is false because a particular individual says that it is false. (The appropriate statistical premiss—most of what the individual says about a particular subject matter S is false—cannot be accepted.) The fallacious forms of *ad hominem* are frequently identified by the special names: abusive *ad hominem,* circumstantial *ad hominem,* and *tu quoque.*

Fallacious Argument from Consensus: Occurs when majority opinion does not constitute a good reason to believe the truth or falsity of a claim.

Fallacy of Circular Reasoning: Occurs when the truth of the conclusion is already assumed in the premises that are supposed to support that conclusion.

Quite a lot of new vocabulary has been introduced in this chapter. In addition to the names of the forms of arguments and fallacies discussed, you should be familiar with the meanings of the following terms:

Attribute Class: The class represented by G in the statistical premiss of the form "X percent of all F's are G's" in a statistical syllogism. The conclusion claims that the individual mentioned in the argument is (or is not, in negative cases) a member of this class.

Reference Class: the class represented by F in the statistical premiss of the form "X percent of all F's are G's" in a statistical syllogism. The other (particular) premiss claims that the individual mentioned is a member of this class.

Syllogism: an argument with two premises.

VIII. EXERCISES

1. The following report contains a statistical syllogism, in which the statistical premiss is supported by an inductive generalization. Reconstruct both arguments, and try to evaluate them in light of the criteria developed in this chapter. Are any other argument forms used to bolster either conclusion?

> For a dozen years, Dr. Joseph Stolkowski has researched a theory that a potential mother can dictate the sex of her baby by regulating her diet.
>
> Dr. Stolkowski is no quack. He is the distinguished chairman of the physiology department of the Pierre and Marie Curie University in Paris. His papers on the preconception selection of sex in humans have been published in the respected medical journals.
>
> He contends that a woman who wants to give birth to a boy should eat foods rich in potassium and sodium—such as meat, fish, vegetables, chocolate, and salt—beginning at least six weeks before she wishes to become pregnant. A woman who wants to have a girl should eat foods rich in calcium and magnesium, such as milk, cheese, nuts, beans, and cereals. . . .
>
> In a study of 47 French couples from 1970 to 1980, he says, 39 of them produced a child of the sex they wanted after the wives had followed special diets. In Canada, a study of 224 couples on special diets reveals an 80 percent success rate with this method.
>
> Asked recently how his research was going, Stolkowski told us: "Better than ever. We now have five health centers in Paris and five outside the city where couples are taking their special diets and producing the boy or girl babies they want. Our success rate is approximately 90 percent."
>
> —Lloyd Shearer, *Parade Magazine*

2. Consider the following inductive generalization and tell whether or not as well as *why* the argument would be strengthened, weakened, or unaffected in strength if it were modified in each way suggested. Where applicable, discuss the importance of background information.

All of the 5,000 swans observed in North America and Europe have been white, and no nonwhite swans have been observed.

All swans are white.

    a. Suppose only female swans had been observed.
    b. Suppose only 500 swans had been observed.
    c. Suppose all observations were made during winters.
    d. Suppose swans had been observed in Africa and Australia as well as in Europe and North America.
    e. Suppose the conclusion was "All European and North American swans are white."
    f. Suppose only adult swans had been observed.
    g. Suppose all observations were made on weekends.
    h. Suppose all observations were made in areas within 300 miles of a city.
    i. Suppose reports from world travelers about black swans had been recorded in seventeenth-century journals, but that no living person had seen a black swan.

3. Samuel Johnson presents the following case supporting the right of a schoolmaster to beat his pupils. What kind of arguments does Johnson employ? Does he commit any fallacies?

> The government of a schoolmaster is somewhat of the nature of a military government; that is to say that it must be arbitrary according to particular circumstances. A schoolmaster has the right to beat, and an action of assault and battery cannot be admitted against him unless there is some great excess, some barbarity. Pufendorf [an outstanding legal scholar in Johnson's day] maintains the right of a schoolmaster to beat his scholars.
>
>   —James Boswell, *Boswell for the Defense*

4. In the following passage, taken from "Joint Custody as a Fundamental Right," what form of argument is the author using? Identify the premises and the conclusion of the argument.

> The fundamental right of parental autonomy [the right of parents to share in the companionship, care, custody, and management of their minor children] arguably is identical both within the traditionally recognized nuclear family unit and outside that traditional family unit so long as the relationships maintained outside the unit are "family-like" in the previously specified sense [both parents have an active interest in making parental decisions, and neither is prevented from doing so by reasons of distance, disability, or any other incapacitating factor]. Since the state's right to interfere with these rights within the family is limited by a principle far more restrictive than "the best interest of the child," it is hard to see why state interference should

become any less restricted after divorce. Normally, the state may interfere with parental rights only to prevent harm or abuse to the child. . . . Why should a comparable limitation on state judicial power not be present after divorce as well?

—Ellen Canacakos, *Arizona Law Review,* 1982

5. The following passage is taken from a newspaper report concerning the efforts of a consumer group to have the government ban Bendectin, a prescription drug used to treat morning sickness associated with pregnancy. The consumer group claims that the drug has been linked to birth defects in humans. On what type of argument supporting the drug's harmful effects does the group base its petition? Discuss any implicit premises.

The consumer group's petition cited an unpublished study from the Max Von Pettenkofer Institute in Germany, which found that 16 of 861 rats exposed to high doses of Bendectin developed a condition in which intestines protrude into the chest through a hole in the muscle separating the lung from abdominal muscles.

The group also cited another study conducted in California that used monkeys. That research raised the possibility of an association between the drug and heart defects, the group said.

—*Pittsburgh Press*

6. In each of the following examples, identify the form of argument used and evaluate each argument according to standards for that form.

a. The pope, the spiritual leader of millions of Roman Catholics, who believe that he speaks infallibly on matters of faith and morals, has—as have previous popes—proclaimed abortion to be a form of murder. Therefore, abortion is murder.

b. In dozens of trials conducted by an independent laboratory, generic brands of laundry detergent performed just as effectively as more expensive name-brand detergents. Therefore, generic brands are just as effective as name-brand detergents for all laundry purposes.

c. In a recent Harris Poll, 47 percent of a sample (carefully matched to the population) of 2,500 American adults said that they approved of the president's economic policies. Therefore, approximately 47 percent of all American adults approve of the president's economic policies.

d. The movie star whose recently divorced young wife receives alimony of $150,000 per year probably won't have to pay it for very long, since most young women who are divorced remarry within a year of the divorce. (Alimony payments cease upon remarriage.)

e. *Background information:* Lead is sometimes added to molten bronze to increase its fluidity. The amounts normally added range from 5 percent to 25 percent of the volume of bronze.

The analyses of Bronze Age Greek artifacts made by Craddock, supplemented by those of Renfrew and the Stuttgart group for the Early Bronze Age, show that most copper, arsenical bronze, and tin bronze objects contain less than 1 percent lead. Indeed, out of a total of 185 analyses of Early and Late Bronze

Age axes, chisels, swords, daggers, knives, spearheads, arrowheads, and fig-
urines, 161 show lead contents of less than 1 percent, and only nine show
more than 3 percent. Catling and Jones found that of 141 Late Minoan II
copper and bronze objects from the unexplored Mansion, Knossos, Crete,
only three objects had as much as 1 percent lead. . . . The evidence that lead
was rarely deliberately added to copper or bronze objects in the Greek
Bronze Age seems compelling and indicates that the lead in ancient copper
or bronze objects below about 1.5 percent (and certainly below 0.5 percent)
is present as an accidental impurity from the copper ore.

—N. H. Gale and Z. A. Stos-Gale, "Bronze Age Copper
Sources in the Mediterranean," *Science* 216(1982):12

f. In the outbreaks of human poisoning from methylmercury in Japan and
later in Iraq, one of the most consistent signs in adults was deficits in
visual function. . . . The visual system of macaque monkeys resembles
that of humans and exhibits the same signs and pathological lesions as
that of humans when exposed to methylmercury. Macaques are therefore
excellent models for testing the effects of methylmercury on the visual
system.

D. C. Rice and S. G. Gilbert, "Early Chronic Low-Level
Methylmercury Poisoning in Monkeys Impairs Spatial
Vision," *Science* 216(1982):759

7. What steps would you take to find an unbiased sample if you wanted to
conduct a poll to determine student opinion at your college or university about
the legalization of marijuana?

8. What kind of argument in the passage below supports the conclusion that
"Over wide areas of Australia the tame dingo was by no means an effective
hunting dog and it contributed relatively little to the Aborigine's larder."

At Warburton, the Aborigines denied ever having used dingoes in hunting,
especially when pursuing large animals, and this view was echoed by Jan-
kuntjara informants [in South Australia, at the southeastern end of the Western Desert] interviewed by Hamilton. Nor were dingoes ever used for hunting by the desert-dwelling Aborigines we observed in the Clutterbuck Hills-
Tikatika region in 1966–1967 or at Pulykara, near Mt. Madley, in 1970.

—R. A. Gould, *Living Archaeology*

9. Can you think of any plausible example in which the opinions of most Americans would constitute the basis for a nonfallacious argument from consensus?

10. Recently, the city of Pittsburgh decided to enforce collection of a personal
property tax on stocks and bonds held by city residents. All residents who own
such property are supposed to file statements listing their property. The city's
resources for detecting ownership of these properties are practically nonexistent, since the city does not have access to federal income-tax returns filed
by residents. Despite this, a letter claiming to know that stocks and/or bonds are
owned was sent by the city to each head of household whose earned income

exceeded $40,000 per year. (A city income tax is deducted from wages, so these persons were identifiable.) On what type of argument do you think the city based its claim to know that persons earning more than $40,000 owned stocks or bonds?

11. In the following, name the mistake in reasoning that the author of the letter accuses Gajdusek of making. Also tell what form of argument Schryer employs against Gajdusek.

> I must question the relevance of Gajdusek's argument that "the whole of Australia knows these people are cannibals"... [This] may well be true, but proves nothing. At one time virtually the whole population of Europe and much of Britain and America "knew" that witches existed and countless persons were not only arrested but put to death for allegedly practicing witchcraft. Nevertheless, it is now generally acknowledged that witches, defined as persons with supernatural powers of diabolical origin, do not exist and never did. Gajdusek may or may not have other proof for the existence of cannibalism in New Guinea, but he does his case no good by arguing, in effect, that if a lot of people, including civil authorities, believe in the occurrence of some questionable practice then it must be so.
>
> —Letter from D. R. Schryer in *Science* 233(1986):926

12. Current debates flourish about the wisdom of raising the automobile speed limit in certain areas from 55 to 65 miles per hour. Both sides agree that preventing traffic accidents and saving lives are worthwhile goals. Proponents of the measure argue that the increase in the speed limit helps to save lives because it will promote smoother traffic flow and will reduce the time in which motorists are on the road and exposed to accidents. Opponents of the measure can agree that higher speed limits promote smoother traffic flow and reduce accident exposure time, while insisting that statistics have shown that the years in which the 55 mph limit was strictly enforced were years in which deaths from traffic accidents were greatly reduced. On the basis of these statistics, they argue that the lower speed limit saves lives. Proponents do not deny the statistics, but say that the figures have been misinterpreted and even manipulated and that this has resulted in a falsification of the true picture.

Can you construct (or reconstruct) some pro and con inductive arguments on the basis of the information available above or from other sources? In your opinion, which side has the stronger support? WHY?

Causal Arguments

C H A P T E R 4

I. INTRODUCTION

Many of the arguments discussed thus far have been causal arguments. The conclusions of such arguments state that a causal relationship holds (or fails to hold) between two types of things or events. For example, one argument in Chapter 3 concluded that birth-control hormones may affect brain development and another that obliterating the high-contrast wing stripes on tropical butterflies does not affect wing damage or flight patterns.

Statements about causes (causal claims) occur as the conclusions of different forms of argument. Some causal arguments have the form of inductive generalizations; others are arguments from analogy. Arguments from authority, which, when correct, are statistical syllogisms, are also used to support causal conclusions. In this chapter, we will pay special attention to a variety of ways of establishing causal claims. We will call any argument in which the conclusion is a causal claim a *causal argument*, but we should remember that the term "causal argument" does *not* refer to any single *form* of argument.

Concern with causal connections is prevalent in everyday life. When cars or other mechanical appliances break down, when buses are late, when classes are cancelled, when we do poorly in an examination, or when personal relationships improve or take a turn for the worse, we normally seek the cause or causes of what has happened.

Research by psychologists R. Nisbett and L. Ross (*Human Inference*) shows that people readily generate causal accounts of events on the basis of very limited evidence when asked to do so and that spontaneous causal analysis is remarkably common in ordinary conversation.

In one experiment, the investigators "bugged" 13 haphazardly selected conversations at singles' bars, at a picnic for economically underprivileged senior citizens, and at student bull sessions. Using a set of categories that included "gives information," "gives evaluation," "gives advice or suggestion," "makes prediction," and "gives causal analysis," they classified each utterance of a speaker. On the average, statements expressing or requesting causal analysis accounted for 15 percent of all utterances recorded. Even though, as the investigators admit, this was not a carefully controlled scientific study, the proportion of ordinary speech devoted to causes was impressive. The search for causes is not confined to scientific investigations in laboratories and offices. Obviously, concern with causes is a primary influence in our everyday lives.

In Chapter 4, we will look closely at causal reasoning and at some methods that have been proposed as aids to discovering causes and supporting causal claims. Although the *discovery* of causes is an important part of everyday life, logic is more particularly concerned with the *justification* of causal claims than with how causes can be discovered. Frequently, causal claims are put forth in the absence of any evidence for them. As critical thinkers, we should be concerned with the quality of the evidence supporting causal claims, or, in other words, with how arguments with causal conclusions are to be evaluated. We should also be aware of common mistakes in causal reasoning (causal fallacies) and learn to avoid them.

II. MILL'S METHODS FOR ESTABLISHING CAUSAL CLAIMS

The problem of justifying causal claims is primarily a problem in *inductive* logic. The reasons offered for the existence of a causal connection are usually less than conclusive, although some causal arguments are better than others. Inductive logic is a much newer branch of knowledge than deductive logic. The latter has been studied in schools continuously since it was first developed—almost single-handedly—by the Greek philosopher Aristotle about 2,300 years ago. (Of course, people reasoned logically even before Aristotle formulated the principles of logical reasoning.) In the nineteenth century, John Stuart Mill—well known for his works *Utilitarianism*, *On Liberty*, and *On the Subjection of Women*—made a serious and significant attempt to systematize inductive logic by spelling out its rules and principles, just as Aristotle had done for deductive logic.

Mill recognized that scientific knowledge is based on inductive reasoning and that causal reasoning is central to acquiring such knowledge. He was distressed with the flimsy and inadequate basis for many causal claims put forward by scientists of his own day, and he tried to formulate standards that would represent sound scientific practice. Mill thought that causal claims should be based on careful observation and experiment; he believed that if he could make these principles explicit, then people could follow the rules and become more skilled at causal reasoning. The methods that Mill outlined, although they did not always measure up to his exaggerated claims for their success, now provide an important basis for contemporary scientific methodology.

Mill's methods are also useful in ordinary causal reasoning. Although Mill outlined and discussed five methods, we will examine only the four that are most commonly used. Mill saw his methods as aids to discover causes and instruments to justify causal claims. Scientists in fact use them both ways.

1. The Method of Agreement

Just after a recent Japan Air Lines flight from Tokyo to Europe landed in Copenhagen, 144 passengers were hospitalized and another 51 were treated but did not require hospitalization. All of the passengers who were ill exhibited symptoms of a gastrointestinal disorder. Doctors immediately suspected that food poisoning was the cause of the illness. The passengers had eaten food taken aboard during a refueling stop in Anchorage. All those who later became ill had eaten omelets prepared by a single cook who worked for the airline's catering service in Anchorage. During a two-week investigation, it was learned that this cook had an infected sore on his finger. Officials concluded that bacteria from this infection had been the source of contamination and the cause of the food poisoning suffered by the passengers.

The investigators' pattern of causal reasoning, as reported above, exemplifies *Mill's Method of Agreement*. When we use the Method of Agreement to identify the cause of some event or condition, we look at *antecedent circumstances* (the events or conditions that occurred earlier) to see whether there is some antecedent circumstance common to each occurence of the event for which a cause is sought. If only one common antecedent circumstance can be identified, then it is likely to be the cause—or a part of the cause—of the event or condition under investigation.

Finding a common antecedent circumstance is not sufficient to justify a causal claim, however, for there may be many such circumstances that are causally irrelevant. In this case, for example, all the passengers who became ill boarded the plane in Japan. Causal reasoning is guided by general background knowledge about the types of causes that bring about the condition or event in question. In the airline incident, the illness was diagnosed as *food poisoning*. This diagnosis structures the search for a cause, for it is known that food poisoning is caused by eating food contaminated by certain bacteria. It is also known that contamination can arise in a number of ways. Harmful bacteria can grow when food is not stored at the proper temperature. Food can also become contaminated through contact with unclean utensils or other things that harbor harmful bacteria, including the hands of cooks, servers, or other foodhandlers. The important point of *agreement* among the antecedent circumstances of the hospitalized passengers was that before becoming ill, all of them had eaten omelets prepared by the cook with an infected finger.

Schematically, the Method of Agreement can be presented in the following form, where E represents the event or condition for which the cause is sought, and $S-Z$ represent a selection, guided by general background information, of antecedent conditions. The left-hand column numbers each separate case in which E occurs.

Case	Antecedent Circumstances	Event for Which Cause Is Sought
1	X, Y, Z	E
2	X, U, V, Y	E
3	X, W, S	E
4	X, T, Z, W	E
etc.	$X, \ldots$	E

In this schematic representation, X is the only antecedent circumstance in which all occurrences of E agree. In such cases, the use of Mill's Method of Agreement affirms that X is the cause—or a part of the cause—of E. In our example, the number of cases is 195, the total number of cases of food poisoning (E). The antecedent circumstance X represents the circumstance of eating an omelet prepared by the cook with an infected finger. The other letters represent various other antecedent circumstances that were possible causes of the disease; in our example, these antecedent circumstances would include foods and beverages, other than the cook's omelets, that were taken by passengers who became ill.

The use of the Method of Agreement does not guarantee that a cause will be discovered nor does the method constitute an absolute guarantee that the *suspected* cause is the *real* cause of the illness. (This is an inductive form of reasoning, not a deductive form.) There is always the possibility that the investigators overlooked the true source of contamination and that the cook's sore finger was only coincidentally connected with the illnesses. However, this investigation was thorough and the evidence was quite strong, so officials felt there was little room for doubt about the true cause of the passengers' illness.

When we draw up a list of antecedent circumstances, we should confine our attention to possible causal agents—not to every antecedent circumstance. We are faced with an unlimited number of antecedent circumstances in most cases of causal inquiry. Without some previous notion of the type of cause sought, there would be no manageable way to use the Method of Agreement.

At the same time, through ignorance or error, a possible cause may be overlooked in constructing the list of antecedent circumstances. If the true cause is not on the list, the Method of Agreement will not disclose it. In such cases, the use of this method may support a false conclusion.

The method is most likely to lead to a true conclusion when we possess general information about the types of causes that bring about the condition or event in question, as we do in cases of food poisoning. When this is so, the method is used to narrow the search for a cause within that general framework. Such general information is called a *causal theory*. In our example, the causal theory that guides the search for a cause of the illness is the general information about the nature and causes of food poisoning. It is known that symptoms appear several hours after eating and that the disease is generally caused by consuming food that is bacterially contaminated. It is also known that in certain foods cooked at rather low temperatures—such as omelets, custards, and cream sauces—harmful bacteria can multiply very rapidly. Such foods receive special scrutiny during investigations of food poisoning.

Exercises

For each of the following situations, suggest some possible common antecedent circumstances that you might investigate to find the cause of the event described.

1. You have a flat tire on the way to work. When you finally get to work, you find that three of your coworkers also had flat tires on the way to work.

2. When you arrive home in the early evening, you try to turn on some lights and find that none of them work.

3. Although it is early summer, all of the trees in the woods near your home are turning brown.

4. When you go to a concert downtown and try to park in the lot you normally use, you find that it is full. All of the other parking lots in the area are full as well.

5. Your dog refuses to eat the food you give him four nights in a row.

6. When you turn on a faucet, the water has a rusty color. Your neighbors complain about the same condition in their water.

2. The Method of Difference

Although the newspaper report from which the food poisoning example was taken did not present all the details, the investigation to find the cause of the illnesses undoubtedly used another of Mill's methods, the *Method of Difference*, to eliminate some possible causes of the disease. Once the illness was diagnosed as food poisoning, the search for a cause concentrated on foods eaten by the various passengers. According to the report, everyone in the first-class section of the plane was served an omelet prepared by that cook, but many of the tourist-class passengers were not. The cook prepared between 207 and 215 omelets, but only 195 passengers became ill. No one, however, who had not eaten an omelet prepared by the cook with the infected finger became ill.

Mill's Method of Difference tells us that to find the cause of an event or condition E, we should look at antecedent circumstances when E is present, and compare these to antecedent circumstances when E fails to occur to see how the antecedent circumstances in the two cases differ. Schematically, the Method of Difference can be represented:

Case	Antecedent Circumstances	Event for Which Cause Is Sought
1	X, S, T, U, V, W	E occurs.
2	S, T, U, V, W	E does not occur.

Suppose, for example, that a husband and wife were on the Japan Air Lines flight together and were served identical meals. Suppose, further, that the wife was allergic to eggs, so she did not eat the omelet, although she ate all the other foods, and—except in that one respect—ate the same things as her husband. If she did not become ill, and her husband did, the omelet would be judged to be the cause of the food poisoning according to Mill's Method of Difference. The only difference between Es occurring and failing to occur is the presence of X (eating an omelet that was prepared by the cook with an infected finger) in the antecedent circumstances of E. Under these conditions—since unless X occurs, E fails to occur—Mill's Method of Difference states that X is the cause, or an indispensable part of the cause, of E.

The Method of Difference is subject to the same limitations as the Method of Agreement. If the real cause is not listed in the antecedent circumstances, the method cannot detect it. Similarly, the choice of antecedent circumstances in our example is guided by a well-established causal theory concerning possible causes of food poisoning. In the presence of such causal theories, uses of Mill's methods constitute strong evidence for causal claims.

Exercises

For each of the following situations, suggest some antecedent circumstances that might account for the presence of the effect on the one hand and its absence on the other.

1. A friend gives you two tomato plants, which you set out in your garden. One plant produces two dozen tomatoes; the other plant fails to yield a single one.

2. You and a friend go on a hike together. The next day she breaks out with a case of poison ivy, but you don't have any signs of it.

3. You bake a birthday cake and it turns out just right. You make a second cake a week later, but this one fails.

4. You normally fall asleep within ten minutes of going to bed, but last night you lay awake for at least two hours before you fell asleep.

5. Your new cotton shirt fit perfectly the first time you wore it two weeks ago, but it is now too tight around the collar and its sleeves are an inch too short.

6. You and a friend submit identical solutions to a puzzle contest. He wins a prize, but you do not win a prize.

3. The Joint Method of Agreement and Difference

In many causal investigations Mill's Method of Agreement and Method of Difference are combined. Obviously, if both methods point to the same cause, support for a causal claim is strengthened. Furthermore, the Method of Difference strictly permits a comparison of only two cases—one in which the event or condition under investigation occurs, and one in which it does not. However, the use of just two cases would constitute rather weak evidence, particularly when information about many cases is available. We know, for example, that some people have a natural resistance to disease and that they do not become ill even when they are exposed to the known causal agent of a disease. In most investigations, the Method of Agreement is actually applied to all cases in which the condition occurs and to all cases in which the condition does *not* occur; the Method of Difference is then used to compare the two sets of cases.

The two methods are combined so often that a special name—*The Joint Method of Agreement and Difference*—is given to the combination. Schematically, the joint method looks like this:

Cases	Antecedent Circumstances	Event for Which Cause Is Sought
1–h	X, S, T, U	E occurs.
i–n	S, T, U, V	E does not occur.

In the schematic representation, the cases $(1-h)$ in which E occurs are grouped together. (In our example, these cases would be the 195 cases of food poisoning.) The cases $(i-n)$ in which E does not occur are also grouped together.

The newspaper report from which our example was taken did not specify the number of cases in which passengers did not become ill, but the plane was a jumbo jet and carried many such persons. The letters $S-U$ represent foods eaten by each passenger. The letter V represents an alternative food to X (for example, an omelet prepared by another cook or a different type of main dish). Although V represents a difference between the two groups, it is not judged to be the cause of the illness, because persons who ate V did not become ill.

The Joint Method of Agreement and Difference is extremely important in studying the causes of and cures for diseases and is a far more powerful tool than either method used alone. For example, if just two persons are given a flu vaccination and one escapes the flu but the other is stricken, we know little about the effectiveness of the flu vaccine. There are exceptional cases in which exposure to a cause does not produce the effect. The person who did not get the flu may have had a natural immunity. (We know also that vaccination itself can, in some cases, be a cause of the disease it is designed to prevent.) If everyone in a rather isolated community receives a flu vaccine and there is little or no incidence of flu, use of the Method of Agreement would tell us the vaccine was effective. But we cannot be too confident about this result, for the community may simply not have been exposed to the flu virus. If, however, hundreds of students are vaccinated for the flu at the student health clinic and only a few of them get the flu, but a very large proportion of hundreds of unvaccinated students at the same school get the flu, the Joint Method of Agreement and Difference tells us that there is good reason to believe the vaccine is effective in preventing flu.

Although Mill's methods are most effective when they are applied within the structure of a specific causal theory to provide evidence for causal claims, they can also be used to guide and restrict the search for causes when no specific causal theory is available. In this way Mill's methods help investigators formulate causal theories that can be subjected to further testing. Early studies of cholera, discussed by B. MacMahon and T. Pugh (*Epidemiology*), illustrate this point. Even before the germ theory of disease was developed, observers noted that cholera spread when persons came into contact with infected persons and that the occurrence of cholera was associated with poverty, overcrowding, refuse, and filth. Use of the Method of Agreement suggested that the common factor was exposure to the fecal discharges from cholera patients.

In 1854, a perceptive observer, John Snow, noticed that despite a cholera epidemic in London, a group of people in one area were attacked by the disease with much less frequency than their neighbors. Five years earlier, in 1849, all groups in London had been uniform with respect to frequency of the disease. Using the Joint Method of Agreement and Difference, Snow looked for antecedent circumstances that would account for the different frequencies of cholera present in the two groups in 1854. He discovered that the area was served by two different water companies. The families supplied by one of the companies, the Southwark and Vauxhall Company, had a much higher incidence of cholera than those supplied by the Lambeth Company. In the years between 1849 and 1854, the Lambeth Company had changed its sources of supply from a place near where the Southwark and Vauxhall Company took its water to a place higher up on the Thames River. As a result of its move, the Lambeth Company no longer drew its water from an area near where large amounts of sewage poured into the river. Snow believed this confirmed his suspicion that fecal contamination was the cause of cholera.

In the wake of Snow's investigations, efforts were made to provide the citizens of London with clean drinking water, and the incidence of cholera declined significantly, even though the exact cause of the disease (the specific germ) was not known until much later. This use of Mill's methods by Snow was an important step in the development of the germ theory of disease, rather than a use that depended on that theory.

In the history of medicine, the search for causes and cures of disease often begins when investigators notice differences in the geographic distribution of a disease. When a disease is prevalent in one area and much less common in another area, it is natural to look for causes in such general features as differences in diet, soil (which affects food grown there), and water supplies.

Not all attempts to use Mill's methods as aids to discover causes have been as successful as Snow's work on cholera. An incident reported in the *Diary* of Samuel Pepys shows the perils of using Mill's methods in the absence of a causal theory.

During a raging epidemic of the bubonic plague in London in the 1660s, it was noted that not a single London tobacco seller died of the plague. On these grounds, reasoning by what is now called the Joint Method of Agreement and Difference, authorities at Eton, outside London, ordered all school boys to smoke tobacco as a preventive measure when the plague reached that area. Eton is one of the few boarding schools in history where boys were flogged for failing to smoke! Unfortunately, smoking did not prevent the occurrence of bubonic plague at Eton; the use of tobacco was totally unrelated to avoidance of the disease. It was a strange coincidence that London tobacconists had been spared during the epidemic.

We now know that the bubonic plague virus is transmitted through the bite of fleas which are carried on rodents. The fleabites infect the rats, and after the rats die of the disease, the hungry fleas begin to bite humans. The great plague episodes in England during the seventeenth century resulted when rats escaped into the cities from ships which brought the rats—and the disease—from foreign ports. This causal connection between rats, fleas, and plague was not discovered, however, until a hundred years after the worst plague epidemics—and it was much later before the immediate cause, a specific virus, was isolated.

In our own time, medical research expends many resources to discover causes and cures for cancer. Mill's methods are frequently applied at various levels of modern cancer research. It has been observed, for example, that cervical cancer is almost nonexistent among nuns, although it is a rather common form of cancer among women in general. Use of the Joint Method of Agreement and Difference leads investigators to suspect that some aspect of sexual activity or the reproductive process is causally related to cancer of the cervix.

4. The Method of Concomitant Variation

The Method of Difference and the Joint Method of Agreement and Difference are applicable only when the suspected causal source can be observed to be present in some cases and absent in others. In the investigation of the cause of food poisoning, the suspected foods were eaten by some passengers but not by others. In the study of cholera, some households received water from one company; some, from another company. In these cases, as in all cases for which the Method of Difference and the Joint Method of Agreement and Difference are applicable, there is a distinction between exposure and nonexposure to the suspected cause.

The event or condition that results from the cause may be an increased or decreased *rate* or relative frequency of occurrence in a group of persons, rather than specific individual occurrences of the condition for each exposure to the causal agent. This is true in the cholera example. The disease was not present in each case in which the suspected cause (contaminated water) was present. Nevertheless, the water supply was judged to be the cause (or part of the cause) of cholera since the probability of contracting the disease in 1854 was greater for customers of Southwark and Vauxhall than for customers of the Lambeth Company. The term "cause" is widely used in this probabilistic sense. (We will examine this and various other uses of the term "cause" in Section IV.)

Sometimes when we wish to investigate a causal question, we are faced with circumstances in which the suspected causal agent is present in all cases. Neither the Method of Difference nor the Joint Method of Agreement and Difference are useful here. The Method of Agreement may be used, but if there are several common antecedent circumstances, this method may not offer strong justification for a causal conclusion. If, however, the condition or event under investigation *varies in degree or strength* from one case to another, the *Method of Concomitant Variation* may be a useful aid to discovering causes and justifying causal claims.

For example, high blood pressure (hypertension)—a widespread condition among people in all parts of America—is regarded as a major contributor to fatal heart attacks. According to a newspaper report in the *Arizona Daily Star*, an estimated 23 million Americans—10 percent of the population—suffer from high blood pressure. Two scientists noted that the death rate from hypertension-related heart attacks in Tucson, Arizona, was 41 percent below the national average. They suggested that the lower death rate could be explained by the causal relationship between a relatively high content of selenium in Arizona soil and lower incidence of hypertension in the population of Arizona residents.

Selenium is a metal found in small quantities in almost all soils, and it finds its way into the human body in minute amounts (it is a "trace mineral") through incorporation into the food chain. Current physiological theory acknowledges the role of trace minerals in preventing diseases. The scientists studied 45 cities. They used the selenium levels measured in grazing food or forage crops as a gauge for amounts of selenium present in state soils. Tucson was among nine cities in seven Western states with high selenium levels and relatively low hypertension-related death rates. The death rates attributed to high blood pressure in selenium-poor states (Connecticut, Illinois, Ohio, New York, Oregon, Massachusetts, Rhode Island, Pennsylvania, Indiana, and Delaware) are three times greater than these rates in selenium-rich areas.

In this example, the association between selenium levels in the soil (the antecedent circumstance) and death rates from high blood pressure (the condition for which a cause is sought) suggests that selenium may be a causal factor in the prevention of fatal high blood pressure. The method used to discover this connection—or to justify the claim that a causal connection exists between higher selenium levels in the soil and lower incidence of fatal high blood pressure—is Mill's Method of Concomitant Variation. Here is a schematic representation of this Method:

Cases or Groups	Antecedent Circumstances	Event or Condition for Which Cause Is Sought
1	$X+, Y, Z, \ldots$	$E+$ (or $E-$)
2	$X-, Y, Z, \ldots$	$E-$ (or $E+$)

The far left-hand column represents individuals, events, or circumstances—or groups of the same—classed according to the severity or degree of strength of the condition under investigation. There may, of course, be more than two such cases. For example, instead of dividing the individuals into two groups according to whether a condition is present in severe or mild degree, we might divide the individuals into three groups—severe, mild, and moderate. The letter X represents the antecedent circumstance that varies in strength—either in the same direction as the condition under investigation or in the opposite direction. In our example, the death rate from hypertension decreased ($E-$) as the selenium level increased ($X+$). The letters Y, Z, and so on, represent any other common antecedent circumstances that might be suspected to be causally connected with the condition under investigation. In the newspaper report from which our example is taken, no other antecedent circumstances—such as trace minerals other than selenium or average hours of sunshine per day—were mentioned.

Another study of disease provides a striking example of the use of the Method of Concomitant Variation. In a large city, such as London, it is usual for a number of deaths due to respiratory problems to occur each day. Until rather recently, most people were unaware of how strongly these deaths were influenced by air pollution. In counting the number of deaths that occurred during a time of severe atmospheric pollution (formerly called "London fog") from November 29 to December 16, 1952, it became apparent, based on Mill's Method of Concomitant Variation, that the intense smog had caused approximately 4,000 deaths. Information concerning the antecedent circumstances (pollution measured in parts per million of sulphur dioxide, SO_2) and the event whose cause is sought (increase in number of deaths) is reproduced in Figure 4-1. This graph shows clearly that the increases and decreases in the number of deaths ($E+$) almost exactly match the increases and decreases in parts per million of sulphur dioxide in the atmosphere ($X+$).

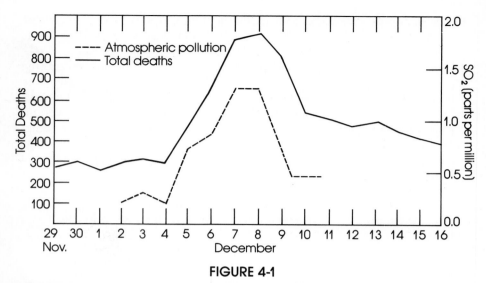

FIGURE 4-1

Atmospheric pollution (in parts per million of sulfur dioxide) and numbers of deaths per day in London, from November 29 to December 16, 1952.

Source: B. MacMahon, T. Pugh, and J. Ipsen, *Epidemiologic Methods* (Boston: Little, Brown, 1960), page 6.

The Method of Concomitant Variation, like Mill's other methods, is most useful within the framework of a specific causal theory. Such a causal theory provides guidance as to which antecedent circumstances among an indefinite number of available antecedents are plausible candidates for causes. If little is known about the specific causal nature of a widespread disease, such as cancer or hypertension, and different frequencies appear to be present in different geographic areas, investigators use the Method of Concomitant Variation to select broad environmental features that vary with intensities that match the variation in frequency of the disease. By doing this, frequently they can control the disease to a certain extent, even when the precise causal agents are unknown.

Exercises

In each of the following exercises:

> (1) Identify the condition or event for which a cause is sought. Be sure to tell whether specific occurrences or rates (relative frequencies of occurrence) are being investigated.
> (2) Identify all antecedent circumstances mentioned in the example.
> (3) State which of Mill's methods is being used.
> (4) Identify the cause, according to the use of Mill's methods.

Note that some of the exercises are taken from newspaper reports and that less than complete information is available. If more background information is required to make a judgment, discuss why this is so. Being aware of what is needed to pass critical judgment on a problem is part of critical thinking! The evidence we receive in newspapers, magazines, and other sources is often incomplete with respect to the conclusions stated there.

1. From a report in *The New York Times* on the use of a new antiviral drug, called "ara-A," in the treatment of herpes simplex encephalitis:

> Of 28 cases of the disease, 18 received ara-A, and 10 were given an inert substance for 10 days. Five persons in the first group died, and seven in the second group. Thus the mortality rate of the untreated group was 70 percent; the rate of the treated group was 28 percent.

2. Alzheimer's disease is a serious form of senility that afflicts between 5 and 10 percent of all persons over age 65. Recently, researchers discovered that patients who die of Alzheimer's disease have much smaller amounts of a particular enzyme in the cortexes of their brains than persons the same age who do not suffer from the disease. The loss of this enzyme activity has been suspected as a cause of the lesions found on the brains of Alzheimer's patients. In postmortem examinations of five Alzheimer's patients and five people without the disease, it was found that all the diseased patients had lost neurons from the nucleus basalis (a tiny area deep in the brain; its function is not understood by neurologists), while all the people without the disease had the normal number of cells in this area. Scientists who conducted this study believe that the loss of neurons from the nucleus basalis may be responsible for the decreased activity in the cortex.

3. An anti-smoking campaign aimed at junior high school students has shown significant results.... The study involved 750 Houston seventh graders. One group of students was asked about smoking habits—31 percent said they had smoked at least one cigarette in the previous month—and was asked the same question again ten weeks later. No anti-smoking instruction was given to them. [They are members of the control group.] Other groups of students were asked the same question [the report does not tell how they responded], and then participated in various kinds of anti-smoking instruction. By the end of ten weeks, 18.3 percent of the control group—those who were not shown anti-smoking propaganda—had taken up smoking. Among the other groups, fewer students had started smoking—ranging from 8.6 percent to 10.3 percent.
> —*Arizona Daily Star*

4. *Background information:* We now know that the disease beriberi is caused by a dietary deficiency in the B complex of vitamins, particularly vitamin B_1. Whole grains provide a common source of this vitamin. The episode described here occurred before anything was known about vitamins. The research was conducted in an asylum for the insane. Cured rice is rice that has been treated to preserve some of the outer hull. Uncured rice (now usually called "polished rice") is rice from which the outer hull—which contains most of the vitamins—is removed.

> The lunatics are housed in two exactly similar buildings on opposite sides of a quadrangle surrounded by a high wall. On December 5, 1905, all the lunatics at that time in the hospital were drawn up in the dining shed and numbered off from the left. The odd numbers were subsequently domiciled [housed] in the ward on the east side of the courtyard, and no alteration was made in their diet. They were still supplied with the same uncured rice as in 1905. The even numbers were quartered in the ward on the west of the

quadrangle and received the same rations as the occupants of the other ward with the exception that they were supplied with cured rice. . . . On December 5, there were 59 lunatics in the asylum; of these, 29 were put on cured rice and 30 on uncured rice. The next patient admitted to the asylum was admitted to the cured rice ward, and the one admitted after him to the uncured rice ward, the next to cured, and so on alternately to the end of the year.

In the middle of the year, the patients in the east ward were moved to the west ward and those in the west ward to the east, but they continued to receive the same diets. By the end of 1906, among 120 patients eating uncured rice, there had been 34 cases of beriberi and 18 deaths. Among the 123 patients assigned to cured rice, there had been only 2 cases and no deaths, and both cases had been manifested at the time the patients were admitted to the asylum.

—B. MacMahon and T. Pugh, *Epidemiology*

5. In England, which imports most of its sucrose [sugar], records of the last 100 years show a steady increase in per capita consumption of sucrose, from about 20 pounds per year in 1820 to over 100 pounds per year today. Present consumption of sucrose in the United States is about the same. This represents 15 to 20 percent of an individual's caloric requirements. Concomitant with this increased consumption of sucrose has been an almost parallel rise in the prevalence of caries [cavities]. Conversely, surveys in Europe and Japan demonstrated that caries was dramatically reduced during periods of wartime restrictions of sugar, syrup, and all sugar products.

—E. Newburn, "Sugar and Dental Caries: A Review of
Human Studies," *Science* 217(1982):418

6. In the newspapers several years ago, there was a story about a doctor in New Jersey who was suspected of—and later tried and acquitted for—murdering a number of patients in a private hospital. Empty vials that had contained curare ("arrow poison") were found in the doctor's locker. The doctor claimed that the curare was used for experiments on dogs, but the man who was supposed to have supplied the dogs denied that he had given or sold any dogs to the doctor. The bodies of the patients, all of whom had been in the hospital for minor operations and who had been in good health otherwise, were exhumed. Sophisticated tests found traces of curare in each of the bodies. On the basis of this evidence, other doctors at the hospital and the authorities insisted that a warrant be issued for the arrest of the suspect.

7. An alarming number of malignant skin cancer cases have been discovered among members of the District of Columbia Police Dept. who were repeatedly exposed to tear gas during the riots and demonstrations of 1968–1971 here.

Dr. Robert F. Dyer, director of the D.C. Police and Firemen's Clinic, said Thursday that one chemical component of tear gas apparently causes cancer.

"Over the past five years I personally have collected a series of 12 patrolmen with malignant melanoma [a form of skin cancer], which in a group of 4,800 men is higher than I would expect," Dyer said.

All 12 officers reported being present at one or more of the many riots and demonstrations quelled with tear gas between 1968 and 1971, he said.

—*Washington Star*

8. Aspirin, taken in large doses by sufferers of arthritis, is being looked at for its effect on the liver.

Gall [the physician conducting the research] said his interest in aspirin and the liver began when a 20-year arthritis sufferer, who had taken aspirin for many years, was found to have high levels of an enzyme in her blood, usually one indicator of hepatitis, a disease of the liver.

When doctors took the woman off aspirin, the high enzyme levels dropped back to normal, Gall said. The test was conducted several times, and each time, the high enzyme levels corresponded to the times when aspirin was taken.

—*Arizona Daily Star*

9. A federal study of 46 cities has concluded that fluoridating water to prevent tooth decay has no adverse effect on public health.

The study by the Center for Disease Control in Atlanta was undertaken to investigate claims that fluoridation is linked to higher cancer rates.

"There is no evidence to suggest that fluoridation does any harm," Dr. J. David Erickson, who conducted the study, said in an interview.

Erickson studied the causes of death of 922,000 people over three years in 46 American cities—24 of them with fluoridated water and 22 without.

After taking into account differences in race, age, sex, education, and population density between the people in the two groups of cities, Erickson found that there was virtually no difference in the death rates. There were 1,124 deaths per 100,000 persons per year in the cities with fluoridated water and 1,137 in those without.

The death rate from cancer was 195 in cities with fluoride and 197 in the cities without.

—Associated Press

10. In a study at Vipeholm, a mental institution in southern Sweden, 436 adult patients on a nutritionally adequate diet were observed for several years. They were found to develop caries [cavities] at a slow rate. Subsequently, the patients were divided into nine groups to compare the effect of various changes in their carbohydrate intake. Sucrose was included in the diet as toffee, chocolate, or caramel, in bread, or in liquid form. Caries increased significantly when food containing sucrose was ingested between meals. Not only the frequency but the form in which sucrose was ingested was important: sticky or adhesive forms were more cariogenic [cavity-producing] than forms which were rapidly cleared from the mouth. After two years on the test diets, the patients were again placed on the control diet, and the caries activity reverted to the pretest pattern.

—E. Newburn, *Science* 217(1982):419

11. Headline: LUNG CANCER FROM "SMOKY COAL" IN CHINA

Women in China's Xuan Wei County heat their homes and cook their meals with "smoky" coal (coal which when burned releases enormous numbers of tiny organic carcinogenic particles that remain airborne for a long time and can eventually lodge in the residents' lungs). . . . Lung cancer incidence is higher among the women who spend their time indoors than among the men, most of whom are farmers and spend the day outside.

—*Science* 235 (1987):139

12. Note: Pheromones are discrete chemicals produced by insects to communicate with other members of their own species. Insects signal the presence of food, enemies, or willing mates by ejecting pheromones. The chemicals can be produced in laboratories and sprayed on crops to the confusion of the insects that produce the chemicals naturally. Scientists who are concerned about damage to the environment hope that the use of pheromones will provide a safer alternative to toxic pesticides.

In the San Joaquin Valley of California, cherry tomato plots were treated with a pheromone that disrupts mating between tomato pinworm moths. Peak infestation during the long growing season was less than 3%. On the control fields sprayed with insecticides, infestation reached 33%.

—*Science* 239(1988):135

III. CONTROLLED EXPERIMENTS

Many of the preceding exercises employed *controlled experiments* to establish causal claims. The use of controlled experiments is closely related to Mill's Joint Method of Agreement and Difference and the Method of Concomitant Variations. In a controlled experiment the investigator studies two groups that are similar to one another, except for their exposure to the suspected cause, and observes whether the groups exhibit a difference in the effect.

For example, in a controlled experiment to study the effects of a birth-control hormone on brain development in rats, two groups of 100 laboratory rats are selected from the relatively uniform population of laboratory rats. The two groups are treated the same in all respects, except that one (the experimental) group's food is supplemented with doses of the birth-control hormone, and the other (the control) group's food is not. If retarded brain development (or a higher rate of retarded brain development) occurs after this treatment in the experimental group, but fails to occur in the control group, the experiment supports the claim that the birth-control hormone is the cause of retardation in laboratory rats. If after this treatment, however, there is no difference in the presence of retardation in the two groups, the experiment does not support the causal claim.

Mill's Joint Method and controlled experiments both use inductive generalization. The experimental group of rats in a study like the one just described is randomly selected from the population of laboratory rats, and the sample is representative of the population from which it is drawn. Thus, what happens to the experimental group in the experiment provides a basis for generalizing to what *would* happen to any population of laboratory rats, all of which were exposed to the hormone. Similarly, the control group is another randomly selected representative sample of rats, and the results obtained from the experiment can be generalized to what would happen to the population of laboratory rats if they were not exposed to the hormone. Being able to say what *would* happen under various circumstances is especially important in causal reasoning, for when we make a causal claim (for example, birth-control hormones cause brain damage in rats), we mean to say not merely that taking hormones was correlated with brain damage in the rats that were studied, but that *if any population of rats were exposed to the hormone, then those rats would suffer a greater rate of brain damage than a population not so exposed.*

The type of controlled experiment performed on the rats described above is called a *randomized experimental study*, because the experimental group and the control group were randomly chosen from the population they represent before being manipulated for the purposes of the experiment.

In the physical sciences, it is possible to perform similar randomized experiments to study various properties of physical substances. Any bit of pure sodium is a representative sample of that metal, so that it is not difficult for investigators to perform controlled experiments to discover the causal properties of sodium. (Sometimes, however, scientists find it difficult to isolate the item on which they wish to perform a controlled experiment. Nobel Prize winner Marie Curie had to handle tons of pitchblende to isolate enough radium to perform her experiments on radioactive materials.)

Obviously, the use of randomized experimental studies on humans is subject to moral and legal restraints. Many of you probably felt uneasy when you read about the treatment of "lunatics" in the beriberi experiment described in the last section. It seems unfair and cruel to compel a group of helpless people to eat a diet suspected of causing a serious disease like beriberi. We must recognize in fairness to the researchers who first suspected a diet deficiency as the cause of beriberi, however, that a diet of polished rice was not unusual for many people outside institutions at that time as well. Nevertheless, restrictions imposed by the federal government would not allow such an experiment today. The government enforces strict guidelines for any experiments involving human subjects, with the result that experiments in which humans are forced to participate are less likely to occur. Federal regulations also require that subjects who do volunteer for experiments be informed about any suspected dangers so that they can give informed consent.

Some other types of controlled studies do not impose possibly harmful treatment on the individuals studied. In *prospective studies*, for example, the experimental group is formed from individuals who have already been exposed to the suspected causal factor, often by "self-selection." The control group in a prospective study is then "matched" to the experimental group in all features thought to be relevant to occurrence of the effect (except the causal factor under consideration). Instead of manipulating the experimental group, as in a randomized experimental study, the experimenter just observes both groups and waits to see what happens. This type of controlled study has been used to investigate the harmful effects of smoking. A sample of persons who already smoke (the experimental group) is matched for such features as age, sex, occupation, place of residence, ethnic background, history of disease, and so on with a sample (control group) of nonsmokers, and both groups are observed over a period of time to see whether rates of various illnesses (or death rates from those illnesses) are different in the two groups. Such studies can be very costly because of the time required for the effects to develop.

In *retrospective studies*, which are quicker than prospective studies, the experimental group is chosen from a population that already exhibits the suspected *effect* and is matched to a control group that is similar in relevant respects (except for the effect). Then a backward-looking study of the histories of the two groups is conducted to justify the claim that some difference in antecedent circumstances between the two groups is the cause.

A recent retrospective study investigated the cause of a particular type of disturbed sleep in infants. The experimental group of 28 newborn infants all showed more rapid-eye-movement sleep and less quiet sleep than the 30 newborns in the control group. The infants in the experimental group had been chronically exposed in the womb to low doses of methadone. (The mothers were former heroin addicts on a methadone maintenance program.) The control group of infants were children of mothers whose care during pregnancy, nutrition, age, and other properties believed to affect the welfare of newborns were similar to the mothers of infants in the experimental group, except that none of these mothers were on drugs.

Although prospective studies and retrospective studies avoid some of the moral and legal objections to randomized experimental studies on humans (and animals), these studies are flawed by possible bias. The samples in both types are *not* randomly selected and are in all likelihood not representative. In prospective studies, the apparent "self-selection" of the experimental group may mask some other underlying cause for the effect. For example, smokers may not freely choose to smoke, but to be drawn to smoke because of some underlying condition. Retrospective studies are subject to the same bias as prospective studies, and they have the added problem of possible errors in the records and reports that are used to reconstruct antecedent circumstances.

When we can study the difference between a control group that is a representative sample of a population, none of which are exposed to the suspected causal agent, and an experimental group that is a representative sample of a population, all of which are exposed to the suspected causal agent, then we have strong justification for concluding that the results of the study will yield reliable information about what *would* happen if the population were exposed to the suspected causal agent. Insofar as samples are not representative, conclusions are less strongly supported.

Many prospective and retrospective studies of human disease draw on hospital patients as subjects, but this practice is almost sure to produce biased samples. Some hospitals attract patients from one economic group of the population; others, from different economic classes. People who enter a hospital for the treatment of one disease may be more susceptible than the general public to other diseases. In evaluating the effects of curative or preventive treatments, it is important to know about the medical history of a patient's family, but this information is often difficult to obtain. For these reasons, medical scientists are very cautious about projecting the results of controlled studies of hospital patients onto the general population.

Another problem and possible source of bias associated with controlled studies of humans is the difficulty of obtaining large enough samples. In the study which concluded that the sleep of newborn infants was affected by drugs taken by their mothers when the infants were in the womb, experimenters made an effort to select two groups of babies who were as alike as possible except for their sleep patterns, but both the experimental group and the control group were rather small. It is often difficult to obtain samples that are large enough to be representative of even a special subgroup of the human population, such as the subgroup of newborns.

Studies performed on experimental animals often meet the ideal conditions of a randomized experimental study. The animals are bred for uniform characteristics, so that almost any group of animals is a representative sample of the population. Such animals are not, however, a representative sample of the *human* population—only the population of laboratory rats, guinea pigs, or whatever experimental animal is used. If we want to use the results of animal studies to draw conclusions about humans, we need to construct arguments from analogy as well. Any relevant differences then between the experimental animals and humans will weaken the conclusions that we draw.

One further problem that should be mentioned in connection with controlled studies of humans is the need to eliminate psychological influences that might affect the purity of the results. It is well known that human illnesses often improve when the patient *believes* in the treatment that is being administered, regardless of any specific physical causal influence of the drug or whatever physical means are employed to effect a cure. The technique of a *double-blind experiment* is adopted to try to eliminate such psychological influences in judging the effectiveness of possible cures. In an experiment to test a new drug, members of the control group are given some inert substance (called a *placebo*) such as a sugar pill, and members of the experimental group are given the drug being tested. The people receiving these substances do not know whether they are members of the control group or the experimental group; they are "blind" to the type of substance they receive. In addition, the investigators are administering the drugs and placebos "blindly"; the substances are identified by codes, and those performing the study cannot tell the placebo from the drug at the time of the experiment. In this way, the experimenters are able to make judgments about success of treatment in each case and learn who received the drug and who received a placebo only after the experiment is completed.

Double-blind experiments are used in many drug tests, and in other tests as well. Recently, the United States government completed a three-year study of the effectiveness of cloud seeding in enhancing rainfall. The technique of seeding clouds involves flying over them and sprinkling them with fine particles of silver iodide. None of the experimenters in the study "knew at the time on which days they were actually seeding clouds with fine silver iodide particles, and on which they were merely sprinkling them with an inert sand 'placebo'" (R. A. Kerr, "Test Fails to Confirm Cloud Seeding Effect," *Science* 217 (1982):234). Neither those who decided which clouds to seed nor those who judged the amounts of rain that fell from seeded clouds knew whether the clouds had been seeded with silver iodide or sand. After three years, a locked vault that held the secret record of the silver iodide seedings was opened. The experimenters were disappointed to find that this particular double-blind experiment failed to confirm the effectiveness of cloud seeding, but they planned further, more refined experiments and were convinced that weather-modification researchers must continue to use such controlled experiments to test the effectiveness of various weather-modification procedures.

Despite all these problems with controlled experiments, however, studies of both humans and animals play an extremely important role in causal investigations. We do not really have any better method for ferreting out causal relationships.

Exercises

1. Review the set of exercises at the end of the previous section on Mill's methods, and note any that exemplify controlled experiments. When you identify the controlled experiments, describe the experimental group and the control group and say whether the study is randomized experimental, prospective, or retrospective.

2. The following report suggests that there may be a causal connection between severe head injury early in life and violent behavior. What types of controlled

experiments are suggested to substantiate this? What are the moral constraints on such experiments?

> A study of 13 men and 2 women convicted of murder and awaiting execution in American prisons has shown that all had experienced severe head injuries earlier in life.
>
> Asked to comment on these findings, Dr. J. Engel of UCLA, a specialist in seeking the roots of violence, noted the difficulty in assessing the relative roles of environmental factors and physical damage to the brain. Individuals such as those examined in the studies, he pointed out, often grow up in a world in which they both witness violence and are subjected to it.
>
> Animal studies have shown that damage to certain areas of the brain can lead to violent behavior, but, Dr. Engel said, "Humans are much more complex than a cat or rat." To identify whether a person's environment or physical damage is more important, he added, would require a series of studies. For such studies, those who suffered specific brain damage and became violent without having been subject to emotional abuse would be matched with a comparable population lacking brain injury. Likewise, those who became violent after a childhood of exposure to violence, but without physical injuries to the brain would be compared statistically with a nonviolent population of similar background.
>
> —*New York Times*

3. Tell how the following study, reported in *Parade* magazine, might have been improved by the use of a controlled experiment:

> A Chinese worker developed a toothpaste that was mixed with the Chinese herbs traditionally presecribed for colds. The toothpaste was tested clinically on 3,600 persons who had colds. The Chinese said that 63 percent of the subjects tested reported marked improvement.

4. Find a description of a controlled experiment in an outside reading source. (Some good sources are the magazines *Science* and *Scientific American* and the "Science" sections of weekly newsmagazines. Other possible sources are newspaper stories and Sunday supplements, such as *Parade*.) Characterize the important features of the experiment (whether it was double-blind, how the control group was matched to the experimental group, and so on).

5. Design a controlled experiment to test a causal claim that interests you.

IV. DIFFERENT USES OF "CAUSE"

> For want of a nail, the shoe was lost,
> For want of a shoe, the horse was lost,
> For want of a horse, the battle was lost,
> And all for the want of a horseshoe nail.
> —Nursery rhyme

Our references to "the cause" of some event or condition conceal the different meanings of the word "cause" and the complexity of most causal situations. How we use "cause" depends on how much we know about a situation and on our practical or theoretical interest in a causal relationship.

Consider a murder trial in which the defendant is accused of shooting the victim. The prosecuting attorney, who is interested in showing that the defendant is legally responsible for the gunshot wound that led to the victim's death, says that the defendant's action was the cause of death. But the medical examiner has a different interest. If the victim died immediately after being shot, for example, the cause cited might be "massive internal bleeding." If the victim did not die immediately, but was taken to surgery and suffocated after an allergic reaction to an anesthetic, the medical examiner's report would cite suffocation as the cause of death. There is no real conflict between the causal stories of the lawyer and the coroner; although suffocation was the *proximate* physical cause of death (the causal physical circumstance closest to the event), the action of the defendant was an important earlier part of the causal chain that led to the suffocation. The law is interested in one part of that chain (*who* is to blame), and the medical specialist is interested in another (which of the body's systems stopped working).

The causal chain leading to the victim's death undoubtedly contains more links. The ambulance that took the victim to the hospital may have been delayed by traffic. The anesthetist may have failed to check the victim for allergies. The shooting may have been provoked (caused) by a quarrel resulting from the victim's attentions to the defendant's spouse; the victim's attentions might have been encouraged by the spouse; and so on. All of these events and conditions were a part of the complex causal process leading to the death of the victim. Only a special interest in some part of the complex set of events and processes (such as who is legally responsible or what should be put on the death certificate) leads us to refer to one part of this complex process as "the cause."

This account of the *chain* of causal events that results in the death of the victim is actually oversimplified, for it fails to consider various other chains of events that might be interwoven with these events and that could reinforce or counteract them. For this reason, it seems more appropriate to use the analogy of a "causal network" rather than that of a "causal chain" to characterize the complex process.

Different interests of the lawyer and the medical examiner in the example above lead them to focus on one aspect of the causal network rather than another. Sometimes, an aspect is singled out as "the cause" because it is more susceptible to control than other aspects of the causal process. In yellow fever, for example, the anopheles mosquito is usually cited as "the cause." Actually, the mosquito transfers the disease from one human to another by taking up or injecting the specific yellow-fever virus into the bloodstream when it bites, but programs to control yellow fever are aimed at eliminating the mosquito rather than controlling the specific virus.

The importance of naming the part of the causal process that is susceptible to our control "the cause" is shown by an interesting contrast between identifying "the cause" of diseases in some plants and in humans. Many humans have a natural immunity to various diseases. All of us have known some of those lucky ones who never seem to catch the flu, even when they haven't had shots and almost everyone around them comes down with the disease. We do not, however, try to control the spread of human diseases through selective breeding, and a lack of natural immunity is almost never cited as "the cause" of human disease. In contrast when a disease-resistant strain of some plant is discovered, plant breeders immediately try to propogate the new strain and market it for this valuable property. Breeding resistant strains rather than attacking the specific organism responsible for the disease is an accepted and effective method of controlling diseases in plants. Because of this, we do sometimes say that a plant succumbed to disease *because* it lacked the immune characteristic.

The mosquito carrier of yellow fever is a "necessary causal condition" of the disease. Without the mosquitos the disease does not occur in nature. A condition is called "necessary" if the effect cannot occur without that condition. The presence of oxygen, for example, is a necessary causal condition for the existence of fires. Our attention often focuses on causally necessary conditions when we are interested in *eliminating* some undesirable effect. When medical scientists try to eliminate a disease, they often look for some necessary causal condition, such as the mosquito carrier of yellow fever. No one, however, would think of trying to prevent forest fires by reducing the oxygen in the atmosphere near forests, even though this would be an effective measure. Unlike the mosquito in the yellow-fever example, oxygen is never referred to as "the cause" of forest fires even though, like the mosquito, it is a causally necessary condition. The difference between the two cases is that the mosquito is something we can eliminate to prevent the problem; oxygen is not.

When we are interested in bringing about some effect, rather than eliminating an effect, we often look for a causally sufficient condition that we can control. A condition is "causally sufficient" for some effect if whenever the condition is present the effect must occur. Decapitation of a person, for example, is a causally sufficient condition for that person's death. Atmospheric testing of nuclear bombs is a sufficient causal condition for producing levels of radiation that are hazardous to humans and other animals in the areas near the test sites. Scientists search for wonder drugs ("magic bullets") that will bring about causally sufficient conditions for curing human diseases.

It is unusual, however, to be able to isolate a single causally sufficient condition. Frequently, the term "suffecent condition" refers instead to some important causal factor that, against a background set of necessary conditions, is especially proximate, or interesting, or easy to control.

For example, it is reasonable to claim that bringing water up to a temperature of 100° Celsius is sufficient to make that water boil. This is true, however, only when certain necessary background conditions, such as relative freedom of the water from impurities and normal atmospheric pressure, are operative. When the background conditions are fairly standard, or are not subject to great fluctuation, or are not usually under our direct control, we can ignore them and use the term "sufficient causal condition" to refer somewhat loosely to an event or process that we can control directly and that, under standard background conditions, will produce the desired effect.

Sometimes we say that a set of causal conditions is "individually necessary and jointly sufficient" for some event to occur. The conditions individually necessary and jointly sufficient to cause germination in viable grass seed, for example, are (1) adequate water, (2) suitable temperature, (3) oxygen, and (4) light. When all of these conditions are present jointly in the appropriate degree (proportions vary for different types of grasses), germination occurs.

It is rather unusual, however, to be able to specify complete sets of conditions that are individually necessary and jointly sufficient even when we know a lot about the causes of some type of event. An example follows.

Dental caries, the localized destruction of tooth tissue by microorganisms, is a process familiar to most of you, and this process is well understood by medical scientists. There are three main causal factors: (1) the hosts (saliva and teeth), (2) the microorganisms (particularly one called *Streptococcus mutans*, which is found in dental plaque), and (3) the diet.

Experiments have shown that rats fed through stomach tubes do not get cavities even when the caries-producing *S. mutans* is present. Similarly, rats do not get cavities when they are fed orally if their mouths are kept sterile. It would seem then that the presence of teeth, microorganisms, and food are individually necessary and jointly sufficient for cavities in rats. However, rats do not *always* develop cavities under these circumstances—although they do develop cavities at "the normal rate." Some rats, like some humans, apparently are able to resist cavities better than others. For this reason, we cannot say that the presence of the three necessary conditions (teeth, microorganisms, and a food supply) jointly form a sufficient causal condition for the disease.

Some further necessary conditions may be specifiable in this case (for example, lack of fluoride protection and genetic susceptibility to the disease), but frequently the causal situations are simply too complex to permit us to identify a complete set of conditions. The effort medical scientists are willing to expend in search of additional necessary conditions for a particular type of event depends largely on practical concerns, such as how much knowledge is necessary to *control* the causal process, rather than on theoretical concerns, such as achieving knowledge of a set of jointly sufficient conditions. Although diet has received emphasis recently in the study of dental caries, research formerly focused primarily on host factors (fluoride treatment of teeth and drinking water) and on microorganisms (the possibility of immunization).

We have been looking at some of the different ways in which the term "cause" is used. The point of this discussion is that there are a number of correct uses of the term. Different uses of "cause" are suitable in different circumstances. It is important for us to understand the various ways that "cause" is used so that we can identify and understand important causal relationships.

We want especially to be aware that there can be causal connections in which the cause is neither a sufficient nor a necessary causal condition for the effect. Cigarette smoking, for example, is neither necessary nor sufficient for the contraction of lung cancer. It is possible to contract lung cancer even if you do not smoke; and you may escape lung cancer even if you are a heavy smoker. Yet, it would be foolish, with all the evidence now available, to deny that smoking causes lung cancer. Smoking is a *probabilistic* cause of the disease. We call a causally antecedent condition a *probabilistic cause* when its presence makes the occurrence of the condition under investigation more probable than it would be in the absence of the antecedent condition. There is very good evidence that smoking is an antecedent condition that is related to lung cancer in this way. Many of the controlled experiments that are examined in this chapter provide evidence for assigning probabilistic causes.

Here is an example, taken from a syndicated newspaper medical advice column, of the dangers of confusing probabilistic causes and sufficient causal conditions:

> Dear Dr. Steincrohn: Thinking about premature death has caused a serious depression in my husband. Although only 38, and, according to our doctor, physically sound he lives in fear of dying early.
>
> He blames it on his poor heredity. His father died of a coronary attack at the age of 59 and his mother had a stroke at about the same age. One uncle suffers from extremely high blood pressure.
>
> With that kind of family history, he asks, "What chance have I got?" As a result he smokes too much. Drinks a lot. Has let himself get fat.
>
> He figures how he lives won't make any difference. Have you run into similar problems?

In answering this letter, the doctor correctly notes that "there may be a hereditary disposition to stroke and heart attacks," but he points out that the man is not inevitably doomed to an early death. He cites records of patients who had good family histories and poor living habits who died earlier than their counterparts who had bad heredity traits. The husband, at least if his wife's description of the situation is accurate, seems to regard his poor heredity traits as causally sufficient for an early death rather than as factors that increase the probability of early death. As a result of this misunderstanding, he ignores other factors, such as not smoking, which could counteract a possible predisposition to cancer.

Exercises

For each of the following causal claims, discuss whether "cause" is used in the sense of:

(1) A proximate or nearest cause in a chain or network of causes,
(2) An agent causally responsible for some action or event,
(3) A necessary causal condition,
(4) A sufficient causal condition,
(5) A sufficient causal condition against a background of accepted, stable necessary conditions,
(6) A probabilistic cause.

1. Martha failed the exam because there wasn't enough time to finish it.

2. Jason will graduate in June because he passed every course he took this year.

3. William went to the party because Jean invited him.

4. An arsonist caused the fire at the museum.

5. The house burned down because oily rags were stored in a closet.

6. The criminal confessed because he was promised a light sentence.

7. Nathan caught the measles because he played with the boy next door who had the measles.

8. The crops are poor this summer because there hasn't been enough rain.

9. Rice takes much longer to cook at the observatory because it is on top of an 8,000-foot mountain. At that altitude, the boiling point of water is considerably less than it is at sea level.

10. The ice on the sidewalk is melting because salt was thrown on it.

11. Terence caught a cold because he wasn't dressed for the storm.

12. Rats that were injected with massive doses of saccharine developed tumors at a much greater rate than a control group of rats that did not receive saccharine, thereby demonstrating that saccharine causes tumors in rats.

13. The assassination of Archduke Ferdinand at Serajevo in August, 1914, was the cause of World War I.

14. The heavy penalties imposed by the Allies on the Germans after the First World War caused the Second World War.

15. Worry about the national deficit caused the crash of the stock market in October, 1987.

V. HUME'S ANALYSIS OF CAUSATION

Thus far in our discussion, we have not attempted to offer a definition of "cause" that would cover the various uses of the term. It is very difficult to define "cause" in a satisfactory way, even though we all seem to grasp the meaning of the term in an intuitive way. In the eighteenth century, David Hume offered an analysis of the meaning of statements of the general form "A causes B." Hume was trying to solve the problem of how to justify causal inferences. For the purposes of simplicity, he analyzed the type of causal relationship that held between two rather uncomplicated events, or types of events (the striking of two billiard balls and their movement after the collision). Hume could find nothing in the *ideas* of striking and subsequent motion to connect the two events. That is to say, the concepts of striking and of motion are not related in the way that the concept of bachelor and the concept of unmarried male are related. When Hume turned to experience for a possible justification of causal claims, he said the features we could *observe* in such relationships were:

1. *A* and *B* are joined with one another in space and time. ("No action at a distance.")
2. *B* follows *A*. (The "effect" does not precede the "cause.")
3. Whenever *A* occurs, *B* occurs; and vice-versa. ("Constant conjunction.")

Hume realized that all three of these relationships might be observed between two events that were only coincidentally connected with one another. (Remember the London tobacconists' avoidance of bubonic plague.) Hume therefore felt that his analysis failed to uncover any "real"—as distinguished from coincidental—connection between the two events. His analysis pushed the matter still further, for he showed that there is no logical reason—no correct deductive or inductive argument—to support the view that constant conjunctions that have been observed in the past will continue to hold in the future.

Hume was not entirely satisfied with his results, and he challenged others to find a "real connection," but his own conclusion was skeptical: The inference from cause to effect is based on a psychological habit of expectation, formed as a result of observing the connections in the past. The inference, Hume said, is apparently not grounded in *reasoned* knowledge of real connections but in habit or custom. Since we tend to think that our knowledge of causes, especially what we have learned from scientific investigations, is based on more than mere habit, Hume's well argued and startling conclusion has troubled all who have thought seriously about this problem.

In this text, we cannot discuss Hume's arguments in detail, nor can we consider various attempts to solve the problems he raised. Many serious thinkers reluctantly accept Hume's skeptical conclusion that there is no logical reason to support the view that constant conjunctions that have been observed in the past will continue to hold in the future. Despite this fact, most people also believe that genuine causal connections can be understood as something more than constant conjunction and the habit of expecting repetitions of these conjunctions.

It is important to understand that Hume was *NOT* recommending that we cease making causal investigations and causal claims or that we give up causal reasoning altogether. He thought that this would be not only foolish but also psychologically impossible. Many philosophers and scientists have adopted the following pragmatic stand in view of Hume's analysis:

Although we have no logical reason for believing that the future will resemble that past, *if* it does, then our causal judgments that are based on observations of continued regularities (using reasoning of the sort recommended by Mill) will be the ones that provide useful and important information about the world. If the world changes in such a way that the present regularities no longer hold, no other method now available can give us any better information about what regularities—if any—we can expect in the future.

You may have noticed that in Hume's analysis of what it means to say that "*A* is the cause of *B*," he was using the notion of "causally sufficient condition." This is expressed in the third statement of his analysis: "Whenever *A* occurs, *B* occurs." Another term that is used to distinguish this type of cause from a cause that is probabilistically related to its effect, is "deterministic" cause. A *deterministic cause* inevitably results in its effect.

Determinism is the philosophical principle that everything that happens is a result of causally sufficient conditions. Determinism does not claim that we know, or even that we will someday know, what these conditions are in each case. Determinism is a view about what the world is like, not a view about the knowledge we can obtain about that world. According to the principle of determinism, the fundamental causal structure of the world is deterministic, and references to probabilistic causes are due to ignorance of some part of the causal complex—some "hidden factors" that, if understood, would complete the causal story.

Whether or not all fundamental causes are deterministic is another difficult—and, as yet, unanswered—philosophical question. If the causal structure of the universe is fundamentally deterministic, then our talk about probabilistic causes may simply reflect our ignorance of hidden, deterministic causal factors. In Hume's time, the most advanced science of the day was Newtonian physics. Newton's genius had unearthed an impressive set of deterministic causes, expressed in his Law of Universal Gravitation and in his three Laws of Motion. In view of Newton's successes, it was widely believed that future scientific advances would uncover more and more deterministic causes in cases where previous knowledge had been probabilistic.

Consider our view that smoking is a probabilistic cause of lung cancer. It is certainly possible that further scientific investigation may uncover a genetic property, present in some but absent in others, that predisposes humans to lung cancer when they smoke heavily. Medical scientists might someday be able to specify a set of individually necessary and jointly sufficient causal conditions for the disease.

Nevertheless, there are some areas of modern science, particularly quantum physics, in which—unlike the situation in Hume's time—the best theories available not only have probabilistic causes at the most fundamental level but also cannot even accommodate the discovery of "hidden factors." This point is rather difficult to understand without an appropriate background knowledge of quantum physics. Nevertheless, it is so important that some scientists have considered it the most revolutionary feature of modern science—comparable to Newton's great discoveries in the seventeenth century. Many scientists hope that eventually a different—and, to their minds a more satisfactory—deterministic theory of quantum physics may be discovered. But they recognize that the present theory cannot be expanded or modified to become a deterministic theory without giving up even more firmly held principles about causality, such as *an effect cannot occur earlier than its cause*. The finest experimental results currently available cannot be accounted for by deterministic causes.

Thus, quantum physics differs from medical science. Medical scientists have discovered that specific microorganisms are causally responsible for such diseases as cholera, plague, tuberculosis, and Legionnaires' Disease and that deficiencies in specific substances (vitamins) are causally responsible for such diseases as beriberi, rickets, and scurvy. Medical theory is heavily committed to the discovery of such specific causal agents, which when present or absent—against a standard background of necessary causal conditions—are sufficient for the occurrence of specific diseases. In other words, the history of medical science can be viewed in terms of searches for deterministic causes and success in finding such causes. Seventeenth-century physics, which reached its peak in Newton's work, enjoyed similar success in identifying deterministic causes. Until quite recently, Newton's (deterministic) physics represented the most advanced science. The most advanced theory of physics in the twentieth century, however, depends on probabilistic causes.

Probabilistic causation would remain important even if all fundamental causes were deterministic, for at any given time in a subject area, probabilistic knowledge may be the most accurate knowledge available. Furthermore, the search for deterministic causes is frequently guided and motivated by the observance of probabilistic (statistical) regularities. As a practical matter, in science as well as in everyday life, we will continue to be concerned with probabilistic causes.

One final remark: Hume's worries about causation are not solved by replacing a deterministic notion of causality with a probabilistic one. Hume's arguments apply to conjunctions that hold only with probability as well as they apply to constant conjunctions.

VI. CAUSAL FALLACIES

Mistakes in causal reasoning, or *causal fallacies*, can arise through inattention to some important aspect of the nature of causal relationships. Causes are *repeatedly* connected with their effects (although the connections may be probabilistic rather than deterministic). This feature of the causal relationship holds whether we are talking about causally necessary conditions, causally sufficient conditions, proximate causes, or any other special type of cause. We expect causes and their effects to occur together with some degree of regularity. Another standard feature of any causal relationship is that a cause does not occur later in time than its effect.

1. Confusing Coincidental Relationships with Causes (*Post Hoc*)

Sometimes people focus on the second standard feature just mentioned, and infer that A is the cause of B simply because event B occurs later than event A. To reason this way is to commit a causal fallacy. The fallacy is common enough to be given the special name *post hoc*, which is derived from the first two words of the Latin expression that describes the fallacious pattern of reasoning: "*Post hoc, ergo propter hoc*" ("After this, therefore because of this").

When we think carefully about the matter, we are not likely to claim that a causal connection exists between two events merely on the basis of the fact that one event occurred later than the other. In our critical moments, we realize that it may have been coincidental that one event followed the other in time. But sometimes when the events are striking, unusual, or important to us, we mistake a coincidence for a true causal connection, particularly if such a connection fits more or less within some accepted causal framework. If, for example, an air conditioning unit breaks down the day after it receives routine maintenance service involving a change of filter, cleaning, and oiling, we might suspect a causal connection between the service and the breakdown and blame the serviceman. Further investigation may show, however, that the cause of the breakdown was unrelated to the maintenance work (say, the failure of a timing switch that had not been touched and that showed no signs of any problem).

Post hoc reasoning underlies many superstitious beliefs. If, for example, I receive bad news on three successive Wednesdays and conclude that Wednesday is my unlucky day (that this day of the week somehow causes me to receive bad news) I am committing a *post hoc* fallacy. If I eat a special breakfast (say bacon and eggs) when I usually have cereal and then do brilliantly on a math examination that afternoon, it would be a *post hoc* fallacy to conclude that the special breakfast was the cause of my unusual performance on the examination.

In addition to constructing unwarranted causal connections between two events that are unusual, or important, and that occur in close succession, the belief that an effect must somehow *resemble* its cause—or that the cause must somehow *contain* whatever is in its effect—is a possible source of *post hoc* fallacies. Mill was especially scornful of this mistake, which he considered to be an undesirable holdover from medieval attempts at scientific reasoning. Mill maintained that proponents of this view might as well argue that pepper had to be in the cook, since there was pepper in the soup! Belief in the efficacy of many folk medicines is based on this kind of reasoning. A causal relationship is considered plausible on the basis of some resemblance, usually between the form of plant and the part of the body that is afflicted. The leaves of the wildflower Hepatica (Liverwort) are shaped something like the human liver, so the plant was used as a cure for liver ailments. The leaves of Pulmonaria (Lungwort) resemble human lungs, and were therefore considered to be an effective lung medicine. Undoubtedly, the supposed "cure" seemed to work in some cases. Many human illnesses clear up regardless of treatment—or lack of treatment—however, and it cannot simply be assumed that a causally efficacious cure has been found simply because improvement follows treatment in a few cases.

The best way to distinguish coincidental relationships from causal ones is to perform controlled experiments when this is possible. If a controlled experiment is not practical, then we should try to make further observations to determine whether or not the regularities persist. After tobacco use failed to prevent the plague at Eton in the seventeenth century, for example, observers realized that the connection between using tobacco and avoiding the plague was not a genuine causal connection but merely a coincidence, and sustained observation proved this to be true. Mill understood that it was important to use his methods repeatedly to test suspected causal connections. His views are reflected in the modern use of controlled experiments and observations. In controlled experiments, irrelevant factors can be eliminated, and the essential components of a causal process—that is to say, a causal theory—may be grasped. If opportunities for checking the persistence of regularities are not available, it is wise to suspend judgment about whether a connection is coincidental or causal.

2. Ignoring a Common Cause

Even when observation and experiment assure us that a regular connection exists between a suspected cause and some effect, we must be careful to distinguish among various direct and indirect causal connections. For example, when archaeologists excavate sites in Central and North America, they find that sites that contain bits of pottery also usually contain fragments of grinding-stones (used for grinding corn). But they do not conclude that the presence of pottery causes the presence of grinding-stones or that the presence of grinding stones causes the presence of pottery. To do so would be to commit the fallacy of *ignoring a common cause*. Pottery fragments and grinding-stone fragments are not directly causally related to one another. Their joint occurrence is a result of an underlying common cause, namely human habitation of those sites.

Examples of regular associations that depend on a common cause are frequently encountered. The measles virus causes both red spots and fever in those people who are afflicted with the disease; although the spots and fever are regularly connected, neither directly causes the other. The regular association between storms and falling barometers is due to a common cause—a sharp drop in atmospheric pressure. The tips of many pine trees in my city turned brown recently. This was not the result of some pine trees infecting others; it was the result of a common cause—an atmospheric inversion that allowed atmospheric fluorides to concentrate in the foliage of the pines.

3. Confusing Cause and Effect

A third causal fallacy, the *fallacy of confusing cause and effect*, arises when a direct causal relationship exists between two types of events, but a mistake is made in judging the *direction* of the relationship. An example of this fallacy occurs in one of Graham Greene's spy novels, *The Human Factor*. In one part of the book, a pair of secret agents are discussing a method to "eliminate" a colleague suspected of leaking secrets. One of the agents suggests using peanuts, and offers the following account to his baffled coworker:

> "Peanuts when they go bad produce a mold. Caused by *aspergillus flavus*— but you can forget the name. It's not that important, and I know you were never any good at Latin."
> "Go on, for heaven's sake."
> "To make it easy for you I'll concentrate on the mold. The mold produces a group of highly toxic substances known collectively as aflatoxin. And aflatoxin is the answer to our little problem."

The spy who is so condescending to his colleague has no reason to be smug, since he is guilty of confusing cause and effect. The peanuts do not *produce* a mold when they go bad. The mold attacks the peanuts and is the *cause* of their going bad. The mold, in other words, is a cause—not an effect—of spoiled peanuts.

Effects cannot precede their causes, so the way to avoid the fallacy of confusing cause and effect is to pay special attention to the *temporal order* of two events that have a directly causal relationship to one another. For example, it is well known that the rise in the incidence of lung cancer and the increase in cigarette smoking have been regularly connected over the past 50 years. Most people believe that there is a direct causal relationship between these two events—that the increase in tobacco use is the cause, and the increase in cancer is the effect. However, some people have said that the rise in the incidence of lung cancer may have caused the increase in smoking, because having cancer may create a craving for tobacco. This seems to be a case of the fallacy of confusing cause and effect, for we know that most smokers who develop lung cancer have smoked heavily for years. Their smoking habits were fixed long before they contracted the disease. There is no evidence that people who contracted lung cancer increased their smoking thereafter.

Although the question of which came first—smoking or lung cancer—seems a fairly easy one to answer, it is difficult in many causal situations to determine which part of the causal complex occurs earlier in time. For example, there is archaeological evidence that certain areas of the southwestern United States were occupied for a prolonged period of time by one group of people, who disappeared rather abruptly and were succeeded by an ethnically different group of people. The temporal order of this series of events is subject to interpretation. The invasion of the newcomers might have caused the former residents to abandon these areas, or the influx of the newcomers might have been caused, or partially caused, by the decision of the former residents to leave these areas.

Another example of the difficulty of sorting out cause and effect occurs in studies of schizophrenia. There is a well-supported, regular association between schizophrenia in young adults and unstable or disturbed relationships in the families of those who suffer from schizophrenia. But it is not known whether the unhappy family situation is a cause, or part of the cause, of schizophrenia or whether the hardship of living with a schizophrenic tends to cause disturbance in the family. Both schizophrenia (or at least the most obvious symptoms of the disease) and unhappy family situations usually develop over an extended period of time. In such situations, it is almost impossible to determine which event occurred first.

In some cases, further observation and/or controlled experimentation that attempts to interfere with some part of the causal process can enable us to determine the direction of a causal relationship. It is on the basis of many studies of the development of lung cancer and the smoking history of victims of this disease that the claim that cancer causes an increase in smoking can be rejected. In their studies of the abandonment of pueblos in the Southwest, archaeologists look for evidence of warfare and evidence of unfavorable conditions for agriculture, as well as for other evidence—such as the exact dates of leaving and arrival of the different groups—that would help them to decide whether invasion by new people was the cause of pueblo abandonment or an effect of the abandonment.

In some cases, such as with schizophrenia, it is very difficult to use experiments to determine causal direction. One experiment that could be performed would be to remove the schizophrenic from the family situation and then to use Mill's Method of Difference to observe whether or not family relationships improved. The results of such an experiment might not be entirely convincing, however. The family situation may have deteriorated during the time spent with the schizophrenic to the point that family patterns of uncooperative behavior may have become too fixed to be changed simply by the removal of the original source of the difficulty.

Although no effect can precede its cause, we must recognize that many causal relationships are complex. Multiple, interacting causes can reinforce and counteract one another to such a degree that isolating the various parts in order to observe or control them separately may not be feasible. In such situations, awareness of the possibility of an underlying common cause, or of the possibility that cause and effect may be confused with one another, can prevent us from accepting unsupported or inadequately supported causal claims.

4. Genetic Fallacy: Reasons and Causes

The term "genesis" is synonymous with "origin." The *genetic fallacy* is a mistake in reasoning that occurs when some factor concerning the origin or causal source of a claim is confused with evidence for the truth of that claim. Unlike the three causal fallacies just considered, the genetic fallacy does *not* involve some misunderstanding of the form of evidence required to support a causal claim. The genetic fallacy is treated in this section because, after our discussion of the nature of causes, we are in a better position to understand the difference between the *cause* of holding a belief and the *evidence* for the truth of that belief.

When evidence is presented in a logically correct argument, the evidence consists of statements that, if true, provide *reasons* for accepting the conclusion as true. Sometimes, however, beliefs are not held on the basis of reasons but are held because of psychological factors that cause the belief. Among these factors are devotion to the person from whom the belief was acquired, social pressures to conform, and the implantation of a belief at an early age. Any of these factors can be a causal source of a belief, and can be cited in an explanation of why someone holds the belief, but none of them is a reason for the truth of the belief.

An adult who is afraid of the dark may believe physical harm will come to him or her from being in a dark room. This belief may be the result of being locked in the closet as a child. The frightening childhood experience is part of a causal explanation of that person's fear of the dark and—as a causal explanation—is probably correct. We have good evidence that such treatment causes fears that persist into adulthood. However, this is not evidence that being in the dark will physically harm that person. To suppose that the causal explanation of the fear is a reason (in the sense of evidence) for believing that physical harm will result from being in a dark room is an example of the genetic fallacy.

Fallacious appeals to authority, fallacious appeals to consensus, and fallacious *ad hominem* arguments are also forms of the genetic fallacy, for they involve mistaking some feature of the genesis of a claim (the person who is the source of the claim) as evidence for (or against) the truth of that claim. If I argue that my senator's description of some proposed legislation is false because he is a pompous windbag, then my so-called argument is a fallacious abusive *ad hominem*, and I also commit the genetic fallacy.

5. Confusing the Harm or Benefits that Result from Holding a Belief with Evidence for It

Closely related to accepting or rejecting a claim because of its source (rather than because of evidence) is accepting or rejecting a claim because of the harm or good that might be caused by holding the belief. This fallacy has no special name but occurs all too frequently when our desires intrude on our reasons for belief. Suppose, for example, that I am a heavy smoker, and that I want very much to continue smoking. If I can make myself believe, despite all the evidence, that cigarette smoking will not harm me, then why should I give up smoking? Here, holding the belief that smoking won't harm me has the benefit of continuing my pleasure in smoking, and because of that result, I believe it. (Of course, smoking is harmful, whether I believe it or not; confusing the benefit of holding a belief with evidence for the belief can be dangerous.)

Swindlers and confidence men offer preposterous claims about easy money-making schemes and depend on the greed of their "targets" to override any evidence against the truth of those claims. If we want very much the great riches that would result if a claim were true, it is more difficult to pay attention to evidence.

Some fundamentalist religious groups have rejected Darwin's theory of evolution not because of evidence against it, but because they believe that if the biblical account of creation is not accepted as literal truth, a drastic relaxation of standards of morality will result.

Holding beliefs is not always cost-free. If I believe that a friend is loyal, I enjoy a benefit. If someone presents me with evidence that the friend has betrayed me, I have a problem. If I admit that the friend has betrayed me, I pay the price of lost or diminished friendship. It is not hard to understand why I do not want to pay that price. But if I take avoiding that cost as a justification (in the sense of evidence) for denying the betrayal, I confuse the effect of holding a belief with a reason for the belief, and I engage in fallacious reasoning.

Just as we must distinguish the causal source of a belief from reasons for it to avoid the genetic fallacy, we have to distinguish the resultant harm or benefit of holding a belief from reasons for it to avoid this other fallacy.

VII. REVIEW

The aims of Chapter 4 have been to increase understanding of the complexity of causal reasoning, to provide some standards for assessing causal arguments, and to point out some common types of fallacious causal reasoning. The new terminology introduced included the names of four of Mill's methods for discovering causes and justifying causal claims: the *Method of Agreement*, the *Method of Difference*, the *Joint Method of Agreement and Difference*, and the *Method of Concomitant Variation*. Look again at Section II, in which these methods are discussed, and be sure that you are able to recognize examples of the use of these methods.

In our discussion of the term "cause," several types of causes were distinguished:

Necessary causal condition: *A* is causally necessary for *B* means that without *A*, *B* will not occur.

Sufficient causal condition: *A* is causally sufficient for *B* means that whenever *A* occurs, *B* will also occur.

Deterministic cause: sufficient causal condition.

Probabilistic cause: *A* is a probabilistic cause for *B* if the presence of *A* increases the probability that *B* will occur.

Proximate cause: the causal condition in a causal complex that is nearest in time or space to the event caused.

Another important concept discussed in this chapter is the **controlled experiment**. In a controlled experiment, an experimental group is subjected to a suspected causal agent and a control group is not. The controlled experiment provides a context for the application of Mill's Joint Method of Agreement and Difference or the Method of Concomitant Variations. The technique is especially valuable because every effort is made in a controlled experiment to see that the control group and the experimental group differ only with respect to the suspected causal agent; in all other respects the two groups should be similar. In one type of controlled experiment, the **randomized experimental study**, the control group and the experimental group are selected in such a way that they form representative samples of the population. Thus, it is reasonable to infer by inductive generalization that what happens to these groups in the presence or absence of the suspected cause would also happen to the population they represent. Since it is immoral to subject humans to unpleasant and possibly harmful causal agents, these studies are usually performed on experimental animals. If we want to make inferences about what would happen to humans on the basis of these animal studies, analogical arguments are required.

Another type of controlled study is the forward-looking **prospective study**, in which an experimental group that has already been exposed to the suspected cause is matched with a control group that has not been exposed. The experimenter then waits to see what happens in each group. These experiments are inferior to randomized experiments for demonstrating causal claims, because there is some reason to believe that the experimental and control groups are not representative samples. Nevertheless, these studies provide valuable information. Since humans "self-select" themselves into the population from which the experimental group is drawn, these studies avoid the moral objections to performing randomized experiments on humans. They also circumvent the need for additional analogical arguments to draw conclusions about humans.

Retrospective (backward-looking) studies are another type of controlled study. In these, the experimental group is chosen from individuals that already exhibit the effect. A matched control group is chosen, and the histories of the two groups are examined to see whether there is a difference in past exposure to the suspected causal factor. These studies suffer from all the problems of prospective studies, and introduce additional bias into the samples. They are the weakest form of controlled study, but because they give quicker results than prospective studies, they can provide useful information, such as early warnings about the dangers of some medical treatment or guides for conducting a more thorough prospective study.

Causal fallacies discussed in this chapter include:

1. **Post Hoc:** the fallacy of arguing that *A* is the cause of *B* just because *B* comes later than *A*. A relationship that is coincidental is judged—on the basis of insufficient evidence of a regular connection—to be causal. Many superstitious beliefs involve this fallacy.

2. **The Fallacy of Ignoring a Common Cause:** When evidence supports the view that there is a regular connection between two events or types of events, the nature of the connection must be investigated before making a causal judgment. *A* and *B* might be regularly connected through some common underlying cause *C*. In such cases, neither *A* nor *B* directly causes the other. Both *A* and *B* are effects of a common cause.

3. **The Fallacy of Confusing Cause and Effect:** When two events or types of events are regularly connected and do not result from a common cause, care must be taken to define which is cause and which is effect. Effects cannot occur earlier than their causes. In complex causal relationships, however, the temporal order of the various parts of the complex may be difficult to investigate.

4. **Genetic Fallacy:** This fallacy occurs whenever something about the genesis (origin, source or cause) of a claim or a belief is taken as evidence for it.

5. The fallacy that involves **mistaking some harm or benefit that results from holding a belief with evidence for it.**

VIII. EXERCISES

1. Some people have argued that both smoking and lung cancer are caused by some unknown factor, perhaps an obscure hereditary condition. Which fallacy

would these people say that those who claim smoking is the cause of lung cancer are committing?

2. Identify any fallacies involved in the following arguments:
   a. Mrs. Jones, who is 89 years old, died two days after receiving a flu shot. Therefore, the flu shot caused her death.
   b. Psychologists who have tested thousand of people working in American businesses have discovered that top executives generally have much larger vocabularies than lower-level employees do. Therefore, if you want to rise to the top in business, you can make this happen by developing a very large vocabulary.
   c. Every time little Johnny approaches the supermarket door, he says "Abracadabra" and then the door swings open. Johnny concludes that saying this magic word causes the door to open.
   d. The results of surveys conducted by a typewriter company indicate that college students who own typewriters are, on the average, better students than college students who do not own typewriters. So if you want to succeed in your college studies, you should get a typewriter.
   e. It has been widely observed that when young children who are usually well-behaved become irritable and difficult, they exhibit the symptoms of a cold or viral infection the next day. It is clear that their misbehavior causes these illnesses.
   f. During the looting and rioting in Detroit in the summer of 1967, the items most commonly stolen were color television sets. Some people argued that one way to prevent such riots would be to distribute free color television sets to those who want them.
   g. Tom is being quite reasonable when he regards all his coworkers with suspicion and fear because he feels that they are trying to take over his responsibilities. After all, he grew up in a tough situation and had to fight for everything he has achieved. He became impressed at an early age that others were out to get him.
   h. Some people argue that emotional distress is the cause of cancer. Their evidence is the well-known fact that many patients with terminal cancer are severely depressed and unusually irritable.
   i. Two students in a large class turn in identical term papers. The teacher accuses them of copying from one another, even though the students can prove that they did not know one another and had no access to one another's work. The teacher maintains that copying could be the only cause of the identical papers. (What fallacy does the teacher commit?)
   j. A number of legislators are opposed to legalized abortions on the grounds that women undergoing abortions may be damaged psychologically. We can dismiss the truth of their claims, however, for these legislators are Catholic, and everyone knows the Catholic Church is opposed to abortion.
   k. A football coach who is trying to bring his team out of a slump studies the statistics of past games. His research on several teams over a number of years shows that many more passes and attempted passes are almost

always made by the losing team than by the winning team. From this information, the coach infers that he can make his team win by restricting the number of passes they throw.

l. "Since modern civilization came into being through Christianity, it would not survive once its supernatural basis were removed."
—Evelyn Waugh.

m. Computers cannot really *think*, because if we were to admit that there are thinking machines that would mean that we humans might be mere machines as well, a very degrading situation!

3. The following examples are taken from Friedrich Nietzche's *Twilight of the Idols*, in which he discusses errors in causal reasoning. Identify the fallacy in each example.

a. Everybody knows the book of the famous Cornaro in which he recommends his slender diet as a recipe for a long and happy life—a virtuous one too. . . . The worthy Italian thought his diet was the *cause* of his long life, whereas the precondition for a long life, the extraordinary slowness of his metabolism, the consumption of so little, was the cause of his slender diet.

b. The church and morality say: "A generation, a people, are destroyed by license and luxury." [I] say: when a people appproaches destruction, when it degenerates physiologically, then license and luxury *follow* from this (namely, the craving for ever stronger and more frequent stimulation, as every exhausted nature knows it).

c. This young man turns pale early and wilts; his friends say: that is due to this or that disease. I say: that he became diseased, that he did not resist the disease, was already the effect of an impoverished life or hereditary exhaustion.

d. The newspaper reader says: this [political] party destroys itself by making such a mistake. [I] say: a party which makes such mistakes has reached its end; it has lost its sureness of instinct.

4. In each of the following, identify the causal fallacies that the reader is warned against making.

a. Has sodium been getting a bum rap? For a decade health organizations, government agencies and physicians have urged everyone to cut back on the intake of all forms of sodium.

R. Curtis Morris, Jr., of the University of San Francisco's General Clinical Research Center, thinks such recommendations may be wrong. "It has never been demonstrated," he says, "that any form of sodium other than sodium chloride [table salt] can raise blood pressure." This means, for example, that the sodium ingested as sodium bicarbonate in baked goods or antacids probably does not affect blood pressure and should not be lumped together on food labels with the sodium of sodium chloride.
—*Scientific American* 258:2,32

b. Breast cancer patients are more likely to survive the disease if they have a happy, positive frame of mind than if they feel hopeless and depressed, according to a study by a team of scientists at Pittsburgh and Yale University. . . .

[Dr. Sandra] Levy emphasized that the findings do not necessarily mean that cancer can be cured by making patients happy. The scientists don't know whether happy feelings cause longer survival, perhaps through an enhancing effect on the body's own healing process, or whether the patient's positive feelings are simply an effect, possibly resulting from an inherent stamina.

—H. Pierce, *Pittsburgh Post-Gazette*

Probabilities and Inductive Logic

C H A P T E R   5

I. INTRODUCTION

We know that in a correct inductive argument the conclusion is *probably* true if its premises are true. We also know that inductive arguments vary in strength. The conclusions of some inductive arguments are highly *probable*; the conclusions of other inductive arguments are *probable*, but not highly probable. So far, we have trusted our common-sense understanding of the meaning of "probable." In this chapter, we will take a closer look at the concept of *probability* and its relationship to inductive logic.

In the statistical syllogism, a form of inductive argument discussed in Chapter 3, we noted that sometimes statistical premises are stated numerically; for example, "90 percent of all freshman are state residents." When the reference class of such a premiss embodies all the available relevant information, we can state the numerical *probability* that a given freshman (for example, Maria) is a state resident.

When we want to take some action, such as investing money or placing a bet, we have a practical interest in knowing exactly *how probable* some conclusion is. Consider, for example, that argument that a blind draw from a standard deck of cards will result in a nonheart (that is, a spade, a diamond, or a club being drawn):

> Most cards in a standard deck are nonheart cards.
> *a* is a card drawn "blind" from a standard deck.
> _____
> *a* is a nonheart card.

This argument is a reasonably strong statistical syllogism. If, however, we are going to *bet* that a nonheart will be drawn, we want to know the exact probability of the outcome "*a* is a nonheart," so we can set the proper betting odds.

Given our background information about the composition of standard decks of cards, we know that a deck contains 39 nonhearts and 13 hearts. Therefore, the first premiss could be stated quantitatively: 39/52 (or 75 percent) of the cards are nonhearts. With this information—which encompasses all relevant available information, given blind drawing of the card—we can say that the probability of drawing a nonheart is 75 percent, or 3/4.

We then use the probability of the outcome to determine proper betting odds. In an even-money bet, the amount won or lost is equal to the "stake" (the amount that is put at risk). An even-money bet is proper when, as in the toss of a fair coin, there are two possible outcomes, and each outcome has a probability of 1/2. When the probabilities of various outcomes are not equal, the betting odds must be altered in an appropriate way to preserve the standard of fairness. For example, betting odds of "3 to 1," in which the return for a winning bet is three times the stake, are fair for an outcome with a probability of 1/4, or 0.25. The "odds" refer to the difference in favor of one side and against the other. For an outcome with a probability of 1/4, such as blindly drawing a heart from a standard deck that contains 39 nonhearts and 13 hearts, there are three times as many ways of losing as there are of winning. In other words, the odds are 3 to 1 *against* winning. A payoff of 3 to 1 balances this disadvantage and makes the bet fair. For an outcome with a probability of 3/4 (drawing a nonheart), the odds are 3 to 1 *in favor* of winning, so a payoff of 1 to 3 balances this advantage.

Numerical probabilities can sometimes be attached to the conclusions of inductive generalizations. In our discussion in Chapter 3, we noted that by increasing the sample size, we can reduce the margin of error while retaining the same *confidence level.* Alternatively, we said that we can retain the same margin of error and increase the confidence level. The confidence level attached to such arguments can be understood as the *probability* that the conclusion will be correct. We saw that under certain circumstances, we can state these probabilities in numerical terms. In one example, we looked at a sample of 100 students to determine voting behavior, and based on preference that 60 percent of the sample showed for the Liberals, we said our conclusion that between 50 percent and 70 percent of the student population would vote for the Liberals carried a confidence level of 0.95. This means that there is a probability of 95 percent that the conclusion is correct.

Probabilities play an important role in judging the outcomes of controlled studies, for as we have seen, inductive generalization is used in such experiments to tell us about what would happen in the population, based on what happens in the experimental and control groups. Probabilities are required to judge whether or not an outcome of a study is *statistically significant.*

We know that the properties of random samples rarely match *exactly* the properties of the populations from which they are selected. But, within a margin of error, samples should resemble the population most of the time. For example, assume a coin you hold is fair, and begin a series of tosses. Stop after five tosses. This series is your sample. Suppose further that the sample contains no heads. This is not impossible, but it happens relatively infrequently. The probability of getting no heads in five tosses of a fair coin is just over 3 percent (1/32). In other words, you can expect at least one head in five tosses of a fair coin with a probability greater than 95 percent. Your sample in this case is *statistically significant* at the 0.05 level because it is the kind of sample you would expect less than 5 percent of the time if the assumption (fair coin) is correct. Statistical significance is obviously dependent on sample size. In a series of two tosses of a fair coin, finding no heads would *not* be significant at the 0.05 level—heads fail to turn up about 25 percent of the time.

Although traditionally, a criterion of statistical significance at the 0.05 level (corresponding to a 95 percent confidence level) is adopted for most scientific studies, use of statistical significance at the 0.01 level is not uncommon. A result is statistically significant at the 0.01 level if the probability of obtaining such a result is less than 1 percent. For example, a series of ten tosses of a fair coin that results in no heads has a probability of less than one in a thousand. A sample composed of such a series would be statistically significant at the 0.01 level and would call into question (at least) the assumption that the coin is fair.

A branch of mathematics, called *the probability calculus*, provides us with rules for figuring out unknown probabilities when some probabilities are known. If we know, for example, that the probability of obtaining a head on a single toss of a fair coin is 1/2, then we can use the mathematical theory of probability to calculate the probability of obtaining all heads on two, three, or more tosses of a fair coin. Since the method of calculating unknown probabilities on the basis of known probabilities is a part of mathematics, it belongs properly to deductive logic rather than to inductive logic. However, the probability calculus has such important applications for inductive reasoning that serious studies of inductive logic always include some treatment of probabilities.

The mathematical theory of probability was developed during the seventeenth century to solve two different types of problems. On the continent, where gambling with cards and dice was a major form of amusement for rich young noblemen, there was a lot of interest in setting fair betting odds for complicated gambling situations. One such situation involved tossing a pair of dice. Each die has six sides; whatever side is up is called the "face," and 36 different combinations of two faces are possible when a pair of dice is tossed. Only one of these possibilities shows six dots on the faces of both dice. Thus, the probability that one toss of a pair of fair dice will result in double sixes is 1/36. Obviously, an even money bet on showing double sixes in one toss would be unfair. Professional gamblers were offering even money bets that at least one pair of double sixes would show in 24 tosses. The Chevalier de Méré, wondering whether these betting odds were fair, put the following question to his friend the mathematician Blaise Pascal:

> How many tosses are required for the probability to be at least 1/2 of getting a double six?

The concept of "probability" used to assign initial probabilities in most games of chance takes a set of equally possible alternatives (for example, each card is equally likely to be drawn from a deck; each face on a die has an equal chance of showing), and identifies the probability of any of these alternatives as the *ratio of favorable to possible outcomes*. Remember that the mathematical calculus of probability is used to calculate probabilities on the basis of some initially known probabilities. In coin tossing, if the coin is fair, there are two equally possible outcomes: heads or tails. Whichever one of these two outcomes is chosen is favorable. The ratio of favorable to possible outcomes in a fair coin toss is therefore 1/2. In dice, each die has six sides. Assuming the die is balanced, the outcome of a particular face showing in a roll of a single die is 1/6. In card games, a standard deck contains 52 cards, divided into 4 suits, with 13 cards in each suit. The probability of blindly drawing a particular single card from a well-shuffled deck is 1/52; of drawing any card of a particular suit, 13/52 (1/4); of drawing a particular number, such as an ace, 4/52 (1/13).

It requires considerable mathematical skill to use the known probability of obtaining a double six on a single toss of a pair of fair dice to determine how many times that a pair of dice must be tossed to yield a probability equal to 1/2 of obtaining at least one double six. In working out answers to complicated problems such as this, French mathematicians constructed the foundations of the mathematical theory of probability. The usefulness of their results goes far beyond allowing us to be sophisticated gamblers. The techniques developed to solve de Méré's problem are also used, for example, to figure out how large a sample needs to be in order for our conclusion about the population from which the sample is taken to be correct with a probability of 0.95.

At the same time that mathematicians were helping the gamblers in France, a different interest motivated studies in mathematical probability in England. There, the problem was not how to figure fair betting odds for games of chance but rather to determine the fair cost of insurance to cover burial expenses. This was the beginning of *actuarial science*—the calculation of risks and premiums for insurance purposes.

The Great Plague struck London in 1664–1665. Previous epidemics of this disease (bubonic plague, sometimes called "black death") had wiped out between one-fourth and three-fourths of the population. When the plague arrived this time, people formed associations to share the burden of funeral and burial expenses. Even after the plague ended, interest in this type of insurance continued. To determine fair costs of membership in burial associations, it was necessary to know, for example, the probability that a prospective member would survive another 5, 10, 15, or 20 years. Obviously, the understanding of "probability" as a ratio of favorable to possible types of outcomes was not appropriate in these circumstances. Years of life are not parceled out like cards from a deck, with any year being viewed as an equally possible year for death to occur. A different concept of probability from the one used in connection with games of chance was required.

"Probability" in this context is connected with the observed *frequency with which events of a certain type occur*. Information about the ages at which death had occurred for persons living in various areas and following assorted trades and occupations was gathered, mostly from church records, by the burial associations. The information was compiled in "mortality tables," which were used to determine the *relative frequency* with which persons in given situations survived to reach various ages. On the basis of the information in a mortality table, for example, it could be observed that 90 percent of the 25-year-old carpenters living in London survived their thirtieth birthdays. A burial association might then use this information to assign a probability of 0.9 (or 90 percent) that Hawkins, a 25-year-old carpenter from London, would be able to pay dues in the association for at least five years and to charge accordingly for his five-year membership.

Mortality tables are still used by insurance companies to determine the cost of life-insurance premiums. Of course, the information compiled in modern tables is far more extensive than the data contained in seventeenth-century tables. Similar types of tables, based on records of automobile ownership and accidents, are used as a basis for determining automobile-insurance premiums. The statistical records show, for example, that males under twenty-five years of age have more accidents than females in the same age category. Male drivers are charged correspondingly higher rates. Health-insurance costs also are based on actuarial tables that are compiled from meticulous records of the frequency of various illnesses and diseases and the costs associated with their treatment.

The two meanings of "probability"—the ratio of favorable to equally possible outcomes and the relative frequency of events of a particular type in some reference class of events—lend themselves naturally to *quantitative* (numerical) expressions of probability values. When probabilities are expressed quantitatively, the probability that the sentence describing an event is true is stated as a single real number (integer, fraction, or irrational number) between 0 (the lowest value) and 1 (the highest value). A probability may be expressed as a ratio between two numbers (1/4), as a decimal (0.25), or as a percentage (25 percent).

A third meaning of "probability" is also common. When, for example, I say there is an extremely low probability that my mother will attend a Rolling Stones concert during the rock group's next United States tour, "probability" does not mean "ratio of favorable to possible outcomes"; nor is my probability assignment based on the relative frequency of her attendance at Stones' concerts. Instead, I am using probability as a measure of the *degree to which it is rational to believe certain statements*. My evidence for the belief that my mother won't go to hear the Stones is comprised of a set of beliefs about her taste in music, her lack of interest in pop culture, her dislike of crowded places, and numerous other beliefs about how she prefers to spend her leisure time. The "degree of rational belief" concept of probability can be expressed numerically, but it does not lend itself as naturally to numerical quantification as the other meanings of "probability." If numerical values are assigned to these probabilities, however, the mathematical rules for calculating unknown probabilities on the basis of known probabilities are applicable to degrees of rational belief, just as they are to other probabilities.

II. THE RULES OF PROBABILITY

Before we look at the mathematical rules, we should note that any assignment of a probability value is based on conditions of specific evidence or general background information. Probability assignments are always conditional on the assumed truth of some such information. Thus, the probability of "a single toss of a die shows six dots on the face" being equal to 1/6 is conditional on the die being balanced or fair. Statements of probability values are often standardized as

$$\Pr(h|e) = n$$

which can be read, "The probability of a statement h, on evidence e, is equal to n." Sometimes, however, when it is clearly understood that a probability value is conditional on general background information and not on any special evidence, we write

$$\Pr(h) = n$$

omitting any reference to evidence.

Rule 1.   The value n in a sentence of the form

$$\Pr(h|e) = n$$

must be a single real number between 0 and 1, inclusive.

In view of Rule 1, the following assignments of probabilities are improper:

Pr(Jones will win the Sweepstakes | Jones bought a Sweepstakes ticket) $= -1$.

(No probability values can be negative numbers.)

Pr(The Democrats will win the next presidential election) $= 1.25$.

(No probability value can be greater than 1.)

Rule 2. If h follows deductively from e, then

$$Pr(h|e) = 1$$

To say that h follows deductively from e means that if e is true, then h must be true also. If this is so, then the probability of h, on evidence e, is 1.

Examples

(a) Pr(Mrs. Jones is married | Mrs. Jones has a spouse) $= 1$.
(b) Pr(A black or a red card is drawn | A card is drawn from a standard deck) $= 1$.

In this probability sentence, e is "A card is drawn from a standard deck" and h is "A black card or a red card is drawn." If a card is drawn from a standard deck, that card will be either black or red; no other possibilities exist. Thus, $n = 1$.

The probability value of 1 is not reserved exclusively for sentences that follow deductively from the available evidence. Sentences that are certainly true ("sure things") are assigned a probability equal to 1. The type of certainty that is involved here may be practical certainty, rather than certainty based on strict relationships of deductive logic.

Example

Pr (A six-year-old child, using materials found in an ordinary home workshop, cannot build a spaceship that will reach Mars) $= 1$.

Notice that no statement of evidence (e) is given in this example; here, the probability is conditional on general background information. This sentence is so likely to be true on the basis of everything we know (it has "practical certainty") that the assignment of 1 to n is appropriate.

Similarly, the lowest probability value (0) is assigned to sentences that are inconsistent with the evidence sentence or that are false as a matter of "practical certainty."

Examples

(a) Pr(5 aces are drawn | 5 cards are drawn, without replacement, from a standard deck) = 0.

Here, the sentence "5 aces are drawn" is *inconsistent* with the evidence that the deck is standard. (Standard decks contain only 4 aces, and the cards are drawn without replacement.)

(b) Pr(A human being, without any artificial aids, can leap tall buildings in a single bound) = 0.

Given our background knowledge of human physiology, we have "practical certainty" that this sentence is false.

Rule 3. If two sentences h_1 and h_2 are *mutually exclusive* (if they cannot both be true), then, on the same evidence in both cases, the probability that their *disjunction* (h_1 or h_2) is true is equal to the *sum* of their individual probabilities.

A disjunction occurs when the components of a compound sentence are connected by "or," as in "The coin came up heads or the coin came up tails." Symbolically, Rule 3 can be expressed

$$Pr(h_1 \text{ or } h_2 | e) = Pr(h_1 | e) + Pr(h_2 | e)$$

Although this rule is stated for any *two* mutually exclusive sentences, it can be generalized to any number of mutually exclusive sentences. This rule allows us to calculate the unknown probability of a disjunction when the probabilities of all the individual disjuncts are known.

Examples

(a) Using as evidence the claim that a fair die is tossed a single time, we know that the probability of throwing a six is equal to 1/6, and that the probability of throwing a two is 1/6. Since the sentences "A six is thrown" and "A two is thrown" are mutually exclusive for a single throw, Rule 3 tells us that the probability of "A six is thrown *or* a two is thrown," is 1/6 + 1/6, or after performing the addition [2/6] and reducing the fraction, 1/3.

(b) Using the evidence in (a), the probability of "A six *or* a two *or* a three is thrown," is equal to (1/6 + 1/6 + 1/6), or 1/2.

Rule 4. The probability of the *conjunction* of two sentences is equal to the probability of the first sentence *multiplied* by the probability of the second sentence on the condition that the first sentence is true.

A conjunction occurs when the components of a compound sentence are connected by "and," or some other expression such as "moreover," or a semicolon, that indicates that the sentence as a whole is true just in case all of its components are true. "A six showed on one face of a pair of dice, and a five showed on the other face" is an example of a conjunction. Rule 4 allows us to calculate the probability of a conjunction when the probabilities of the individual conjuncts are known. Symbolically, Rule 4 can be expressed

$$\Pr(h_1 \text{ and } h_2 | e) = \Pr(h_1 | e) \times \Pr(h_2 | e \text{ and } h_1)$$

Like Rule 3, Rule 4 can be generalized to any number of cases, but for simplicity here, it is stated to cover only two conjuncts. When more than two conjuncts are involved, the probability of each successive conjunct is conditional on the truth of all the preceding conjuncts.

Examples

(a) Suppose that a fair coin is tossed twice (the evidence sentence). What is the probability that both tosses yield a head?

Rule 4 tells us to multiply the probability that the first toss will yield a head (1/2) by the probability that the second toss will be a head, on the condition that the first toss yields a head. This probability is also 1/2, since what happens on the first toss has no effect on the second toss (the probability on the second toss is 1/2 regardless of whether the first toss is a head or a tail). Multiplying 1/2 by 1/2 gives us 1/4, which is the probability of "two heads appear on two tosses of a fair coin."

(b) Suppose that two cards are drawn blindly from a standard deck and placed in a drawer together (the evidence). What is the probability that both cards are aces?

We want to know the probability of the conjunction "The first card is an ace *and* the second card is an ace." The probability that the first card is an ace is 4/52. (There are four aces in a standard deck of 52 cards.) The probability that the second card drawn is also an ace, if the first card drawn is an ace, is 3/51. (At the time of the second draw, the deck contains 51 cards; if the first card drawn is an ace, only three aces remain in the deck.) Multiplying 4/52 by 3/51 gives us 12/2,652. This fraction can be reduced to 1/221, which is the probability of drawing two aces from a standard deck in two draws (without replacing the first card drawn).

In example (b), unlike example (a), the probabilities are not the same for the first and second conjuncts. In coin tossing, what happens on a second or a third toss is *independent* of what happens on any previous toss. When cards are drawn from a deck without replacement after each draw, the probabilities of drawing a particular card are not the same for successive draws. The deck is different after any draw. What happens on the second draw is *not independent* of what happens on the first draw. Of course, if the cards are replaced and the deck is shuffled after every draw, the outcome of each draw is independent of previous draws from the deck.

(c) What is the probability of drawing three aces in three draws from a standard deck without replacement?

Here, we want to apply Rule 4 to more than two conjuncts. The probability that the first draw is an ace is 4/52. The probability that the second draw is an ace, given that the first card drawn is an ace is 3/51. The probability that the third card is also an ace, given that the first and second cards drawn are aces is 2/50. Multiplying these three probabilities (a calculator is helpful for such problems), we find that the probability of three aces being drawn from a standard deck in three draws without replacement is equal to 24/132,600. This fraction can be reduced to 1/5,525.

In these examples of the application of Rule 4, it is not difficult to tell whether the events being considered are independent or not. Tosses of coins and rolls of dice are independent events. Draws from a deck, when cards previously drawn are replaced and the deck is reshuffled, are also independent. When cards drawn from a deck are *not* replaced or, as in games such as 21 (Blackjack), when cards that are exposed are then placed on the bottom of the deck and the deck is *not* reshuffled, successive draws are not independent. In applying Rule 4 to many real-life situations, we must pay particular attention to the independence of events. For example, suppose that the probability of getting a busy signal when calling any one of your close friends is 0.05. The probability of getting a busy signal when you call one friend and then getting another busy signal when you call a second friend is *not* equal to 0.05 x 0.05 if those two friends are also friends of one another, because the busy signals are then not independent events. If your first friend is on the phone, this raises the probability that you will also get a busy signal when you try to call the second friend. When we are not dealing with such simple matters as dice and card games, it is often difficult to assign probabilities for nonindependent events, but we should at least be aware of the possibility that nonindependence can affect the calculation of probabilities.

Rules 1–4 (sometimes called *axioms*) form the entire basis of probability theory, just as the axioms of geometry form the basis for that area of mathematics. We will not derive any theorems here, but we will take notice of one useful theorem that makes calculations simpler than they would otherwise be:

Theorem

$$\text{If } \Pr(h|e) = n, \text{ then } \Pr(\text{not } h|e) = 1 - n.$$

Here, "not *h*" is the negation, or denial, of the sentence *h*.

Examples

(a) What is the probability of not drawing an ace from a standard deck when a card is drawn blindly?

Since the probability of drawing an ace is 4/52, the probability of not drawing an ace is $1 - 4/52 = 48/52 = 12/13$.

(b) What is the probability of obtaining at least one head in two tosses of a fair coin?

Rule 3 is not applicable in this problem because "a head occurs on the first toss" and "a head occurs on the second toss" are not mutually exclusive sentences. Heads could occur on both tosses. If we were (mistakenly) to add the probabilities of obtaining a head on the first toss and of obtaining a head on the second toss, the probability would be equal to 1. Obviously, this is incorrect, because it is by no means certain that a head will occur in two tosses. However, the sentence "At least one head occurs in two tosses of a fair coin," is equivalent to the sentence "Tails do not occur on both tosses of a fair coin." We can use Rule 4 to calculate the probability of obtaining tails on both tosses ($1/2 \times 1/2 = 1/4$). Then, we can use the theorem to calculate the probability of *not* obtaining a tail on both tosses ($1 - 1/4 = 3/4$).

The *Rasmussen Report*, the most complete study by the United States government on the safety of nuclear power, issued in 1975, offers an interesting and important application of this theorem. This report has been called into question by critics of nuclear power. One criticism is that the report presents the probability of a serious accident at a nuclear-power plant (a core-melt accident) in a misleading way (K. S. Shrader-Frechette, *Nuclear Power and Public Policy*).

According to federal government figures, the probability of a serious accident is 1/17,000 per year, per reactor. "Serious accident" in this context refers to a core melt, which, again, according to government estimates, would be equivalent to 1,000 Hiroshimas. The probability of 1/17,000 per year, per reactor may sound like a very low probability. However, critics point out that each reactor presently operating at 65 nuclear power plants has an estimated lifetime of 30 years. The critics feel we should be concerned with the probability that a serious accident will occur at any one plant during its 30-year lifetime.

We can apply the preceding theorem twice to calculate the probability that a serious accident (a core melt) will occur in at least one of these 65 nuclear-power plants over their 30-year lifetimes. This probability is equal to 1 minus the probability that there will be *no* serious accidents in any of these plants during their 30-year lifetimes. The probability that there will be *no* core melts—using the government probability of 1/17,000 per year, per reactor that there will be a serious accident *and* assuming that the events (core melts per year, per reactor) are independent—is equal to

$$[1 - (1/17,000)]^{65 \times 30}$$

or

$$(16,999/17,000)^{1950}$$

which is equal to 0.8916.

We can then apply the theorem a second time to determine the probability that there will be at least one serious accident. "There will be no serious accidents (core melts)" is the denial of "There will be at least one serious accident." To calculate the probability that there will be at least one serious accident, we subtract the probability that there will be no serious accidents (0.8916) from 1:

$$1 - 0.8916 = 0.108$$

Thus, the probability that the United States will be faced with a nuclear-power disaster equivalent to 1,000 Hiroshimas is, according to the government's own figures, slightly more than 10 percent.

The assumption of *independence* for per year, per reactor core melts is questionable. Nuclear reactors are built along similar designs and have almost identical safety devices. Thus if the threat of a serious accident is connected with the design of the reactor itself or the failure of its protective devices, such accidents could not be considered independent. There are, of course, other possible sources of serious accidents, such as sabotage. We would probably judge an isolated instance of a sabotage-caused accident as independent, but it could be a part of a terrorist campaign against nuclear power reactors or the publicity about the sabotage could be a causal factor in other instances.

Another difficult question is whether or not the lack of independence would *raise* or *lower* the estimate of the probability that an accident will occur in at least one plant during its 30-year lifetime. In addition, we can ask whether it is reasonable to assume that the probability of a serious accident in a nuclear-power plant is the same throughout each of its 30 years of use. Some critics of nuclear power have also objected that the figure of 1/17,000 is an unrealistically low estimate of the probability of a serious accident per year, per reactor.

Such questions cannot be answered by simply applying the rules to calculate probabilities. The assignment of initial probabilities and the determination of whether events are dependent or independent require the assemblage and evaluation of evidence, using means far beyond the probability calculus. With suitable evidence in hand, many of the argument forms we considered in earlier chapters—inductive generalizations, statistical syllogisms, and analogies—may be useful in assigning appropriate initial probabilities.

Exercises

1. What is the probability of obtaining either an ace or a king in a single, blind draw from a standard deck of cards?

2. What is the probability of *not* obtaining either an ace or a king in a single, blind draw from a standard deck of cards?

3. What is the probability of obtaining three heads in three tosses of a fair coin?

4. What is the probability of obtaining at least one tail in three tosses of a fair coin?

5. What is the probability of obtaining either a head or a tail in a single toss of a fair coin?

6. What is the probability of drawing an ace and a king in two blind draws from a standard deck without replacement?

7. Consider a Health Club with 100 members (60 men and 40 women). Each member uses the club for just one favorite activity, and men and women are equally likely to engage in any of the activities. Twenty members of the club are swimmers; 30 play racquet ball; 24 take aerobics classes; 16 lift weights; and 10 play indoor tennis.
   a. Suppose a member of the club is randomly selected:
      (1) What is the probability that the member selected is a weight-lifter?
      (2) What is the probability that the member is either a swimmer or takes aerobic exercise classes?
      (3) What is the probability that the member selected is either a tennis player or a racquet-ball player or a weight lifter?
      (4) What is the probability that the member selected is a woman weight lifter?
      (5) What is the probability that the member selected is a man who takes aerobic classes?
   b. Suppose that two members of the club are randomly selected:
      (1) What is the probability that both are tennis players?
      (2) What is the probability that the *first* one selected is a tennis player and the *second* one selected is a racquet-ball player?
      (3) What is the probability that a tennis player and a racquet-ball player are selected?

8. Suppose the probability that a 22-year-old male will survive his forty-seventh birthday is 0.840 and the probability that a 22-year-old female will survive her forty-seventh birthday is 0.910. A man and a woman, who have been close friends at college, are both graduating at the age of 22. They promise to meet each other at their twenty-fifth reunion.
   a. What is the probability that both friends will be alive to keep that promise?
   b. If these good friends fall in love and marry one another after college, would this affect the independence of each friend living another 25 years?

9. Assuming that you know what your birthday is but do not know what mine is, what is the probability that we share the same birthday (day only—not year!)?

10. Suppose that you hold three aces and two different small cards in a game of draw poker. If you discard the two small cards, what are your chances of improving your hand on the draw? The hand will be improved either by drawing another ace and some other card or by drawing a pair. (*Hint:* Since this is a fair game and you do not know what cards are in the other players' hands, treat their cards as if they were part of the deck.)

11. If my chances of being apprehended for committing some crime are 0.7, my chances of being convicted if I am apprehended are 0.6, and my chances of serving time if I am apprehended and convicted are 0.5, what is the probability that I will serve time if I rob the local grocery store?

III. USING PROBABILITIES TO PLAN A COURSE OF ACTION— DECISION THEORY

"Probability," as Bishop Butler remarked in the eighteenth century, "is the very guide of life." None of us can see what the future holds. We make most choices, decisions, and plans as best we can in the face of less than complete knowledge about what the world will be like and what others will do. Probabilities play an important role in many of these decisions, because we are often in a position to *judge* the probabilities of various outcomes before we make decisions. If we care about seeing a movie from the beginning, we try to arrive at the theater before the show is scheduled to begin because it will probably start on time. We pursue college educations because we believe that what we learn in college will probably enhance the quality of our lives in various ways.

However, the probability that some event or condition will occur is not the *only* consideration on which we base our decision to take a particular course of action. We are concerned with costs and benefits as well. In Exercise 11 in Section II, the probabilities given for apprehension, conviction and incarceration were not unrealistic, based on government crime statistics. If anything, they were slightly higher than the norm. The probability that someone would actually serve time for robbing a store was quite small (0.21), but even in the absence of any moral or social considerations, a person contemplating such a robbery should surely reflect not only on the probability of serving time but also on the severe unattractiveness of that prospect. It is prudent to avoid even a fairly small risk of falling into such an unhappy situation. Conversely, we think it is reasonable to try to achieve some goals, even though the probabilities of attaining them are small, if the potential benefits are very attractive.

The term *utility* is often used to refer to the desirability (*positive* utility) or undesirability (*negative* utility) of a situation. The term *value* (which can also be positive or negative) is sometimes used as well. We will adopt the somewhat more neutral term *utility*. Thus, we could say that serving time in prison has great negative utility and that this utility should be considered along with the probability of serving time when contemplating an action that could result in a prison sentence.

Decision theory is the area of study that focuses on how decisions are made in contexts that vary with respect to the degree of knowledge available. (Here, a "decision" is a decision to take some action.) The goal of decision theory is to develop criteria for rational (reasonable) decision making. In our necessarily brief look at decision theory, we will consider three types of general contexts in which decisions occur:

1. *Decisions under risk*: Contexts in which we can assign various probabilities to the outcomes of our actions. Our knowledge in these contexts is said to be partial or incomplete.
2. *Decisions under certainty*: Contexts in which we know the exact outcomes of our actions. In these contexts, our knowledge has "practical certainty."

3. *Decisions under uncertainty*: Contexts in which various outcomes of our actions are possible and we are unable to assign to those outcomes any probabilities.

1. Decisions Under Risk

In one example in the discussion of statistical syllogisms in Chapter 3, a patient whose doctor had suggested an ear operation was trying to make a decision under risk. The operation had three possible outcomes, and each outcome had an assigned probability (improvement to "very good": 0.85; no improvement: 0.10; further damage to ear: 0.05). Although the probabilities in this case are clearly stated, no utilities for the various outcomes are mentioned. Obviously, the first outcome has the greatest utility as well as the highest probability; the second outcome has a lower utility (the hearing problem is unimproved and the patient must endure the pain and expense of an operation); and the third outcome has the lowest utility. If the patient decides against the operation, there is only one outcome to consider (no change in the ear condition). The utility of this outcome ranks higher than utilities of having an unsuccessful operation (no improvement or no improvement and further damage) but ranks lower than the outcome of an operation that results in hearing improvement. Should the patient have the operation or not?

The patient could act as if the most probable outcome of the operation will be the one to occur. However, "Always act as if the most probable outcome of an action will occur," is a poor decision-making rule, since it ignores the utilities of various outcomes and it will lead to apparently irrational decisions in some cases. Following this rule, for example, would lead an immoral robber to hold up the local grocery store on the grounds that no prison sentence was the most probable outcome of that action. Following this rule would also lead a home-owner to refuse to purchase fire insurance, even a very inexpensive policy, because the probability (based on statistics) that a given house will catch fire is very low.

Another possible decision rule for our patient is "Always choose the action with a possible outcome that has a higher utility than any other possible outcome." If the patient follows this rule, the operation will be chosen, for a complete restoration of hearing is clearly the outcome with the highest utility, and this outcome is possible only if the patient has the operation, not if any other action is taken. But this rule ignores the known probabilities involved in making a decision under risk, and like the rule "Always act as if the most probable outcome of an action is the one that will occur," it can lead to decisions that most of us would regard as foolish.

To illustrate that this rule is not effective, consider the following case. Suppose that someone has $10,000 to cover college costs. This person places a high utility on having money but also wants a college education very much, and college would be out of the question if this $10,000 were lost. Someone offers this person a chance to invest that $10,000. There is a 10 percent probability that the $10,000 investment will return a profit of $100,000 and a 90 percent probability that the original $10,000 will be lost. Given the high value placed on a college education, most people would consider it unreasonable to invest the $10,000 under these circumstances, even though one possible outcome of this action (money for education and a lot left over for other things) has the greatest utility.

To evaluate decisions under risk correctly, a rule that accounts for both utilities and probabilities is required. "Choose the action that maximizes *expected utility*" is such a rule. To understand this rule, we need to know how to calculate *expected* utilities. Before this can be done, however, we must be able to quantify, or measure, utilities; only then can a calculation be performed.

The problem of measuring utilities is by no means simple. How can we place a numerical value on hearing properly, or on undergoing an unsuccessful operation, or on losing one's hearing? Objectivity is not the issue here. The measurements of utilities need not be objective in the sense that the assigned quantities must be acceptable to any reasonable person. All that is required is that the person confronted with the decision measure his or her utilities, but even that is very difficult in many cases.

Studies of decision theory often begin with examples of decisions that involve money, such as decisions concerning bets or investments. There is a certain sense in which an investment that will return $30,000 is—all other things being equal—three times as desirable as (has three times the utility of) an investment that will return $10,000. If units of money are correlated in this manner with units of utility, it is not difficult to assign a measure of the utility of various amounts of money lost or won, for money already comes in measurable units. We will consider a problem that involves only money to illustrate how expected utilities work; then we will return to the problem of the operation, in which units of utility cannot be identified with dollar amounts.

I am committed to go to a school fair and spend at least $2 there playing a game of chance. I have to decide whether to risk $2 on a punch board or on a dice game. A $2 punch buys the following possible outcomes with associated probabilities: 0.05 for $10, 0.10 for $5, 0.20 for $2, 0.65 for $0. In the dice game, if I roll any matched pair, I win $10; otherwise I win nothing. To make the problem of measuring utilities correspond to measuring the amounts of money won or lost, I assume that the dice game is no more or no less amusing to me than the punch board and that my sole desire is to gain as much money as possible from my $2 play.

The *expected utility* of a $2 punch is calculated by multiplying each payoff with its associated probability, summing the results, and subtracting the $2 cost:

$$[(10 \times 0.05) + (5 \times 0.10) + (2 \times 0.20) + (0 \times 0.65)] - 2 =$$
$$(0.50 + 0.50 + 0.40) - 2 = -0.60.$$

In the dice game, the expected utility is also calculated by multiplying payoffs with their associated probabilities, summing the results, and subtracting the $2 cost. In general, the rule for calculating the expected utility of some decision is to multiply the probability of each possible outcome by the number of units (the total amount) of utility associated with that outcome. The sum of these products, minus the initial cost (also measured in units of utility), if any, is the expected utility of that decision.

In the dice game, the probability of rolling a pair of ones, twos, threes, fours, fives, or sixes is 1/6. This probability can be calculated in several ways. The probability of rolling any one pair is 1/36. You can win by rolling any of six mutually exclusive pairs, and (1/36 + 1/36 + 1/36 + 1/36 + 1/36 + 1/36) = 1/6. Or the problem can be viewed another way. The first die shows some number on its face. The probability that the second die will show the same number is 1/6, and this is also the probability that you will roll a pair.

The utility associated with rolling a pair (the payoff) is $10. The probability of *not* rolling a pair is 5/6 (1 minus the probability of obtaining a pair). The payoff for not rolling a pair is $0. Since $10 × 1/6 = $1.67 and 0 × 5/6 = 0, we sum these amounts and subtract the $2 cost (1.67 + 0 − 2 = − 0.33). Thus, the expected utility (measured in money) of a play on the punch board is − $0.60 and the expected utility of the dice game is − $0.33. If I followed the rule of maximizing expected utilities, I would choose the dice game and thereby cut my losses.

Now we will return to the problem of measuring the utilities associated with the ear operation. Remember that the measures I assign are my own in such a situation. You might react differently, and could not be criticized for doing so. The units I assign are just "units of utility." The arithmetic operations of addition, subtraction, multiplication and division can be performed on these units of utility, but they need not—and perhaps cannot—be translated into monetary amounts.

    (i) Units of utility associated with possible outcomes of operation (probabilities are enclosed in parentheses):

Hearing improvement to "very good":	10 (0.85)
No improvement:	− 2 (0.10)
Further damage:	− 10 (0.05)

    (ii) Units of utility associated with possible outcome of no operation:

No change:	0 (1)

Using these figures and the associated probabilities, the expected utility of the operation is [(10 × 0.85) + (− 2 × 0.10) + (− 10 × 0.05)] = 7.8. The expected utility of not having the operation is (0 × 1) = 0. The "cost" of the operation was not calculated separately here; it was "figured in" when the utilities were assigned to various outcomes. Following the rule of maximizing expected utility, if I were the patient, I would choose the operation.

In considering candidates for the best rule to follow when making decisions under risk, we saw that different rules can lead to the same decision in some cases. By far the most probable outcome of the operation was also the outcome that clearly had the greatest utility. But the rule "Choose the action that maximizes expected utility" is adequate when other proposed rules appear to offer unreasonable advice. This happens frequently when an outcome with a low probability has a very high utility, or when an outcome with a high probability has a very low utility. That is why the rule for maximizing *expected* utility is generally accepted as a good rule for rational decision making when the probabilities of the possible outcomes of an action are known. This rule is applicable not only when another rule would lead to the correct decision but also when other rules would lead to decisions that seem unreasonable.

2. Decisions Under Certainty

In some situations, we must choose among various actions and each action has only one possible outcome. These decisions are called *decisions under certainty*, but this is something of a misnomer, because the future is never absolutely certain. The world around us might change in a dramatic and unpredictable way between the time of the decision and the outcome of the action. For example, your decision might be between studying for a test in your room and studying for a test in the library. Ordinarily, there is only one possible outcome to each choice—you study in your room if that is your decision, or study in the library if that is your choice. It is, however, *possible* that you decide to study in the library, but find that it is closed owing to an unusual and totally unexpected electrical power failure. This is, of course, an unlikely occurrence. In general, when we talk about decisions under certainty, we simply ignore such unusual possibilities.

Decisions under certainty do not require the calculation of any probabilities. The probability associated with the single possible outcome of each action under these circumstances is 1. The rule to apply when making decisions under certainty is simple: "Choose the action that has the highest utility." If no single action has the highest utility, it is reasonable to choose any of the actions that have the highest utility.

Although we do not have to calculate probabilities for decisions under certainty, sometimes we have to think carefully about how to compare utilities. For example, some products (such as automobile tires and batteries) are sold at different prices that depend on the how long the guarantee lasts. If I buy tires with a two-year guarantee at a specified price, I can calculate the cost per year and compare it to the cost per year of tires with a three-year guarantee. But other factors may enter into the decision. How long will I keep my car? How much trouble is it to replace worn tires? Are both sets of new tires equally safe throughout their guarantee period? Comparing utilities almost always involves more than purely monetary considerations, and these additional factors should not be ignored just because they may make the decision more difficult. In many cases (as in the tire-buying decision), the consideration of additional factors involves probabilities (for example, whether or not your car will last two or three more years is uncertain and can be assigned a probability of less than 1) that can change a decision under certainty into a decision under risk.

In one way, it is simpler to compare utilities for decisions under certainty than it is to compare utilities for decisions under risk. To make the kind of comparison that is required to evaluate decisions under certainty, the utilities need only be ordered by rank (highest, second highest, and so on). Since you do not multiply the amounts of utility by probabilities, there is no need for *units* of utility. In other words, in a decision under certainty, we do not need to be concerned with whether the highest utility is ten times higher than the next highest utility, or six times higher, or exactly how much higher. Units of utility are required, however, to perform arithmetic operations such as multiplication, for these operations make no sense otherwise.

3. Decisions Under Uncertainty

When we face decisions under conditions of uncertainty, we are aware that various outcomes of our actions are possible, but we have no way of assessing the probabilities associated with these outcomes. Such situations may be rather unusual; in most cases, we are in a position to make at least very rough assignments of probabilities on the basis of past experience or information gathered from other sources. If we can make even rough probability judgments, we should follow the rule for making decisions under risk (choose the action that maximizes expected utility). For the sake of completeness, however, most accounts of decision theory consider the categories of decisions under certainty and decisions under uncertainty as well as decisions under risk.

When we make decisions under uncertainty, since we have no information about probabilities, we base our choices entirely on our consideration of the utilities that are assigned to various outcomes. As usual, the problem of assigning utilities may be difficult. Just as when we make decisions under certainty, in many cases of decision under uncertainty, we need only to order the various utilities by rank (highest, second highest, and so on) rather than to measure them in units that can be multiplied, divided, added, and subtracted—as we must when we apply the rule for decisions under risk. One decision rule for decisions under uncertainty does require units of utility, but this rule need not be used in every case.

In a decision under uncertainty, sometimes one action has a possible outcome that is better than the outcomes of any other action and also has no possible outcome that is worse than any other outcome. For a simple decision between two actions, each of which has two possible outcomes, this situation can be represented:

Actions	Outcomes Ordered by Rank (1 is highest)	
	I	II
I	4	3
II	2	1

In this table, Action I has two outcomes, ranked lowest and second-lowest in utility. Action II also has two outcomes, ranked highest and second-highest in utility. Clearly, Action II is the "best action" and should be chosen; either possible outcome of Action II is better than either possible outcome of Action I.

In the following case of a decision under uncertainty, a "best action" is available. A football player is offered two nonathletic scholarships—one at State University and one at Out-of-State University. He doesn't know what his chances are of making the team at either university. He'd like to play ball, but he wants the best education he can get, regardless of whether or not he plays ball, and he believes the academic program at State is better. His utilities are ranked (1) play ball at State, (2) be a nonplayer at State, (3) play ball at OSU, (4) be a nonplayer at OSU. Thus, he will be better off at State, whether or not he plays ball. Since a best action is available to him, he should choose it and go to State.

Suppose, however, that another football player assigns his first priority to playing ball. Faced with the same scholarship offers, his ranking of utilities would be (1) play ball at State, (2) play ball at OSU, (3) be a nonplayer at OSU, (4) be a nonplayer at State. In this decision under uncertainty, there is no "best action." Going to State not only has the outcome with the highest value but also has the outcome with the lowest value. Since no best action is available, the next question is whether there is just one *satisfactory* action—an action that has all acceptable outcomes and no unacceptable ones. If the second player would be satisfied with a utility ranked three or higher but would not be satisfied with a utility ranked lower than three, then choosing State would not be a satisfactory action for him to take. He should follow the rule: "Choose the action that is satisfactory," and go to OSU.

Suppose, however, that no utility is completely unacceptable to the football player. He could be happy even as a nonplayer at State, although for him that outcome has the lowest utility. The rule for choosing *the* satisfactory action does not apply if there is *more than one* satisfactory action. At this point, several strategies (rules for decision) are open to the player.

In cases in which there is no "best action" and no single "satisfactory action," there is no one best decision-making rule to follow. Which strategy our football player follows will depend in part on what sort of person he is. Decision theorists categorize three different types:

1. *The Gambler:* In situations in which only one action has an outcome with the highest utility, one decision strategy is to take that action. The gambler is willing to take a chance to get the best. If our player is a gambler, he'll go to State.

2. *The Cautious Player:* The cautious player determines the lowest, rather than the highest utility for each outcome. The choice is based on which action has the *highest of the low utilities*. The cautious player wants to protect against losses, to "maximize the minimum." Using this strategy, our football player will choose OSU, for the lowest utility associated with that action is 3, whereas the lowest utility associated with State is 4.

3. *The Calculator:* The calculator has to take the trouble to assign units of utility in order to calculate the *average* utilities of the various actions. An average utility cannot be determined merely on the basis of a rank

ordering. The strategy is to choose the action with the *highest average utility*.

If our football player is a calculating type, he might assign the following units of utility: play at State (10); be a nonplayer at State (2); play at OSU (8); be a nonplayer at OSU (6). The average utility of an action is calculated by adding the utilities of each possible outcome for that action and dividing the total by the number of possible outcomes. The average utility of the decision to go to State is then $(10 + 2)/2 = 6$, and the average utility of the decision to go to OSU is $(8 + 6)/2 = 7$. Following the rule of choosing the action with the highest average utility, our player will go to OSU.

If we examine the calculator's decision-making rule, we can see that when average utilities are assigned, the decision under uncertainty is similar to a decision under risk in which each possible outcome is considered to be just as probable as any other outcome. This method would not be appropriate if available information indicated that one outcome was much less or much more likely to occur than another outcome. In these situations, the problem should be treated as a decision under risk, and probabilities should be assigned in a suitable way.

4. The Prisoner's Dilemma

An interesting puzzle about decisions under uncertainty, entitled "The Prisoner's Dilemma," has been widely discussed by decision theorists. Here is one statement of the problem:

A man and a woman are arrested on suspicion of operating a ring of thieves who burglarize homes. The police have sufficient evidence to make the arrests, but the District Attorney doubts that there is enough evidence to convict the pair. In an effort to obtain further evidence, the prisoners are prevented from consulting with one another, and each is offered the following proposition by the District Attorney:

Confess to the crime. If your partner does not confess, you will receive a light sentence of one year in prison, but your partner will receive the maximum sentence of five years.

Each prisoner wants to know what will happen if he or she does confess and the other partner also confesses. The District Attorney tells each prisoner that if both confess, each will receive a three-year-sentence. The District Attorney also reveals that if neither partner confesses, the case will collapse, but that there is sufficient evidence to convict both partners of a lesser crime, for which they will each receive the maximum sentence of two years.

In making such a bargain, the District Attorney is confident that both partners will confess, even though they would be better off if neither partner confessed! Can you see why this is so?

We have assumed that each partner is unable to assign any probability to whether or not the other partner will confess. Thus, each partner is faced with a decision under uncertainty. If units of (negative) utility are correlated with the length in years of the possible prison terms, each prisoner is faced with the following choice of actions and the utilities associated with the possible outcomes of those actions (utility rankings are shown in parentheses):

	Partner Confesses	Partner Does Not Confess
Confess	−3 (3)	−1 (1)
Do Not Confess	−5 (4)	−2 (2)

In this situation there is no "best action," for one outcome of confessing carries a lower utility than a possible outcome of not confessing, and vice versa. If there is a satisfactory action, it is to confess, for the lowest utility of all is associated with one outcome of not confessing. If either partner follows the rule of choosing the satisfactory action, that partner will confess. However, if there is no satisfactory action and either partner follows *any* other rule for making decisions under uncertainty, the prisoner will also confess.

The gambler's strategy would be to take the action that has the outcome associated with the highest utility; one of the possible outcomes of confessing has the highest utility. The cautious strategy would be to maximize the minimum utility—in this case, also, to confess. (The worst outcome would then be to spend three years in prison, versus a possible five-year prison term for not confessing.) The calculator would determine that the average utility of confessing is

$$(-3 + -1)/2 = -2$$

whereas the average utility of not confessing is

$$(-5 + -2)/2 = -3.5$$

and would also confess.

The District Attorney feels that both partners will make a *reasonable* decision. Whatever reasonable rule they follow, both partners will confess.

The Prisoner's Dilemma raises many interesting problems in decision theory. It is crucial to note that separating the partners, thereby preventing their communication and cooperation, affects their decisions. It is a condition of the problem as a decision under uncertainty that the partners are not able to work out a solution between themselves that would be to their mutual benefit. Nevertheless, if they were able to communicate with one another, each partner would be faced with the problem of whether or not the other partner could be trusted to carry out the mutually agreed on plan. If each partner's decision as to whether or not to trust the other partner is a decision under uncertainty, the dilemma arises again.

The Prisoner's Dilemma is an artificial problem, but the same sort of situation often arises in real life. Consider, for example, the problem facing a group of prosperous manufacturers located along a river in which they dispose of manufacturing wastes. The river is in danger of becoming polluted owing to their dumping practices, and if pollution levels rise significantly, the manufacturers will be charged stiff penalties. The profits of all manufacturers would increase if their plants could be expanded and no penalties had to be paid. If all manufacturers expand, however, the pollution levels will be high enough to result in penalties, which will reduce profits below their present levels.

The Board of Directors of Plant X is considering expansion. The members of the board figure that if they expand but no other plant expands, the pollution levels will not rise too noticeably and Plant X can count on a 10 percent increase in profit. If Plant X does not expand, but the other plants do, then Plant X not only will have to pay a share of the penalty but, unlike the other plants, will not accrue any additional revenue from an expanded facility to help offset this loss. In such a case the profits of Plant X would sink 10 percent below the present level, but the profits of the other plants would sink to only 5 percent below the present level. In the absence of any information about the other manufacturers' plans, the board members of Plant X are in a situation similar to "The Prisoner's Dilemma"; moreover, each manufacturer considering expansion is in the same state as Plant X.

	Others Expand	Others Do Not Expand
X Expands	$P - 0.05\,P$	$P + 0.10$
X Does Not Expand	$P - 0.10\,P$	P

5. The Petersburg Paradox

Another famous problem in the history of probability and expected utilities, the Petersburg Paradox, raises questions about equating units of utility with units of money within the context of a game of chance. The problem and a solution to it were formulated in the seventeenth century by the great Swiss mathematician Daniel Bernoulli, one of the many famous scholarly guests of the Russian Empress Catherine the Great at her court at St. Petersburg.

The game is played this way. A person begins by tossing a fair coin and continues to toss the coin as long as the tosses result in heads. As soon as a tail shows, the game is over. If the first toss is a tail, the game is over and there is no payoff. If only one head shows before a tail appears, the payoff is $4. If two heads show, the payoff is $8. If three heads show, the payoff is $16, and the payoff doubles for each successive head that occurs before a tail appears.

The paradoxical aspect of the game arises when we attempt to determine a fair price to charge for a play of the game. Normally, in games of chance, a price is considered fair if it is equal to, or reasonably close to, the expected value of a play of the game. If units of utility are equated with dollars, the expected utility of a play can be calculated in the usual way—by multiplying the probability of each possible outcome of the game by the associated payoff for that outcome and summing the results. A play of the Petersburg game can be considered to be a set of mutually exclusive outcomes, since a game ends after one toss, or after two tosses, or after three tosses, or after an indefinite number of tosses (n). The probability that a game will end after one toss (that a tail will appear on the first toss) is 1/2, and the associated payoff is \$0; the probability that a game will end after two tosses (H, T) is 1/4, and the payoff is \$4; the probability that a game will end after three tosses (H, H, T) is 1/8, and the payoff is \$8; and so on. In other words, the expected utility in dollars is

$$(1/2 \times 0) + (1/4 \times 4) + (1/8 \times 8) + (1/16 \times 16) + \ldots + (1/n \times n)$$
$$+ \ldots$$

Each of the terms after the first term in this series is equal to 1, and since there is no mathematical limit to the number of tosses, the mathematical sum of the series is an infinite number of dollars! It would seem that the game is worth playing no matter how much a play costs, for any finite cost would be less than the infinite expected utility of the game.

It is highly unrealistic to view a coin-tossing game as if it had no end to the number of possible tosses. But the situation is hardly less puzzling if some reasonably large limit is placed on the length of a game. For example, let us say that the maximum number of tosses in a play is 1001 tosses. The expected utility of that game is \$1,000; however, only the most reckless gambler would pay \$1,000 to play such a game.

Many different solutions to the Petersburg Paradox have been proposed. You may be able to think of a few yourself. Bernoulli's solution is particularly interesting because in it he introduced a significant concept in economic theory—the diminishing marginal utility of money.

Bernoulli distinguished the "physical" value of money from its "moral" (or "practical") value to explain why the addition of a certain fixed amount of money to a large fortune has less value (except to a miser) than the addition of the same amount of money to a small fortune. The principle of the diminishing marginal utility of money can be stated:

> If a certain gain is added to an initial fortune f_0, the utility of this gain decreases as f_0 increases.

According to this principle, a person whose initial fortune is \$100 will place a greater value on an additional \$100 than a person whose initial fortune is \$100,000 will place on receiving another \$100. The "physical" value of the \$100 is the same in both cases, but the "moral" value is much greater in the first case than in the second. In deciding what price to pay for a play of the Petersburg game, a reasonable person who is aware of the decreasing marginal utility of money will consider the moral value, as well as the physical value, of the expected winnings, and will also consider the moral value of the money that must be risked to play the game. In terms of moral value, the loss of even a small amount of his fortune could be very hard on a poor man; the win of a large amount might not mean much to a rich man. (See John Maynard Keynes, "The Application of Probability to Conduct," in J. R. Newman's *The World of Mathematics*, for further discussion of solutions to the Petersburg Paradox.)

6. The Law of Averages and the Gamblers' Fallacy

If a fair coin is tossed repeatedly, then "on average" roughly half the tosses will result in heads, and as the series of tosses grows longer (that is, the sample grows larger), the proportion of heads moves ever closer to one half. Suppose you toss a coin and get a head on the first toss and tails on the next eight tosses. Should you use the law of averages to argue that the next toss will be a head? Many people not only argue this way but bet money on the basis of such reasoning.

If the next toss is another tail, that would be the ninth in a row. A series of nine tails in nine tosses has a very low probability $[(1/2)^9 = 1/512]$. Nevertheless, such series do occur (about once in 500 times). If the coin is fair, the probability that the next toss will be a head is 0.50, the same as for any other toss. What happens on earlier tosses has no effect on the next toss, since the events are independent. The law of averages tells us that if the series of tosses is long enough, the eight tails in a row will eventually become insignificant. After a thousand tosses, for example, there may still be a slight excess of tails over heads, but the proportion will be roughly half and half. The law of averages does not have anything to say about what happens in the tosses that immediately follow the improbable series of eight tails. To suppose otherwise is to commit the *gamblers' fallacy*.

The explanation of the correct understanding of the law of averages above was based on the assumption that the coin was fair and that the tosses were independent. Suppose those assumptions are false. Then would it be reasonable to assign a high probability to the next toss being a head? If the coin is weighted and the tosses are independent, then based on the evidence of eight tails in a row, the probability that the next toss will be a head is *less* than 0.50. The coin gives the appearance of being weighted for tails. If the coin is cleverly designed so that a hidden magnet controls which side lands up, and is programmed so that after a certain number of tails, a head appears, then the tosses are not independent. In the absence of any information about this magnet or how it is adjusted though, it is not reasonable to assign a probability of greater than 0.50 to heads on the next toss.

Another instance of the gamblers' fallacy occurs when statistical records are misused in the following way. Suppose your favorite baseball player has ended his past four seasons with batting averages that range between 0.330 and 0.340. This means that he gets hits "on average" about one out of three times at bat. It is now about the middle of the season; his average so far this year is 0.330; but he's in a slump and hasn't had a hit in his last fifteen times at bat. Unlike the coin tosses, hits are not independent events. Psychological factors such as a burst of confidence after several hits or physiological factors such as an injury that becomes progressively more painful each time the batter takes the box can affect the probability of the next hit. If we are going to use past performance as our guide to the future, then we take account not only of the published statistics, but also the hot streak or the slump. We commit the gamblers' fallacy if we think that the batter has somehow used up his allotted number of failures, and will have proportionately more (or fewer) hits from now on to keep his average intact.

IV. REVIEW

In Chapter 5, we have considered applications of the mathematical calculus of probability to inductive logic. The term "probability" may be used to refer to the ratio of favorable to possible outcomes of some action or event, to the relative frequency with which events of a certain type occur in some series of events, or to the degree to which it is rational to believe certain statements. Whatever "probability" means, the mathematical rules of probability apply. These rules allow us to calculate unknown probabilities when some probabilities are known.

Probabilities play an important role in everyday decision-making. Decision theory is a rather new area of study in which criteria for making rational decisions are the chief concern. Several rules or strategies for making decisions under various conditions of available knowledge were proposed as guidelines for making rational decisions. The rule "Choose the action that maximizes expected utility" is the most acceptable rule for choosing among actions when the probabilities of the various outcomes of these actions are known. The rule "Choose the action with the highest utility" is a reasonable rule to use when choosing among several actions which have only one outcome each and the outcomes are known. In deciding among actions that have more than one outcome when the probabilities of the outcomes are unknown, the rule "Choose the best action" should be followed if there is a best action. If there is no best action, but one satisfactory action is available, the satisfactory action should be chosen. If there is no best action and no satisfactory action, or if there is no best action and more than one satisfactory action, it is reasonable to make decisions using either the gambler's strategy, the cautious strategy, or the calculating strategy.

Decision theory can be used to establish the criteria for making reasonable decisions, depending on the type of information available, but it cannot be relied on to provide the *information* required for making sound decisions. Obviously, our everyday decisions would be inappropriate and even dangerous if we did not attempt to obtain the most accurate information possible before we made them. The following letter from the president of the Travelers Aid Association, published in a syndicated newspaper column by Ann Landers, makes this point quite strongly:

> Since January, vast numbers of job-seekers have gone to the Deep South in search of employment. Recently, it came to our attention that many of these people are victims of a heartless scam. Ads in newspapers and flyers are offering thousands of fabulous jobs in the offshore oil industry. Information for these jobs costs $10 to $12. For this, the advertiser sends a list of offshore oil companies in Texas and Louisiana.
>
> Travelers Aid Societies in Houston, New Orleans and elsewhere are seeing an enormous increase in clients who have spent the last of their money on

a bus ticket, only to be bitterly disappointed after weeks of fruitless searching for a job.

The unemployed who were desperate enough to risk their last savings on the search for a job thought they were making a reasonable decision, for it appeared, on the basis of deceptive advertising, that the probabilities of finding work were very high. In terms of following the rule of maximizing expected utilities, they did not act unreasonably. However, when the stakes are so high (as they were in this case), it is imprudent—and a violation of the principles of critical thinking—to make judgments about the probabilities of various outcomes on the basis of such poor sources of information. Newspaper advertisements, paid for by profit-seeking organizations, cannot be considered authoritative sources of information. People who base a probability judgment on such a source are apt to be making a fallacious appeal to authority (see Chapter 3). The appropriate way to establish probabilities in such cases is to use strong inductive generalizations, statistical syllogisms (including legitimate appeals to authority) or arguments from analogy. When no reliable probabilities can be established and utilities are so high, decisions can be perilous.

A list of some important terms introduced in Chapter 5 follows:

Best Action: In a choice among several actions, if one of the actions has an outcome that has a higher utility than the outcome of any other action in the set and also has no outcome with a utility lower than the outcome of any other action in the set, then that action is a best action.

Conjunction: A compound sentence that is true just in case all its component sentences are true. "And," "but," and "moreover" are commonly used to join sentences to form conjunctions.

Decision Under Certainty: A choice in which the only possible outcome for each action is known.

Decision Under Risk: A choice in which the probabilities of the various outcomes of the actions are known.

Decision Under Uncertainty: A choice in which the probabilities of the various outcomes of the actions are not known.

Disjunction: A compound sentence that is true if any of its component sentences is true, but is false if all its component sentences are false. "Or" is commonly used to join sentences to form a disjunction.

Expected Utility: The utility of some event is its value, which may be positive or negative. For purposes of comparison and calculation, we assign units of utility to various events. The expected utility of an action is calculated by multiplying the probability of each possible outcome of the action by the utility associated with that outcome, and summing the results.

Independent Events: Events are independent of one another when the occurrence of one event does not affect the probability of the occurrence of the other event. Tosses of a fair coin are independent of one another; draws from a deck of cards without replacement and reshuffling are not independent of one another.

Mutually Exclusive Events: Events are mutually exclusive if the occurrence of one rules out the possibility of the occurrence of the other. On a single roll of a pair of fair dice, rolling a total of six points mutually excludes rolling a total of five points. Sentences are mutually exclusive when the truth of one rules out the truth of the other. If the sentences that form a disjunction are mutually exclusive only one of them can be true.

Satisfactory Action: In a choice among several actions, if there is no best action, but there is an action with no outcomes that have less than an acceptable level of utility, that action is a satisfactory action.

V. EXERCISES

1. The state in which you live operates a lottery. The proceeds of the lottery are used to supplement the state's unemployment insurance fund. You can play the lottery for $1. To play, you choose a three-digit number from 000 to 999, inclusive, and receive an official ticket with that number printed on it. Each evening, a ball is drawn blindly from a container that holds 1,000 balls, each with a different three-digit number on it. If your number is selected in the daily drawing on the date you play, you receive $500 for your ticket. Otherwise you receive nothing.
   a. What is the expected utility (in dollars) of a single play?
   b. Suppose that you decide to play three times in one day, and that you choose the same number each time. (You hold three tickets at a cost of $3.) What is the expected utility (in dollars) of your triple play?
   c. Suppose that you decide to play three times in one day, and that you choose a different number each time. What is the expected utility (in dollars) of this triple play?

2. An investor has $1,000 to invest for a period of one year. She must decide whether to invest the money in a recommended stock or in a money-market fund. If she invests in the fund, she will collect $1,200 (her original $1,000 + a profit of $200). If she invests in the stock and there is a merger, she will realize $1,800 (her original $1,000 + a profit of $800). If she invests in the stock and there is no merger, she will receive only $900 (a loss of $100). The probability that there will be a merger is 0.40. Assume that units of utility can be correlated with dollars (no other utilities are involved in this decision).
   a. What is the probability that no merger will occur?
   b. What is the expected utility of investing in the money-market fund?
   c. What is the expected utility of investing in the stock?
   d. What decision rule should the investor use?
   e. What is the rational decision in this case?

3. You are in charge of organizing a dinner party that is being held for the sole purpose of raising money for a worthy cause. You must decide whether to schedule an outdoor picnic or an indoor buffet supper. This event must be planned so far in advance that you have no way of assigning a probability of rain on the day of the party. On the basis of past events of this type, you have the following information:

   If it does not rain the outdoor picnic will yield a profit of $500, and the indoor buffet supper will yield a profit of $170.

If it does rain, the outdoor picnic will yield a profit of $80, and the indoor buffet supper will yield a profit of $440.

    a. Is this a decision under risk, a decision under certainty, or a decision under uncertainty?
    b. Is it reasonable in this case to correlate units of utility with dollars gained for the worthy cause?
    c. What decision rule would you follow in this case?
    d. Apply the decision rule, and state what decision you would make. (Show your work.)

4. The same conditions stated in Exercise 3 exist, *except* that on the basis of weather records for the date of the party, you can reasonably assign a probability of 1/3 to rain on that date.
    a. What type of decision are you faced with now?
    b. What decision rule should you follow?
    c. On the basis of that rule, what is the proper decision? (Show your work.)

5. You are a restaurant manager who is responsible for planning the "daily specials." You are considering whether or not to introduce a new Thursday special. If the special is successful, the restaurant will show a profit of $250 for the night; if the special is not successful the restaurant will lose $50. If you serve the usual Thursday special, the restaurant will show a profit of $100. You determine that the probability that the new dish will be a success is about 1/2. You've been doing a good job at the restaurant, so you are not afraid that you'll be fired if you make the wrong decision this time. However, you share in the profits, so the decision does affect your pay.
    a. What decision rule would you use in this situation?
    b. What would your decision be? (Show your work.)

6. A famous problem in decision theory, called "Pascal's Wager," was formulated by the French mathematician and philosopher Blaise Pascal in the seventeenth century. Pascal, who was a devout Christian, offered several formulations of the problem. Here is one way of looking at "Pascal's Wager":

> There are two possible states of the world: either God exists, or He does not. You are faced with two choices: Believe in God, or refuse to believe. If God does exist and you are a believer, you will be rewarded with infinite happiness in Heaven. If God does not exist and you believe He does, your life will be as usual, without any supernatural benefits or penalties. If, on the other hand, you refuse to believe and God exists, you can expect everlasting punishment in Hell. If you do not believe and there is no God, your life will be the usual rewards of life with no Heaven or Hell to face.

    a. Is this version of "Pascal's Wager" a decision under certainty, uncertainty, or risk?
    b. If you accept this formulation, is there a "best action"?
    c. Do you think that this way of presenting the problem is reasonable? For example, are there just two choices and two outcomes for each action?

Is "life as usual" the same for the believer and the nonbeliever? Does Pascal make any assumptions about what God is like?

7. Flu shots can offer valuable protection against the flu, particularly in an epidemic year. The shots, however, are not entirely unproblematic. In some people, flu shots can cause an allergic reaction—a kind of miniflu. This reaction is less severe than a real case of flu and lasts a much shorter time. Another problem is that in order to be effective, the flu shot must be administered before it is known whether or not an epidemic is on the way.

Suppose that you are trying to decide whether or not to get a flu shot. Based on statistical data, there is a probability of 0.6 that this year will be an epidemic year in your city. You have never had flu in a nonepidemic year and believe the probability that you will get flu is 0 if there is no epidemic. If an epidemic strikes your city and you are not vaccinated, your chances of getting the flu are 0.4, and you will be ill with the flu for nine days. If you are vaccinated, there is a probability of 0.1 that you will have a reaction and be ill for two days.

Flu vaccination is free at the student health clinic, and you do not particularly mind getting shots. Thus, it is reasonable to equate units of (negative) utility for this decision with days of illness.
- a. What is the probability that you will get the flu if you are not vaccinated?
- b. What is the expected utility of not being vaccinated?
- c. What is the expected utility of being vaccinated?
- d. If you follow the rule of maximizing expected utilities, will you get the flu shot or not?

8. Suppose that a person who needs $1,000 to stay in business (the business is the person's only means of support) is offered the choice between a $1,000 gift or a gamble on a prize of $100,000 if any number but a six is rolled on a single throw of a fair die (but nothing if the six shows). Also suppose that the person has no other way of obtaining the money needed to stay in business.
- a. Is it rational for the person to choose the gamble rather than the gift?
- b. Why or why not?
- c. What does this problem suggest about the practice of equating units of utility with units of money?
- d. What does this problem suggest to you about considering risks as well as possible gains when contemplating an action?

Deductive Reasoning: Conditional Arguments

I. PROPERTIES OF DEDUCTIVE ARGUMENTS: VALIDITY AND THE IMPORTANCE OF LOGICAL FORM

The distinguishing feature of (correct) deductive arguments is their ability to preserve truth. That is to say, if the premisses of a deductive argument are all true, then the conclusion must be true as well. When an argument is truth-preserving it is said to be a *valid* deductive argument. Strictly speaking, if we *define* deductive arguments as truth-preserving, then all deductive arguments are valid arguments. However, terminology varies; some logicians distinguish two types of deductive argument: arguments that are truth-preserving, or valid, and arguments that fail to preserve truth but which are put forth as valid by their proponents. These arguments that merely *purport* to be valid are called *invalid deductive arguments*.

The term "valid" has many uses in ordinary English. We hear people speak of valid beliefs, valid reasons, and valid claims. In our study of logic, however, "valid" and "validity" are used to refer to the truth-preserving property of deductive arguments. One of the chief concerns of deductive logic is to understand the nature of validity. Logicians try to determine how this property relates to other properties of arguments, and they develop methods for testing the validity of various types of arguments.

Although "validity" refers to the truth-preserving character of deductive arguments, arguments can be valid even if their premisses or their conclusions are *not* true. An argument can be truth-preserving even though it contains no truth (its premisses and conclusion are all false) to be preserved. To say that an argument is valid is to claim that regardless of whether or not the premisses are actually true, if all of its premisses were true, then its conclusion would be true also.

Because of the definition of validity, it is impossible to construct a valid argument in which all of the premisses are true and the conclusion is false. Valid arguments can, however, contain a false premiss (or premisses) and a true conclusion. Here, for example, is one such argument:

(1)

| No mammals can fly. | (false premiss) |
All dogs are mammals.	(true premiss)
No dogs can fly.	(true conclusion)

There are also valid arguments with false premisses and false conclusions. Here is one:

(2)

No mammals can fly.
All birds are mammals.

No birds can fly.

In the presentation of arguments (1) and (2), nothing has been done to *prove* that they are valid. At this point, we are relying on intuitive ability to see that if the premisses of these arguments were true, then their conclusions would be true also. Later on, we will prove that these arguments are valid.

If we present a deductive argument to persuade someone that the conclusion is *true*, we want the argument not only to be valid but to have true premisses as well. Valid arguments in which all of the premisses are true are called "sound arguments" (see Chapter 2). Soundness is obviously an important property of arguments that are used in everyday life. Nevertheless, the property of validity is so interesting that it—rather than the truth of premisses—is the chief focus of deductive logic.

In ordinary life, too, we are sometimes interested in the validity of arguments apart from the truth of their premisses. Occasionally, we may want to trace the consequences (the conclusions that follow deductively) of a variety of premisses, not all of which can be true. We might ask ourselves what would follow if A and B were true and, alternatively, what would follow if A were true and B were not true. Sometimes we want to identify the consequences of sentences but have no way of determining their truth or falsity at the time the argument is constructed. If we do not know whether some premisses are true, but we see that they lead deductively to some false conclusion, then—because of the definition of deductive validity—we can say that at least one of those premisses must be false.

The validity of deductive arguments is closely connected with their *logical form*. Logicians take the position that any argument that is deductively valid has this property by virtue of being an instance of some valid form of argument.

In earlier chapters, we looked at various forms of inductive arguments: analogy, inductive generalization, and statistical syllogism. The form, or structure, of an argument refers to certain logical features that pertain to the argument regardless of its particular subject matter or content. Statistical syllogisms, for example, have two premisses: a statistical generalization that relates an attribute class to a reference class, and a particular sentence that says a given individual is a member of that reference class. The conclusion of a statistical syllogism is another particular sentence that places the individual mentioned in the premiss in the attribute class. (Or, symbolically, "X percent of Fs are Gs. a is an F. Therefore, a is a G.") The form of deductive arguments (1) and (2) above can be represented, using our familiar symbols for class terms in generalizations, as

> No Fs are Gs.
> All Hs are Fs.
> ———————
> No Hs are Gs.

In a fundamental sense, the strict dependence of validity on the *form* of argument makes it simpler to evaluate deductive arguments than to evaluate inductive arguments. When we tried to evaluate inductive arguments, we had to consider the forms of those arguments, but we also had to take into account all sorts of background information that could affect the strength of the argument. We had to be concerned, for example, with the size of samples, the lack of bias, the relevance of analogies, and other matters. We then had to make judgments about whether or not the premises supported the conclusion, and if so, how strong the support was.

In evaluating deductive arguments, we do not need to consider any background information beyond the information required to state implicit premises. If an argument is an instance of a *valid argument form*, then that argument is valid. Moreover, unlike the degrees of strength in correct inductive arguments, validity is an all-or-nothing affair. An argument is either valid or not valid; there are no degrees of validity.

In the following sections, we will discuss conditional sentences, introduce some common forms of valid conditional arguments, explain what it means for an argument to be an instance of a valid form, and discuss some fallacies associated with deductive forms of argument.

II. CONDITIONAL SENTENCES

Conditional arguments are arguments that contain conditional sentences as premises, as conclusions, or both. Before we discuss these arguments, we will take a closer look at conditional sentences. *Conditional sentences* are used when we want to say that the truth of one claim depends on (is conditional on) the truth of another claim. Here are some examples:

1. If I study, then I will pass my math exam.
2. Maisie will recover from mono, provided that she takes care of herself.
3. John wouldn't have done that if he had not been forced.
4. You will break your leg climbing that way unless you are careful.

1. The Structure of Conditionals

Each of these conditional sentences (or, briefly, *conditionals*) is a *compound* English sentence—a sentence that contains another sentence as one of its parts. A sentence that is not compound is called *simple*. Conditionals are made up of (at least) two sentences—one that states the condition, and one that depends on the stated condition. In the vocabulary of logicians, the sentence that states the condition is called the *antecedent* and the dependent sentence is called the *consequent*. Antecedents and consequents are themselves sometimes compound, but we will first consider conditionals with simple antecedents and simple consequents.

In example (1), the antecedent is "I study" and the consequent is "I will pass my math exam." In (2), the antecedent is "she takes care of herself" and the consequent is "Maisie will recover from mono." In (3), the antecedent is "he had not been forced" and the consequent is "John wouldn't have done that." In (4), the antecedent is "you are (not) careful" and the consequent is "you will break your leg climbing that way."

Even this small sample reveals some of the variety of ways in which conditionals are expressed in English. Different verb tenses (past, present, and future) and moods (indicative and subjunctive) are used. Various terms indicate the presence of a conditional: "if . . . then," "provided that," "unless." Sometimes the word that signals the presence of the conditional also functions in another way in the sentence. "Unless," for example, connotes negation; it means the same as "if not." Sometimes, as in (1), the antecedent comes before the consequent; sometimes the antecedent follows the consequent, as in (2), (3), and (4). Subjunctive conditionals are most often used in English to express what would have occurred if something else had occurred, when, in fact, that something else did not occur. These subjunctive conditionals, like example (3), are called *counterfactual conditionals.*

Since the validity of an argument depends on its form, and the form of an argument in turn depends to some extent on the form, or structure, of the sentences that are its premises and conclusion, logicians are concerned with representing the form of conditional sentences in a standard way. To do this, they must ignore all sorts of rhetorical subtleties that are present in the different ways of stating conditionals in English. For the sake of clarity and precision in the study of arguments, logicians forego such refinements.

From the logician's point of view, it is important to know which sentence is the antecedent and which sentence is the consequent in a conditional. A relationship between antecedent and consequent is the crucial logical relationship in these sentences, just as relationships between classes are the crucial relationships in universal generalizations (see Chapter 3). When conditionals that occur in arguments are written in the standard way—"If (antecedent), then (consequent)"—their form is readily apparent. This practice makes it easier to recognize the structure of conditional arguments. We can rewrite examples (2), (3), and (4) above in this way (example [1] is already in standard form):

2. If Maisie takes care of herself, then she will recover from mono.
3. If he had not been forced, then John wouldn't have done that.
4. If you are not careful, then you will break your leg climbing that way.

Other English expressions besides those in the examples above are used to indicate conditionals. Here are some of them:

1. Whenever I see a kangaroo, I run. (If I see a kangaroo, then I run.)
2. I run only if I see a kangaroo. (If I do not see a kangaroo, then I do not run.) Note that this is *not* the same as (1) but that it is the same as "If I run, then I see a kangaroo."
3. Given that I see a kangaroo, I run. (Same as [1].)
4. A sufficient condition of my running is my seeing a kangaroo. (Same as [1].)
5. A necessary condition of my running is my seeing a kangaroo. (Same as [2].)
6. I don't run unless I see a kangaroo. (Same as [2].)

2. The Truth of Conditionals

In English, conditionals are used to express various kinds of relationships between the antecedent and the consequent. The conditional "If Maisie takes care of herself, then she will recover from mono" is used, for example, to express a *causal* connection between Maisie's caring for herself and her recovery. Conditionals are also used to express *logical*, or *definitional*, connections between sentences, as in "If two and two are added, then they equal four" or "If porpoises are aquatic, then they live in water." For a causal conditional to be true, there must be a real causal connection between the situation described in the antecedent and the situation described in the consequent. Similarly, if a conditional is intended to express a logical or definitional relationship, it will not be regarded as true unless that connection holds between the antecedent and the consequent.

Another type of connection occasionally expressed in English conditionals is called the *material conditional*. An example of a material conditional is "If there is human life on Jupiter, then my great-grandmother was an astronaut." Obviously there is no causal, definitional, or logical connection between the antecedent and consequent in this conditional. The point of this sentence, and others like it in English, is to emphasize the falsity of the antecedent. It is a way of expressing, forcefully or humorously, that there is no human life on Jupiter.

Occasionally, we encounter conditional sentences in which the truth of the consequent does not really depend at all on the truth of the antecedent, since the consequent is true whether or not the antecedent is true. An example is

> If Jake continues to smoke, he will eventually die.

Jake will *eventually* die whether or not he continues to smoke—although "eventually" may come a bit sooner if Jake smokes than if he doesn't smoke.

Although material conditionals are used rather infrequently in English, we can learn something logically important about the role of conditionals in valid arguments by examining the circumstances under which material conditionals are true or false.

In a material conditional, the "if . . . then . . ." that connects the component sentences is called a *truth-functional connective*. This means that the truth of the sentence as a whole is completely determined by (is a function of) the truth of the component sentences. The only circumstances under which we can say a material conditional is false is when it has a true antecedent and a false consequent. That is why the compound sentence "If there's human life on Jupiter, then my great-grandmother was an astronaut" can be used to state the falsity of "there is human life on Jupiter." The consequent of the conditional ("my great-grandmother was an astronaut") is obviously false. Yet the sentence as a whole is taken as true. But if the antecedent were true, then the conditional would be false, for it would have a true antecedent and a false consequent.

When we look at the *form* of a sentence, we ignore its *content* (the *meanings* of the component parts of the sentence). We are interested merely in the logical relationships between, for example, the subject and the predicate of the sentence or between the various sentences that make up a compound sentence. For example, when we express the form of generalizations such as "All *F*s are *G*s," we ignore the meanings of the terms that *"F"* and *"G"* represent. Similarly, when we express the form of a conditional—"If (antecedent), then (consequent)" we ignore the content of its component sentences.

If we do not pay attention to the content, however, we have no way of knowing whether a conditional is a causal conditional, a logical conditional, or a material conditional. This matters for some purposes, but it is balanced in the logicians' view by the advantages of treating the validity of all conditional arguments in a similar way.

Causal conditional sentences and definitional conditional sentences resemble material conditionals in the sense that if their antecedents are true and their consequents are false, then they are false conditionals. (For example, the causal conditional "If the match is struck, then it will light," is shown to be false if the match is struck and the match does not light.) Causal conditionals, however, unlike material conditionals, cannot be judged true just because they have true antecedents and true consequences. For a causal conditional to be true, the appropriate causal relationship must hold between antecedent and consequent. But to know this requires knowledge of the world as well as knowledge of the meanings of the component sentences. Similarly, for a definitional conditional to be true, the appropriate relationship must hold between the meaning of the antecedent and the meaning of the consequent. Counterfactual conditionals pose special problems for understanding since their antecedents are always false, and if their antecedents were true, they would not be *counterfactuals*. We will avoid the special problems raised by counterfactuals by excluding them from our discussion of conditional arguments.

To determine the validity of disparate conditional arguments on the basis of their *forms*, logicians ignore such "extralogical" considerations as the meanings of the component sentences and look only at what happens for various possible assignments of truth or falsity to the component sentences.

The truth-functional relationship between the antecedent and the consequent in material conditionals fits this requirement, and greatly simplifies the study of the validity of conditional arguments. We can learn important things about validity and the structure of arguments in a simplified system that treats all conditionals as materials conditionals.

We do not mean to say that all conditionals *really* are material conditionals or that other types of conditionals are unimportant to logicians. The logic of truth-functional connectives, such as the material conditional, does however provide a relatively simple introduction to deductive reasoning. More complicated logical systems attempt to handle the complexities of causal conditionals and the arguments that employ causal conditionals, but these topics are beyond the scope of a beginning text.

In summary, remembering that our primary purpose is the study of the validity of arguments, we can state the general circumstances under which a conditional statement is regarded as true by considering only the truth or falsity of its component parts. The only four possibilities are listed in the following table:

Antecedent	Consequent	Conditional Sentence
True	True	True
True	False	False
False	True	True
False	False	True

Exercises

1. Rewrite each of the following sentences in standard conditional form: *If* (antecedent), *then* (consequent).
   a. You can do well in math and logic classes only if you keep up with the assignments.
   b. Unless you want a ticket, you won't park in the faculty parking lot next to the classroom building.
   c. Whenever you want something very much you work hard to achieve it.
   d. You will get the job provided that you complete your degree this term.
   e. Without complications, life is uninteresting.
   f. In case the teacher asks about her, Jane missed the test because she was ill.
   g. You can pass this class if you really want to pass it.
   h. Having a grade-point average of C or better is a necessary condition for a student's being graduated.
   i. Passing one course in logic is a sufficient condition for a student's fulfilling the logic requirement.
   j. Only if you care little for your safety will you ride a bicycle on Main Street during rush-hour traffic.

2. In the following exercises, the letters *"p"* and *"q"* represent component sentences in conditionals. Suppose that *"p"* is a true sentence, and *"q"* is a false sentence. Rewrite each conditional in standard form, and state whether the conditional is true or false. (You may wish to refer to the preceding table.)
   a. *p* if *q*.
   b. *q* if *p*.
   c. *q* if *q*.
   d. If *p*, *q*.
   e. *p* provided that *q*.
   f. *q* whenever *p*.
   g. *p* is necessary for *q*.
   h. *q* is sufficient for *p*.
   i. *p* unless *q*.
   j. *p* only if *q*.

III. CONDITIONAL ARGUMENTS

In this section, we will examine two common forms of conditional arguments. Each of these forms has two premisses, one of which is a conditional sentence. In neither of these forms is the conclusion a conditional sentence.

1. Affirming the Antecedent

The argument

> If we drive nonstop to the coast, we will need two days to recover.
> We are driving nonstop to the coast.
> _____
> We will need two days to recover.

is an example of *affirming the antecedent.* Like many common argument forms, it has a Latin name, *modus ponens,* which can be roughly translated "the way of affirming." One premiss of the argument is a conditional. Using the letters "*p*" and "*q*" to represent the component sentences of the conditional, and the same letters to represent the same sentences when they occur elsewhere in the argument, we can exhibit the form of the argument in the following way:

> If *p*, then *q*.
> *p*.
> _____
> *q*.

Stated in English, this argument is so simple that its validity is readily apparent. If the premisses of the argument are true, it is easy to see that the conclusion must be true as well. However, now that we understand material conditionals, we are in a position to prove that any argument that has this structure (form) must be valid. We need to show only that there are no circumstances under which the sentences represented by "If *p*, then *q*" and "*p*" are both true and "*q*" is false.

If the second premiss ("*p*") is true, then the antecedent of the conditional premiss is true. But a conditional with a true antecedent is true only if its consequent ("*q*") is true as well. However, "*q*" is not only the consequent of the conditional, it is also the conclusion of the argument. So, if "If *p*, then *q*" and "*p*" (the premisses) are true, then "*q*" (the conclusion) must be true as well.

In showing that this argument form is valid, we did not take into account any meanings of the sentences that the letters "*p*" and "*q*" represent. The validity of the form does not depend on the content of the argument. All that is required to show that the form is valid is an understanding of the circumstances under which material conditionals are true or false and the recognition that one of the premisses is a conditional; the other premiss "affirms the antecedent" (claims the antecedent is true), and the conclusion affirms the consequent of the same conditional.

By showing that this argument *form* is valid, we have also shown that any argument in English that "fits" this form, or is an instance of this form, is also valid. This means that any argument with two such premises (one a conditional; the other, a sentence that affirms the antecedent) and a conclusion that is the consequent of the conditional is valid. It is impossible for an argument with this structure to have all true premises and a false conclusion.

Here are some examples of English-language arguments that are instances of *affirming the antecedent*. These arguments can be rewritten to fit the form without drastically changing the meaning of what is said in English:

1. Sally will go to the dance if Charlie will. But Charlie will certainly go, so Sally will be there.
2. Here comes Rover. Whenever Rover appears, Kitty-cat is not far behind. Therefore, Kitty-cat will be along soon.
3. With persistence, you'll be elected. So you will be elected, for persistence is your strong point.
4. A man cannot be robbed unless he can own, spend, claim, or want money. It is impossible for dead men to own, spend, claim, or want money. Therefore, dead men cannot be robbed. (This is a reconstruction of Gaffer's argument in *Our Mutual Friend* in Chapter 1.)

2. Denying the Consequent

The second type of conditional argument, *denying the consequent*, is also very common and only slightly more complicated than *affirming the antecedent*. The Latin name of this form is *modus tollens* ("the way of denying"). Here is an example:

If Japanese beetles are present in the garden, then leaves take on a lacy, or skeletonized, appearance.
The leaves in the garden are not lacy, or skeletonized.

Japanese beetles are not present in the garden.

In this argument, as in *affirming the antecedent*, there is a conditional premiss. The other premiss *denies the consequent*, or says that the consequent of the conditional premiss is false. The conclusion of the argument says that the antecedent of the conditional is also false. Using the letters "*p*" and "*q*" as we did in the previous argument form, we can represent the form of this argument in the following way:

If *p*, then *q*.
Not *q*.

Not *p*.

Again, we appeal to the circumstances under which material conditionals are true or false to show that this argument form is valid. In addition though, we must consider the meaning of "not." The logical force of "not" is to turn true sentences into false ones, and vice versa. In English, this logical function of *negation* can be accomplished in a number of ways. Sometimes, the term "not" is inserted in a sentence. Other times, sentences are negated by replacing the main verb of the sentence with the negation of that verb: "You can do this."— "You can't do this." A verb that means the same as the denial of the verb in the original sentence may be used: "You passed the test."—"You failed the test." The expression "it is not the case that" may precede the sentence to be negated: "You can do this."—"It is not the case that you can do this." Although "it is not the case that . . ." is an awkward phrase, it is favored by logicians because it can be placed at the beginning of any sentence to negate the sentence that follows it without tampering with the structure of the original sentence. All of this is familiar to competent speakers of English, but here are a few more examples to remind us of the variety of ways in which negation can be accomplished:

1. Harry is happy. Harry is unhappy.
2. She will do it. She won't do it.
3. Jack loves Jill. It is false that Jack loves Jill.
4. Skeletonized leaves are present. Skeletonized leaves are absent.

As in their treatment of conditionals, logicians ignore various subtleties of English usage and concentrate on the logically important feature of negation. Negation is an operation that changes a true sentence into a false one, or changes a false sentence into a true one. This is the feature that is important to the validity of arguments. Thus, we adopt a standard way of writing the negation of a sentence in argument forms: write "not" in front of the letter that stands for the sentence that is negated ("Not *p*.").

Now we are ready to consider the validity of the form of *denying the consequent*. One premiss of the argument says that the consequent of the conditional premiss is false. Thus, if the conditional premiss is true, it must have a false antecedent. But the conclusion of the argument simply states that the antecedent of the conditional premiss is false. So, if both premisses are true, the conclusion must be true as well.

Any English-language argument that fits the form (is an instance of) *denying the consequent* is a valid argument, just as any that fits the form of *affirming the antecedent* is valid. Here are some examples of arguments in English that are instances of *denying the consequent*.

1. Without complications, life is uninteresting. But life is interesting, so there are complications.
   The argument could be stated

   If there are no complications, then life is uninteresting.
   It is not the case that life is uninteresting.
   _____
   It is not the case that there are no complications.

2. If you really wanted that car, you would get a job to pay for it. So you must not really want the car, since you won't get a job.

3. Stupid savages could not devise complex languages without God's help. The languages of these people are complex. Therefore, God helped to construct the languages.

This is a reconstruction of Dobrizhoffer's argument in Exercise 11 at the end of Chapter 1. Like example (1) above, it involves double negation when the conditional is written in standard form:

If God did not help to construct the languages of savages, then these languages could not be complex.
It is not the case that these languages are not complex.

It is not the case that God did not help to construct the languages of savages.

3. Unstated Premisses in Conditional Arguments

Often in written works and ordinary speech we find incompletely stated conditional arguments of the forms *affirming the antecedent* and *denying the consequent*. Frequently, either the nonconditional premiss or the conclusion is omitted. Occasionally, both the conclusion and one of the premisses is missing, and we must depend on the context to tell us that an argument, rather than just a statement of facts, is intended. This is acceptable in many situations because the forms of conditional argument are so well understood. For example, in the Bible, St. Paul is obviously arguing for the truth of Christ's resurrection from the dead when he says "If Christ has not risen, vain then is our preaching, vain too is your faith (I. Cor. 15)." Paul intends the argument to be interpreted in the form of *denying the consequent*. Can you supply the missing premiss?

When premisses are not actually stated, there is always some danger that what is intended as a *modus tollens* may be interpreted as a *modus ponens*. For example, John Wesley (the founder of the Methodist Church), counting on his listeners' faith, is supposed to have said "If you give up belief in witches, then you give up belief in the Bible." Complete Wesley's argument—first as a *modus ponens* (*affirming the antecedent*), and then as a *modus tollens* (*denying the consequent*). Which form do you think Wesley intended? With respect to Wesley's conditional, Bertrand Russell once said "I agree." How did Russell interpret Wesley's argument? (Russell was not a Methodist!)

IV. FALLACIES ASSOCIATED WITH CONDITIONAL ARGUMENTS

Arguments sometimes are offered as deductive but fail to meet the truth-preserving standards for deductive validity. When these invalid arguments bear a superficial resemblance to valid arguments, they are called *deductive fallacies*.

Whether an argument is offered as deductive is sometimes difficult to determine but is an important consideration. Although inductive arguments are not truth-preserving, it would be inappropriate to regard all inductive arguments as fallacious. Inductive arguments are not meant to be deductive, and the standards for assessing the strength of inductive arguments differ from the standards for evaluating deductive arguments.

1. Fallacious (Invalid) Forms of Arguments

Before we address the question of fallacious arguments in English, we will consider what it means when we say that an *argument form* is "invalid." An argument form is *invalid* (not valid) if it is possible to find an instance of that form with all true premises and a false conclusion. Invalid argument forms that closely resemble valid argument forms are called *fallacious* forms of argument. The following form, which resembles *affirming the antecedent*, is an invalid form of argument:

$$\text{If } p, \text{ then } q.$$
$$q.$$
$$\overline{}$$
$$p.$$

To show that this form is invalid, we need to note only that if "*q*" were true and "*p*" were false, the conclusion would be false but both premisses would be true. This is because a material conditional with a false antecedent is true whether its consequent is true or false. This fallacious form is called (not surprisingly) *affirming the consequent.*

It is not difficult to supply an argument in English with two true premisses and a false conclusion that is an instance of this form:

If Cincinnati is the capital of Ohio, then Cincinnati is in Ohio.
Cincinnati is in Ohio.
_____

Cincinnati is the capital of Ohio.

The second fallacious form of argument, which is somewhat similar to *denying the consequent*, is called *denying the antecedent.*

$$\text{If } p, \text{ then } q.$$
$$\text{Not } p.$$
$$\overline{}$$
$$\text{Not } q.$$

The invalidity of this form is evident if we consider that the second premiss denies the antecedent of the conditional premiss (says it is false). But conditionals are true when their antecedents are false, whether they have false consequents (as the conclusion states) or true ones. Since the truth of the premisses cannot guarantee the truth of the conclusion, the argument form is not valid. Again, it is easy to supply an argument in English with true premises and a false conclusion that is an instance of this form:

> If bats are birds, then bats have wings.
> Bats are not birds.
> _____
> Bats do not have wings.

To show that an *argument form* is invalid, we need only to show that it is logically possible for an argument with all true premises and a false conclusion to fit (or be an instance of) that form. We can do this abstractly, for example, by discussing the circumstances under which sentences of a certain form are true or false. Or we can actually exhibit an English-language argument that fits the form but that has obviously true premises and an obviously false conclusion. This latter method is called "providing a counterexample."

2. Invalid and Fallacious Arguments

Incorrect arguments are normally called "fallacious" if they somehow resemble correct arguments. Arguments that resemble deductively correct arguments but are invalid are called "deductive fallacies." Unless an argument has premises that are all obviously true and an obviously false conclusion, it is more difficult to show that a given *argument* is invalid than it is to show that an *argument form* is invalid. An argument that is offered as deductive is invalid only if it is not an instance of *any* valid argument form. (Of course, no inductive argument, no matter how strong, is an instance of a valid form. In this discussion of fallacies, we are only considering arguments that somehow resemble valid deductive arguments.)

There are an infinite number of valid argument forms. Thus far, we have considered only two valid argument forms—*affirming the antecedent* and *denying the consequent*. Obviously, we cannot prove an argument is fallacious by showing that it fails to fit either of these forms. For example, the following valid argument does not fit either form:

> All men are mortal.
> Socrates is a man.
> _____
> Socrates is mortal.

One problem we encounter is that a single English-language argument can fit several different argument forms. Forms of argument reflect certain structural features of the components of the argument. Sometimes we are interested in structural (formal) relationships *among* various simple sentences in an argument, as when we analyze conditional arguments. In other arguments, validity depends on structural relationships *within* the simple sentences that make up the argument, such as the relationships between the subject and the predicate in a sentence. The syllogism about Socrates is an example. If the validity of a given argument depends on *intra*-sentence structures, we will not prove that it is valid by representing its form in terms of *inter*-sentence structure.

If an English-language argument has obviously true premisses and an obviously false conclusion, we know that it is invalid, for it could not be an instance of any valid form. For this reason, it is safe to call the earlier example of English-language arguments that were instances of *affirming the consequent* and *denying the antecedent* fallacious. In addition, since deductive validity is a matter of form, when we are more familiar with the various types of argument structure and when we can be reasonably certain we have not overlooked any hidden structure by virtue of which some arguments could be valid, we may say that it is highly probable that these arguments are fallacious, even though they may not have true premisses and false conclusions. For the time being, however, we are on safer ground when we speak of fallacious *argument forms*. When we are presented with an English-language argument that is an instance of one of the known fallacious forms, we should *suspect* it of being fallacious, and it is reasonable to challenge whoever is presenting the argument to prove that it is not.

V. REVIEW

Since the most important material in Chapter 6 can be described in the new vocabulary that was introduced here, the chapter can be reviewed by listing those new terms and their meanings:

Compound Sentence: A sentence that contains another sentence as one of its parts.

Conditional Argument: An argument that contains at least one conditional sentence as a premiss. Some conditional arguments (not the ones studied in this chapter) also have conditionals as conclusions. In this chapter, we studied two valid forms of conditional argument: *affirming the antecedent* (or *modus ponens*), and *denying the consequent* (or *modus tollens*):

Modus ponens	Modus tollens
If p, then q.	If p, then q.
p.	Not q.
_____	_____
q.	Not p.

We also studied two invalid or fallacious forms of conditional arguments:

Affirming the consequent	Denying the antecedent
If p, then q.	If p, then q.
q.	Not p.
_____	_____
p.	Not q.

Conditional Sentence (*Conditional*): A compound sentence consisting of an *antecedent* (the sentence that states the condition) and a *consequent* (the sentence that depends on the stated condition). The standard form of a conditional is: "If (antecedent), then (consequent)."

Deductive Fallacy: An invalid deductive argument that somehow resembles a valid argument.

Invalid Argument (*Invalid Deductive Argument*): An argument is invalid if it is meant to be truth-preserving, but fails to meet the standards for deductive validity. An invalid argument is not an instance of any valid form of argument.

Invalid Argument Form: An argument form is invalid if it is possible for an argument in that form to have all true premisses and a false conclusion. Invalid argument forms that resemble correct forms are called *fallacious* forms.

Material Conditional: A conditional sentence in which the connection between the antecedent and the consequent is merely truth-functional, rather than some "real" causal, definitional, or logical connection. A material conditional is false only when its antecedent is true and its consequent is false.

Truth-Functional Connective: In a compound sentence that is connected by a truth-functional connective, the truth or falsity of the compound sentence depends entirely on the truth or falsity of its component parts. "If . . . then," *when interpreted in the sense of a material conditional,* is a truth-functional connective. "Not" is also a truth-functional connective. If a sentence "*p*" is true, then "Not *p*" is false. If a sentence "*p*" is false, then "Not *p*" is true. In contrast, "if . . . then" in subjunctive counterfactual conditionals (for example, "If Nixon had not resigned, then he would have been impeached") is not a truth-functional connective. The truth of a counterfactual conditional is not a function of the truth of its component parts.

Valid Argument: An argument is valid if it is impossible for all of its premisses to be true and its conclusion to be false. "Valid" is the term applied to correct deductive arguments, those that actually preserve truth rather than merely purport to preserve truth. Any instance of a valid argument form is a valid argument.

Valid Argument Form: An argument form is valid if it is impossible for an argument in that form to have all true premisses and a false conclusion.

VI. EXERCISES

I. Each of the following exercises contains a conditional argument. Treat all the conditionals as material conditionals. Assume that all the arguments purport to be deductive, and rewrite each argument (in English) so that its premisses and conclusion are on separate lines. If the conditional premiss is not in standard form, rewrite it. Supply missing premisses or conclusions, if necessary. When doing so, adopt a principle of "charity" and give the proponent of the argument the benefit of the doubt. Then tell whether the rewritten argument is in the form of *affirming the antecedent, denying the consequent, affirming the consequent,* or *denying the antecedent.*

1. If our school's team wins all its football games this season, then they'll be invited to play in a postseason bowl game. They will be invited to play in a bowl game. Thus, they will win every game this season.

2. State will play in a bowl game only if State has a winning season. State will not have a winning season, so State won't play in a bowl game.

3. Headlines on the *Pittsburgh Press* sports pages on two successive days:

IF STEELERS BEAT OILERS, THEY GO TO PLAYOFFS
STEELERS BEAT OILERS; GO TO PLAYOFFS

4. You can do well in math and logic classes only if you keep up with the assignments. You keep up with the assignments, so you do well in math and logic classes.

5. The picnic will be held on Thursday, provided that it doesn't rain. But according to the weather reports, there will be no rain on Thursday, so we'll have the picnic.

6. If primitive peoples did not cross the Pacific Ocean, there would not be a strong resemblance between Polynesian artifacts and South American artifacts. But there is a strong resemblance between these artifacts, so primitive peoples did cross the Pacific Ocean.

7. Since there are holes in the carpet, there must be moths in the house; for if there are moths in the house, then they make holes in the carpet.

8. Coyotes howl only when there's a moon, but there's a moon tonight, so they'll be howling.

9. All forms of pantheism [which involves the belief that man is a part of God] must be rejected, because if man is actually a part of God, the evil in man is also in God. But there is no evil in God.

—Bishop of Birmingham,
quoted in *Religion and Science*, Bertrand Russell

10. If 2 is not a prime number, then there is a positive integer smaller than 2 and greater than 1 which evenly divides 2. But there are no positive integers smaller than 2 and greater than 1. Therefore, 2 is a prime number.

11. If morals could be taught simply on the basis that they are necessary to society, there would be no social need for religion. But morality cannot be taught in that way.

—Patrick Lord Devlin, *The Enforcement of Morals*

12. We would not be at the trouble to learn a language when we can have all that is written in it just as well in translation. But as we cannot have the beauties of poetry but in its original language, we learn it.

—Samuel Johnson

13. The earth is spherical in shape. For the night sky looks different in the northern and southern parts of the earth, and this would be so if the earth were spherical in shape.

—Aristotle, *Physics*

14. A judgment of acquittal by reason of insanity is appropriate only when a jury verdict of guilty would violate the law or the facts. We cannot say that this was the situation in Washington's case. Therefore, the district court did not err in its refusal to enter a judgment of acquittal by reason of insanity.

—Bazelon, *Washington vs. United States*

15. All history shows that the progress of humanity is accomplished not otherwise than under the guidance of religion. But if the race cannot progress without the guidance of religion—and progress is always going on, and also in our own times—then there must be a religion of our times.

—Leo Tolstoy, *What Is Art*

16. One could argue that given raw materials of more-or-less equally ideal qualities for axemaking, a simple utilitarian model would predict a wide but more-or-less even pattern of dispersal of axes in all directions from the quarry source. However, such uniformity of dispersal of greenstone [for making axes] from Mt. Williams is emphatically what one does not find in southeastern Australia.

—R. A. Gould, *Living Archaeology*

17. Because the financial burden of radioactive waste storage is simply taken on by the government [and not by the operators and customers of nuclear power plants], the taxpaying public is the victim of an inequitable practice. . . . If the public as a whole bears the cost of waste storage, but only a subset of society receives the benefits of atomic power, then the costs and benefits of nuclear generation of electricity are not borne equitably.

—K. S. Shrader-Frechette, *Nuclear Power and Public Policy*

II. The following compound sentences are not truth-functional compounds:
   a. Jake believes that Sally won the marathon.
   b. Frank admires Gloria because she is brave.
   c. Rita phoned Larry before she went to his apartment.

1. Identify the component sentences in the compound sentences (a), (b), (c), and explain why the compound sentences are not truth-functional compounds.

2. Formulate at least three other compound sentences that are not truth-functional compounds.

Confirmation of
Hypotheses

C H A P T E R   7

I. HYPOTHESES

The first time I baked muffins, they tasted fine but looked peculiar. They were cracked, crooked, wobbly, and peaked. When I told an experienced cook about my muffins, she said they had been baked in an oven that was too hot. This surprised me, for I had followed cookbook directions carefully, but I decided to test her claim. If she is right, I thought, and if I make the muffins the same way but bake them at a lower temperature, they should turn out all right. I baked another batch, lowering the oven temperature 50°. This time the muffins looked the way they were supposed to, and I believed the cook had been correct in saying that my first muffins had been baked in an oven that was too hot.

This experience illustrates the type of reasoning we will examine in this chapter. To check whether or not a claim—such as the cook's claim that the oven was too hot—is true, we often find a way to "test" the claim, by making a prediction based on the claim and seeing whether or not the prediction comes out true. We call these claims "hypotheses." Webster defines "hypothesis" as "a supposition used as a basis from which to draw conclusions." "Hypothesis" has several different uses in ordinary language. Sometimes, it means a guess or suspicion that something is the case: "Our hypothesis is that it will rain on graduation day." Other times, "hypothesis" is used to refer to a belief that is not well established: "The existence of life on any other planet in our solar system is only a hypothesis." In our discussion of hypotheses, we will use the term to refer to any sentence that we want to test by finding a prediction that follows from it and checking the truth of that prediction. The conclusions that scientists draw when they test hypotheses are predictions, the truth of which can be checked by performing experiments or making observations. The results of such tests usually cannot conclusively establish hypotheses. They can, however, inductively support (*confirm*) the claims or they can inductively undermine (*disconfirm*) them. In this chapter we will examine the logic of confirmation, which is an important part of inductive logic.

Hypotheses can be formulated about any subject matter. Many hypotheses are causal claims. (We have already said something about using Mill's Methods to test causal claims. There are close relationships between the use of these methods and the form of reasoning we will discuss here.) Hypotheses may take different logical forms. Some are universal generalizations: "All human languages have terms for kinship relations." There are also statistical hypotheses: "49 percent of all Americans would say they approve of the way the president is handling foreign affairs." Hypotheses that are not generalizations can also be tested: "A mouse is in the kitchen."

Conditional arguments, introduced in Chapter 6, play an important part in the logic of confirmation, for a conditional sentence expresses the relationship between the hypothesis and the prediction that follows from it, and a nonconditional sentence states whether or not the prediction is true. Yet, arguments of confirmation are not, as we will see, conditional deductive arguments, for they combine aspects of deductive and inductive reasoning. We have postponed discussing arguments for the confirmation of hypotheses until after our introduction to conditional arguments so that we could better understand the logic of hypothesis testing.

II. THE HYPOTHETICO-DEDUCTIVE METHOD

Most introductory science classes in both high school and college discuss hypothesis testing. Texts used in these classes often refer to the *hypothetico-deductive method* of testing scientific claims. In its simplest form it is presented thus: To see whether a hypothesis is true, derive some prediction from it. If the prediction is true, then the hypothesis is confirmed. If the prediction is false, then the hypothesis is disconfirmed. In this chapter we will show that this presentation of hypothetico-deductive reasoning is an oversimplification of scientific reasoning, and we will develop an account that more nearly reflects scientific practice.

The form of reasoning we want to examine can be illustrated with a famous example—Galileo's use of the telescope to check a prediction based on the hypothesis that the earth and other planets revolve around the sun.

The prevailing sixteenth-century view of the arrangement of the sun, the earth, and other planets had been proposed 1,400 years earlier by Ptolemy, a Greek astronomer who worked in Alexandria. The Ptolemaic system was *geocentric*; Ptolemy placed our immobile earth at the center of the universe with the other planets and the sun revolving around it. Although the orbits of celestial bodies were complicated to compute under this geocentric system, astronomers who used it were able to predict the positions of stars and planets quite accurately over the centuries.

In 1543, Copernicus, a Polish astronomer, proposed a new system of planetary orbits that avoided many complexities of the Ptolemaic system. Copernicus did not base his system on any new observations. By placing the sun at the center with the planets, including earth, revolving around the sun, however, the *heliocentric* Copernican system postulated more regular (nearly circular) orbits and accounted for the same observations as the Ptolemaic system. The Copernican system also used simpler mathematics to calculate the paths of celestial bodies.

About 50 years after the work of Copernicus was published, a Danish astronomer, Tycho Brahe, introduced still another planetary system in which the earth was motionless, the sun orbited the earth, and the other planets orbited the sun. The Tychonic system had the same mathematical advantages as the Copernican system—it offered simpler orbits with easier calculations than the Ptolemaic system—and it was in accord with all observational evidence. Moreover, in a time when scripture was considered by many scholars to be a source of information about such things, the Tychonic system agreed with Biblical remarks about the immobility of our earth, found in such passages as Psalm 104: "O Lord my God . . . who laid the foundations of the earth, that it should not be removed for ever." (See O. Gingerich "The Galileo Affair," *Scientific American*, 247:2, 133.)

All three of these planetary systems were proposed before 1609, the year the telescope was invented. Galileo did not invent the telescope, but he built one that same year and was the first to use the telescope for astronomical observations. Soon after Galileo built his instrument, one of his students suggested to him that if the Copernican system was correct, then Venus, which is between the sun and the earth, should show a full range of phases similar to the phases of the moon—from almost dark to crescent to nearly full. Galileo turned his telescope on Venus, and, over a period of several months, he was

FIGURE 7-1

Phases of Venus

In the Copernican system, Venus can appear nearly full as it passes behind the sun, and its size varies greatly.

Source: Richard S. Westfall, *The Construction of Modern Science: Mechanisms and Mechanics* (Cambridge, UK: Cambridge University Press, 1971). Used by permission of the publisher.

able to observe the full set of phases. (You can observe this yourself with a good pair of binoculars.) Galileo interpreted this data as evidence that the Copernican (heliocentric) system was correct—that the apparently immobile earth actually revolved around the sun.

As a first approach to understanding the hypothetico-deductive method, we can reconstruct Galileo's argument in the following way. His hypothesis is "The Copernican system is correct." On the basis of this hypothesis, Galileo (with the help of his student) deduced a prediction that can be checked by observation. That is to say, there is an observable prediction that must be true if the hypothesis is true. The prediction in this case is "Venus will show phases."

Galileo's argument can be stated

> If the Copernican system is correct, then Venus will show phases.
> Venus shows phases.
> _____
> The Copernican system is correct.

In this argument, the first premiss is a conditional sentence; its antecedent is the hypothesis, and its consequent is the observable prediction. The second premiss says that the prediction was observed to be true. The conclusion asserts the truth of the hypothesis.

Galileo's argument for his hypothesis, thus formulated, fits one of the patterns of conditional arguments discussed in Chapter 6. A similar argument can be used for any hypothesis, and can be stated generally

If the hypothesis is true, then the prediction is true.
The prediction is true.

The hypothesis is true.

This argument is an instance of *affirming the consequent*:

$$\text{If } p, \text{ then } q$$
$$q$$

$$p$$

Affirming the consequent is, as we know, a fallacious argument form. An argument that is intended to be deductive and is in this form is suspected of being fallacious unless the argument is also an instance of some valid form of argument.

We should remember, however, that arguments provided in support of hypotheses are intended to be inductive arguments, not deductive arguments. The truth of their premises only makes it probable that their conclusions are true. These arguments are said to *confirm* hypotheses. *Confirmation* refers to positive inductive support, rather than to a guarantee of truth.

Nevertheless, it would not be satisfactory to regard fallacious deductive forms of argument as satisfactory inductive forms. Fortunately, it is not necessary to do so. The form of reasoning we use to confirm hypotheses is actually more complicated than *affirming the consequent*, and requires premises not represented in that invalid form.

III. COMPLEXITIES IN THE HYPOTHETICO-DEDUCTIVE METHOD

The *deductive* part of the hypothetico-deductive method refers not to the overall structure of the arguments, but rather to the *connection* between the hypothesis and an observable prediction that is deduced from it. To say the connection between the hypothesis and the observable prediction is deductive means that if the antecedent (hypothesis) is true then the consequent (prediction) cannot be false. The conditional sentence that states this relationship is one premiss in a confirmation argument.

1. Auxiliary Hypotheses

In Galileo's test of his hypothesis, some additional assumptions are required to connect the hypothesis deductively with the observable prediction. These assumptions, called *auxiliary hypotheses*, must be true if the observable prediction is to follow deductively from the hypothesis, but they are usually unstated. Typically, these premises are unstated because they are claims that form part of a generally accepted theoretical background or standard claims about the conditions of the observation or experiment. Although they are assumed to be true in the context of testing the hypothesis for which they are auxiliaries, they can themselves be tested in other contexts. One of Galileo's assumptions (auxiliary hypotheses) was "Venus lies between the earth and the sun." Another was "The telescope is a reliable instrument for observing celestial bodies." The conditional premiss in Galileo's argument, if these auxiliary hypotheses were stated rather than assumed, would read

> If the Copernican system is correct, and if the telescope is a reliable instrument of observation, and if Venus lies between the earth and the sun, then Venus will show a complete set of phases.

There are two important types of auxiliary hypotheses. One type has to do with *proper testing conditions*. In general, these auxiliary hypotheses are concerned with whether or not all of the equipment and materials to be used in a test are in proper working order and the observers of the outcome of the test are capable of correctly assessing the outcome.

The second type of auxiliary hypothesis has to do with *theoretical background knowledge*. Most hypothesis testing is carried out against a background of some other claims that are assumed to be true. Tests of hypotheses concerning the curative powers of many drugs assume that certain theories of human physiology and microbiology are true. The physical theory of optics plays a background role in any tests that use microscopes or telescopes. When theoretical knowledge is not itself being tested but its truth is assumed in a test of some other hypothesis, it is used in the form of auxiliary hypotheses.

When we remember that Galileo was the first person to use a telescope to observe the heavens, we can see that hypotheses about the reliability of telescopes could easily be questioned. In the tremendous controversy that followed Galileo's discovery (he was censored, then silenced, and finally tried by the Inquisition and placed under house arrest by the Catholic Church), he suggested that his critics look through the telecope to observe what he had seen. With his remarkable new instrument he had observed not only the phases of Venus, but also the moons of Jupiter and the mountains on our own moon. Many critics refused to look, on the grounds that what was seen through a telescope did not constitute observation because telescopes could not be relied on to show what was really there.

In Galileo's time, the questions raised about his telescope were chiefly theoretical. That is to say, not just the accuracy of Galileo's own instrument, but the principles of optics on which the construction of telescopes were based, were doubted by some influential thinkers. It seemed too implausible that putting together two curved lenses—each of which would distort the appearance of objects—could enable an observer to see far-away objects more clearly. Prior to the invention of the telescope, people had used curved lenses and mirrors for the explicit purpose of distorting images, in a way similar to that employed by "fun houses" in amusement parks today.

When a widely held belief is apparently overturned by a new test, it often happens that auxiliary hypotheses are questioned. When things occur pretty much the way we expect them to and when our beliefs are confirmed by tests, we don't take the trouble to ask what assumptions are involved. But those assumptions—auxiliary hypotheses—nevertheless play an important part in hypothesis testing.

In the dispute between those who believed the Copernican system was correct and those who denied it, the reliability of some auxiliary hypotheses was unquestioned by both parties. No one, for example, doubted that Venus was positioned between the earth and the sun. This was an assumption shared by all the then-current theories.

The importance of auxiliary hypotheses for the logic of confirmation requires us to revise the simplest form of hypothetico-deductive reasoning, which only mentions the hypothesis and the observational prediction. We can represent the form of the revised argument, in which H denotes the hypothesis that is being tested, $A_1, \ldots, A_n$, represent auxiliary hypotheses (there may be any number of these), and P stands for the observable prediction:

> If H and $A_1, \ldots, A_n$, then P.
> P is true.
> _____
> H and $A_1, \ldots, A_n$ are true.

This form of argument is not deductively valid. It is an improvement over the first version of an argument for confirmation, however, because it includes the auxiliary hypotheses in the premises, and makes the role of these hypotheses in the argument explicit. Further revisions, however, are required.

2. Alternative Hypotheses

The form of argument to support the truth of hypotheses we have just examined is more complicated than the simplest arguments of confirmation, but it still does not represent the full complexity of the logic of hypothesis testing because it fails to account for the importance of *alternative hypotheses*. An alternative hypothesis is one that, along with the same auxiliary hypotheses, would yield exactly the same observational prediction as the hypothesis that is being tested.

In Galileo's time, three competing planetary systems were proposed by leading astronomers. Tycho's system, which was a different *geocentric* system from Ptolemy's system, predicted *the same phases of Venus that Galileo observed.* Tycho's system agreed with the Copernican system in *all* points of observation that could be obtained using the telescopes of that day. Our previous account of confirmation, even with the added complexity of auxiliary hypotheses, does not say anything about how to choose among incompatible alternative hypotheses with the same observable predictions. Since both Tycho's system and the Copernican system predict the phases of Venus, how do we choose one rather than the other?

To see that problem more clearly, let us look at another example in which an alternative hypothesis plays an important role.

The question of when humans first came to America is perplexing. It is widely believed that the first American immigrants came from Asia, across the Bering Strait, probably over an "ice bridge." From there, they (or their descendants) spread out all over the North and South American continents. The big question—When did this happen?—is especially puzzling because there is a lot of good evidence indicating that humans were all over both continents about 12,000 years ago. Presumably, only rather small numbers of humans crossed from Asia, so it must have taken a long time for this widespread settlement to occur. However, there is almost no evidence that humans were anywhere in North America much before 12,000 years ago, and what little evidence there is has been highly disputed.

Several years ago, two archaeologists (W. Irving and C. Harrington, "Upper Pleistocene Radiocarbon-Dated Artifacts from the Northern Yukon," *Science* 179(1973):335) made an important discovery that they took as confirmation of the hypothesis "Humans were in Beringia [Alaska] 27,000 years ago." They found mammoth bones that showed traces of having being shaped by humans. Bones can be "worked" (shaped into tools) only when they are in a fresh state. After a relatively short time, they become so brittle that they splinter. Mammoths did coexist with humans for a time in the New World, but they have long been extinct. The worked bones, when subjected to radiocarbon dating, showed that this mammoth had died approximately 27,000 years ago. (The correctness of radiocarbon dating is an important auxiliary hypothesis.)

Nevertheless, many archaeologists did not accept these dated worked bones as confirmation of the hypothesis that humans were in America 27,000 years ago. They pointed out that an alternative hypothesis could accommodate the dates of the worked bones just as well. This hypothesis is that the bones were from an animal that died 27,000 years ago but was frozen in the tundra for approximately 15,000 years. Then, during a thawing period around 12,000 years ago, the mammoth remains were found by newly arrived humans, who worked the bones. The long freeze had preserved the bones from brittleness, so that when they thawed, they could be worked just like fresh bones.

This alternative hypothesis may seem a bit farfetched, but actually it is not. In recent times, long-frozen mammoths were heaved from the earth in Siberia during thawing and freezing cycles. Their meat was eaten; their ivory tusks were sold on the market; their stomachs were examined to see what food they had eaten before they died; and people made tools from their bones. Since archaeologists knew about these occurrences and since at the time of the discovery of the worked bones, there was no solid evidence to support the presence of humans in that region before 12,000 years ago, they believed the hypothesis that the bones had been frozen for 15,000 years before being worked was initially more plausible than the hypothesis of early occupation of the area by humans.*

Let us return to our question of how we choose among alternative hypotheses that have the same observable predictions. If we agree with the reasoning in the last example, we can say that when the same true prediction follows from several different hypotheses, then the hypothesis that was more plausible (or

---

*This situation may change. Archaeologists are diligently searching for remains of early man, and new and better evidence may be found at any time. Recent discoveries, for example, show that humans were in Australia—long thought to be the most recently populated continent—some 40,000 years ago.

had a higher *prior probability*) before the test occurred is the hypothesis confirmed by the test.

Prior probabilities—the probability that a hypothesis is true prior to (before) taking account of a particular test of that hypothesis—play an important role in the logic of confirmation. Not only do these probabilities help us to decide which hypothesis among several alternatives is confirmed by a particular test, they also help us to decide which hypotheses are worth taking the trouble to test. If a hypothesis is wildly implausible (if its truth is almost impossible to imagine) scientists are reluctant to spend any time, effort, or money on testing it. Furthermore, if a hypothesis has a very high prior probability—such as the geocentric hypothesis in Galileo's time—then, even when tests apparently disconfirm it, efforts are made to "save the hypothesis" by questioning auxiliary hypotheses. The debate between supporters of the heliocentric system and the geocentric system went on for nearly 100 years after the Copernican system was first published, and for much of that time, the prior probabilities favored the geocentric hypothesis. The Law of Universal Gravitation and the Laws of Motion, formulated by Newton, who was born the year Galileo died, severely undercut the geocentric hypothesis. These laws, which showed that the proposed geocentric systems required motions that were impossible, were accepted by almost all scientists. It took that work—and some further important observations (such as stellar parallax) with better instruments—to finally overturn the geocentric hypotheses.

The prior probabilities of hypotheses depend on a number of factors. Previous studies or tests may have contributed to the probability of a hypothesis. The prior probability of a hypothesis that is compatible with well-established scientific theories is greater than the prior probability of a hypothesis that conflicts with accepted views. A hypothesis proposed by a legitimate "authority" has greater prior probability than a hypothesis proposed by a crank. In some cases, only rough estimates of prior probabilities can be made. In others, precise quantitative values can be assigned, as we will see in Section VI on Bayesian confirmation.

3. Form of Inductive Arguments of Confirmation

We can now present the structure of reasoning that is used to confirm hypotheses. It is considerably more complex than the first simple formulation of the hypothetico-deductive schema, which treated arguments of confirmation as simple conditional arguments. This new formulation shows how conditional arguments play a part in reasoning about hypotheses, but it also exhibits the overall inductive structure of these arguments.

The structure of arguments to confirm hypotheses can be summarized:

1. The hypothesis is initially plausible. (It has some degree of prior probability.)
2. If the hypothesis, and the auxiliary hypotheses, are true, then the observable prediction is true.

3. The observable prediction is true.
4. No alternative hypothesis has as high a prior probability as the hypothesis that is being tested.
5. Therefore, the hypothesis is true.

In these arguments of confirmation, there are four premises. The first premiss states the plausibility of the hypothesis to be tested. The second and third premises are the same premisses as those in the simple conditional argument form. The conditional premiss states the deductive connection between hypothesis and prediction, and the third premiss states the truth of the prediction. The fourth premiss again appeals to prior probabilities. If a test confirms a number of alternative hypotheses, the hypothesis that is best confirmed *after* the test is the one that *started out* with the greatest degree of plausibility. A positive prediction that follows deductively from several hypotheses confirms each of them; after the test, however, the hypothesis that was most probable before the test remains most probable. The only way to change this relative ranking is by negative (disconfirming) evidence, as we will see in Section V.

Although the conclusion of the confirming argument is "the hypothesis is *true*," we must remember that since the argument is inductive, the strength of support that the premises can give to the conclusion is variable. In a case, for example, where there are several alternative hypotheses with prior probabilities only slightly lower than the hypothesis being tested, the argument for the truth of the hypothesis will not be very strong. The hypothesis will be only a little better supported after the test than it was before. In another case, where there are apparently no other plausible alternatives, the argument can be very strong.

Another factor to consider in how strongly a hypothesis is supported by an argument of this type is the nature of the hypothesis itself. On the one hand, a low-level empirical hypothesis, such as "There's a mouse in the kitchen," can be strongly supported by a small amount of the right kind of evidence; if we predict mouse "tracks" on the countertop and find them, there is little doubt that the hypothesis is correct. On the other hand, a theoretical hypothesis as high-level and wide-ranging as the Copernican hypothesis will not be strongly confirmed by a few observations with a telescope. Although we will have some things to say about the quality of evidence, a discussion of the amount and type of evidence it takes to support broad theoretical hypotheses is beyond the scope of our text. The general framework for confirmation arguments developed here, nevertheless, is intended to apply to both high-level and low-level hypotheses.

Finally, any conclusion that a hypothesis about what the world is like is *true* is revisable in the face of further evidence. This should be clear from our insistence that inductive arguments can be strengthened or weakened by the inclusion of additional evidence. Ptolemy's theory was strongly supported for a very long time by all the available evidence. Some of our own best-supported theories will undoubtedly go the way of Ptolemy's, and new ones will take their places.

4. Confirming a Causal Hypothesis

Edward Jenner's confirmation of the hypothesis that an attack of cowpox confers immunity to smallpox is classic in the history of medicine.

Smallpox is a very serious disease that has long been the source of wide-spread death and disfigurement. Recently, the World Health Organization announced that smallpox has at last been completely eliminated; there is not a single case of the disease in the entire world. Since smallpox spreads only by contact among humans (no other carriers of the disease are known), this is a significant step toward the achievement of worldwide health.

Smallpox is highly contagious. When a few of Columbus's sailors first brought it to America, whole tribes of Indians, who had never been exposed to smallpox, were destroyed by the disease. Smallpox epidemics were common in Europe and the Middle East before the twentieth century, and the disease was a serious problem in some parts of the world until just a few years ago. Within the last 30 years, New York City was thrown into near panic when it became known that a foreign traveler with an active case of smallpox had spent several hours in Grand Central Station.

For centuries, doctors tried to discover a way to prevent smallpox. It was long known that people who survived an attack of the disease were immune to further infection. It was also well known that some persons contracted a relatively mild form of the disease. Thus, one method of trying to protect against a severe case of smallpox was to be scratched with the infectious material from a sore from someone with a mild case of the disease. This method, called "inoculation," was extremely hazardous and frequently resulted in the very condition it was designed to prevent. Nevertheless, it was widely practiced in the Middle East as early as the seventeenth century.

In England, persons who lived and worked near dairy farms were susceptible to a somewhat similar but much milder disease, "cowpox," that attacked both cows and humans. The disease was never fatal, and left only a few faint scars. Jenner—a doctor who lived and worked in the dairy country of Gloucestershire—was aware of the belief, commonly held in that area, that an attack of cowpox conferred immunity not only to further attacks of that disease, but to smallpox as well.

Jenner decided to test the hypothesis "An attack of cowpox confers immunity to smallpox." A report of his test is given by Isaac Asimov in *The Intelligent Man's Guide to the Biological Sciences*:

> In 1796, he [Jenner] decided to chance the supreme test. First, he inoculated an eight-year-old boy named James Phipps with cowpox, using fluid from a cowpox blister on a milkmaid's hand. Two months later came the crucial and desperate part of the test. Jenner deliberately inoculated young James with smallpox itself.
> The boy did not catch the disease. He was immune.

We can reconstruct Jenner's argument, using the model for confirmation listed in the preceding section.

1. *The hypothesis "An attack of cowpox confers immunity to smallpox" is initially plausible.*

It was widely believed in Gloucestershire that an attack of cowpox produced this benefit. Dairymaids and others who worked around cows, although very susceptible to cowpox, never seemed to get smallpox, even during raging epidemics. Another factor influencing the plausibility of the hypothesis was that mild attacks of smallpox conferred immunity to further attacks, and cowpox produced symptoms similar to those of *extremely* mild cases of smallpox. All of this made the hypothesis worth testing.

2. *If an attack of cowpox confers immunity to smallpox, then Phipps, who has had cowpox and is inoculated, is immune.*

The consequent follows deductively from the antecedent, with three auxiliary hypotheses:

(i) The smallpox matter with which Phipps was inoculated had not lost its potency.
(ii) Jenner knew how to inoculate, and he was qualified to observe whether or not Phipps actually had cowpox and whether or not he contracted smallpox.
(iii) Persons who are inoculated and who do not contract even a mild case of smallpox are immune.

The first two auxiliary hypotheses refer to the conditions of the test; the third is a theoretical background assumption, based on past experience with the disease.

3. *The observable prediction is true.* Phipps was immune.
4. *No alternative hypothesis has as high a prior probability as the hypothesis that is tested.*

Jenner's hypothesis is a causal hypothesis (having cowpox *causes* immunity to smallpox). Causal hypotheses are especially difficult to test because there are usually a number of alternative possible causes for what is observed. For example, some persons have natural immunities to some diseases. Phipps may have been one of those fortunate few who are naturally immune to smallpox. The alternative causal hypothesis "Phipps has natural immunity to smallpox," along with the same auxiliary hypotheses, has exactly the same observable prediction: Phipps is immune (even though he is inoculated).

The hypothesis of natural immunity, however, has a lower prior probability than the cowpox hypothesis. Although exact statistics were unavailable, it was known that natural immunity to this highly contagious disease was relatively rare.

5. *Therefore, an attack of cowpox causes immunity to smallpox.*

The hypothesis is confirmed.

Exercises

In each of the following:

(1) Identify the hypothesis.
(2) Try to state some observable predictions that follow from the hypothesis. Identify any auxiliary hypotheses that are required for your predictions.
(3) Try to formulate an alternative hypothesis to account for what has been observed.
(4) Compare (in a rough, non-numerical way) the prior probabilities of the original hypothesis and the alternatives you suggest. Indicate the sources on which your probability assignments are made. (For example, you might assign a very high prior probability to H because it fits well with established scientific theories; or you might assign a very low prior probability to H on the basis of your past experience with similar types of hypotheses.)

1. Medical scientists have noticed recently that the incidence of severe heart attacks in young and middle-aged men is far greater in a particular small area of Finland than in any other region of the world. Most of these men work as lumberjacks. Their diets consist of large amounts of meat, eggs, cream, and rich pastries—foods that are high in cholesterol. Medical scientists believe that diet is the cause of the high incidence of heart attacks.

2. A plastic surgeon who specializes in face-lifts recently commented that his youngest patients are frequently actresses. He believes that actresses seek face-lifts at an earlier age than other women because actresses' faces "fall" as a result of extensive massaging when they put on and take off their makeup.

3. In the chapter from S. J. Gould's *The Mismeasure of Man*, entitled "The Real Error of Cyril Burt," Gould discusses the views of one of the leading developers of "intelligence testing." Answer questions about Burt's hypothesis.

> [Burt] wonders about the intellectual achievements of Jews, and attributes it, in part, to the inherited myopia [nearsightedness] that keeps them off the playing fields and adapts them for poring over account books.

4. On the basis of annual data, Mr. Ehrenhalt [Regional Commissioner for the Bureau of Labor Statistics] said, fewer teen-agers (16 to 19 years old) in proportion to the youth population are working in New York City than in other central cities. While New York is at the bottom in the proportion of its young people actually holding jobs, he said, the city's rate of unemployment for that group has run below that in the major middle western cities hard hit by the recession.
The seeming contradiction, he explained, stems from the fact that a large element of youths here in the 16- to 19-year-old bracket have not been looking for jobs and, in many cases, have probably not even been thinking about working because jobs for young people are so hard to get here. Consequently, they are not counted as unemployed in population surveys, he said.

—Damon Stetson, *The New York Times*

5. Counseling and home placement programs can substantially reduce the number of juveniles locked up for minor status offenses, according to a federally funded study.

The study, done by University of Southern California researchers, evaluates a program undertaken at eight sites where efforts were specifically made to help juveniles stay out of detention facilities.

The Southern California researchers reported there was a reduction of 43 percent from preprogram levels in the total number of juvenile status offenders placed in detention at the eight sites.

Their evaluation added "Although this does not constitute proof that the program caused the reduction, since such reductions were part of the larger national trend in any case, knowledge of particular program activities makes us confident that a substantial portion of the reductions can be attributed to the program."

—Howard Benedict, Associated Press

6. [John Ferguson McLennan (1827–1881)] was interested in the early history of society, and charged that no one before him had attempted to reconstruct the social conditions of primitive peoples....

His major item of reconstruction was bride capture, which is still carried out in mock battles in some contemporary societies. Thus, among the Kalmucks, a prospective groom would go to the village of his bride, pay the bride price, and then carry the girl away on his horse, while the people of her village pursued them or made mock resistance. Or again, among the Welsh, the groom and his friends engaged in a mock battle with the friends of the bride, until the latter inevitably lost. Postulating that these customs were survivals from former actual situations of bride capture, McLennan set out to explain why women should have been taken in this manner. He arrived at the logical conclusion that there must have been a shortage of women [due to the practice of female infanticide.]

—A. de W. Malefijt, *Images of Man*

7. A rare Amazon "sea cow," one of only two manatees of its kind in the nation, died yesterday at the Pittsburgh Zoo.

The 200-pound, $5\frac{1}{2}$-foot creature was found dead in its tank at 8 A.M. It had been in apparent good health.

An autopsy by Robert Wagner, zoo veterinarian, failed to reveal the cause of death, but zoo officials speculated that a drop in water temperature during a heating failure Monday night might have been a contributing factor.

"It wasn't an old animal, as manatees go," Goodlett [Director of the Aquazoo] said. "They're believed to live about 35 years." [The 15-year-old manatee had been in the zoo for 13 years.]

Goodlett said the building's furnace went off at about midnight Monday night. Tuesday morning, the water temperature stood at 64°F., he said. The water is usually kept at 75–78°F.

—H. Pierce, *Pittsburgh Post-Gazette*

8. In the following excerpt from *The Bog People*, P. V. Glob is referring to studies of three Iron Age men, found in Danish peat bogs, where they had been buried for nearly 2,000 years. The circumstances of the burials, as well as their location, showed that the men had been deliberately killed, probably in conjunction with some ceremony. Bog water, which is saturated with soil-acids, prevented deterioration of the bodies, and the contents of the stomachs and intestines of the three men were examined and analyzed.

> In each of these last meals no trace was found of summer or autumn fruits, such as strawberries, blackberries, raspberries, apples, or hips; nor was there any trace of greenstuffs. There are thus grounds for thinking that all three

men met their deaths in winter or early spring, before everything had come into leaf. From this we may conjecture that the deaths took place at the time of the mid-winter celebrations whose purpose was to hasten the coming of spring. It was on just such occasions that bloody human sacrifices reached a peak in the Iron Age.

9. Catfish slime, a gel-like substance secreted by the fish, has remarkable properties that help heal wounds. . . . Richard S. Criddle, a professor of biochemistry and biophysics at the University of California at Davis, said that when a local Gulf species of catfish is caught, it secretes a slime over its entire body.

"I have used it myself on cuts," he said. "They heal entirely in 3 days, instead of the usual 10."

—S. Blakelee, *The New York Times*

10. Headline: EMOTIONAL PREPARATION AIDS SURGICAL RECOVERY. A study of 60 men undergoing coronary bypass grafts at the University of Iowa Medical Center was conducted recently. The men were divided into two groups. One group received the hospital's standard preparation for patients about to undergo surgery: a brochure on the procedures and a short visit from a nurse to answer questions. The other group watched a videotape called "Living Proof" that followed a patient through the operation and recovery. While 75 percent of those with the standard preparation suffered after the surgery from acute hypertension—a condition that can endanger coronary bypass patients in the first 12 hours after surgery—only 40 percent of those who viewed the tape had the problem.

—*New York Times*

IV. INCREMENTAL CONFIRMATION AND "ABSOLUTE" CONFIRMATION

Tests such as Jenner's test of the cowpox hypothesis and Galileo's test of the heliocentric hypothesis confirm usually in a relative or *incremental* sense. This means that the probability of the hypothesis *after* such a test is greater than it was *prior* to the test. A hypothesis is said to be confirmed in the "absolute" sense only when it is so strongly supported by evidence that it is almost certainly true. (Its probability is close to 1.) Many tests may have to be performed before a hypothesis is "absolutely" confirmed.

Even when a hypothesis is "absolutely" confirmed, there is always the possibility that new evidence will prove that it is false. Before Europeans learned about platypuses, the hypothesis "All mammals bear live young" was considered absolutely confirmed. When Europeans first heard reports of Australian egg-laying mammals, they assumed that the aboriginal Australians who described these strange animals were either mistaken or dishonest. However, the aboriginals were correct; platypuses are mammals that lay eggs.

Newton's Laws of Motion, long regarded as universally applicable and absolutely confirmed, are now—in light of Einstein's work on relativity—either regarded as only approximately true or considered restricted in their application to particles that are not moving at speeds close to the speed of light or that are not located in strong gravitational fields. To say hypotheses are "absolutely" confirmed means they are very strongly supported, and there is no evidence available that counts against them. It does not mean that there is no chance that they will be rejected in light of future evidence.

Controlled experiments and Mill's methods are often used to test causal hypotheses. Observable predictions deduced from hypotheses are often predictions about the outcome of controlled experiments. The Method of Difference and the Joint Method of Agreement and Difference are sometimes useful in eliminating alternative hypotheses. In controlled experiments, special attention is paid to auxiliary hypotheses that might affect the outcome of a test. The use of varied samples and the repeated use of Mill's methods play a role in the confirmation of hypotheses, for no important hypothesis is firmly accepted or rejected on the basis of a single test.

Any observable prediction that can be deduced from a hypothesis can be used to test it, but some predictions are more important than others. Consider, for example, the hypothesis that the mastadons and other very large mammals (megafauna) that once roamed North America and Australia became extinct because man "overhunted" them. One "prediction" that follows from the over-hunting hypothesis is that these mammals coexisted with man over a period of time. Archaeological investigation has proved this to be true. But this evidence does not confirm the overhunting hypothesis nearly so strongly as archaeological evidence of massive "kill sites" or "butchering sites" would, and such evidence has not been found. In fact, many archaeologists believe that the long period of coexistence between man and these animals counts *against* the overhunting hypothesis, and indicates an ecological balance between hunters and hunted.

In general, we can say that the more unlikely it is for a prediction to be true *unless* the hypothesis is true, the better the truth of that prediction confirms the hypothesis. In some cases, it would be very surprising if a prediction turned out to be true unless the hypothesis which gave rise to it were also true. A long period of coexistence for humans and megafauna would not be particularly surprising or unlikely, even if the animals became extinct as a result of some cause other than overhunting by humans. We know that extinctions sometimes occur as a result of destruction of habitat—which may be a result of human activities or of some natural force, such as severe droughts—rather than from human predation. Giant Pandas in China are now threatened with extinction, despite human efforts to prevent this, from loss of a suitable habitat. Thus, the evidence of coexistence does not weigh very heavily either for or against the overhunting hypothesis.

Proponents of pseudoscientific theories often try to find acceptance for their theories by pointing to successful predictions based on these theories. An example of this is found in *dianetics*—a pseudopsychological theory that predicts the remission of neurotic symptoms for people who undergo the therapy prescribed by dianetic theory (see W. Salmon: 1967, p. 119). Many persons who submitted to this treatment did improve, so we can say that the predictions of dianetics were true. The spontaneous remission of neurotic symptoms, however, is very common. Many people recover from their neuroses with no treatment at all, so the true predictions of dianetics do not constitute strong confirmation for the theory.

Astrology attracts many believers, who faithfully read their "horoscopes," follow the advice given, and note that many of the predictions contained therein turn out to be true. Consider some typical examples of these astrological forecasts, which are printed in many daily newspapers:

> What appeared to be immovable will now prove to be flexible.
> Apparent obstacle actually proves to be a stepping-stone toward goal.
> Be ready for significant change which could ultimately result in journey.
> Member of opposite sex does care, will plainly show it.
> Many people miscalculate when judging your capabilities.

All of these "predictions" are couched in such vague terms that they can be applied to many different types of situations that are not at all unusual or surprising in the lives of most people. The truth of such "predictions" does nothing to confirm the hypothesis that our lives are influenced by the positions of the stars and planets.

Exercises

1. For the following example, adapted from *Fads and Fallacies*, by Martin Gardner,
   a. Identify the hypothesis at issue.
   b. Identify any mistake in reasoning.

   > Mr. Smith is unable to get rid of an annoying cold. He decides to try a new doctor he has heard about. The doctor's methods are unorthodox, but he has been strongly recommended. The doctor assures Mr. Smith that his cold will be cured. The treatment requires Mr. Smith to take off his shoes and stockings and let the doctor shine infrared light on his feet for ten minutes. Mr. Smith returns for several more treatments at a cost of $15 each. After a week or so, Mr. Smith's cold has vanished, and he becomes one of the doctor's loyal boosters.

2. Find an example of a prediction made by some pseudoscientific theory, and explain why the prediction either does or does not support the theory.

V. DISCONFIRMATION

It is often said that scientific hypotheses cannot be *proved*; they can only be *disproved*, and that scientists should therefore try to falsify, or disconfirm, hypotheses rather than try to confirm them. Let us look at this suggestion in connection with the heliocentric-geocentric controversy.

According to the Ptolemaic system, Venus will not show a full set of phases; it will always have a crescent appearance, although the crescent will vary somewhat in width (see Figure 7-2).

Galileo could have used the following argument to *disconfirm* the hypothesis "The Ptolemaic (geocentric) system is correct." The observable prediction that follows deductively from this hypothesis is "Venus will not show a full set of phases."

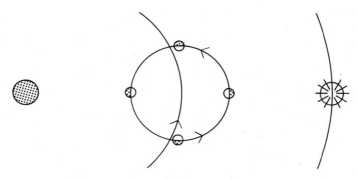

FIGURE 7-2

In the Ptolemaic system, Venus must always appear more or less crescent-shaped.

Source: Richard S. Westfall, *The Construction of Modern Science: Mechanisms and Mechanics* (Cambridge, UK: Cambridge University Press, 1971). Used by permission of the publisher.

If the Ptolemaic (geocentric) system is correct, then Venus will not show a full set of phases.
Venus does show a full set of phases.

The Ptolemaic system is not correct.

In the conditional premiss of this argument, the hypothesis is the antecedent and an observable prediction—which must be true if the hypothesis is true—is the consequent. This time, however, the observable prediction turns out to be false. The argument fits the *valid* conditional form of *denying the consequent*:

> If p, then q.
> Not q.
> ___
> Not p.

Thus, there is an apparent difference between *confirmation* of hypotheses, which we have said depends on inductive reasoning, and *disconfirmation* of hypotheses, which can be deductively valid. This discrepancy accounts for the greater enthusiasm that many scientists hold for the method of disconfirming hypotheses. The method looks particularly attractive when it seems that by the method of elimination, the true hypothesis will emerge. For example, if the geocentric hypothesis is rejected deductively, then the heliocentric hypothesis wins by default. However, as we have seen in looking at the geocentric-heliocentric controversy in its historical context, proponents of a hypothesis can try to "save" it by rejecting one or more of the auxiliary hypotheses that are required to connect the hypothesis with the unfavorable prediction. Although the Ptolemaic system is now rejected by astronomers, in Galileo's time its prior probability was too great to be outweighed by observations with an instrument that was not considered by many to be reliable. If the disconfirming argument were fully stated along with the important auxiliary hypotheses, it would read

If the Ptolemaic system is correct, and if the telescope is a reliable instrument of observation, and if Venus lies between the earth and the sun, then Venus will not show a complete set of phases.
Venus does show phases.

Either the Ptolemaic system is incorrect, or the telescope is unreliable, or Venus is not between the earth and the sun.

Faced with this conclusion, many of Galileo's contemporaries were willing to reject the reliability of the telescope rather than the Ptolemaic system. (See Galileo's own argument for the reliability of his telescope, Exercise #6, Chapter 1, Section III.)

The general form of this argument for disconfirmation is:

If H and $A_1 \ldots A_n$, then P.
P is false.

Either H is false or A_1 or $\ldots$ or A_n is false.

In this argument form, the conclusion follows deductively from the premises, but the conclusion is not simply a rejection of the hypothesis. The conclusion says merely that either the hypothesis is false or one of the auxiliary hypotheses is false.

In scientific practice, it is considered inappropriate to reject some auxiliary hypothesis *just to* "save the hypothesis" that would otherwise be disconfirmed. The arbitrary rejection (or addition) of an auxiliary hypothesis to save a favored hypothesis is called "*ad hoc* reasoning" and is regarded as fallacious. While everyone agrees that arbitrary rejection of auxiliary hypotheses is inappropriate, they do not always agree about whether or not a particular rejection is "arbitrary." Galileo thought his opponents were being arbitrary because they refused to look through the telescope. His opponents did not think they were being arbitrary because they knew that curved lenses distorted images, and so did not think that what they saw through a telescope could support Galileo's case.

When an auxiliary hypothesis is called into question and can be tested, it should be. It cannot be tested in isolation, however, any more than the original hypothesis could be. When an auxiliary hypothesis becomes the focus of attention, still other auxiliary hypotheses will have to be called in to connect it with its predictions. It is this sort of complexity that often makes the rejection of hypotheses no less complicated than their acceptance.

Even when the auxiliary hypotheses are accepted, trying to derive the true hypothesis with deductive certainty by eliminating incorrect hypotheses will not work. There is no theoretical limit to the number of possible false hypotheses that have to be eliminated. While we are not usually faced with an abundance of *plausible* hypotheses for testing, we may nevertheless overlook or be unaware of some that should be tested. A situation in which there are only two plausible competing hypotheses and in which the rejection of one "forces" us to accept the other hypothesis occurs far less often than we would like. Even if Galileo succeeds in rejecting Ptolemy's geocentric hypothesis, for example, the Copernican hypothesis is not thereby established, for Tycho's geocentric hypothesis is also compatible with the full set of phases of Venus.

1. Crucial Tests

Occasionally, scientists do find themselves in the happy situation of agreeing about auxiliary hypotheses and being faced with an observable prediction that confirms one of only two competing hypotheses at the same time it disconfirms the other. These *crucial tests* have received much attention in the history of science. Jenner's test of the cowpox hypothesis on young Phipps comes close to the ideal situation. There was a very small chance that Phipps was naturally immune to smallpox, but this was so unlikely that the inoculation seemed to settle the issue between the two real contenders: "Cowpox confers immunity to smallpox," and "Cowpox does not prevent smallpox."

In this case, as in most examples of crucial testing, the test that seems to settle the question definitively in favor of one of the hypotheses becomes possible only after prolonged investigation and many noncrucial tests. It is unrealistic to call even this kind of scientific reasoning "purely deductive," for the deductive rejection of one hypothesis is embedded in a series of complex inductive arguments. These inductive arguments serve to support the truth of auxiliary hypotheses, to establish prior probabilities, and to eliminate some alternative hypotheses. Such work is usually necessary before reaching the stage of performing a crucial test. The following example illustrates what typically happens in attempts to disconfirm well-established hypotheses. Like arguments of confirmation, arguments for disconfirmation of a hypothesis involve considerations of prior probabilities and the availability of alternative hypotheses as well as the relation between the hypothesis, auxiliaries and the observable prediction.

2. Disconfirming a Causal Hypothesis

Different Indian groups, each with distinct languages and cultures, live in the region of the Amazon River. Some of these groups are extremely hostile to neighboring tribes and are constantly engaged in violent warfare. The Yanomamö are known to be among the most warlike of the groups. Many anthropologists have long believed that the cause of their hostile behavior is the scarcity of protein in their diets. The warlike tactics, say those anthropologists, enable the Yanomamö to compete for scarce resources in an environment that is inadequately supplied with enough protein for those who live there.

However, when the hypothesis "Warlike behavior among the Yanomamö is caused by a diet deficient in protein" was recently tested, it was rejected by the two anthropologists who conducted the test (N. Chagnon and R. Hames, "Protein Deficiency and Tribal Warfare in Amazonia: New Data," *Science* 203(1979):910).

Chagnon and Hames spent 13 months living with the Yanomamö, carefully recording the foods they ate and calculating the amounts of protein in those foods. They found that the protein intake of the Yanomamö was greater than standard minimum daily requirements—that their diet was not deficient in protein. The argument for disconfirmation can be reconstructed as follows:

1. *The hypothesis has initial plausibility.*
      The truth of this hypothesis was the prevailing view among the anthropologists who had studied these people. This hypothesis is consistent with a widely accepted theoretic approach to the study of human culture, which views the material conditions in which people live as the chief factors in determining their behavior. It is also known that protein deficiencies have various effects not only on human physiology but also on human behavior.
2. *If warlike behavior among the Yanomamö is caused by a diet deficient in protein, then the diet of the Yanomamö will exhibit protein deficiency.*
      The observable prediction of protein deficiency in the Yanomamö diet follows deductively from the hypothesis and three auxiliary hypotheses:

   (i) The methods used by the investigators to measure amounts of available protein in the diet of the Yanomamö were accurate.
   (ii) The field study that lasted 13 months was long enough to provide a correct picture of the normal eating patterns of the Yanomamö.
   (iii) The "minimum daily requirement of protein" is a good measure of the amount needed to avoid protein deficiency.

      The first two auxiliary hypotheses refer to the conditions of the test. The third auxiliary hypothesis is derived from generally accepted theoretical knowledge of human nutritional requirements—the theory that is the source of information you see printed on boxes of breakfast cereal.
3. *The diet of the Yanomamö is not deficient in protein.*
      The observable prediction is false.
4. *Therefore, warlike behavior among the Yanomamö is not caused by protein deficiency in their diet.*
      Although the observation that the diet is not deficient in protein disconfirms the hypothesis, it does not conclusively establish that this hypothesis is false. This argument, like the arguments that confirm hypotheses, is inductive—if we regard the falsity of the hypothesis as its conclusion. Deductively, all we can say is that either the hypothesis is false or some auxiliary hypothesis is false.

Some anthropologists have questioned the second auxiliary hypothesis, that is, whether the 13-month study was long enough. Those who study the diets of people who live by hunting and gathering, as do the Yanomamö, have found that there are often sharp variations in the the amounts of available protein from one year to another. Excessive rains or droughts or epidemic diseases in animals that are hunted (events that do not occur on a yearly basis) greatly affect the amounts of available protein-rich food. Hunter-gatherers cannot count on steady supplies when environmental conditions are unusually severe. This particular study may have been conducted in an unusually good year for gathering and hunting.

Obviously, the results of this 13-month study are important. However, this one result is not enough to convince those who believe that the prior probability of the protein-deficiency hypothesis is very high. Additional tests, carried out over a period of years, would (if the results were similar to the results of the 13-month study) eventually overturn the hypothesis. In a situation such as this one, it is difficult to see what sort of crucial test could be devised to help us choose between the hypothesis being tested and some other hypothesis. No other causal hypothesis (except the negative "Warlike behavior is not caused by protein deficiency") was even formulated in this study.

Exercises

For each of the following, identify the hypothesis that is disconfirmed, and reconstruct (insofar as possible) the disconfirming argument, with reference to plausibility, disconfirming observations, and alternative hypotheses.

1. A student tells the teacher that a family crisis may require a trip out of town at the time of the next class period when a test is scheduled. The student fails to appear for the test, and the teacher surmises that the student left town to deal with the crisis. Then, immediately after the test ends, the teacher sees the student with a group having lunch at the Student Union.

2. You oversleep and are concerned about missing an appointment, so you dress hurriedly, skip breakfast, and leave the house as quickly as you can. When you return in the evening, you find the front door ajar and immediately suspect that a burglar is responsible. When you go inside, however, nothing is disturbed. The house looks exactly the way it did when you left in the morning, so you stop worrying about a burglar.

3. Cauterization was the only known treatment [for gangrene]; sometimes the patient was cured by it and sometimes the gray slough would reappear. Most surgeons regarded hospital gangrene and the other septic diseases as inescapable scourges, without troubling to do more than to speculate about their causes. Young Lister, [Joseph Lister, 1827–1912, who revolutionized surgery by the introduction of antiseptics] however, examined the results of the cautery treatment and reasoned that if some patients recovered and some did not, though all had been exposed to the oxygen in the air which most doctors vaguely assumed to be the cause of the trouble, then oxygen could not be responsible.

—A. Young, *The Men Who Made Surgery*

4. Researchers [at the national Centers for Disease Control] say they are convinced that, despite earlier worries, the [new hepatitis B] vaccine is not linked to the deadly acquired immune deficiency syndrome.

The vaccine, which became generally available last July, prevents one common type of hepatitis, a viral infection that causes inflammation of the liver.

Of more than 200,000 people who have been given the vaccine, only 118 became ill. Fifty-six of the illnesses were found to be unrelated to the vaccine. Only six of the people were seriously ill, the centers said.

The centers found no cases of immune deficiency in people who had received the vaccine since July, and just two cases, both in homosexual men, in the initial study and trial of the vaccine. . . .

Hepatitis B vaccine, first licensed in 1981, is made from the blood plasma of donors who have hepatitis B, most of whom are homosexual men. Because most of the donors are homosexual men, the centers said, there has been concern that the vaccine could be linked to acquired immune deficiency.

—*The New York Times*

5. In an attempt to make ecological sense out of a diversity of practices, including food choices and taboos, much attention has been given to protein as a necessity in potentially short supply. These various studies identify a particular potential for protein scarcity in a given situation and seek to demonstrate that the ecologically most important effect of certain aspects of behavior is the alleviation of this scarcity. Support for these interpretations has been offered in the form of the almost universal preference for meat over plant foods, a preference that, while not instinctual, is "biologically and culturally conditioned" and makes good nutritional sense as well.

Yet this general "Protein Hypothesis" faces a number of problems. Proteins per se are not recognized by most peoples of the world and thus are not considered in their evaluations. Furthermore, all meat is not preferred over all plants, and preference orders among animal foods do not correspond to protein contents. Certainly, high-quality protein is a requirement for survival, but since many people can give reasons for their food preferences, and since these reasons do not include the protein content of different foods, it becomes necessary to explore the link between stated preferences and nutritional consequences that include protein intake. One possible link between the two is the suggestion that, for lack of a better name, may be called the "Fat Hypothesis."

There are numerous examples of stated preferences for fat as a major attribute of food desirability. Animal foods are often clearly ranked according to fat content.

—M. A. Jochim, *Strategies for Survival*

6. *Background information:* Some birds, such as Clark's nutcracker, hide seeds and recover them later.

> Few people would want to wait several months near a nutcracker's cache, hoping to learn whether it was eventually dug up by the bird that buried it.
>
> Diana Tomback of the University of Colorado at Denver reasoned, however, that much could be learned from the way Clark's nutcrackers search for caches. She took advantage of the fact that birds leave a record of their searches in the form of beak marks in the snow and the earth where they dig. Moreover, successful searches can be identified by the presence of pinon-seed coats next to the holes from which seeds were taken. If nutcrackers search at random, successful probe holes and clusters of unsuccessful holes should be more or less evenly distributed over landscapes where the birds have searched. Tomback found, on the contrary, that unsuccessful probes were clumped around successful ones. The pattern indicated that nutcrackers were not searching for caches by trial and error. Furthermore, in the early spring (before rodents had found many of the caches), about two-thirds of the probes were successful, far more than one would expect of a random search.
>
> Tomback's observations do not prove unequivocally that the birds could remember where their caches were. They might have smelled them (although

again it is an unlikely possibility). Alternatively, they could have searched mainly in places of the kind that are likely to contain caches. Recent laboratory studies done by Stephen B. Vander Wall at Utah State University seem to rule out these possibilities.

—S. J. Shettleworth, "Memory in Food-Hoarding Birds,"
Scientific American 248:3, 106

7. In 1678 the Dutch physicist Christian Huyghens suggested [contrary to the accepted theory that light was made up of tiny particles] that light consisted of tiny waves. If it was made up of waves, there was no difficulty about explaining the different amount of refraction of different kinds of light through a refracting medium, provided it was assumed that light traveled more slowly through the refracting medium than through air. The amount of refraction would vary with the length of the waves: the shorter the wavelength, the greater the refraction. This meant that violet light (the most refracted) had a shorter wavelength than blue light; blue, shorter than green; and so on. It was this difference in wavelength that distinguished colors to the eye. And of course, if light consisted of waves, two beams could cross without trouble. (After all, sound waves and water waves crossed without losing their identity.)

But Huyghens' wave theory was not very satisfactory either. It didn't explain why light rays traveled in straight lines and cast sharp shadows, nor why light waves could not go around obstacles, as water waves and sound waves could. Furthermore, if light consisted of waves, how could it travel through a vacuum, as it certainly did in coming to us through space from the sun and stars? What medium was it moving?

—I. Asimov, *The Intelligent Man's Guide to the Physical Sciences*

8. Most any textbook [on the subject of pre-Neanderthal man] tells us that the men of Choukoutien cooked meat over hearths, predominantly ate venison, but also ate elephants, rhinoceroses, beavers, bison, and wild pigs, and on occasion one another.

Evidence for the use of fire was summarized by Teilhard de Chardin as so extensive as to need no further comment! In this judgment I must agree, but the evidence hardly justifies the picture one gets from textbooks of early man seated around his hearth roasting meat and carrying on a fireside chat.

The thickest layer of ash, in the upper-middle part of the cave deposit is up to *six meters* [more than 19 feet] deep. Stone tools and fossilized small vertebrates—rats and bats—were numerous in this layer, *sometimes indeed forming their own layers*. The ash deposit here is not in piles, but spread out in even layers, apparently the result of water movement. In the lower-middle part of the cave deposit, the ash layer is thicker near the south wall. *At its maximum, it is four meters deep.* It was around the fringe of this ash layer that most of the human fossils and stone tools were unearthed.

—Lan-Po, *The Cave Home of Peking Man*
—L. Binford, *Bones*

Note: The emphasis in the quoted passage is Binford's. His alternative hypothesis to the claim that early man was a cave-dwelling hunter of large animals is that early man was more of a scavenger who used caves, but who did not live in them, and who feasted mainly on the marrow in bones left by animal predators.

9. Hot water bottles, electric heaters and warm blankets may be no help at all to people suffering the effects of extreme cold, according to six Canadian researchers who found out the hard way. . . . They sat in tubs of ice water for one to two hours, until their body temperatures dropped as much as 8 degrees Fahrenheit, from the normal of 98.6 degrees.

Then they tried three alternative methods of getting their temperatures back up from those dangerously low levels. They sat in front of heaters. They exercised. Or they just shivered.

Shivering warms the body from the inside by letting muscles produce waste heat. It worked surprisingly fast—about three times faster than previous researchers have found.

Surprisingly, external heat appeared to make no difference. "We surmise that the heat blunted the shivering response," said Gordon Giesbrecht [one of the researchers]. "Paradoxically, when we kept the skin cool, it maintained the shivering stimulus and let the body do what it does best."

Exercise, which hypothermia [extreme cold] victims cannot always manage, was best of all, warming the body three times faster than shivering alone.

—James Gleick, *New York Times*

10. Until 1967, when a measles vaccine was licensed, about 500,000 cases of the disease were reported each year in the United States.

The disease was believed to be headed for eradication in 1983, when only 1,497 cases were reported, but the case count surprised researchers by rising in 1984, 1985, and 1986 [6,255 cases].

Nearly half the cases reported in the first six months of 1987 were in patients who had been vaccinated against measles.

One-third of those people had been vaccinated at 12 to 14 months of age. Researchers now believe that at that age the vaccine may be less effective.

—Associated Press

VI. BAYESIAN CONFIRMATION

When arguments for confirmation and disconfirmation are supplemented with considerations of prior probabilities, as suggested in preceding sections of this chapter, and when the requisite probabilities can be expressed quantitatively, *Bayes's Theorem*—a theorem of the mathematical calculus of probability (discussed in Chapter 5)—provides a formal model for arguments of confirmation and disconfirmation. In this section, we will look at Bayes's Theorem first, and then we will see how arguments similar to those we have already examined can be analyzed along Bayesian lines.

1. Bayes's Theorem

The probability calculus is used to calculate unknown probabilities on the basis of some already known probabilities. Thus we can use the "multiplication rule" (Rule 4, Chapter 5, Section II) to calculate the probability of a conjunction, when the probabilities of individual conjuncts are known:

$$\Pr(h_1 \text{ and } h_2|e) = \Pr(h_1|e) \times \Pr(h_2|e \text{ and } h_1)$$

Sometimes, we have information about a "set-up," such as the composition of a deck of cards, and we are interested in the probability of some outcome that has not yet occurred, such as drawing an ace. Such "pretrial" problems were discussed in Chapter 5. Other times, however, we may have already observed an outcome, such as four successive tosses of a coin resulting in a head, and we may be interested in what kind of set-up gave rise to that outcome. (For example, was the coin that was tossed and landed heads four times in a row a fair coin?)

Bayes's Theorem, which can be derived from the four rules of probability presented in Chapter 5, enables us to calculate these "inverse" or "post-trial" probabilities when certain other probabilities are known. To illustrate the theorem, we will consider the question just raised about whether a coin that lands heads four times in a row is fair.

Before we can use Bayes's Theorem, some prior probabilities must be known. In our example, we need to know the prior probability that the coin is fair as well as the prior probability that the coin is unfair. (Here, let's say that "unfair" means the coin is weighted to yield a head on every toss.) These prior probabilities are usually not the result of calculations, but are assigned on the basis of some background knowledge. If the coin is received in change from the grocery store, then there is a very high prior probability that it is a normal, fair coin. But if the coin is in the possession of person who is known as a prankster or a slick gambler who seems to be winning heavily, we might reasonably assign a very low prior probability to the fairness of the coin. For the sake of our example, we will assume the slick gambler holds the coin and that the prior probability that it is fair is only 0.1. Then, since the coin is either fair or not fair, the prior probability that it is *not* fair is $1 - 0.1 = 0.9$.

The next probabilities we need to know are the *likelihoods* that the observed outcome (four heads in a row) would have happened if the coin was fair and if the coin was not fair. If the coin is fair, the probability of obtaining four heads in a row is $(1/2)^4$, or 0.0625. If the coin is unfair (weighted to show only heads when it is tossed) the likelihood of getting four heads in a row is 1. If the *evidence statement* follows deductively from a hypothesis, then its likelihood is 1.

In addition, we need to know the probability that the observed evidence would occur without regard to whether or not the hypothesis is true. This is called the *total probability* for the evidence statement. It is based on the prior probabilities of each of the hypotheses that could give rise to the observed evidence as well as the probability that the evidence would occur, given the truth of each of the hypotheses. Suppose, for example, that we want to know the probability that a white ball will be drawn (e) when the ball may be drawn blindly from either of two jars (h_1) or (h_2). Let us say that each jar has an equal probability of being selected (the prior probability for h_1 is equal to the prior probability for h_2, and both are 1/2). But suppose that the first jar contains 50 white balls and 50 black balls, and the second jar contains 75 white balls and 25 black balls. If the ball is drawn from the first jar, the probability that it will be white is 1/2; but if it is drawn from the second jar, the probability that it will be white is 3/4. The total probability of drawing a white ball, regardless of which jar is selected is

$$[Pr(h_1) \times (Pr(e|h_1)] + [Pr(h_2) \times Pr(e|h_2)]$$

which, in this case, is $[1/2 \times 1/2] + [1/2 \times 3/4]$. This is equal to $1/4 + 3/8$, or 5/8, which is the total probability of "A white ball will be drawn, given that it is drawn from one of the two jars, each with a probability of 1/2 of being selected, one of which contains 1/2 white balls and the other of which contains 3/4 white balls."

Finally, Bayes's Theorem is applicable only when the prior probability of the hypothesis that is tested is greater than zero. The reason for this will be clear when we look at the mathematical formulation of the theorem.

We now return to our problem about whether or not the coin held by the slick gambler is fair. In the following representation of Bayes's Theorem, let h represent the hypothesis "The coin is fair," let $\sim h$ (not h) represent the other hypothesis "The coin is unfair," and let e represent the evidence "Four heads appeared in four tosses of the coin." Thus, $\Pr(h)$ is the prior probability that h is true, and $\Pr(\sim h)$ is the prior probability that $\sim h$ is true. $\Pr(e|h)$ is the likelihood that four heads will appear if the coin is fair, and $\Pr(e|\sim h)$ is the other likelihood. Finally, $\Pr(h|e)$ is the *inverse probability* that we want to calculate—the probability that the coin is fair, given the evidence of four heads appearing in four tosses.

Bayes's Theorem. Assuming that $\Pr(h)$ is not equal to 0

$$\Pr(h|e) = \frac{\Pr(h) \times \Pr(e|h)}{[\Pr(h) \times \Pr(e|h)] + [\Pr(\sim h) \times \Pr(e|\sim h)]}$$

(The probability in the denominator is the total probability for e. It is the probability that four heads will occur, regardless of which hypothesis is true. Also, we can see that if $\Pr(h)$ were zero, then the value on the left would be zero as well.)

Inserting the values for likelihoods and prior probabilities just assigned into this equation gives us

$$\Pr(h|e) = \frac{0.1 \times 0.0625}{[.1 \times 0.0625] + [0.9 \times 1]} = 0.0068$$

The quantity on the right, called the *posterior probability* of the hypothesis that the coin is fair, is lower than the prior probability of that hypothesis. In other words, after examining the evidence of four heads in a row, the probability that the coin is fair has been reduced from the prior probability of 0.1 to a posterior probability of 0.0068. The hypothesis that the coin is fair is thus disconfirmed.

Exercises

1. Among 300 freshmen attending a certain college, 100 are from out of state and 200 are state residents. Cars are owned by 50 of the out-of-state students and by 50 of the state residents.
   a. If a student is selected *randomly* (if each student has an equal probability of being selected), find:
      (1) The probability of selecting an out-of-state student without a car.
      (2) The probability of selecting a state resident without a car.
      (3) The probability of selecting a student with a car.

b. If the student who is selected randomly has a car, find:
   (1) The probability that the student is an out-of-state student.
   (2) The probability that the student is a state resident.

2. A total of eight points on a pair of dice can be rolled the "hard way" (4–4), or the "easy way" (3– 5,5–3,2–6,6–2). There is a prior probability of 1/36 of rolling an eight the hard way, but a prior probability of 4/36 of rolling an eight the easy way. (Can you see why this is so?)

   Suppose you know that someone has rolled an eight (this is the evidence), but you did not see the way the dice came up. What is the probability that the eight was rolled the hard way?

3. The object of a game of chance is to draw a white ball blindly from one of two jars, each of which contains 100 balls. One of the jars contains 75 white balls and 25 black balls. The other jar contains 25 white balls and 75 black balls. The outcome of a toss of a fair die determines from which jar the ball is to be drawn. If the die shows a six, the ball is drawn from the jar with 75 white balls. If any other face shows, the ball is drawn from the jar that contains only 25 white balls. Suppose you agree to play the game.
   a. What is the prior probability that you will be able to draw from the jar with 75 white balls?
   b. What is the prior probability that you will have to draw from the jar that contains only 25 white balls?
   c. What is the likelihood that you will draw a white ball if you draw from the jar containing 75 white balls?
   d. What is the likelihood that you will draw a white ball if you must draw from the jar containing only 25 white balls?
   e. What is the total probability that you will draw a white ball (the probability of drawing a white ball no matter which jar is selected)?
   f. Suppose that someone ahead of you plays the game and loses by drawing a black ball. What is the probability that your opponent's ball came from the jar containing 75 white balls and 25 black balls?

4. A candidate for state office is supposed to appear at a dinner in a city at the other end of the state from where she has a breakfast meeting. Her campaign manager goes ahead of her to help with arrangements for the dinner, and the candidate plans to fly over in time for the dinner, but her flight is cancelled. She figures that if she drives, her chances of arriving on time for the dinner are fifty-fifty (Pr = 0.50). Someone offers to fly her in a small plane, but she loathes small aircraft and is reluctant to accept the offer even though it means that she would be practically certain of of making the dinner that way. She calls her campaign manager, and he tries to persuade her to accept the small plane ride. He figures that his arguments had only about a 40 percent chance of winning her over. He goes to the dinner not really expecting to see her and she walks in on time. What is the probability that she took the small plane?

2. Using Bayes's Theorem to Test a Hypothesis

In this section, we will see how Bayes's Theorem can be used to disconfirm a hypothesis concerning prehistoric agriculture in America: "The diet of people in Ecuador during the Valdivian Phase (6th century) was based on intensive maize agriculture." The prehistoric beginnings of agriculture are of great interest to anthropologists, and the claim that maize agriculture was practiced at this early date in coastal Ecuador has been strongly defended by some investigators. This hypothesis was also initially very plausible because the ecological setting in coastal Ecuador is similar to many other areas in which there is evidence of early agricultural activity. Although in this case—unlike the exercise in which the prior probability of selecting one of the jars depended on the outcome of a toss of a fair die—we have no precise way of assigning a prior probability, we do know that the prior probability is rather high, so we will assign 0.7 to it. Then, the prior probability that the diet was not agriculturally based is $1 - 0.7 = 0.3$. Bayes's Theorem formally requires that $\Pr(h)$ be greater than zero, and this is reflected in our informal requirement that there is at least some plausibility for the hypothesis to be tested.

Anthropologists can learn what prehistoric peoples ate by examining their skeletal teeth. Dental caries (cavities), for example, are most frequent and severe in people whose diets are agriculturally based, less severe in gathering-collecting-hunting peoples, and least severe among strictly meat-eating hunters. (This is an important auxiliary hypothesis.)

The agricultural hypothesis was tested by a physical anthropologist, Christy Turner ("Dental Caries and Early Ecuadorian Agriculture," *American Antiquity* 43(1978):694), whose evidence consisted of a sample of 76 teeth recovered from six crania of individuals who had been buried in a Valdivian-period cemetery. These individuals were judged to have lived to an age at which they would be susceptible to caries (another auxiliary hypothesis). Two additional auxiliary hypotheses were stated by Turner:

(i) Maize, as it is usually prepared for eating, has strong cariogenic potential (it clings to the teeth and causes cavities).

(ii) T. D. Stewart's dental pathology review (*American Journal of Anthropology*, 1931) provides a good measure for incidence of dental caries among prehistoric Central American Indians whose diet was agriculturally based. (According to Stewart's review, 15.5 percent of all teeth of these individuals have one or more carious lesions.)

Using the agricultural hypothesis and these auxiliaries, the observable prediction was that in a sample of 76 teeth, approximately 12 (76 × 0.155) should have had at least one cavity. However, when the teeth were examined, there was not a single cavity on any of the teeth. (This is the evidence *e*.)

Using the expected average of 12 bad teeth in a sample of 76 to determine the likelihood of finding no cavities when our hypothesis is true and making certain assumptions about the randomness of the sample and the normal distribution of cavities in the population, there is only about one chance in 100 of finding no cavities in a sample of 76 teeth: $\Pr(e|h) = 0.01$.

Because our auxiliary hypotheses assure us that the incidence of cavities is much lower when the diet is not agriculturally based, let us assign the likelihood of 0.1 to discovering no cavities if the diet is not agriculturally based:

$$\Pr(e|\sim h) = 0.1$$

Now we are ready to apply Bayes's Theorem to determine the posterior probability of the hypothesis in light of the evidence:

$$\Pr(h|e) = \frac{0.7 \times 0.01}{[0.7 \times 0.01] + [0.3 \times 0.1]} = \frac{0.007}{0.037} = .19$$

The posterior probability that the diet was agriculturally based during the Valdivian period has been dramatically reduced by this test—from 0.7 to 0.19. The probability that the diet was not agriculturally based (since that is the only alternative) has been correspondingly enhanced—up from 0.3 (its prior probability) to 0.81.

The role of alternative hypotheses, which was not explicit in the first simple formulation of the hypothetico-deductive method, is apparent in Bayesian confirmation. To know what support some piece of evidence lends to a hypothesis, we need to know how probable the evidence would be if the hypothesis were false—that is, if some alternative hypothesis were true. For simplicity in our example, we considered only two alternatives, but we could have treated each alternate hypothesis about subsistence strategy (hunter-gatherer-collector, hunter, and agriculturalist) separately by assigning each one a prior probability and considering the likelihood that the evidence would occur for each case.

Bayes's Theorem helps us to understand why some tests are more valuable for confirming or disconfirming hypotheses than other tests. The evidence of no cavities is particularly damaging to the hypothesis because this would be so unlikely (only one chance in 100) if the hypothesis were true. Furthermore, there are many cases of hypotheses that we would like to test, but that do not deductively imply any observable predictions even when we consider the auxiliary hypotheses. In these cases, it is reasonable to ask how *likely* (or probable) a certain prediction would be if the hypothesis were true or if some alternative hypothesis were true. Bayes's Theorem helps us to see how these *likelihoods* raise or lower posterior probabilities by various amounts. The posterior probability is not as affected by an outcome that is very likely to occur whether or not the hypothesis is true as it is by an outcome that would be very surprising unless the hypothesis were true. Thus, this Bayesian pattern, or model, for arguments of confirmation and disconfirmation seems to capture our insights and intuitions about using the outcomes of predictions to judge whether a hypothesis is true or false.

Exercises

1. Approximately one out of every twenty American women develops breast cancer by age 50. For women whose mothers had breast cancer, the risk is higher (one out of ten). Early detection is important to prevent fatalities. Suppose that doctors develop an early warning screening test that is inexpensive and "non-invasive" (it does not involve X-rays or any surgical technique). The test, however, is not very reliable. So far, it has produced a false positive reading 20 percent of the time. When a test is positive, the patient is advised to undergo further testing with X-rays. Mrs. Griffen, age 50, has no symptoms or history of breast cancer in her family but she is considering having the screening test performed.
   a. What is the prior probability that Mrs. Griffen has breast cancer?
   b. Suppose that Mrs. Griffen has the test and that the result is positive. What is the posterior probability that she has breast cancer?

2. Suppose you see an announcement that all cars of your make and model are being recalled to correct a suspension problem. These models were produced at two plants: X and Y. You have no way of checking to determine which plant produced your model, but plant X produced about 80 percent of the make and model of your car, whereas plant Y produced only 20 percent. The automobile manufacturer estimates that about 90 percent of the models produced by plant Y have the suspension problem but that only 50 percent of the models produced by plant X have this problem.
   a. What is the probability that the suspension in your car will be defective?
   b. Suppose you take your car in to be tested and find out that the suspension is defective. What is the probability that your car was produced by plant X?

3. Based on recent statistics, the probability that a smoker who lives in a rural area will die from lung cancer is 0.00065. The probability that a smoker from an urban area will die from lung cancer is 0.00085. The probability that a non-smoker from an urban area will die of lung cancer is 0.00015; while the probability that a rural nonsmoker will die of lung cancer is 0.00001. Approximately 70 percent of the population live in urban areas, and about 30 percent live in rural areas. Assume that 20 percent of urban dwellers are smokers and that 10 percent of rural dwellers are smokers.
   a. What is the probability that an urban dweller will die of lung cancer?
   b. What is the probability that a person from a rural area will die of lung cancer?
   c. Given only the information that a person died of lung cancer, what is the probability that this person was an urban dweller?
   d. Given only the information that an urban dweller died of lung cancer, what is the probability that this person was a smoker?

4. A murder has been committed, and the police have brought in two suspects on the basis of circumstantial evidence. The suspects are similar in physical appearance, but one is a redhead and the other has brown hair. The police feel that one of the two suspects almost certainly committed the crime, but they think

there is a greater chance (80 percent) that the redhead, who has a previous record, is guilty. A witness who saw someone running from the scene of the crime says that the person had brown hair, so the brunette is brought to trial. The defense attorney insists that the witness be tested for reliability, and a test is set up. In lighting and other circumstances similar to those in which the crime occurred, the witness is correct about 90 percent of the time in distinguishing redheads from brunettes.

    a. Taking the performance of the witness into account and accepting the prior probabilities offered by the police, what is the probability that the brunette is guilty?

    b. If the witness had correctly distinguished the redhead from the brunette in 50 percent of the test cases, what would be the posterior probability that the brunette is guilty?

5. Recently, an advisory group of the National Cancer Institute turned down a proposal to study the possible link between breast cancer and fat consumption. The proposal was for a 10-year prospective study of women across the country, 10,000 of them on a low-fat diet to see whether their risk of breast cancer was lower than the additional 22,000 women who would form the control group. The reason the panel of experts gave for the turn-down, according to *Science* was "The hypothesis that dietary fat is a cause of breast cancer among women is plausible, but only weakly supported at present." Explain, in terms of the Bayesian model of confirmation, why the consideration raised by the expert critics is important.

VII. REVIEW

This chapter provides an introduction to the logic of confirmation. This methodology is based on the concept that certain claims that are not accessible to direct observation can be inductively supported or undermined by checking the truth or falsity of *observable predictions* based on those claims. Confirmation is of the utmost importance in scientific reasoning, and is also commonly used in everyday life. Confirmation often employs deductive arguments as well as inductive arguments, but its overall structure is inductive. The conclusions reached by using this form of reasoning may be false even though the premises are all true. This is to be expected, since these arguments make claims about what is unobserved on the basis of observations: future observations can lead us to reject claims that we currently consider to be highly confirmed. Several simple formulations of the *hypothetico-deductive method of confirmation* were considered but these were shown to be in need of supplementary features (prior probabilities and recognition of the role of alternative hypotheses) if they were to reflect sound scientific practice. This supplemented version of the hypothetico-deductive method can be viewed as a *Bayesian model of confirmation*, developed informally in Section III and formally in Section VI.

    Brief definitions of the key concepts examined in this chapter follow.

Ad hoc reasoning: This fallacious form of reasoning occurs when auxiliary hypotheses are rejected (or brought in) arbitrarily, merely to save a favored hypothesis.

Alternative Hypotheses: Hypotheses that are distinct from the hypothesis being tested, but that could yield the same observable predictions.

Auxiliary Hypotheses: Claims (often unstated) that are assumed to be true in the context of a test of a hypothesis. Auxiliary hypotheses are used in conjunction with the hypothesis being tested to derive observable predictions. There are two chief categories of auxiliary hypotheses: (1) those that claim that the conditions of the experiment or observation are "normal" (that reliable instruments are used by competent observers, and so on), and (2) theoretical auxiliary hypotheses that assume the truth of background theories.

Bayesian Confirmation: A method of confirmation that, like the hypothetico-deductive method, considers the observable predictions derived from the hypothesis and the auxiliary hypotheses. In addition, Bayesian confirmation requires taking into account the prior probabilities not only of the hypothesis being tested but also of the alternative hypotheses. A true prediction confirms the hypothesis if that hypothesis had a higher prior probability than any of the alternative hypotheses. This method of confirmation also accommodates observable predictions that follow inductively rather than deductively from the hypothesis and the auxiliary hypotheses. When numerical values can be assigned to certain probabilities, *Bayes's Theorem* provides a quantitative model for Bayesian confirmation.

Confirmation: Positive inductive support for hypotheses. "Confirmation" is used in both an *incremental* and an "absolute" sense. Hypotheses are incrementally confirmed by tests that raise their probability. Hypotheses are considered to be "absolutely" confirmed only when there is overwhelmingly strong support for them and when there is no available evidence against them. However, it is always possible for an "absolutely" confirmed hypotheses to turn out to be false.

Crucial Test: A test that confirms one and disconfirms the other of two plausible but incompatible hypotheses that are the only candidates for acceptance.

Disconfirmation: Inductive support for rejection of a hypothesis. Like "confirmation," "disconfirmation" is used in both an incremental and an "absolute" sense.

Hypothesis: A sentence to be tested by finding a prediction that follows from it and checking the truth of that prediction.

Hypothetico-Deductive Method: A method of testing hypotheses by deriving an observable prediction from the hypothesis along with any auxiliary hypotheses. The simplest version of the method says that if the prediction is true, the hypothesis is confirmed; and if the prediction is false, the hypothesis is disconfirmed. To provide a realistic account of scientific method, the simple version must be supplemented by considerations of initial plausibility of the hypothesis and by how the tested hypothesis compares to alternative hypotheses with the same observable predictions.

Likelihood: The probability of a piece of evidence relative to the truth of some hypothesis. Likelihoods are one of the types of probabilities required for using Bayes's Theorem as a model of confirmation.

Posterior Probability: The probability that a hypothesis is true after taking into account the results of a particular test. When Bayes's Theorem is used as a model of confirmation, the hypothesis is said to be confirmed if the posterior probability is higher than the prior probability, and disconfirmed if the posterior probability is lower than the prior probability.

Prior Probability: The probability of a hypothesis before taking into account the results of a particular test or observation.

VIII. EXERCISES

1. Suppose some hypothesis **H** is similar to other well-supported scientific hypotheses and that it does not conflict with any well-confirmed hypotheses. How is this information relevant to the confirmation of **H**?

2. Can prior probabilities be based on objective evidence rather than on personal beliefs about how likely a hypothesis is to be true? Give an example to support your answer.

3. Give an example of a hypothesis that you believe to be FALSE but which can be used as a basis for true predictions. Be sure to say what one of the predictions is.

4. When different alternative hypotheses have the same observable predictions, how can you choose among them?

5. Can true predictions establish conclusively a scientific hypothesis? Explain why or why not.

6. In the hypothetico-deductive method, is the argument from the truth of the observable prediction to the truth of the hypothesis deductive or inductive?

7. Is it usually possible to deduce an observable prediction directly from a scientific hypothesis without any additional assumptions as premisses? Explain why or why not.

8. "No matter how carefully a scientific hypothesis is tested, there is always a possibility that it may be rejected later in light of the discovery of new evidence." If this sentence is true, does it follow that hypotheses can never be confirmed but can only be disconfirmed or rejected?

9. Is it true that in most cases, there is only one scientific hypothesis that is compatible with all the available evidence? Explain your answer.

10. If a hypothesis has a very strong degree of confirmation, do further successful predictions raise its probability very much? Explain why or why not.

11. Is it always possible to construct and carry out a crucial test to determine once and for all which of two competing hypotheses is correct?

12. Are good scientific hypotheses typically nothing more than a summary of the observable evidence on which they rest?

13. When testing a hypothesis, can we simply assume that all of the auxiliary hypotheses required to support the observable prediction are true?

14. Can auxiliary hypotheses ever be tested? Explain.

15. If the prior probability of a hypothesis is zero, then why is it not suitable for testing using the Bayesian method of confirmation?

16. Can a hypothesis have a very low prior probability initially but become strongly confirmed as a result of a single favorable test? Explain.

17. Under what circumstances can a series of favorable tests fail to raise the probability of a hypothesis very much?

18. Suppose that you are taking a course in which you have done well on the midterm exams and homework, and that you studied for the final and thought you did well in that too, but then you receive a "D" when your grade report arrives. What prior probability would you assign to "There was an error in the grade report"?

Arguments in Which Validity Depends on Connections among Sentences

---

C H A P T E R   8

I. INTRODUCTION

In this chapter we will continue our analysis, begun in Chapter 6, of deductive arguments in which validity depends on *truth-functional* connections among sentences. We have already discussed *affirming the antecedent* (*modus ponens*) and *denying the consequent* (*modus tollens*)—as well as the fallacious forms that mimic these valid forms of inference. Two sentential connectives—often expressed by "if . . . then" and "not" in English—were introduced in Chapter 6. The truth-functional sense of "if . . . then" is given in the following table, where *p* and *q* represent any two sentences:

p	*q*	If *p* then *q*
True	True	True
True	False	False
False	True	True
False	False	True

The table can be summarized by noting that the conditional is true whenever the antecedent is false or the consequent is true.

The truth-functional meaning of negation is given in the following table:

p	Not *p*
True	False
False	True

The table can be summarized by noting that a negation is false whenever the original sentence is true, and vice versa.

Other connectives (terms used to form compound sentences)—expressed in English by "or," "and," and "if and only if"—can be assigned truth-functional definitions also, thereby allowing a large class of English-language arguments to be analyzed in truth-functional terms. We will begin by introducing a few more common forms of truth-functional arguments, and then present a general method for determining the validity or invalidity of *any* argument form in which validity depends on truth-functional connections.

It may be useful to point out that this area of logic, called "truth-functional logic," "sentential logic," or "propositional logic," is based on two important principles:

1. Every sentence is either true or false.
2. No sentence is both true and false.

The first principle is sometimes called "the principle of the excluded middle"; the second principle, "the principle of contradiction." The first principle assures us that a sentence such as "It is raining" is either true or false; the second principle assures us that the sentence "It is raining" cannot be both true and false. It should be understood that these principles apply to sentences in a *specific context of utterance*. For example, the time and place to which the claim "It is raining" refers is either understood or expressed. If this were spelled out explicitly, the sentence would be something like "It is raining on March 15, 1984, at Washington Square in New York City." Obviously, the sentence "It is raining" is true when it applies to places and times when it is raining, and it is false when it applies to places and times when there is no rain, but when the sentence is understood as referring to a particular time or place, the principles apply. Some sentences (generalizations) are understood as implicitly referring to all times and all places ("All men are mortal"). Properly understood, the principles of the excluded middle and contradiction seem obvious enough, and we will accept them in our study of logic.

1. Hypothetical Syllogisms

Hypothetical syllogisms have two conditional premises, and a conditional conclusion. The following argument is an example of a hypothetical syllogism:

> If inflation can be controlled, then businesses will expand.
> If businesses expand, then unemployment will decrease.
> _____
> If inflation can be controlled, then unemployment will decrease.

As in the conditional arguments discussed in Chapter 6, the conditional sentences in hypothetical syllogisms are treated as *material conditionals*. The connective "if . . . then" yields a false compound sentence only if the antecedent is true and the consequent is false. We can represent the form of this argument by letting "p", "q", and "r" stand for the antecedents and consequents in the premises and conclusion, using the same letter for the same simple sentence in each case:

> If p, then q.
> If q, then r.
> _____
> If p, then r.

For this argument form to be *invalid*, it must be possible for the conclusion to be false while both premises are true. However, this is impossible, since the only way the conclusion could be false would be for p to be true while r is false. But if p is true, then q must also be true for the first premise to be true. If the second premise has a true antecedent (q), then its consequent (r) must also be true, or it will not be a true premise.

In other words, if p is true, the sentence represented by "r" would have to be categorized as "false" in the conclusion and as "true" in the second premise for this argument form to be invalid. But no sentence can be both true and false, so the argument form is valid. The English argument just presented is an instance of this valid form, so it is a valid argument. In offering proofs of validity, we will follow this general procedure: we show that the attempt to assign truth and falsity to component sentences in such a way that true premisses and a false conclusion results will lead us to assign some component sentence contradictory values.

2. Dilemmas

In English the term *dilemma* is often used to refer to a situation in which a choice between two disagreeable alternatives must be faced ("Tom is in a dilemma; he must either give up the big party weekend or fail some of his midterms next week"). The original meaning of the term "dilemma" refers to a form of argument in which one of the premisses states the choice between the two alternatives. The two meanings are connected, for someone like Tom who is in a dilemma often faces the following sort of argument:

If I spend the weekend partying, then I will fail some midterms.
If I spend the weekend studying, then I will miss out on some good times.
I will party this weekend, or I will study.

I will fail some midterms, or I will miss out on some good times.

This argument is valid. (Remember that for an argument to be valid the premisses do not have to be true. If it is impossible for the argument to have all true premisses and a false conclusion, then the argument is valid.)

You have probably noticed that this argument is similar to, but slightly more complicated than arguments that take the form of "affirming the antecedent." In this dilemma form of argument, called the *constructive dilemma*, there are two conditional premisses. The third premiss states that one or the other of the antecedents is true, and the conclusion states that one or the other of the consequents is true. Using letters to represent simple sentences, this form of argument can be symbolized:

If p, then q.
If r, then s.
p or r.

---

q or s.

Before we show that this argument form is valid, we need to consider the truth-functional meaning of the sentential connective "or." Compound sentences that are connected by "or" are called *disjunctions*. Some disjunctions are *exclusive*, in which case "or" is understood to mean "one or the other, but not both." When a menu says "Soup or salad is included in the price of the meal," we understand that the disjunction is exclusive. If you want both soup and salad, you must pay extra.

Other disjunctions are *inclusive*. In these sentences, "or" means "one or the other, or possibly both." When a road sign says "This bridge is open to automobile or truck traffic," we understand that the disjunction is inclusive. The

English "or" is thus ambiguous; it has two distinct meanings. Some languages, such as Latin, have two different words for the two senses of "or."

For the purpose of analyzing forms of arguments, it is desirable to eliminate ambiguity in the important sentential connectives by agreeing on a single meaning. Logicians have selected the inclusive sense of "or." The truth-functional meaning of the inclusive "or" is given in the following table, where "p" and "q" represent any two sentences:

p	q	p or q
True	True	True
True	False	True
False	True	True
False	False	False

The table can be summarized by noting that a disjunction is true whenever one or both of its components (*disjuncts*) is true, and false only when both disjuncts are false.

Now we can see that the constructive dilemma form of argument is valid, for when the truth-functional meanings of "if . . . then" and "or" are adopted, if all the premisses are true, the conclusion must be true as well. For the disjunctive premiss ("p" or "r") to be true, at least one of its disjuncts must be true. Then, the conditional premiss that has that disjunct as its antecedent must have a true consequent to be true. But this means that "either q or s" (the conclusion) is true if all of the premisses are true. The English argument representing Tom's dilemma is valid, since it is an instance of a valid argument form.

Another version of the dilemma, called the *destructive dilemma*, is closely related to *denying the consequent* (*modus tollens*). Here is an example of an English-language argument that is an instance of a destructive dilemma:

If the reporter was doing his job, he was present at the political meeting.
If the reporter is intelligent, he would have known what was happening there.
Either the reporter wasn't present at the meeting, or he didn't know what was happening there.

Either the reporter wasn't doing his job, or he isn't intelligent.

The form of this argument is represented below:

If p, then q.
If r, then s.
Not q or not s.

Not p or not r.

This argument form is valid. (You can convince yourself that this is so by analyzing the form in a similar way to the analysis of the constructive dilemma just presented.)

There are several other variations of the dilemma form of argument. Frequently, the antecedent of one of the conditionals is the denial of the antecedent of the other conditional, and the disjunctive premiss then takes the form "*p* or not *p*." When this is the case, the disjunctive premiss is often unstated in English, since it is obviously true. In many cases, the conclusion is also unstated.

James Boswell, in his *Journal*, describes such an argument, offered by Pasquale de Paoli, the "George Washington of Corsica," when Paoli was trying to decide whether or not to marry:

> If he [the commander of a nation] is married, there is a risk that he may be distracted by private affairs and swayed too much by a concern for his family. If he is unmarried, there is a risk that not having the tender attachments of a wife and children, he may sacrifice all to his ambition.

Can you complete Paoli's dilemma with an appropriate premiss of the form "*p* or not *p*" and a conclusion?

In another variant of the constructive dilemma, both conditionals have the same consequent:

> If I win a scholarship, I'll have enough money for tuition.
> If I get a part-time job, I'll have enough money for tuition.
> I'll win a scholarship, or I'll get a part-time job.
> _____
>
> I'll have enough money for tuition.

This obviously valid argument illustrates another feature of dilemmas. Dilemmas do not necessarily present *unattractive* alternatives in the disjunctive premiss. We can be in a "happy dilemma," facing two pleasant alternatives, as well as an unhappy one.

3. False Dilemmas

When we are presented with two choices, we often consider the consequences of each and reason about them using one or another of the dilemma forms. When we do so we must be careful not to be misled by this form of reasoning into thinking that no more than two choices are ever available. Suppose, for example, that a young woman has received two proposals of marriage. Suitor A is very charming, but lazy and poor; Suitor B is dull but rich. The woman might construct the following argument:

> If I marry A then I'll be poor.
> If I marry B then I'll be bored.
> I must marry A or B.
> Therefore, I'll be poor or bored.

If she reasons this way, however, she constructs a false dilemma for herself. She can choose to marry neither suitor! She can also tell the lazy charmer that she'll consider his proposal when he settles down to work, or she can persuade the rich suitor to expand his horizons.

4. Disjunctive Syllogisms

In *disjunctive syllogisms*, one of the premisses is a disjunction and the other premiss states the denial of one of the disjuncts. The conclusion affirms the truth of the other disjunct.

Either the home team will win the pennant, or the fans will be unhappy. The home team won't win the pennant.

The fans will be unhappy.

This argument is an instance of the following valid form:

p or *q*.
Not *p*.

---

q

If the first premiss is true, then at least one of the disjuncts ("*p*", "*q*") must be true. The second premiss says that one of those disjuncts is false ("*p*"). The conclusion simply says that the other disjunct ("*q*") is true, which must be so if both premisses are true.

A variation on the disjunctive syllogism is

p or *q*.
Not *q*.

---

p

In this form, the second disjunct, rather than the first, is denied in the second premiss, and the conclusion affirms the truth of the first disjunct.

Because we have agreed to interpret "or" in its inclusive sense, the following argument *form*, which resembles disjunctive syllogism, is *not* valid:

p or *q*.
p

Not *q*.

Since "*p* or *q*" is true not only when one of the disjuncts is true but also when both disjuncts are true, affirming the truth of one of the disjuncts in the second premiss does not rule out the truth of the other disjunct. However, the conclusion in this argument form states that the other disjunct is false.

Nevertheless, the following English-language argument is valid:

> Joshua either failed the exam, or he passed it.
> Joshua failed the exam.
> _____
> Joshua did not pass the exam.

In this argument, "or" is clearly understood as exclusive, because it is impossible for Joshua to both fail and pass the same exam. However, since we have agreed to use "or" only in its inclusive sense, we cannot represent the form that demonstrates the validity of this argument unless we find another way to express the meaning of the exclusive "or." We could do this by introducing a *new* connective (we could call it "eor"):

p	q	p eor q
True	True	False
True	False	True
False	True	True
False	False	False

This table can be summarized by noting that an exclusive disjunction is true only when one of its disjuncts is true and the other is false.

It is possible, however, to use "or," "and," and "not" in the following way to express "or" in its exclusive sense:

> p or q, and not both p and q.

The valid form that the English argument is an instance of is:

> p or q, and not both p and q.
> p
> _____
> Not q.

("And" is another important truth-functional connective. Its meaning will be discussed in the next section.)

In our discussion of the *false dilemma*, we said that when we reason with this form of argument, we must be careful not to frame a disjunctive premiss that oversimplifies the options open to us by presenting only two alternatives when more are available. The same caution applies to disjunctive syllogism. Suppose, for example, that you want to buy a car. The owner wants a thousand dollars in cash, and you have only $500. You could argue:

> Either I come up with $1000 or I can't get the car. I can't come up with $1000. Therefore I can't have the car.

While this argument is formally valid, the first premiss probably does not represent all the available options. Perhaps you could persuade the owner to arrange terms that would allow you to pay $500 down and the rest later. Perhaps the owner is willing to come down in price for a quick sale. The mistake of looking only at the two extremes when intermediate alternatives are available is sometimes called "*the fallacy of black-and-white thinking.*"

Exercises

Which of the argument forms discussed in this section fits most closely each of the following English-language arguments?

1. If Roxanne knew that Cyrano spoke to her, she would have fallen in love with him. If she had fallen in love with Cyrano, Christian would have been disappointed. So, Christian would have been disappointed if Roxanne knew that Cyrano was speaking.

2. If stocks go up, bonds go down. If interest rates rise, bonds go down. Therefore, since stocks or interest rates will go up, bonds will go down.

3. Tina has volleyball scholarship offers at State University and at Smalltown College, one of which she'll accept. But she certainly won't take the offer at Smalltown, so she'll go to State University.

4. To pass a logic class, you must work exercises. To get a degree, you must pass a logic class. So if you intend to get a degree, you should do your logic exercises.

5. If the team wins next week, they'll go to the bowl game. If the team ties next week, they'll win the conference championship. But they will either win or tie next week, so they'll go to the bowl game or win the conference championship.

6. Either you buy a lottery ticket for the school library fund, or you care nothing about the library. But surely you care about the library, so you'll buy a lottery ticket.

7. If your lottery ticket wins you'll receive a good book for a prize; if your lottery ticket loses, you'll be supporting the school library fund. So either way, you'll get something good for your ticket.

8. If I stay up late to cram for the exam, I'll do poorly because I am so tired. If I don't stay up late to cram, I'll do poorly because I haven't read the material. So it looks like I'll do poorly on the exam.

9. If I keep up my studies during the term, I won't have to cram for the final exam. If I don't have to cram for the final, I'll do well on it. So if I keep up my studies during the term, I'll do well on the final.

10. Either extraterrestrial visitors have landed in the United States or the honest people who have reported seeing them are liars. But these people are not liars, so the extraterrestrial visitors must have landed in the United States.

II. SYMBOLIZING CONNECTIVES

Since we are treating validity as a matter of logical form, our task of formal analysis will be easier if we introduce symbols to represent truth-functional connectives. This will simplify writing argument forms, and it will also serve to remind us that the truth-functional meanings of such expressions as "if . . . then," "or," and the other connectives are considerably more restricted than the meanings of these terms in ordinary language. The English connective "if . . . then" has various meanings, but we will interpret it as a material conditional connective. Similarly, we will understand "or" in its "weak" or inclusive sense.

In addition to the following truth-functional connectives:

1. *Arrow* ($\rightarrow$): The connective "if . . . then" will be represented by a "$\rightarrow$" (called an "arrow") between two sentences.
2. *Tilde* ($\sim$): The connective "not" will be represented by a "$\sim$" preceding the sentence that is negated.
3. *Wedge* (v): The connective "or" will be represented by a "v" between two sentences.

We will also employ the truth-functional conjunction "and", represented by a "$\cdot$" (dot) between two sentences.

In ordinary English, a conjunction with two conjuncts, such as "John went to the movies, and Mary played racquetball," is true just in case both conjuncts are true. Otherwise, it is false. This is the logically important feature of conjunction, and it expresses the whole of the truth-functional meaning of "and," as shown in the following table. (The dot symbol [·] is used instead of "and." "True" is abbreviated by "T", and "false" is abbreviated by "F.")

p	q	$p \cdot q$
T	T	T
T	F	F
F	T	F
F	F	F

In English, we form conjunctions with other words besides "and." Some other conjunctions are "also," "but," "furthermore," "moreover," and "while." Sometimes we use a semicolon to conjoin sentences. Different conjunctions carry varying connotations. For example, "but" implies a *contrast* between the two sentences that are conjoined ("Jane won the election, but John lost"). "And" is sometimes used to connote *temporal succession* in the sense of "and then"

("Rosie finished the marathon and went to a dance that night"). However, as with the other connectives, logicians ignore these subtleties to concentrate on the logical force of conjunction as it affects the validity of arguments. The preceding table, called a *truth table*, assigns an unambiguous meaning to the dot symbol by stating conditions under which sentence forms containing the dot are true or false.

In addition to the truth table for "and" (the dot), the following three truth tables completely define the other truth-functional connectives introduced thus far:

p	$\sim p$	p	q	$p \rightarrow q$	p	q	$p \vee q$
T	F	T	T	T	T	T	T
F	T	T	F	F	T	F	T
		F	T	T	F	T	T
		F	F	T	F	F	F

It is a little unusual to regard negation ($\sim$) as a *connective*, since it does not connect two sentences, but it is similar to other connectives in most ways. Negation is called a "unary" connective; the others are "binary" connectives. Every negated sentence does contain another sentence (the sentence that is negated) so a negated sentence fits our definition of a "compound sentence."

It will be convenient to define one more truth-functional connective—the *material biconditional*. In English, the expression closest in meaning to this connective is "if and only if." The sentence "The roof leaks if and only if it is raining" obviously means that if the roof leaks then it is raining *and* if it is raining the roof leaks. Thus, the material biconditional is equivalent to the conjunction of two material conditionals, in which the antecedent of one is the consequent of the other, and vice versa. Since this is so, we could simply use the arrow and the dot to express this relationship: "$(p \rightarrow q) \cdot (q \rightarrow p)$." The left conjunct represents "p only if q," and the right conjunct represents "p if q." However, the relationship represented by the material biconditional is common enough in argumentation to use a special symbol (double arrow) to denote it. The truth table for the material biconditional is:

p	q	$p \leftrightarrow q$
T	T	T
T	F	F
F	T	F
F	F	T

A material biconditional is true when both components are true and when both components are false; otherwise, a material conditional is false.

III. SYMBOLIZING ENGLISH SENTENCES

For the purposes of analyzing English arguments in which validity apparently depends on truth-functional connections between sentences, we will symbolize the arguments by using letters ("*p*," "*q*," "*r*," "*s*," and so on) to denote simple sentences and the connective symbols ("→," "•," "v," "↔," and "~") to denote truth-functional connectives. When arguments are symbolized, the resulting expressions are argument forms.

Sentence forms are symbolic expressions that consist of letters for sentences and symbols for connectives. The relationship between sentence forms and English sentences is analogous to the relationship between argument forms and English-language arguments.

Before we can symbolize English sentences that contain more than two simple sentences, one last feature of our symbolism must be introduced. Some form of punctuation is necessary to avoid ambiguity in these sentences. In English, various punctuation marks (commas, dashes, semicolons) serve to eliminate ambiguity. Certain terms in English, such as "either," "neither," and "both," also perform this function. Our logical symbolism has just one form of punctuation— parentheses—which are used here just as they are in arithmetic and algebra.

For example, the expression

$$7 + 5 \times 3$$

is ambiguous, because one value is obtained when 7 is added to 5 and then multiplied by 3, and another value is obtained when 7 is added to the product of 5 and 3. When the expression is written

(1) $7 + (5 \times 3)$

the value is clearly 22. When the expression is written

(2) $(7 + 5) \times 3$

the value is 36. Parentheses tell us which expressions belong together and which arithmetic operations we should perform first. To determine a numerical value for an expression, we perform the operation *within* parentheses first and the operation that is indicated by the *main connective* last. Parentheses are used to indicate that the sign for addition in expression (1) and the sign for multiplication in expression (2) are the *main connectives*. In a similar way, parentheses indicate the main connective in sentence form, telling us whether the sentence form in question is a conditional, a disjunction, a conjunction, a biconditional, or a negation.

The following examples illustrate how parentheses are used in translating English sentences into formal symbolism.

1. Either Andretti won the race and the prize money is large, or his backers will not be happy.

p: Andretti won the race.
q: The prize money is large.
r: His backers will be happy.

(1) $$(p \bullet q) \text{ v } \sim r$$

In this sentence, "either" serves to group together all the components that precede "or." Both the occurrence of "either" and the comma prevent us from understanding the sentence in the following way:

(2) $$p \bullet (q \text{ v } \sim r) \text{ (incorrect translation)}$$

Just as in our example with numbers, a difference in the placement of parentheses can make a difference to the *truth value* assigned to the compound sentence. Suppose that "p" is false, "q" is true, and "r" is false. Then "$\sim r$" is true. Since (1) is a disjunction (its *main connective* is "v") that contains one true disjunct, (1) is true. However, (2) is a conjunction (its main connective is "$\bullet$") and the first conjunct ("p") is false; based on the same assignment of truth values to sentence letters, (2) therefore is false.

2. Neither rain nor sleet can keep the postman away, but only Superman could deliver mail in this snowstorm.

p: Rain can keep the postman away.
q: Sleet can keep the postman away.
r: Only Superman could deliver mail in this snowstorm.

$$\sim(p \text{ v } q) \bullet r$$

In this sentence, "neither" and the comma indicate that the main connective is the conjunction (in English, "but"). "Neither rain nor sleet can keep the postman away" has the same meaning as

(1) "It is not the case that either rain can keep the postman away or sleet can keep the postman away," or symbolically,

$$\sim(p \text{ v } q)$$

Alternatively, the "neither . . . nor" could be rendered

(2) "Rain cannot keep the postman away and sleet cannot keep the postman away," or symbolically,

$$\sim p \bullet \sim q$$

We see that expressions (1) and (2) are equivalent by examining the following truth table:

| | | | (1) | | | (2) |
p	*q*	($p \lor q$)	$\sim(p \lor q)$	$\sim p$	$\sim q$	$\sim p \cdot \sim q$
T	T	T	F	F	F	F
T	F	T	F	F	T	F
F	T	T	F	T	F	F
F	F	F	T	T	T	T

In this truth table, as in all standard truth tables, the initial columns display all possible truth values of the relevant sentence letters. There are just two sentence letters in this case ("*p*" and "*q*"). The third column displays the truth value of "$p \lor q$" for each combination of truth values of the sentence letters. The fourth column displays the values of "$\sim(p \lor q)$." The values in this column are opposite to the values in the preceding column ("$\sim$" turns true sentences into false ones, and vice versa.) The fifth and sixth columns display values of the negation of "*p*" (opposite to values in the first column) and the negation of "*q*" (opposite to values in the second column), respectively. The final column, which is identical to the "$\sim(p \lor q)$" column, gives the values of the conjunction of "$\sim p$" and "$\sim q$." Thus, the table shows that whatever values are assigned to the sentence letters "*p*" and "*q*," expressions (1) and (2) always have the same truth value. When this relationship holds between two sentence forms, the forms are said to be *logically equivalent.*

The logical equivalence of expressions (1) and (2) above is an example of *De Morgan's Laws.* The logician Augustus De Morgan (1806—1871) pointed out important similarities between some aspects of logic and ordinary algebra. The laws that bear his name can be stated in English:

1. The negation of a conjunction is logically equivalent to the disjunction of the negations of the conjuncts.
2. The negation of a disjunction is logically equivalent to the conjunction of the negations of the disjuncts.
3. The conjunction of two sentences is logically equivalent to the negation of the disjunction of their negations.
4. The disjunction of two sentences is logically equivalent to the negation of the conjunction of their negations.

In symbols, the laws can be expressed more simply:

1. "$\sim(p \cdot q)$" is logically equivalent to "$\sim p \lor \sim q$"
2. "$\sim(p \lor q)$" is logically equivalent to "$\sim p \cdot \sim q$"
3. "$p \cdot q$" is logically equivalent to "$\sim(\sim p \lor \sim q)$"
4. "$p \lor q$" is logically equivalent to "$\sim(\sim p \cdot \sim q)$"

Exercises

1. Translate each of the following English sentences into the sentence form that most nearly captures the meaning of the English sentence, using the suggested sentence letters and their assigned interpretations. Be sure to use parentheses when necessary to prevent ambiguity.

> p: Logic is easy.
> q: Logic is fun.
> r: Symbols can be used.

a. Logic is fun, but logic is not easy.
b. Logic is not easy unless symbols can be used.
c. Logic is fun only if symbols can be used.
d. Logic is easy, and logic is fun if symbols can be used.
e. Logic is not fun if symbols can't be used.
f.   Symbols can be used, or it is not the case that logic is easy.
g. Logic is fun if and only if it is easy.
h. Logic is neither easy nor fun.
i.   It isn't true that symbols cannot be used.
j.   Logic isn't easy if and only if symbols can't be used.
k. Logic is fun, but it isn't easy.
l.   Logic is easy; moreover, it is fun.

2. Using the preceding interpretations for "p," "q," and "r," translate the following sentence forms into English sentences:

a. $p \bullet \sim r$
b. $\sim(p \bullet r)$
c. $\sim(q \vee r)$
d. $q \leftrightarrow \sim r$
e. $p \bullet (\sim r \rightarrow q)$
f. $(p \vee q) \bullet \sim(p \bullet q)$
g. $r \rightarrow (p \rightarrow q)$
h. $(r \bullet p) \rightarrow q$
i. $q \bullet (p \leftrightarrow q)$
j. $(q \rightarrow r) \bullet (r \rightarrow q)$

3. Construct a truth table to show that the expressions "$p \leftrightarrow q$" and "$(p \rightarrow q)$ $\bullet (q \rightarrow p)$" are logically equivalent. This will be a four-row truth table, like the one that showed the logical equivalence of "$\sim(p \vee q)$" and "$\sim p \bullet \sim q$." Be sure to include separate columns for "$p \rightarrow q$" and "$q \rightarrow p$".

4. Construct a truth table to show whether each of the following pairs of sentences is logically equivalent. Be sure to indicate whether or not your truth table shows they are equivalent.

a. $p \rightarrow q, q \rightarrow p$
b. $p \rightarrow \sim q, \sim(p \rightarrow q)$
c. $p \rightarrow q, \sim(p \bullet \sim q)$
d. $p \rightarrow q, \sim p \vee q$

IV. DETERMINING THE TRUTH VALUES OF COMPOUND SENTENCES

When compound sentences are formed from simple sentences and truth-functional connectives and when the truth values of simple sentences are known, the truth values of the compound sentences can be determined. Consider the following examples of sentence forms, when it is known that "p" is true, "q" is true, "r" is false, and "s" is false.

1. "$r \rightarrow (p \cdot q)$" is true.
   This sentence form is a conditional with a simple sentence as the antecedent, and a conjunction as the consequent. Since its antecedent is false, it is a true conditional. We do not need to consider the truth value of the consequent in this case, because any conditional with a false antecedent is true.

2. "$(p \vee r) \rightarrow (q \vee s)$" is true.
   This sentence form is a conditional with a disjunction as its antecedent and another disjunction as its consequent. The antecedent has a true disjunct ("p"), so it is true. The consequent also has a true disjunct ("q"), so it is true. A conditional with a true antecedent and a true consequent is true.

3. "$p \cdot (r \vee q)$" is true.
   This sentence form is a conjunction. Its first conjunct is a simple sentence ("p"), with a true value. Its other conjunct is a disjunction with one true disjunct ("q"), so this conjunct is also true. The conjunction of two true sentences is true.

4. "$(p \cdot r) \vee s$" is false.
   This sentence form is a disjunction. Its second disjunct is a simple sentence with a false value. Its first disjunct is a conjunction with one false conjunct ("r"), so the conjunction is false. Thus, the disjunction has two false disjuncts and is false.

5. "$p \leftrightarrow \sim q$" is false.
   This sentence form is a material biconditional. One of its components is a simple sentence ("p") that is true. Its other component is the negation of a true sentence, so that component is false. Thus, the two components of the biconditional have different truth values, and the biconditional is false.

The general method for determining the truth values of compound sentence forms is to work from the innermost parentheses out, considering the sentences connected by the main connective last of all.

Exercises

Suppose that "p" is true, "q" is false, "r" is true, and "s" is false. What is the truth value (T or F) of each of the following compound sentence forms?

1. $p \vee q$

2. $q \vee s$

3. $p \cdot (q \vee \sim q)$

4. $(p \cdot q) \vee (r \cdot s)$

5. $(p \cdot r) \vee (q \cdot s)$

6. $p \rightarrow s$

7. $p \rightarrow (s \rightarrow r)$

8. $p \rightarrow (r \rightarrow s)$

9. $(p \cdot s) \rightarrow r$

10. $\sim(r \cdot s)$

11. $r \rightarrow (p \rightarrow (q \vee s))$

12. $r \cdot (q \rightarrow p)$

13. $\sim(r \vee s)$

14. $q \leftrightarrow s$

15. $(q \leftrightarrow r) \rightarrow p$

V. DETERMINING THE VALIDITY OR INVALIDITY OF ARGUMENT FORMS

Truth tables similar to those used to define truth-functional connectives may be used to prove the validity or invalidity of argument forms. Since every valid argument in which validity depends essentially on truth-functional connectives is an instance of a valid truth-functional *argument form*, the truth-table method provides an indirect test of validity for truth-functional *arguments* in English. Consider the following argument:

> If primitive peoples did not cross the Pacific Ocean, there would not be a strong resemblance between Polynesian artifacts and South American artifacts. But there is a strong resemblance, so primitive peoples did cross the Pacific.

Assume that sentence letters "*p*" and "*q*" are interpreted in the following way:

p: Primitive peoples crossed the Pacific Ocean.
q: There is a strong resemblance between Polynesian artifacts and South American artifacts.

Then the English argument is an instance of the following argument form:

$$\sim p \rightarrow \sim q$$
$$q$$
$$\overline{}$$
$$p$$

To prove the validity of this form (and thus the English argument), we need to construct a truth table with four rows to display all possible combinations of the truth values of the component sentence letters (p, q):

(1)	(2)	(3)	(4)	(5)
p	q	$\sim p$	$\sim q$	$\sim p \rightarrow \sim q$
T	T	F	F	T
T	F	F	T	T
F	T	T	F	F
F	F	T	T	T

In addition to the two initial columns for the sentence letters, there will be a column for each sentence form that is a premiss and a column for the sentence form that is the conclusion of the argument. There may also be additional columns for compound sentence forms that are components of the premisses or the conclusion. (In this case, we will have columns for "$\sim p$" and "$\sim q$". This will simplify reading the table, because to determine the truth value of "$\sim p \rightarrow \sim q$" we need only look at the columns for "$\sim p$" and "$\sim q$".)

To check the validity or invalidity of the argument form, look at the premiss *columns* (5) and (2) and the conclusion *column* (1). Note any *rows* in which the premisses are *all* true. (The first row is the only row in which both premisses are true.) Now check that row (or rows) to see whether the conclusion is true as well. If the conclusion is true in each case in which *all* the premisses are true, as in the truth table here, then the argument form is valid. If in some row the premisses are all true but the conclusion is false, then the argument form is invalid. The argument form above is valid. In the first row, the only row in which all the premisses are true, the conclusion is true as well.

Since a truth table displays all *possible* combinations of truth values of the premisses and conclusion, an examination of truth tables settles the question of whether or not it is *possible* for an argument in that form to have all true premisses and a false conclusion. By definition, an argument (also, an argument form) is valid if it is not possible for it to have all true premisses and a false conclusion.

Here is another example of an argument in English that can be tested by the truth-table method:

If we drive nonstop to New York, we'll need at least two days to recover; for if we drive nonstop we'll be on the road for 24 hours, and if that happens we'll need at least two days to recover from the trip.

The conclusion is stated at the beginning of the argument, which is an instance of *hypothetical syllogism*. If we assume that sentence letters "p," "q," and "r" are interpreted

> p: We drive nonstop to New York.
> q: We'll be on the road for 24 hours.
> r: We'll need at least two days to recover from the trip.

then the argument is an instance of the following form:

$$p \to q$$
$$q \to r$$
$$\overline{}$$
$$p \to r$$

This argument form contains three distinct sentence letters. An eight-row truth table is required to display all possible combinations of the truth values of these three letters. (In general, a table of 2^n rows is required when there are n distinct sentence letters.) In addition to the three initial columns for the sentence letters "p," "q," and "r," the truth table contains a column for each premiss and a column for the conclusion:

(1)	(2)	(3)	(4)	(5)	(6)
p	q	r	$p \to q$	$q \to r$	$p \to r$
T	T	T	T	T	T
T	T	F	T	F	F
T	F	T	F	T	T
T	F	F	F	T	F
F	T	T	T	T	T
F	T	F	T	F	T
F	F	T	T	T	T
F	F	F	T	T	T

Here, columns (4) and (5) display truth values of the premisses, and column (6) displays the corresponding truth value of the conclusion. Both premisses are true in only the first, fifth, seventh, and eighth rows. The conclusion is true as well in these rows. Thus, no row contains all true (T) premisses and a false (F) conclusion. This argument form is valid, and any English-language argument that is an instance of this form is valid.

Truth tables can also be used to demonstrate the invalidity of argument forms. *Affirming the consequent* is a fallacious (invalid) argument form:

$$p \to q$$
$$q$$
$$\overline{}$$
$$p$$

with the following truth table:

(1)	(2)	(3)
p	q	$p \rightarrow q$
T	T	T
T	F	F
F	T	T
F	F	T

Here, the premises are given in columns (2) and (3) and the conclusion is given in column (1). Note that in this truth table, as in many others, the initial columns do "double duty." When a sentence letter is either a premise or a conclusion, there is no need to repeat it in a separate column. In the third row, both premises are true but the conclusion is false. The table demonstrates that this argument form is invalid, because it is possible for an argument of this form to have all true premises and a false conclusion.

Although the truth-table method can prove the invalidity of an argument form conclusively, we should remember that such a proof does *not* show that any English-language argument of that form is invalid. Since not all valid arguments are valid truth-functional arguments, the English argument may be an instance of some other valid form. (Some valid forms, for example, depend on connections *within* the sentences in the argument rather than on connections among the sentences.) To prove that an argument is invalid, it must be shown that the argument is not an instance of any valid argument form.

Indirect arguments, also called *proofs by contradiction*, which were discussed in Chapter 2, can be handled by the truth-table methods. In an indirect argument, the proponent tries to prove a sentence by assuming that it is false (taking its denial as a premiss) and then showing that this assumption leads to some absurdity—either an obviously false sentence or an outright contradiction. (In Latin, this type of argument is called *reductio ad absurdum*; the assumed premiss leads to an absurdity.) Since if all the premises are true in a valid argument, the conclusion must be true as well, a valid argument that leads to an obviously false conclusion must contain at least one false premiss.

As we mentioned in Chapter 2, in ordinary language, the claim used as a premiss in an indirect argument is frequently supported by an opponent but rejected by the person constructing the argument. Indirect argument is a powerful method of proof in mathematics. Students of higher mathematics encounter this method frequently and recognize that assuming the denial of what they are supposed to prove provides a convenient starting point for constructing many a proof.

Consider the following example of a proof designed to show that there is no largest prime number:

Suppose there is a largest prime number (K). Let R be the number obtained by multiplying together all prime numbers less than or equal to K, and adding 1 to this product ($R = [2 \cdot 3 \cdot 5 \cdot \ldots \cdot K] + 1$). It is clear that R is larger than

K. R leaves a remainder of 1 when divided by any of the prime numbers less than or equal to K. Moreover, if R itself is not prime, then it is divisible by *some* prime, that is greater than any prime less than or equal to K. Hence, K is not the largest prime number.

To represent the form of this argument, let us use sentence letters as follows:

> p: There is a largest prime number (K).
> q: There is a prime number (R) greater than K.

The conclusion of the argument form is "$\sim p$." To use the indirect method of proof, the denial of the conclusion ("p") is taken as a premiss, and it is pointed out that if this is so, it has as a consequent another sentence "q." In addition, "q" has as a consequent the denial of "p." The form of the argument can be represented thus:

$$p$$
$$p \rightarrow q$$
$$q \rightarrow p$$
$$\overline{}$$
$$\sim p$$

The following truth table shows that this form is valid:

(1)	(2)	(3)	(4)	(5)	(6)
p	q	$\sim p$	$\sim q$	$p \rightarrow q$	$q \rightarrow \sim p$
T	T	F	F	T	F
T	F	F	T	F	T
F	T	T	F	T	T
F	F	T	T	T	T

Columns (1), (5), and (6) are premiss columns and column (4) is the conclusion. In this truth table—unlike the others we have considered so far—there are NO rows in which all the premisses are true. Although this may seem to invalidate the form, in fact it guarantees its validity. If there are no rows in which all of the premisses are true, then there can be no rows in which all the premisses are true and the conclusion is false! There are no rows in which all the premisses are true because the premisses contradict one another; at least one of the premisses must be false. Since the purpose of this argument is to show that the first premiss is false (it is the denial of the conclusion), this should not be too surprising. Any argument in which it is *impossible* for all of the premisses to be true is valid, for in such arguments, it is automatically impossible for all of the premisses to be true and the conclusion to be false.

It should be mentioned that when an argument of this form has more than one premiss, the argument may not indicate *which* of the premisses is false, only that at least one of them must be false. The preceding valid argument is said to guarantee the truth of its conclusion ("There is no largest prime number") because the other premisses are not considered questionable.

Exercises

1. Use truth tables to determine the validity or invalidity of each of the following argument forms. Be sure to say whether the form is valid or invalid.

    a. $p \cdot q$
       p
       $\sim p \text{ v } \sim q$
       ─────────
       q

    b. $(p \text{ v } q) \rightarrow (p \cdot q)$
       $p \cdot q$
       ─────────
       $p \text{ v } q$

    c. $(p \text{ v } q) \rightarrow (p \cdot q)$
       $\sim(p \text{ v } q)$
       ─────────
       $p \cdot q$

    d. $p \rightarrow q$
       $\sim(q \text{ v } r)$
       ─────────
       $\sim p$

    e. $p \rightarrow q$
       $p \rightarrow \sim q$
       ─────────
       $\sim p$

    f. $p \rightarrow q$
       $\sim p \rightarrow q$
       ─────────
       q

    g. $p \rightarrow (q \rightarrow r)$
       $q \rightarrow (r \rightarrow s)$
       ─────────
       $p \rightarrow s$

2. Using sentence letters and connective symbols, symbolize the following arguments and construct truth tables to help you decide whether the resulting argument forms are valid or invalid.

    a. Either the game has been sold out, or it has been canceled. If it's been sold out I won't be able to see it, and if it's been canceled I won't be able to see it. So I won't be able to see the game.

b. Either Jeremy won a scholarship, or he borrowed money for tuition. But he hasn't borrowed money. Therefore, Jeremy won a scholarship.

c. If it doesn't rain for two weeks in June, the garden will fail. If the garden fails, we won't have fresh tomatoes in July. So if it doesn't rain for two weeks in June, we won't have fresh tomatoes in July.

d. If the public is very interested in a sport like baseball, they'll pay plenty to see the games. The public does pay a lot to see baseball, so the public is very interested in baseball.

e. Professional baseball players can command big salaries, and they could do so only if the public supported them strongly. So the public strongly supports professional baseball players.

f. If I buy a new car, I'll be broke (because of the insurance payments). But if I buy an older car, I'll be broke (because of the cost of keeping it in shape). I must buy either a new car or an older car, so I'll be broke.

3. The following passage occurs in Sophocles's play *Antigone*. Antigone has admitted burying her brother, against the tyrant Creon's orders, and has been sentenced to death. Reconstruct her argument as a truth-functional argument, and translate it using appropriate symbols:

> *Antigone*: This punishment will not be any pain.
> Only if I had let my mother's son
> Lie there unburied, then I could not have borne it.
> This I can bear.

4. Reconstruct the following argument from *Les Liaisons Dangereuses* (C. de Laclos, translated by P. W. K. Stone) as a truth-functional argument, and translate it using appropriate symbols:

> Either you have a rival or you don't. If you have one you must set out to please, so as to be preferred to him; if you don't have one you must still please so as to obviate the possibility of having one. In either case the same principle is to be followed: so why torment yourself?

5. Reconstruct the following argument, using truth-functional connectives, and the suggested interpretations of sentences:

> In England under the blasphemy laws it is illegal to express disbelief in the Christian religion. It is also illegal to teach what Christ taught on the subject of non-resistance. [Therefore], whoever wishes to avoid being a criminal must profess to agree with Christ's teaching, but must avoid saying what that teaching was.
>
> —Bertrand Russell

p: You express disbelief in the Christian religion.
q: You break the law.
r: You teach what Christ taught on the subject of nonresistance.

6. Consider the following passage from *Middlemarch*:

> Poor Mr. Casaubon was distrustful of everybody's feelings toward him, espe-
> cially as a husband. To let anyone suppose that he was jealous would be to
> admit their (suspected) view of his disadvantages; to let them know that he
> did not find marriage particularly blissful would imply his conversion to
> their (probably) earlier disapproval. . . . All through his life Mr. Casaubon had
> been trying not to admit even to himself the inward sores of self-doubt and
> jealousy.
>   Thus Mr. Casaubon remained proudly, bitterly silent.
>
> —George Eliot

Try to cast Mr. Casaubon's reasoning into argument form, stating the premises and the
conclusion. Then select sentence letters, with appropriate interpretations, and construct the argument form that this argument fits. Use a truth table to test the validity of
the form.

7. Consider the following argument from *Nuclear Power and Public Policy*:

> Now either nuclear power is safe and catastrophic accidents are impossible,
> in which case no limit on liability is needed to protect the nuclear industry
> from bankruptcy or on the other hand, nuclear power is not safe and cata-
> strophic accidents are possible, in which case a limit on liability is needed
> to protect the nuclear industry from bankruptcy. If the limitation is needed,
> it can only be so because successful claims can be made against the industry.
> But successful claims can be made against the industry only when injury can
> be shown to be the result of a nuclear accident. And if this can be shown,
> nuclear power is not safe. Hence one cannot argue consistently, both that
> there is a need for a limit on nuclear liability and that nuclear reactors are
> safe.
>
> —K. S. Shrader-Frechette

   a. Represent the form of this argument, using the following interpretations of
      sentences:
      p: Nuclear power is safe.
      q: Catastrophic accidents are possible.
      r: A limit on liability is needed to protect the nuclear industry from
         bankruptcy.
      s: Successful claims can be made against the industry.
      t: Injury can be shown to be the result of a nuclear accident.

   b. How many rows are there in the truth table for this argument form?

8. On the basis of the following passage from *West with the Night*, can you construct a
truth-functional argument for the conclusion that elephants dispose of their dead in
secret burial grounds? What is the form of the argument?

> There is a legend that elephants dispose of their dead in secret burial
> grounds and that none of these has ever been discovered. In support of this,
> there is only the fact that the body of an elephant, unless he had been trapped

or shot in his tracks, has rarely been found. What happens to the old and diseased?

—Beryl Markham

VI. TAUTOLOGIES, SELF-CONTRADICTIONS, AND CONTINGENT SENTENCES

Some sentences have the interesting property of being true simply on the basis of their truth-functional structure. An example of such a sentence is "If it is snowing, then it is snowing." This sentence is an instance of the form "$p \rightarrow p$," and it is obviously true regardless of what the weather happens to be. Sentences of this type are called *tautologies*. Truth tables can be used to determine whether or not sentence forms are tautologous. If the column under the sentence form contains only T's, that sentence form is tautologous. If a sentence is an instance of a tautologous sentence form, then that sentence is a tautology.

Some truth tables of tautologous sentence forms follow:

1.

p	$p \rightarrow p$
T	T
F	T

This truth table shows that $p \rightarrow p$ is a tautology. Any English conditional in which the antecedent and the consequent are identical is an instance of this tautologous form.

2.

p	$\sim p$	$p \vee \sim p$
T	F	T
F	T	T

Any English sentence that is a disjunction with two disjuncts, one of which is the denial of the other, is an instance of this tautologous form. Examples are

   a. It is snowing or it is not snowing.
   b. John loves Mary or he does not.

3.

p	q	$q \rightarrow p$	$p \rightarrow (q \rightarrow p)$
T	T	T	T
T	F	T	T
F	T	F	T
F	F	T	T

An English instance of this tautologous sentence form is "If there's gold in the mine, then if the prospector finds gold then there's gold in the mine."

Tautologies belong to the class of sentences that are *logically true*. Their truth is a matter of their logical form and not a matter of what they say about how things are in the world. A sentence such as "If it is snowing, then it is snowing," tells us nothing at all about the weather, or anything else in the world. The meaning of "tautology" in the logician's vocabulary is somewhat different from the common usage of the term to refer to any obvious or uninteresting claim. Because of the empty or uninformative nature of logical tautologies, the two senses are related. Despite the fact that logical tautologies do not provide information about what the world is like, these sentences, which are true as a result of their form rather than their content, are interesting to logicians. One widely held philosophical view of the nature of mathematical truths is that they are all tautologies, and few people would deny the importance of mathematics.

Just as some sentences are true by virtue of logical structure rather than their connections with the way the world is, other sentences are false by virtue of their truth-functional logical structure. These sentences are called *self-contradictions*. In a truth table, the column under a self-contradiction will contain only F's. An obvious example of a self-contradictory sentence form is "$p \cdot {\sim}p$," with the following truth table:

p	${\sim}p$	$p \cdot {\sim}p$
T	F	F
F	T	F

The English sentence "It is snowing, and it is not snowing" is an instance of this self-contradictory form. Obviously, any conjunction that contains one conjunct that is the negation of another conjunct is self-contradictory. However, there are more subtle forms of self-contradictory sentences, such as

$$(p \rightarrow q) \cdot ((q \rightarrow r) \cdot (p \cdot {\sim}r))$$

It may not be apparent, without constructing a truth table, that this is a contradictory sentence form.

When the truth or falsity of a sentence depends not merely on its logical structure but also on how the world actually is, it is called a *contingent sentence*. Because the truth value of these sentences is contingent on actual states of affairs, they may be either true or false. Any truth-functional sentence form that is not a tautology or a self-contradiction is contingent. The truth-table column under such a sentence form will contain a mixture of T's and F's.

The following important relationship holds between the truth-functional validity of arguments and the tautologousness of sentences:

An argument is valid truth-functionally if and only if its corresponding conditional is a tautology.

The *corresponding conditional* to an argument is a conditional sentence with the following structural properties:

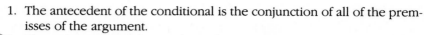

1. The antecedent of the conditional is the conjunction of all of the premisses of the argument.
2. The consequent of the conditional is the conclusion of the argument.

The corresponding conditional to the form *affirming the antecedent* (*modus
ponens*) is

$$((p \rightarrow q) \cdot p) \rightarrow q$$

The corresponding conditional to the form *hypothetical syllogism* is

$$((p \rightarrow q) \cdot (q \rightarrow r)) \rightarrow (p \rightarrow r)$$

Exercises

1. Explain why any argument with a tautologous conclusion is valid.

2. Explain why any argument with a self-contradictory premiss is valid.

3. Explain why there can be no valid argument that has all tautologous premisses
and a contingent conclusion.

4. Is the following claim true? "If two sentence forms are logically equivalent,
then the statement of their material biconditional is a tautology." Explain.

5. Write the corresponding conditionals for each of the following argument
forms:

   a. $p \vee q$
      p
      _____
      $\sim q$

   b. $p \rightarrow q$
      $p \vee r$
      $r \rightarrow \sim s$
      s
      _____
      q

6. Construct truth tables to show whether the following sentence forms are
tautologous, self-contradictory, or contingent. Be sure to say what the truth table
shows.

   a. $(p \rightarrow q) \rightarrow (q \rightarrow p)$
   b. $p \rightarrow \sim p$
   c. $\sim p \rightarrow p$
   d. $q \rightarrow (p \vee \sim p)$
   e. $(p \rightarrow q) \rightarrow (p \rightarrow (p \cdot q))$

7. Using sentence letters to represent simple sentences in English, translate each of the following into an appropriate sentence form that most closely captures the truth-functional structure of the sentence. Use a truth table to decide whether the sentence as translated is a truth-functional tautology, self-contradiction, or contingent sentence.

    a. You can't win if you don't try.
    b. The rain falls on both the rich and the poor.
    c. You win some, and you lose some.
    d. If you really love her, you'll tell her so.
    e. You're either with me, or against me.

VII. LOGIC AND COMPUTERS: APPLICATION OF TRUTH-FUNCTIONAL LOGIC

The ability to perform calculations at incredible speeds is an important feature of modern computers. The speed of computers depends on their electronic components; the calculating ability of computers depends on their logical design. Although computers work at remarkable speeds, they can accomplish their tasks only when the problems they are to solve can be analyzed in terms of basic logical operations, such as negation, conjunction, and disjunction.

    Following a few preliminary remarks, we will briefly discuss the role of truth-functional logic in the logical design of computers, using a rather primitive adding machine as an example.

1. Representation of Numbers

Numerals are symbols that are used to name numbers. You are familiar with *Roman numeral symbols* (I, X, V, L, C, D, M) and with *Arabic numeral symbols* (0, 1, 2, and so on). In addition to the various types of symbols that may be used to name numbers, there are many possible different *systems of numerals*. These numeral systems are distinguished by the number of distinct numeral symbols used to represent numbers.

i. Decimal System

The system familiar to all of you is the *decimal* system. It employs ten distinct symbols (0,1,2,3,4,5,6,7,8,9). The numbers zero through nine can each be represented by a single digit. Numbers greater than nine must be represented by more than one digit, using the familiar *place system*, which employs powers of 10. (Remember 10^0 is equal to 1, 10^1 is equal to 10, 10^2 is equal to 100, and so on.)

    In the decimal system, the *rightmost* digit stands for the number of units (10^0). The place left of that stands for the number of tens (10^1); the place left of that stands for the number of hundreds (10^2); and so on.

Some examples are:

67 represents 6 tens and 7 units, or

$$(6 \times 10^1) + (7 \times 10^0)$$

342 represents 3 hundreds, 4 tens, and 2 units, or

$$(3 \times 10^2) + (4 \times 10^1) + (2 \times 10^0)$$

1001 represents 1 thousand, no hundreds, no tens, and 1 unit, or

$$(1 \times 10^3) + (0 \times 10^2) + (0 \times 10^1) + (1 \times 10^0)$$

The decimal system is sometimes called a *base-ten numeral system*.

ii. Binary System

In the binary system, sometimes called a *base-two numeral system*, there are only two digits (0 and 1). The numbers zero and one can each be represented by a single digit. Numbers greater than one must be represented by more than one digit, and a place system, employing powers of two, is used in which the rightmost digit stands for the number of units (2^0; any number raised to the 0 power is equal to 1). The place left of that stands for the number of twos (2^1); the place left of that stands for the number of fours (2^2); and so on. Some examples are:

1001 represents the number nine, because it signifies

$$(1 \times 2^3) + (0 \times 2^2) + (0 \times 2^1) + (1 \times 2^0).$$

111 represents the number seven, or

$$(1 \times 2^2) + (1 \times 2^1) + (1 \times 2^0).$$

The binary system is not especially convenient for human calculators using paper and pencil, because it requires many more marks than are needed in the decimal system to represent identical numbers. Nevertheless, any number can be represented in either system; the fact that there are only two distinct symbols in the binary system is not a limitation in that sense. Furthermore, under some circumstances, it is more convenient to use a binary system than a decimal system. If information about numbers is transmitted as a series of electrical impulses on a wire, then it is simpler to distinguish only two types (using high current and low current) instead of ten types. Electrical impulses can be transmitted very quickly, so the disadvantage of having to write down long strings of symbols—as a human calculator who uses paper and pencil must—does not apply.

2. Binary Addition

Binary addition works just like addition in the decimal system. In the following addition table, the numbers above the lines (rows p, q) are the numbers to be added; below the lines, the left digit (c) is the carry digit and the right digit (s) is the sum digit:

p	1	1	0	0
q	1	0	1	0
cs	10	01	01	00

To summarize the table, the first column shows us that one plus one is equal to two (10 in binary notation); the second and third columns show us that zero and one added yield one (although it is written down here, the carry digit can be omitted when it is zero); and the final column gives the result of adding two zeros. The information about addition may be viewed in a form analogous to that of a truth table:

p	q	c	s
1	1	1	0
1	0	0	1
0	1	0	1
0	0	0	0

3. Constructing an Adder

To analyze addition as a *logical* operation, we can consider which of our familiar truth-functional connectives can be used to capture the functions represented in the c and s columns.

In the c column, there is a high value (1) when both p and q have the high value; otherwise the value is low (0). If we read 1 as T and 0 as F, the addition table for c is exactly analogous to the truth table for logical conjunction ($\cdot$).

Turning now to the s column, we can see that when p and q have the same value, s takes the low value (0), whereas when p and q have different values, s takes the high value (1). This is exactly the opposite situation from the one represented by the material biconditional connective. So one way of representing this s function is

$$\sim(p \leftrightarrow q)$$

Another way of representing this s function is

$$(p \cdot \sim q) \vee (\sim p \cdot q)$$

Exercise

Construct a truth table to show that these two forms are logically equivalent.

Now suppose that we have electrical switches that can physically realize the logical functions of conjunction, disjunction, and negation. For example:

Conjunction (See Figure 8-1): There are two input wires (*p*, *q*). When both wires carry high current (1), the single output wire from the switch carries high current. When either or both input wires carry low current (0), so does the output wire.

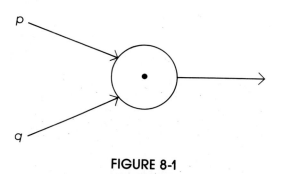

FIGURE 8-1
Conjunction

Disjunction (See Figure 8-2): This switch also has two input wires and one output wire. When either or both input wires carry high current, so does the output wire. When both input wires carry low current, so does the output wire.

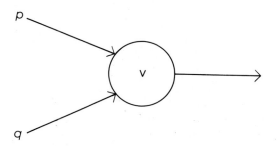

FIGURE 8-2
Disjunction

Negation (See Figure 8-3): This switch has one input wire and one output wire. It changes the current on the input wire from high to low and from low to high.

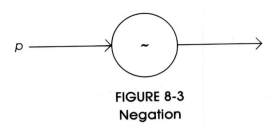

FIGURE 8-3
Negation

Using switches of this type, we can build our simple adding machine. We want to feed numbers, represented by impulses of high and low current, into the machine on the input wires p and q, and to have output wires that represent the carry digit c and the sum digit s.

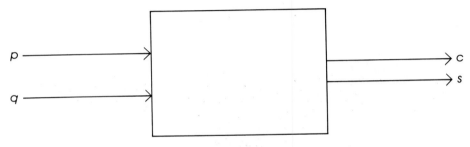

FIGURE 8-4
Adding Machine (external view)

Figure 8-4 is a "black box" representation of such a machine, so-called because although we can observe the inputs and the outputs, we cannot see how the machine works.

The internal workings of the machine are represented in Figure 8-5.

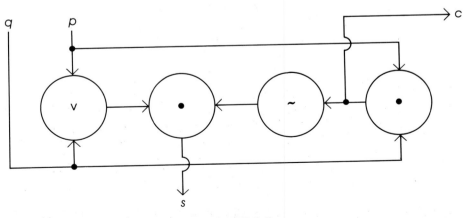

FIGURE 8-5
Adding Machine (internal view)

The simple adding machine, called a half adder, is quite primitive. Although it can add any two digits, it cannot add the carry digit from a previous addition. To construct a *full adder*, we need to consider binary addition for three digits (p, q, and a carry-in digit c_{in} from a previous addition). The following table provides the required information about binary addition:

p	q	c_{in}	c_{out}	s
1	1	1	1	1
1	1	0	1	0
1	0	1	1	0
1	0	0	0	1
0	1	1	1	0
0	1	0	0	1
0	0	1	0	1
0	0	0	0	0

Examination of this table reveals that c_{out} takes the high value in rows 1, 2, 3, and 5 (when all three inputs p, q, c_{in} are high, as they are in row 1, or when any two inputs are high and the third input is low). In row 2, p and q are high; in row 3, p and c_{in} are high; in row 5, q and c_{in} are high. Thus, we can express c_{out} as the following function of p, q, and c_{in}:

$$(p \cdot q \cdot c_{in}) \vee (p \cdot q \cdot \sim c_{in}) \vee (p \cdot \sim q \cdot c_{in}) \vee (\sim p \cdot q \cdot c_{in})$$

The same type of reasoning may be used to formulate s as a function of p, q, and c_{in}. The high value is assigned to s in rows 1, 4, 6, and 7. The high value is assigned whenever an odd number of components (either one or three) takes a high value; otherwise s is low. Thus, we can express s as the following function:

$$(p \cdot q \cdot c_{in}) \vee (p \cdot \sim q \cdot \sim c_{in}) \vee (\sim p \cdot q \cdot \sim c_{in}) \vee (\sim p \cdot \sim q \cdot c_{in})$$

The full adder will have three input wires and two output wires. Using three types of switches to realize the functions of negation, conjunction, and disjunction, the adder might be constructed as shown in Figure 8-6.

Many logical problems of computer design resemble these rather simple problems just presented, although, of course, they can be considerably more complicated.

4. Disjunctive Normal Forms

A *disjunctive normal form* is a disjunction, each disjunct of which is a conjunction. Furthermore, each conjunction contains exactly one occurrence of every sentence letter in that sentence form; the one occurrence may be either negated or unnegated. (The sentence forms for c_{out} and s above are called disjunctive normal forms.) It can be proved that for any truth-functional sentence form, there

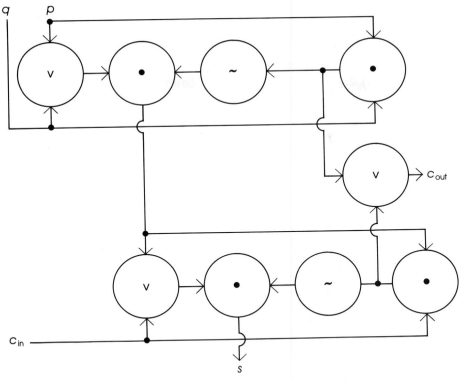

FIGURE 8-6
A Full Adder

is a logically equivalent disjunctive normal form. Sometimes it is desirable to design computers using only three kinds of switches (for negation, disjunction, and conjunction). In such cases, it is useful to have a method for translating sentence forms that contain other connectives into sentence forms that contain only tildes, dots, and wedges. One method for constructing the disjunctive normal form that is logically equivalent to any sentence form was first proposed by Lewis Carroll (*Symbolic Logic*):

1. Construct a truth table for the sentence form.
2. Note any rows in which the truth value of the sentence form is T.
3. For each row in which the sentence form is assigned T, form a conjunction in which each sentence letter occurs exactly once and is negated if and only if the sentence letter is assigned F in that row.
4. Form a disjunction using each of the conjunctions (constructed according to step 3) as disjuncts.
5. This disjunction is in disjunctive normal form and is logically equivalent to the original sentence form.

Exercises

1. Construct logically equivalent disjunctive normal forms for each of the following sentence forms:
   a. $p \rightarrow q$
   b. $p \leftrightarrow q$
   c. $\sim(p \rightarrow q)$
   d. $p \rightarrow \sim q$

2. Sometimes computers are designed with just one kind of switch, called a "nand" switch and symbolized by a stroke "|". This switch represents the negation of a conjunction:

$$\text{"}(p \mid q)\text{" is logically equivalent to "}\sim(p \cdot q).\text{"}$$

It is possible to use only the stroke connective to represent *any* truth-functional connection between sentences. Some examples are:
   "$\sim p$" has the same truth table as "$p \mid p$."
   "$p \rightarrow q$" has the same truth table as "$p \mid (q \mid q)$."
   "$p \vee q$" has the same truth table as "$(p \mid p) \mid (q \mid q)$."

Using only the stroke connective, construct a sentence form that is equivalent to:
   a. $p \cdot q$
   b. $p \leftrightarrow q$

3. Design a circuit with two input wires p and q and one output wire s, using only the connectives "$\sim$," "$\cdot$," and "$\vee$," that functions as an "exclusive or" switch.

4. Many lights are wired in such a way that they can be turned on or off at either end of a room. Use the logical connectives for conjunction, disjunction, and negation to work out a design for the circuit that controls these lights.

VIII. REVIEW

Chapter 8 was devoted to the study of various forms of truth-functional arguments, the translation of English arguments into argument forms, the use of symbols for sentence letters and connectives, and the use of truth-table tests to determine the validity and invalidity of argument forms. The *truth-functional connectives* represented in English by "if . . . then," "and," "or," "not," and "if and only if" were given truth-table definitions. Sentences that are true by virtue of their truth-functional structure (*tautologies*) and sentences that are false by virtue of their structure (*self-contradictions*) were also examined. The truth-table method for settling questions of validity and tautologousness can be cumbersome if many distinct sentence letters occur in the sentence forms and argument forms that are tested. An alternative method for proving validity or invalidity of argument forms and for determining whether sentence forms are tautologies, contingent sentence forms, or self-contradictions is presented in Appendix 1 to this text. This method is more convenient to use if more than four distinct sentence letters occur in an argument form or sentence form. In the last section of Chapter 8, an important application of truth-functional logic—the logical design of computers—was discussed, using the construction of a simple adder as an example.

A list of important definitions and argument forms covered in this chapter follows.

Truth-table definitions of logical connectives:

Conjunction:	p	q	$p \cdot q$
	T	T	T
	T	F	F
	F	T	F
	F	F	F

Disjunction:	p	q	$p \vee q$
	T	T	T
	T	F	T
	F	T	T
	F	F	F

Material Biconditional:	p	q	$p \leftrightarrow q$
	T	T	T
	T	F	F
	F	T	F
	F	F	T

Material Conditional:	p	q	$p \rightarrow q$
	T	T	T
	T	F	F
	F	T	T
	F	F	T

Negation:	p	$\sim p$
	T	F
	F	T

Some important valid argument forms:

Constructive Dilemma:

$$p \to q$$
$$r \to s$$
$$p \lor r$$
$$\overline{}$$
$$q \lor s$$

Destructive Dilemma:

$$p \to q$$
$$r \to s$$
$$\sim q \lor \sim s$$
$$\overline{}$$
$$\sim p \lor \sim r$$

Disjunctive Syllogism:

$$p \lor q$$
$$\sim p$$
$$\overline{}$$
$$q$$

Hypothetical Syllogism:

$$p \to q$$
$$q \to r$$
$$\overline{}$$
$$p \to r$$

Contingent Sentence: The truth or falsity of a contingent sentence depends on its content as well as on its logical structure. A sentence form is contingent if its column in a truth-table contains both T's and F's.

Corresponding Conditional: Every argument (and every argument form) has a corresponding conditional in which the antecedent is the conjunction of all of the premises and the consequent is the conclusion of the argument.

False Dilemma; Fallacy of Black-and-White Thinking: When we ignore a whole range of alternatives and think only in terms of extreme opposites (for example, "He is either my friend or my enemy"—when he could be neutral), we commit this fallacy. We are sometimes tempted to think this way when we construct arguments in the form of dilemmas and disjunctive syllogisms.

Logical Equivalence: Two sentences (or sentence forms) are logically equivalent if they always have the same truth value. If two sentences are logically equivalent, then the statement of their material biconditional is a tautology.

Self-Contradiction: A compound English sentence is a self-contradiction if it is false by virtue of its logical structure, regardless of its content. A sentence form is a truth-functional self-contradiction if its column in a truth-table contains only Fs.

Tautology: A compound English sentence is a tautology if it is true by virtue of its truth-functional structure, regardless of its content. A sentence form is a tautology if its column in a truth-table contains only Ts.

Truth-Table Test for Validity or Invalidity of Argument Forms: Construct a truth-table with an initial column for each distinct sentence letter in the argument. (If there are n such letters, the truth-table will have 2^n rows.) Construct a separate column for each premise and the conclusion. (There may be additional columns for compound components of these sentence forms as well.)

If there is some row in which all of the premises are assigned T and the conclusion is assigned F, the argument form is invalid. If there are no such rows, the argument form is valid.

Valid Truth-Functional English-Language Argument: An English-language argument is valid truth-functionally if it is an instance of some valid truth-functional argument form. (Note that a valid argument may also be an instance of some invalid argument form. An English-language argument is invalid only if there is *no* valid form of which it is an instance.)

Categorical Syllogisms

C H A P T E R 9

I. INTRODUCTION

Discussions of deductive validity in earlier chapters included examples of obviously valid arguments, similar to the following:

(a)

> No bird is a mammal.
> Every bat is a mammal.
> ___
> No bird is a bat.

(b)

> All birds can fly.
> Some mammals cannot fly.
> ___
> Some mammals are not birds.

(c)

> Every president is a politician.
> Some president is a statesman.
> ___
> Some statesman is a politician.

Each of these arguments is an example of a type of argument called "categorical syllogism." In ordinary discourse we rarely meet with arguments that are expressed in the standard form of the above examples. When the arguments are spelled out that way they look so obvious, it seems pointless to state them, let alone to develop a set of rules to determine whether they are valid or invalid. In fact, a seventeenth-century author of a treatise on logic raised doubts about whether the formal rules of syllogistic reasoning, which he admitted to be "the only aspect of logic traditionally treated with any care," are "as useful as is generally believed." For, he says, "If any man is unable to detect by the light of reason alone the invalidity of an argument, then he is probably incapable of understanding the rules by which we judge whether an argument is valid—and still less able to apply those rules" (Arnauld 1964:175). Despite his doubts, however, Arnauld went on to write a long chapter about the subject.

Syllogistic reasoning is worth studying for a number of reasons. These arguments, though not often completely stated, are so pervasive that they underlie a great deal of day-to-day reasoning. We are exposed to syllogisms from a very early age. Children's "why" questions are often given answers that can be construed as syllogistic arguments, for example:

(a)   Why do chickens have feathers?
         Because they're birds and all birds have feathers.
(b)   Do all birds fly?
         No, ostriches are birds, but ostriches can't fly.

Not all syllogistic arguments are so simple to evaluate as the three given at the beginning of this chapter. An understanding of the rules of the syllogism allows us to construct as well as evaluate more difficult syllogisms. Mastery of this common, well-understood type of reasoning also provides access to more difficult types.

In this chapter, the forms of categorical syllogisms will be analyzed and two different methods for determining their validity will be presented.

Categorical syllogisms, like hypothetical syllogisms and disjunctive syllogisms (discussed in Chapter 8), are arguments with two premises. However, categorical syllogisms are *not* truth-functional arguments. Techniques other than truth tables are required to assess the formal validity of categorical syllogisms. All three of the preceding categorical syllogisms are valid. The validity of these arguments, however, does not depend on truth-functional connections among sentences. If we represented the structure of these arguments by using sentence letters to denote simple sentences, each argument would be an instance of the obviously invalid form:

$$p$$
$$\underline{q}$$
$$r$$

Intrasentence structures—connections between classes named by subject terms of categorical sentences and classes named by predicate terms of categorical sentences—must be considered to discover the forms by virtue of which these arguments are valid.

II. CATEGORICAL SENTENCES

In arguments (a), (b), and (c), only four basic types of sentences occur. These are the four types of *categorical sentences*. If we let the letter "*S*" represent the subject terms and the letter "*P*" represent the predicate terms, we can characterize the forms of the four types of categorical sentences in the following standard way:

1. Every *S* is *P*.
2. No *S* is *P*.
3. Some *S* is *P*.
4. Some *S* is not *P*.

The form of the first type of categorical sentence, "Every *S* is *P*," is the already familiar *affirmative universal generalization*, which can also be stated "All *S* are *P*." Sentences of this form state that all the members of the *class* denoted by the term "*S*" are members of the *class* denoted by the term "*P*." Another way of stating the same thing is to say "the subject class is included in the predicate class." (The logic of categorical syllogisms is sometimes called "the logic of classes.") "Every junior at the University is an undergraduate" is an example of an affirmative universal sentence in which "junior at the University" refers to the subject class and "undergraduate" refers to the predicate class.

The second type of categorical sentence, "No *S* is *P*," is a *negative universal generalization*. This type of sentence states that no members of the class *S* are members of the class *P*. Alternatively, this sentence could be interpreted as "the subject and predicate classes do not overlap," or "the subject and predicate classes exclude one another." "No professional football player is a ballerina" is a negative universal sentence in which "professional football players" is the subject and "ballerina" is the predicate.

The third type of categorical sentence, "Some *S* is *P*," is an *affirmative particular generalization*, also called an *affirmative existential generalization*. This type of sentence says that at least one individual is a member of the class *S* and also of the class *P*. (This is a *general* sentence because no member is actually identified; the sentence just says there is *some* such member.) Another way of stating the same thing is to say "the subject and predicate classes overlap to the extent that they share at least one member." "Some dog is brown" is an example of an affirmative particular generalization.

The fourth type of categorical sentence, "Some *S* is not *P*," is a *negative existential* (or *particular*) *generalization*. Sentences of this form state that something (at least one thing) that is a member of the class *S* is not also a member of the class *P*. That is to say, there is at least one member of *S* such that given any individual member of *P*, it is not identical with that member of *S*. This alternate formulation, although quite awkward in English, will be useful in our later discussion of an important feature of the negative existential generalization. "Some dog is not brown" or "There is at least one dog such that no brown thing is identical with it" is an example of a negative existential generalization.

1. The Square of Opposition

Syllogistic logic was developed by Aristotle more than 2,300 years ago. Aristotle made the first attempt to formalize principles of valid arguments and was so successful that much of what he developed has continued to be studied in logic classes from antiquity to the present day. Only the geometry developed by Euclid, at roughly the same time Aristotle achieved his results, has secured a comparable position in western intellectual history. In addition to his interest in the validity of syllogisms, Aristotle was concerned with various relationships among the four types of categorical sentences when each had the same subject and predicate. These relationships can be considered by displaying the four types of sentences in a square of opposition, shown in Figure 9-1.

(A)   Every *S* is *P*.   (E)   No *S* is *P*.

(I)   Some *S* is *P*.   (O)   Some *S* is not *P*.

FIGURE 9-1
Square of Opposition

The letters *A*, *E*, *I*, and *O* have been used since medieval times to denote the four types of categorical sentences. *A*, which represents the universal affirmative, is the first vowel of the Latin "Affirmo," or "I affirm." *I*, which denotes the particular affirmative, is the second vowel of the same Latin word. *E*, which identifies the universal negative, is the first vowel of the Latin "Nego," or "I deny," and *O*, which represents the particular negative, is the second vowel of the same Latin word.

i. Relationships Among Categorical Sentences

According to Aristotle's system of logic, the following relationships hold between pairs of categorical sentences:

1. The *A* sentence and the *O* sentence are *contradictory* to one another, as are the *E* sentence and the *I* sentence.

   To say that two sentences are *contradictories* means that when one sentence of the pair is true, the other sentence must be false. Clearly if "Every *S* is *P*" is true, then it must be false that "Some *S* is not *P*." And if it is true that "Some *S* is not *P*," then it cannot be the case that "Every *S* is *P*." With regard to the *E* and *I* sentences, if "No *S* is *P*, it must be false that "Some *S* is *P*." Similarly, if it is true that "Some *S* is *P*," then it must be false that "No *S* is *P*." The sentence forms that are *diagonally* opposite one another on the square of opposition are "opposites" in the sense that they are logically contradictory to one another.

2. The *A* sentence and the *E* sentence are *contrary* to one another.

   Two sentences are *contraries* when they could not both be true, although they could both be false. The sentences "Every dog is brown" and "No dog is brown" are contraries, and both sentences are false. The sentences "Every football player is an athlete" and "No football player is an athlete" are contraries, but only the second sentence is false. The sentence forms that are opposite one another at the *top* of the square of opposition are "opposites" in the sense that they are logically contrary to one another.

   It is proper to use the terms *contradictory* and *contrary* to apply to pairs of sentences that are not categorical sentences. For example, "My only brother weighs more than my only sister" and "My only sister weighs more than my only brother" are contraries, even though neither sentence is categorical. Both of these sentences could not be true, although they could both be false (if my siblings weigh exactly the same).

   Referring to truth-functional sentence forms, any pair of the forms "*p*" and "~*p*" is a contradictory pair, whether or not "*p*" is a categorical sentence. (Remember that a sentence letter may represent any sentence whatsoever, although when we were interested in capturing structural relationships among sentences, we used sentence letters to represent *simple* sentences.) The sentences "It is raining" and "It is not raining" are obviously contradictories.

   In critical thinking, it is important to be clear about the difference between contradictory and contrary pairs of sentences. It would be a mistake, for example, to conclude "Sally hates me" from the premiss "Sally doesn't love me." Although the sentences "Sally hates me" and "Sally loves me" are contrary to one another, they are not contradictory. Therefore, we cannot conclude that because one of them is false, the other must be true. They could both be false. The English term "incompatible" is ambiguous when it is applied to pairs of sentences that do not "agree" with one another. "Incompatible" sometimes refers to contraries, and sometimes refers to contradictories.

3. The *I* and the *O* sentences could not both be false, but they could both be true.

Sentences that are related to one another in this way are called *subcontraries*. The English sentences "Some dog is brown" and "Some dog is not brown" are subcontraries; both are true. The pair "Some men are mortal" and "Some men are not mortal" are subcontraries, but only the first sentence is true. The sentences on opposite sides of the *bottom* of the square of opposition are "opposite" in the sense that they are subcontraries. Contrary pairs of sentences are frequently mistaken for contradictories but subcontraries are not often mistaken for contradictories. When this mistake does arise, it can often be traced to confusion about the placement of "not" in English sentences. For example, the sentences

> (i)   "Elizabeth II is the queen of England."
> (ii) "Elizabeth II is not the queen of England."

are contradictories. In sentence (i), inserting "not" after the verb has the same logical force as prefixing sentence (i) with "It is not the case that."

Despite similarities, however, particular generalizations are logically different from (i) and (ii), and inserting a "not" after the verb has a different logical force than prefixing "It is not the case that." Consider the following pair of sentences:

> (iii) Some women are queens.
> (iv)   Some women are not queens.

These sentences are not contradictories. They are both true, and they are subcontraries.

4. The *I* sentence is a logical consequence of (is implied by) the *A* sentence; and the *O* sentence is a logical consequence of (is implied by) the *E* sentence (see Figure 9-2).

It seems reasonable to say that if it is true that every *S* is *P*, then some *S* is *P*. Similarly, if "No *S* is *P*," is true, then it must be the case that "Some *S* is not *P*."

This relationship between the *A* and *I* sentences, and between the *E* and *O* sentences is called *subimplication*, because the sentences at the top of the square of opposition *imply* the sentences below them. If the *A* sentence is true, then

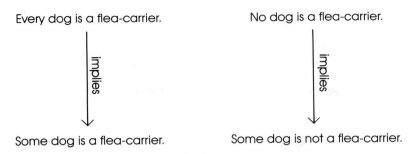

FIGURE 9-2

the *I* sentence must be true as well; if the *E* sentence is true, then the *O* sentence must be true also.

The relationships among categorical sentences in the Aristotelian square of opposition can be represented by arrows, as shown in Figure 9-3.

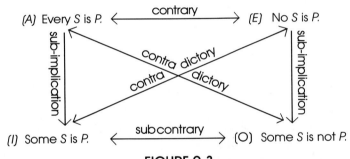

FIGURE 9-3
Aristotelian Square of Opposition

Exercises

1. Using Aristotle's account of the relationships between categorical sentences as presented above, answer each question with a *categorical sentence* in English.
   a. What is the contradictory of "All fiddlers are bass fiddlers"?
   b. What is the contrary of "No politicians are statesmen"?
   c. What is the contradictory of "Some politicians are statesmen"?
   d. What is the subcontrary of "Some cats are Persians"?
   e. What sentence must be true if "All cats are Persians" is true?
   f. What sentence must be true if "No cats are Persians" is true?
   g. What is the contradictory of "Some cats are not domestic"?
   h. What is the contradictory of "No football players are pre-med students"?
   i. What sentence is contrary to "All doctors are rich"?
   j. What is the subimplication of "No rich persons are doctors"?

2. Give an English sentence (it need not be categorical) that is contrary to each of the following:
   a. It never rains in southern California.
   b. Mary Ann has two blue eyes.
   c. His only pet is a dog.
   d. Johnny is rich.
   e. Chocolate desserts are delicious.
   f. Chocolate is my favorite flavor.
   g. You always complain about the homework.
   h. When it rains, it pours.
   i. Many a hero has gone unsung.
   j. Parakeets are the easiest pets to keep.

3. Give an English sentence (it need not be categorical) that is contradictory to each of the following:
   a. Peas are not usually eaten with a knife.
   b. Carrots are orange.
   c. Baseball is less interesting than football.
   d. Every rose has its thorn.
   e. The grass is always greener on the other side of the fence.
   f. This movie glorifies criminals.
   g. Mary Stuart was the only reigning queen of Scotland.

ii. Existential Import

Despite a superficial similarity between universal sentences ("Every S is P," "No S is P") and particular sentences ("Some S is P," "Some S is not P"), their logical structures are distinct. Universal sentences are understood by contemporary logicians to have a conditional structure in which the pronoun in the consequent refers back to the subject of the antecedent clause: "If anything is S, then it is P"; "If anything is S, then it is not P." Particular sentences, in contrast, assert that there is some individual that has some property (or, in the negative case, that lacks the property): "Something that is S is also P"; "Something that is S is not P." The structure of particular sentences resembles a grammatical conjunction rather than a conditional.

A logically important feature of the A and E forms of categorical sentences is that we sometimes use universal generalizations in English when we are aware that there are no members of the subject class ("All ghosts are invisible"). We also sometimes use universal generalizations when we *hope* there will be no members of the subject class ("Every student who does not meet the deadline for term papers will receive a failing grade"). We characterize this feature of universal sentences by saying that they "lack existential import." Particular sentences, in contrast, either assert that some individual has a property or that some individual lacks a property. In either case, the existence of something is asserted. Particular sentences have existential import.

2. The Modern Square of Opposition

Modern logicians view the relationships between categorical statements differently from Aristotle.* If universal generalizations are regarded for purposes of
logical analysis as *material conditionals*, then they will be regarded as true just
in case they do not have a true antecedent and a false consequent. In other
words, any conditional that has a false antecedent is true. Consider the sentence:
"Every ghost is invisible." If we rephrase it in conditional form it becomes "If
anything is a ghost, then it is invisible." But there are no ghosts, so the antecedent
is false. Then, if we interpret the conditional as a material (truth-functional)
conditional, "Every ghost is invisible" is true. The same sort of reasoning, however, applies to the negative universal generalization "No ghost is invisible," and
it is also true because it has a false antecedent. But then the *A* sentence and the
E sentence can both be true, and so they are no longer contraries. If universal
generalizations are understoood as material conditionals in this way, the square
of opposition is drastically simplified. Most of the relations between forms of
categorical sentences with the same subject and predicate terms recognized by
Aristotle no longer hold. Only the contradictory relationships between the pairs
of categorical sentences diagonally opposite one another remain intact. This
modern square of opposition is shown in Figure 9-4.

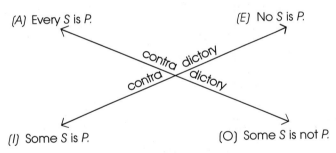

FIGURE 9-4
Modern Square of Opposition

If universal generalizations are interpreted as material conditionals:

> *(A)* If anything is an *S*, then it is a *P*.
> *(E)* If anything is an *S*, then it is not a *P*.

then it is possible for the *A* sentence to be true (when there are no *S*'s) while
the corresponding *I* sentence is false, for the *I* sentence asserts that some *S* is *P*.
The *I* sentence has existential import. Similarly, it is possible for the *E* sentence

*See "Truth-Functional Conditionals and Modern vs. Traditional Syllogistic," R. B. Angell, 1986.

to be true while the corresponding *O* sentence is false. Thus, the relationships of subimplication do not hold in the modern interpretation. Furthermore, the *I* and *O* sentences can both be false, when there are no *S*'s, so the relationship of subcontraries also fails to hold.

Consider the following four categorical sentences in which "unicorn" is the subject term and "white things" is the predicate term:

A: Every unicorn is a white thing.
E: No unicorn is a white thing.
I: Some unicorn is a white thing.
O: Some unicorn is not a white thing.

We know that there are no unicorns. Accordingly, the *A* and *E* sentences are both true, and the *I* and *O* sentences are both false. The *A* sentence does not imply the *I* sentence; the *E* sentence does not imply the *O* sentence. *A* and *E* are not contraries; *I* and *O* are not subcontraries. However, *A* and *O* are contradictories, as are *E* and *I*.

The main reason why modern logicians interpret conditionals as material conditionals is to have the convenience of a uniform interpretation; a cost for this is the suppression of content in favor of purely structural considerations. When we employ sentence forms, such as those presented in the square of opposition, we disregard all *content* in the sense that we do not concern ourselves with the nature of the subject class or the predicate class. All that interests the logician is the relationship between those classes. Does one class include or exclude the other? Do the two classes share a common member? Is there a member of one class that does not belong to the other class? We are already familiar with some advantages of employing sentence forms rather than sentences when we are concerned chiefly with the validity or the invalidity of an argument. However, such abstraction from content requires us to make certain decisions about how terms are to be treated. By treating universal sentences in a way similar to material conditionals, logicians are able to provide a comprehensive system of logic that builds on the symbolic techniques developed to treat sentential arguments and extends these techniques to more complex sorts of arguments.

In Chapter 10, we will develop some of the symbolic techniques that have already been introduced, and then it will be possible to show how simplicity can be gained through modern treatments of the logic of classes. In the rest of this chapter, in our formal treatment of the syllogism we will follow the practice of adopting the modern attitude toward the square of opposition unless otherwise stated. The Aristotelian square of opposition retains its importance, however, because of the aid it provides in understanding ordinary discourse in which universal sentences are not normally interpreted as material conditionals.

Even though we will use the simpler modern square of opposition in our formal treatment of the syllogism, the relationships among categorical sentences in the traditional Aristotelian square of opposition are important in everyday reasoning in ordinary language. For that reason, it repays our careful attention. Arguments in ordinary reasoning often depend on the fact that one sentence is contrary to another, or is subcontrary to another, or is a subimplication of another. We should be able to recognize and assess such arguments.

III. TRANSLATING ENGLISH SENTENCES INTO STANDARD CATEGORICAL FORMS

It should come as no surprise that there are many ways of expressing English-language sentences that have the logical structure of one of the four types of categorical sentences. With sufficiently clever linguistic manipulation, many English sentences that do not appear to be categorical sentences can fit one of these categorical forms. For example, a sentence such as "It never rains but it pours," can be "translated" into "Every time of raining is a time of pouring," which is a standard *A* sentence.

1. *A* Sentences

Consider the following English sentences:

1. All trespassers are persons who will be prosecuted.
2. Trespassers will be prosecuted.
3. Anyone who trespasses will be prosecuted.
4. If anyone trespasses, that person will be prosecuted.
5. No trespasser will fail to be prosecuted.
6. It is false that some trespassers will not be prosecuted.
7. All persons who will not be prosecuted are nontrespassers.

All of these sentences are equivalent to one another in the logically important sense that each sentence states that the class of trespassers is included in the class of persons who will be prosecuted. The following remarks about each of these sentences are designed to make this equivalence apparent:

1. This sentence is clearly equivalent to "Every trespasser is a person who will be prosecuted." "Trespassers" denotes the subject class, and "persons who will be prosecuted" denotes the predicate class. We can regard "All *S* are *P*" as a standard rendering of the *A* sentence.
2. In English, the *quantifier* ("every," "all," or "some") is frequently dropped when context makes clear which quantifier is intended. For example, the sentence "Whales are mammals" is to be understood as "Every whale is a mammal." But in "Watch your language. Children are present," the second sentence is understood to mean "Some child is present." Also, noun phrases such as "persons who," "things which," and similar expressions are frequently dropped from the predicate term.
3. In this sentence, we can easily see that "Anyone who trespasses" means the same as "all trespassers."

4. This is the standard translation of an *A* sentence into a form that makes its conditional nature apparent: "If anything is an *S*, then it is a *P*."

5. This sentence is obviously equivalent to the *E* form: "No trespassers are persons who will not be prosecuted." In addition to changing the "all" in the original sentence (1) to "no," the predicate "persons who will be prosecuted" has been replaced by "persons who will not be prosecuted." In general, an *A* sentence may be transformed to an equivalent *E* sentence in the following two steps:

   a. Replace "every" (or "all") with "no." Changing an affirmative sentence to a negative sentence, or a negative sentence to an affirmative sentence, is called "changing the *quality* of a categorical sentence."

   b. Replace the predicate term of the sentence with its *complement*. The complement of a class is the class of all things that are not in the original class. For example, the complement of the class of cats is the class of noncats; the complement of the class of nonmen is the class of men. The term that refers to the complement class is called the *complement* of the original term.

      The process of changing the quality of a categorical sentence and replacing the predicate term with its complement is called *obversion*. When any categorical sentence (*A*, *E*, *I*, or *O*) is *obverted*, a sentence that is equivalent in meaning to the original sentence results.

6. This sentence is equivalent to the *denial* of an *O* sentence: "*It is not the case that* some trespassers are persons who will not be prosecuted." The *O* sentence that is contradictory to "All trespassers are persons who will be prosecuted" is "Some trespassers are persons who will not be prosecuted." The denial of the contradictory of a sentence is logically equivalent to the original sentence.

7. In this sentence, the subject term is the complement of the predicate term in (1) and the predicate is the complement of the subject term in (1). This transformation is called *contraposition*. The contraposition of *A* sentences yields *A* sentences that are equivalent in meaning to the original sentence.

The relationship between subject and predicate in the *A* sentence can be represented graphically in the *Venn diagram** of the *A* sentence shown in Figure 9-5.

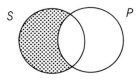

S   P

FIGURE 9-5

---

*After John Venn (1834–1923), an English clergyman who made important contributions to mathematics and logic.

Against a background of all of the types of things in the universe, the over-lapping circles represent two classes, or types of things in that universe: Ss and Ps. These classes may or may not have members. Shading is used to indicate the emptiness of a region. Thus, for the A sentence, the region in the S circle that lies outside the P circle is shaded, for any Ss (if there are any) must lie within the part of the S circle that is included in the P circle.

2. *E* Sentences

Consider the following English sentences:

1. No whales are fish.
2. Whales aren't fish.
3. Nothing that's a whale is a fish.
4. None but nonfishes are whales.
5. If anything is a whale, then it is not a fish.
6. All whales are nonfish.
7. It is false that some whales are fish.

Each of these sentences says that the class of whales and the class of fish is nonoverlapping, or in other words, that no members are common to both classes. Comments on each of these sentences follow:

1. This sentence is in standard E form.
2. This sentence is equivalent to the categorical A sentence "All whales are nonfish." In ordinary English, we might be tempted to say "All whales are not fish," but this sentence is ambiguous; it leaves open the possibility that some whales are fish, but in the original sentence (2), the intent is to deny that any whales are fish. The sentence form "All S are not P" is not a categorical sentence form, and due to its ambiguity, is not equivalent to the categorical "All S are non-P," which is a variant of the A form.
3. "Nothing that's a whale" in this context clearly has the same meaning as "no whales," and "is a fish" agrees better grammatically with this version than "are fish."
4. "None but nonfishes are whales" means the same as "Only nonfishes are whales" or "If anything is not a nonfish, then it is not a whale." This in turn can be seen to be equivalent to "If anything is a fish, then it is not a whale." This sentence states that there is no overlap between the classes of fish and whales, which is what the original E sentence (1) says.
5. This is the standard translation of the E sentence into an equivalent conditional. "No S is P" becomes "If anything is an S, then it is not a P."
6. This sentence represents the standard transformation of an E sentence into an equivalent A sentence by *obversion*. The quality of the sentence

is changed from negative to affirmative, and the predicate term is replaced by its complement.

7. This sentence is the denial of the contradictory of the original *E* sentence (1). In general, the categorical sentence "No *S* are *P*" is equivalent to the noncategorical sentence "It is false that some *S* are *P*."

E sentences (including all the English variants of the standard form of *E* sentence) can be represented by the Venn diagram shown in Figure 9-6.

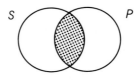

FIGURE 9-6

As in the Venn diagram of the *A* sentence, the two circles represent the classes *S* and *P*. The shading in the overlapping area indicates that this region is empty (that there are no things included in both classes).

Inspection of the Venn diagram should make it clear that the sentence forms "No *S* is *P*" and "No *P* is *S*" are equivalent. This means that the subject term and the predicate term can be interchanged in an *E* sentence without changing the meaning of the sentence. This transformation is called *conversion*. Conversion does not always preserve meaning. When it is applied to *A* sentences, for example, "All elephants are mammals," we see that this does not mean the same as "All mammals are elephants." Examination of the Venn diagram of the *A* sentence makes its lack of symmetry with respect to subject and predicate terms apparent.

3. *I* Sentences

The following are all English variations of the same *I* sentence:

1. Some logical principles are things difficult to grasp.
2. Some logical principles are difficult to grasp.
3. Some things are both logical principles and difficult to grasp.
4. There are logical principles that are difficult to grasp.
5. Some logical principles are not things that are not difficult to grasp.
6. Some logical principles are not easy to grasp.
7. It is not the case that no logical principles are difficult to grasp.
8. It is not the case that all logical principles are easy to grasp.
9. Some things that are difficult to grasp are logical principles.

Some of these equivalencies are discussed below. You should convince yourself of the equivalencies of the rest.

1. This sentence is in the standard *I* form.
3. This form makes the conjunctive nature of *I* sentences apparent.

5. An *O* form that is equivalent to the *I* form can be constructed by changing the quality from affirmative to negative and replacing the predicate term with its complement (obversion).

7. The *E* sentence that is the contradictory of the *I* sentence is negated. The resulting sentence is equivalent to the original *I* sentence.

9. Since the *I* sentence has the logical form of a conjunction and since the order of the conjuncts is irrelevant to the truth of the conjunction, "Some *S* are *P*" is equivalent to "Some *P* are *S*." As in the *E* sentence, the subject and predicate terms in the *I* sentence may be interchanged without changing the meaning of the sentence. Conversion preserves meaning in *I* sentences.

In constructing the Venn diagram for the *I* sentence, two overlapping circles are again used to represent the classes *S* and *P*. An **x** is used to represent the fact that a class has a member. Since the *I* sentence says that the classes *S* and *P* share at least one member, an **x** is placed in the overlapping region, as shown in Figure 9-7.

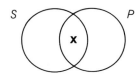

FIGURE 9-7

4. *O* Sentences

The following are all English variations of the same *O* sentence:

1. Some runners are not vegetarians.
2. Some runners are nonvegetarians.
3. Some nonvegetarians are runners.
4. Not all runners are vegetarians.
5. There are nonvegetarian runners.
6. Some nonvegetarians are not nonrunners.

The principles by virtue of which these sentences are equivalent to one another have all been introduced by now. The first sentence (1) is in standard *O* form. The second sentence (2) is the obverse of (1). The quality of sentence (1) is changed from negative to affirmative (that is, from an *O* sentence to an *I* sentence), and the predicate term is replaced by its complement. Sentence (3) is the converse of (2), in which the subject and predicate terms of that *I* sentence are interchanged. Sentence (4) is the denial of the *A* sentence that is contradictory to the original *O* sentence. Sentence (5) exhibits the conjunctive nature of the *O* sentence. Finally, sentence (6) is the *contrapositive* of sentence (1). Contraposition preserves sameness of meaning in *O* sentences as well as in *A* sentences.

Again, using overlapping circles and an **x** to show that a class has some member, the Venn diagram in Figure 9-8 represents all variants of the *O* sentence. In this case, the **x** is drawn outside the *P* circle but within the *S* circle.

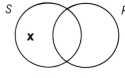

FIGURE 9-8

Exercises

For each of the following English sentences, construct an English sentence in one of the four standard categorical forms that captures the meaning of the original sentence as nearly as possible. Draw a Venn diagram for each sentence and clearly label the subject class circle and the predicate class circle.

1. Only a mother could love him.
2. If students don't keep up with the assignments, they're lost.
3. The longest mile is the last mile home.
4. Happy is the bride the sun shines on.
5. No one may be admitted except juniors and seniors.
6. Not all apples are red.
7. If it isn't genuine, it isn't worth owning.
8. The home team always wins at football.
9. Valuable lessons are never easily learned.
10. Not every good dancer is a good person.
11. American warships are in the Indian Ocean.
12. The easiest course is not always the most satisfying.
13. It never rains in southern California.
14. She brings sunshine everywhere she goes.
15. Cosmic radiation is all around us.
16. Times like these try persons' souls.
17. It's an antique only if it's more than 100 years old.
18. The last exercise is always the best.

IV. TESTING FOR VALIDITY WITH VENN DIAGRAMS

Categorical syllogisms in standard form are arguments with two premises and a conclusion that also have the following properties:

1. Both the premises and the conclusion are categorical sentences in standard form.
2. Only three terms occur in the argument. One of these terms occurs

once in each premiss; each of the other two terms occurs once in one of the premisses and once in the conclusion.

When we represent the forms of these arguments, we will use S to refer to the subject term of the conclusion, P to refer to the predicate term of the conclusion, and M to refer to the term that occurs in both premisses.

Remember that an argument is deductively valid if its conclusion does not contain any information that is not already present at least implicitly in the premisses. If no new information occurs in the conclusion, then it is impossible for the premisses to be true while the conclusion is false.

We have already seen how the information contained in categorical sentences can be represented in Venn diagrams. A Venn diagram can show whether or not one class is included in another, one class excludes the other, classes share a common member, or one class has a member that lies outside the other class (see Figure 9-9).

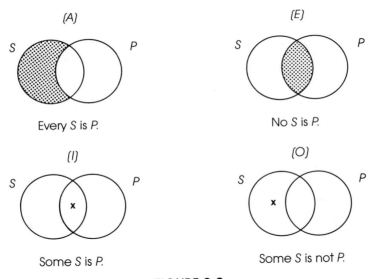

FIGURE 9-9

To apply the Venn diagram technique to categorical syllogisms, we need three overlapping circles—one for each of the three terms in the argument. The circles are arranged in the standard way shown in Figure 9-10.

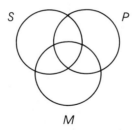

FIGURE 9-10

To test a syllogism for validity, we use shading or **x**s to mark information contained in the premisses on this standard blank diagram. Then we inspect the diagram to see whether or not the information in the conclusion sentence can be "read off" the diagram. If, after the premisses are diagrammed, the conclusion can be "read off" the diagram, then the argument is a valid syllogism. If the conclusion cannot be "read off" the diagram, then the argument is not a valid syllogism.

Examples

(a)

All sensitive persons are dreamers.	All *S* are *M*.
All dreamers are poets.	All *M* are *P*.
All sensitive persons are poets.	All *S* are *P*.

In this argument, *S* is the class of sensitive persons, *P* is the class of poets, and *M* is the class of dreamers.

To diagram the first premiss, we consider only the two circles labeled *S* and *M*. The first premiss is an *A* sentence, with *S* as the subject term. Thus, we shade all of the *S* circle that lies outside the *M* circle, as shown in Figure 9-11.

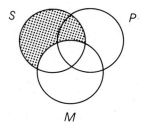

FIGURE 9-11

To diagram the second premiss, we consider the two circles labeled *P* and *M*. The second premiss is also an *A* sentence with *M* as the subject term, so we shade all of the *M* circle that does not lie within the *P* circle, as shown in Figure 9-12.

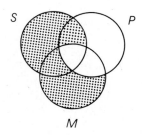

FIGURE 9-12

After diagramming these two premisses, we stop and inspect the Venn diagram to see whether or not we can "read off" the conclusion. The conclusion is an *A* sentence with *S* as the subject term and *P* as the predicate term. On the diagram, all of the *S* circle that lies outside the *P* circle has been shaded. (A part that lies inside the *P* circle has been shaded as well, but this does not conflict with the claim that if anything is an *S* then it is a *P*; it simply provides the additional information that any of the *S*s that are *P*s are *M*s as well.) Thus we can "read off" the sentence "All *S* are *P*" from the Venn diagram, and the argument is shown to be valid.

(b)   All statesmen are honorable persons.   All *S* are *M*.
           Some honorable persons are politicians.   Some *M* are *P*.
           ─────────────────────────────────   ──────────────
           Some statesmen are politicians.   Some *S* are *P*

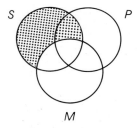

FIGURE 9-13

In Figure 9-13, the first premiss, "All *S* are *M*," is diagrammed by shading the part of the *S* circle that lies outside the *M* circle.

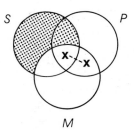

FIGURE 9-14

In Figure 9-14, the information contained in the second premiss, "Some *M* are *P*" is added to the diagram of the first premiss. The overlapping region between the *P* circle and the *M* circle is itself divided into two parts. One of these parts lies within the *S* circle; the other part lies outside the *S* circle. Since the information in the premiss tells us only that there is a member somewhere in this overlap, we cannot locate an **x** definitely in one region or the other.

Instead, we use the "floating **x**" (two **x**s connected by a dashed line) to indicate that a member lies somewhere in that region.

However, when we try to "read off" the conclusion "Some S are P," we see that the diagram tells us only that an **x** *may* lie in the region overlapping S and P or that it *may* lie in the region overlapping P and M but outside of S. Thus, we cannot "read off" the conclusion from the diagrammed premisses, and the syllogism is invalid. It is *possible* for both premisses to be true and the conclusion to be false.

(c)   No unicorns are black things.   No S are M.
            Some black things are dogs.   Some M are P.
            _____   _____

            No unicorns are dogs.   No S are P.

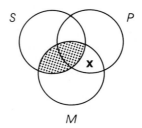

FIGURE 9-15

In the Venn diagram in Figure 9-15, the first premiss requires us to shade the overlapping area between the S and the M circles. An **x** is then drawn in the overlapping area between the M and the P circles to represent the second premiss. In this case, as a result of diagramming the first premiss, we can see that the area of overlap between M and P that also lies within the S circle is empty, so we do not need to use a "floating **x**." The **x** can only be drawn in the area between M and P that is unshaded.

In order for us to "read off" the conclusion from this diagram, the area of overlap between the S and the P circles would have to be shaded. Since this is not the case, the syllogism is invalid.

(d)   No intelligent persons are gluttons.   No P are M.
       Some famous persons are gluttons.   Some S are M.
       _____   _____

       Some famous persons are not intelligent.   Some S are not P.

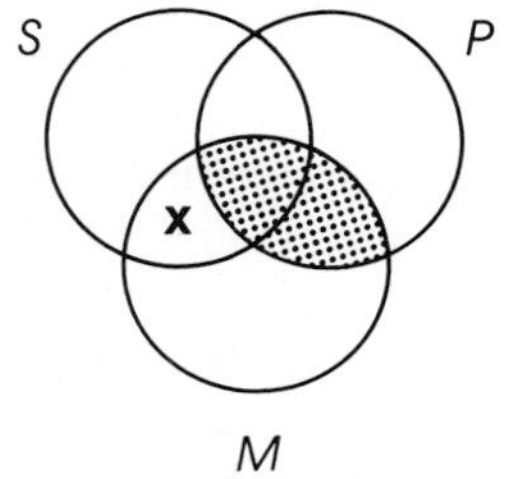

S ⬭⬭⬭ P

M

FIGURE 9-16

The first premiss is diagrammed in Figure 9-16 by shading the overlapping region between the *P* and the *M* circles. The second premiss requires that we place an **x** in the overlap between the *S* and the *M* circles. The **x** is placed in the unshaded portion of this overlap. In order to "read off" the conclusion, there must be an **x** in the portion of the *S* circle that lies outside the *P* circle. This is the case, and so the diagram shows the validity of this syllogism.

(e)   Some animals are furry.   Some *S* are *M*.
          Some furry things are cats.   Some *M* are *P*.
          _____   _____
          Some animals are cats.   Some *S* are *P*.

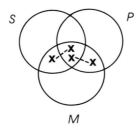

FIGURE 9-17

To diagram the first premiss, we place an **x** in the overlap between *S* and *M*. There are two parts to this overlap—one within the *P* circle and one outside the *P* circle (see Figure 9-17). The premiss does not tell us where to place the **x**, so we must use a floating **x**. The second premiss tells us that there is a member of both *P* and *M* but does not tell us whether or not this member belongs to *S*. Therefore, we must use another floating **x**. The conclusion requires that an "**x** be in the overlapping region between *S* and *P*." But since both **x**s are floating, we cannot tell whether or not either **x** lies in that region. Thus, the conclusion cannot be "read off" the diagram, and the syllogism is invalid.

Exercises

1. For each of the following syllogisms:

    (i) Identify the *S*, *M*, and *P* terms.
    (ii) Draw a Venn diagram.
    (iii) Tell whether the syllogism is valid or invalid.

Diagramming will be simplified if, whenever a syllogism contains both a universal and a particular premiss, the universal premiss is diagrammed first. This will minimize the use of floating **x**s.

    a. All animals feel pain. All things that feel pain are able to think. Therefore, all animals are able to think.

    b. All patriots are chauvinists. Some chauvinists are fanatics. Therefore, some patriots are fanatics.

    c. No good persons are cruel to animals. Some children are cruel to animals. Therefore, some children are not good persons.

d. No elephants are easy to train. Some dogs are not easy to train. Some dogs are not elephants.

e. All messengers who bring bad news are unwelcome. All messengers who bring bad news are punished. Therefore, some unwelcome persons are punished.

f. Some awards are worthless. Some worthless things are fun to have. Therefore, some awards are fun to have.

g. All diets require will power. No things that require will power are simple. Therefore, no diets are simple.

h. Some syllogisms are not valid arguments. All syllogisms have two premisses. Therefore, some arguments with two premisses are not valid.

i. No syllogisms are arguments with four terms. Some arguments with four terms are invalid. Therefore, no syllogisms are invalid.

j. Some arguments are invalid. Some invalid arguments are not syllogisms. Therefore, some arguments are not syllogisms.

2. Consider each of the following pairs of sentences to be premisses. Using an appropriately labeled three-circle Venn diagram, tell what syllogistic conclusion, if any, can be drawn from these premisses.

a. No football players are weaklings.
   No ballerinas are weaklings.

b. Some dogs have fleas.
   Some things with fleas are good pets.

c. No students are boring.
   Some professors are boring.

d. All mariners are sailors.
   All mariners love the sea.

e. Some valuable things are inexpensive.
   Some inexpensive things are not bargains.

f. No valuable thing is free of charge.
   All immunizations at the Health Center are free of charge.

g. All champions are hard-workers.
   Some hard workers are unsuccessful.

h. All birds are egg-layers.
   Some mammals are egg-layers.

i. No birds are cold-blooded.
   All reptiles are cold-blooded.

j. All reptiles are cold-blooded.
   Some dinosaurs are not cold-blooded.

V. DISTRIBUTION OF TERMS

A term is said to be *distributed* in a categorical sentence if and only if that sentence says something about *every* member of the class to which the term refers. In the *A* sentence, for example, the subject term is distributed. When we say that "All logic students are hard-working," we are saying that *every* logic student is a hard-working person. However, the predicate term in the *A* sentence is not distributed, because that sentence does not say something about every hard-working person.

In the *E* sentence, both the subject and predicate terms are distributed. The sentence "No NFL football player is a ballerina" says of every NFL football player that that person is not a ballerina and also says of every ballerina that that person is not an NFL football player.

In the *I* sentence, neither the subject term nor the predicate term is distributed. This sentence says only that the two classes share at least one member. The *I* sentence says nothing about every member of either the subject class or the predicate class.

In the *O* sentence, the subject term is not distributed; as in the *I* sentence, the subject term in the *O* sentence refers to only some member or members ("some" may mean more than one) of the class, not to every member. Although it is not immediately obvious, however, the predicate term is distributed in the *O* sentence. The awkward alternate formulation of the *O* sentence presented earlier ("There is at least one member of *S* such that, given any individual member of *P*, that member of *S* is not identical to that individual") illustrates that the *O* sentence says something about every member of the *P* class—namely, that at least one member of *S* is not identical with it. Thus, the claim that "Some dogs are not brown" has the same meaning as "There is at least one dog that is not identical with any brown thing." It should be clear that the latter sentence says something about every member of the class of "brown things."

These facts about the distribution of terms, which will play an important role in the second method for assessing the validity of categorical syllogisms, can be summarized as follows:

Universal sentences: Subject term is distributed.
Negative sentences: Predicate term is distributed.

Fallacies of distribution can occur if the distinction between using a term distributively (to refer to every member of a class) and using a term collectively (to refer to the class as a whole) is not recognized. Consider the following arguments, neither of which is a categorical syllogism:

1. I infer that this stew will be delicious because each ingredient that went into it is delicious.
2. Mary's room at college must be large, for she lives in a very large dormitory.

In the first of these arguments, the conclusion that a *collective whole* (a stew) has a certain property is based on the information that its *parts* (distributively or individually) have that property. But this type of inference is not reliable. We all know that you can put together a collection of individually fine football players and end up with a poor team, and that you can gather fine singers into a choir that sings badly. What is true of the parts is not *necessarily*— or even *probably*—true of the whole. The mistake of reasoning that what is true of the parts of a whole is also true of the whole, or that what is true of the individual members is true of the class, is called the *fallacy of composition*.

The second argument depends on the principle that what is true of the whole must be true of its parts. But this is also mistaken reasoning. Very large machines can be constructed from parts that are individually very small. A herd of cattle can be small even though none of its members is small. The fallacy involved in argument (2) above is called the *fallacy of division*. Like the fallacy of composition, the fallacy of division involves confusing the distributive use of a term with its collective use.

Exercises

1. The following argument occurs in Book V of Lucretius's (c. 100–55 BC) great philosophical poem *On the Nature of the Universe*. What fallacy does Lucretius commit here?

> In the first place, since the elements of which we see the world composed— solid earth and moisture, the light breaths of air and torrid fire—all consist of bodies that are neither birthless nor deathless, we must believe the same of the world as a whole.

2. Does the following argument commit a fallacy of distribution?

> Science tells us that physical objects are made up entirely of tiny particles— electrons, positrons, neutrons, and so on—that are invisible, although their motions can be detected by sophisticated instruments. Science also tells us that these particles are in constant motion and that there are spaces between them. Yet we can see physical objects, feel their solidity, and see that they are not always in motion. So science must be wrong; physical objects cannot be composed of atomic and subatomic particles.

3. What fallacy occurs in the following passage?

> What is prudence in the conduct of every private family can hardly be folly in that of a great kingdom.
>
> —Adam Smith, *Wealth of Nations*

VI. RULES FOR TESTING THE VALIDITY OF SYLLOGISMS

The use of Venn diagrams provides a general method of determining which conclusions follow validly from premisses in categorical syllogisms. This technique is simple to apply and provides a practical test for validity.

Various other techniques can be used to determine whether syllogisms are valid or invalid. Deductive logicians are not as concerned with assessing the validity of *particular arguments* as they are concerned with formulating and testing *general principles* related to what conclusions follow from what premisses. The truth tables and the proof method discussed in Appendix 1 embody such general principles for truth-functional arguments. A number of different systems of principles governing what follows from what in categorical syllogisms have also been investigated by logicians, beginning with Aristotle.

Aristotle's treatment of syllogisms was quite different from the Venn-diagram method. To understand his approach to the problem, the concept of a *figure of a syllogism* must be introduced. In categorical syllogisms, we see that the *S* term (the subject term of the conclusion) can be either the subject or the predicate of the premiss in which it occurs; similarly, the *P* term (the predicate term of the conclusion) can be either the subject or the predicate of the premiss in which it occurs. Thus, four possible arrangements, or figures of the syllogism can be distinguished:

$$
\begin{array}{cccc}
MP & PM & MP & PM \\
SM & SM & MS & MS \\
\hline
SP & SP & SP & SP
\end{array}
$$

Since the order in which the premisses of an argument are stated has no bearing on the validity of the argument, variations in form that depend on this feature do not need to be considered. Both the premisses and the conclusions of these arguments are sentences in *A, E, I,* or *O* form. There are 64 possible combinations of these four types of sentences taken three at a time (two sentences as the premisses and one sentence as the conclusion), and each of the 64 combinations (called *moods*) can occur in each of the four figures. Thus, there are only a finite number of forms of categorical syllogisms. Although the number is rather large (256), it is possible to use Venn diagrams to test each form. (Only a few of these forms are valid.)

Aristotle's own system of principles for testing validity involved taking as axioms those syllogisms in the first figure that were obviously valid and showing that all valid forms in the other figures could be reduced (by obverting sentences, exchanging subject and predicate terms in *E* and *I* sentences, and other transformations discussed in Section III) directly or indirectly to these obviously valid forms. To show the invalidity of forms, Aristotle used the method of counterexample, providing arguments in those forms with obviously true premisses and obviously false conclusions. Aristotle's treatment of syllogistic logic was therefore similar to Euclid's treatment of geometry as a deductive system and different from the methods for testing validity discussed in this chapter.

1. Three Rules for Valid Syllogisms

In this section, we will consider a system of three rules for testing the validity of categorical syllogisms. This system of rules is an alternative to the Venn-diagram method, and some people find it easier to use than the diagrams.

All of the properties required for a syllogism to be valid can be stated compactly in the three following rules.*

---

*These rules are presented by Wesley Salmon in *Logic,* 3rd ed., and were adapted from a set given by James T. Culbertson, *Mathematics and Logic for Digital Devices.*

1. *The middle term must be distributed exactly once.* (This means that the middle term must be distributed in one of the premisses and must be undistributed in the other premiss.)
2. *No end term can be distributed exactly once.* (This means that the *S* term can be distributed in the conclusion *if and only if* it is distributed in a premiss; the same is true for the *P* term.)
3. *The number of negative conclusions must equal the number of negative premisses.* (That is to say, there can be a negative conclusion *if and only if* there is exactly one negative premiss.)

Although these requirements are not immediately obvious, they are easy to memorize and provide an extremely simple way of testing for the validity of categorical syllogisms.

If a categorical syllogism violates *none* of these three rules, then it is valid. If *any* one of these rules is violated, then the syllogism is invalid.

Understanding what it means for a term to be distributed is crucial to understanding why these rules work. However, all we need to know to *apply* these rules to syllogisms is *which* terms are distributed—not what "distribution" means.

If a term is distributed in the conclusion, then the conclusion says something about every member of the class to which the term refers. In any valid syllogism, the occurrence of that term in the premiss must be distributed as well; otherwise, the conclusion would "go beyond" the premiss in the sense that the conclusion—but not the premiss—would say something about every member of that class.

For similar reasons, one of the occurrences of the *middle term* (the *M* term, which occurs in each premiss but not in the conclusion) must be distributed, because it is through the middle term that the *S* and *P* terms (*end terms*) are connected. This connecting function of the middle term shows up clearly in Venn diagrams. If one of the premisses did not say something about every member of a class, then there might be no connection between the subject term and the predicate term of the conclusion, for the subject class might be connected with one part of the class denoted by the middle term while the predicate class might be connected with a separate part of the class denoted by the middle term.

The preceding remarks offer *partial* justification for the rules. A justification has been given for why the middle term must be distributed *at least* once, but nothing has been said about why it must be distributed *at most* once. It has been shown why an end term that is distributed in the conclusion must be distributed in the premiss, but it has not been shown why an end term that is distributed in the premiss must also be distributed in the conclusion. All of the other less obvious features of the rules can be justified, but the proofs are often tedious "proofs by cases," in which one must go through all the possible figures of the syllogism in which the rule is applicable to show why it works.

For example, to show that no valid categorical syllogism can have two negative premisses, we note that each negative premiss either states that the middle term and the end terms completely exclude one another or that some member of one of these classes does not belong to the other class. From this, however, it may not be apparent that nothing at all can be said with certainty in the conclusion about the relationship between the two end terms. In a "proof by cases," we can use Venn diagrams to consider the following possibilities.

(i) Both premisses are *E* sentences.

Since the subject and the predicate terms are interchangeable in *E* sentences, we do not need to consider each figure separately. The Venn diagram for any syllogism with two *E* premisses looks like the one shown in Figure 9-18.

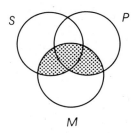

FIGURE 9-18

An inspection of the Venn diagram shows that no conclusion relating the end terms can be drawn from such premisses.

(ii) Both premisses are *O* sentences.

If the middle term is not the predicate term in at least one of the *O* sentences, then the middle term is undistributed. Thus, the third figure is invalid:

$$MP \quad (O)$$
$$MS \quad (O)$$
$$SP$$

For the other three figures, Venn diagrams will show that no syllogistic conclusion can be drawn from two *O* premisses.

(iii) One premiss is an *E* sentence, and the other premiss is an *O* sentence.

There are two possibilities:

(a) The premiss containing the *P* term is the *E* sentence. Two Venn diagrams are relevant here (see Figure 9-19). The left one diagrams "Some *S* are not *M*"; the right one diagrams "Some *M* are not *S*." Neither shows a syllogistic conclusion.

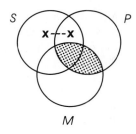

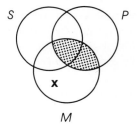

FIGURE 9-19

(b) The premiss containing the *S* term is the *E* sentence. Two Venn diagrams are relevant here (see Figure 9-20). The left one diagrams "Some *P* are not *M*"; the right one diagrams "Some *M* are not *P*." Neither yields a syllogistic conclusion.

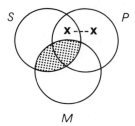

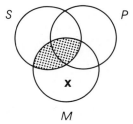

FIGURE 9-20

A *part* of the third rule has thus been justified in this "proof by cases," for we have shown that any syllogism in which the number of negative premisses is *greater than* the number of negative conclusions is invalid. (Obviously, any syllogism can have only one conclusion.)

Exercise

Show, by a demonstration similar to the preceding "proof by cases" that any syllogism in which the number of negative conclusions is greater than the number of negative premisses is invalid. (Show that any valid syllogism with a negative conclusion must have at least one negative premiss.) Be sure to consider all possibilities.

2. Examples of Using the Rules to Test Validity

Remember that the subject terms are distributed in universal sentences and that the predicate terms are distributed in negative sentences. All distributed terms will be denoted by the subscript d in the argument forms.

(a)   All soldiers are brave persons.   All M_d are S.
       Some soldiers are not daredevils.   Some M are not P_d.
       ———————————————————————   ————————————————
       Some brave persons are not daredevils.   Some S are not P_d.

1. The middle term is distributed in the first premiss but not in the second premiss. Thus, the middle term is distributed exactly once.
2. S is not distributed in the first premiss or in the conclusion. P is distributed in both the second premiss and in the conclusion. Thus, no end term is distributed exactly once.
3. The second premiss is the only negative premiss. The conclusion is negative. Thus, the number of negative premisses is equal to the number of negative conclusions.

The syllogism is valid.

(b)   All football fans are fanatics.   All P_d are M.
       Some fanatics are silly people.   Some M are S.
       ———————————————————————   ————————————————
       Some silly people are football fans.   Some S are P.

1. The middle term is not distributed in either of the premisses.

The syllogism is invalid. (Violation of one rule is sufficient to show invalidity. However, notice that the second rule is also violated, since P is distributed exactly once.)

(c)   No difficult subjects are worthless.   No M_d are P_d
       Some logic classes are not difficult.   Some S are not M_d.
       ———————————————————————   ————————————————
       Some logic classes are not worthless.   Some S are not P_d.

1. The middle term is distributed in both premisses.

The syllogism is invalid. (Also note that the third rule is violated. There are two negative premisses and one negative conclusion.)

Exercises

1. Identify the premisses and the conclusions of the following categorical syllogisms. Put the premisses and the conclusions into standard categorical form. Use the rules you have learned in this section to determine the validity or invalidity of the arguments. If a syllogism is invalid, say which rule or rules it violates.
   a. Some birds are nonflyers, for ostriches are birds and all ostriches are nonflyers.
   b. No persons who aren't in great shape are runners, so no smokers are runners, for all smokers are persons who aren't in great shape.

c. Not all generals are warmongers, but some admirals are warmongers; so no admirals are generals.
d. Some bridge games are interesting to observe, but no canasta games are interesting to observe. Hence, some bridge games are not canasta games.
e. Whales have lungs, but no fish do; so whales aren't fish.
f. All gemstones are expensive, but some cubic zirconias are not expensive; so cubic zirconias are not gemstones.
g. All feminists supported the ERA, but some women did not support the ERA. Hence, some feminists are not women.
h. All porpoises are mammals, but no fish are mammals; so no porpoises are fish.
i. Ostriches never fly, but birds always do; so ostriches aren't birds.
j. Not all sofas are beds, but some beds are uncomfortable; so some sofas are uncomfortable.

2. Some systems of rules for valid syllogisms include the following rule:

No syllogistic conclusion can be drawn from two particular premisses.

Provide a justification for this rule. (*Hint*: You may provide a "proof by cases," using Venn diagrams to support each case. Or you may appeal to the set of three rules for a valid syllogism and show that this rule follows from that set.)

VII. REDUCING THE NUMBER OF TERMS IN SYLLOGISMS

By definition, a categorical syllogism cannot contain more than three terms. However, many arguments that do contain more than three terms can be transformed to equivalent categorical syllogisms. *Synonyms* are often used in ordinary-language arguments for rhetorical purposes. Language is more interesting if the same term is not repeated several times. Obviously, when we wish to reconstruct these arguments to assess their validity, synonyms can be treated as different occurrences of the same term.

In other cases, arguments contain both pairs of a complementary set of terms. In such cases, it may be possible to reduce the number of terms by obverting (changing the quality and replacing a predicate term with its complement) some categorical sentence. Since obversion can reduce the number of terms only when the extra term occurs in the predicate position, it may be necessary to exchange the subject and predicate terms before obverting. (Remember, this exchange is legitimate only in *I* and *E* sentences!) Consider the following argument, in which both premisses are categorical sentences and the conclusion is a categorical sentence, but in which there are four terms:

All puzzles are interesting.
All logic exercises are puzzles.

No logic exercises are uninteresting.

First, we note that the terms "interesting" and "uninteresting" are complementary. If the first premiss is obverted, it becomes "No puzzles are uninteresting." This categorical sentence is equivalent to "All puzzles are interesting." The number of terms in the new equivalent syllogism is now only three, and the syllogism can be tested by the rules for a valid syllogism or by the Venn-diagram method:

> No *M* are *P*.
> All *S* are *M*
> ───────────
> No *S* are *P*.

A different way to reduce the number of terms in this English argument is to obvert the conclusion instead of the first premiss. Then, the conclusion becomes "All logic exercises are interesting." Again, a categorical syllogism results, but of the following form:

> All *M* are *P*.
> All *S* are *M*.
> ───────────
> All *S* are *P*.

(In this form, the *P* term is "interesting," whereas in the preceding form, the *P* term is "uninteresting.") Is this a valid form of syllogism?

The following argument contains five terms:

> Some nonbelievers are freethinkers, because no believers are atheists and some atheists are nonfreethinkers.

Letting *P* represent freethinkers, *S* represent believers, and *M* represent atheists, we can represent this argument as follows:

> No *S* are *M*.
> Some *M* are non-*P*.
> ───────────
> Some non-*S* are *P*.

First, we obvert the second premiss. We change the *I* sentence to an *O* sentence, and change non-*P* to *P*:

> Some *M* are not *P*.

Next, we reduce the pair of terms *S* and non-*S*. We begin by exchanging the subject and the predicate terms in the conclusion. This is legitimate, since the conclusion is an *I* sentence:

> Some *P* are non-*S*.

Then, this sentence can be obverted to yield

Some *P* are not *S*.

The reconstructed argument, which contains only three terms, has this form:

No *S* are *M*.
Some *M* are not *P*.
_____
Some *P* are not *S*.

Is this a valid form of syllogism?

Exercises

Reconstruct each of the following arguments as a categorical syllogism in standard form. Test each syllogism for validity, using either the rules for a valid syllogism or Venn diagrams.

1. Some men are nonsexists, since all sexists oppose equal rights for women and some men do not oppose equal rights for women.

2. Some strong persons are sensitive, but no poets are insensitive. Hence, some poets are strong persons.

3. All modern-style architecture is stark, but some recently constructed buildings are ornate; so not all new buildings are in the modern style.

4. Some edible things are nonpoisonous, for all insects are edible and some insects are poisonous.

5. No man is willing to die; but women aren't men, so some women are not unwilling to die.

6. No one who speaks Latin lives in Latin America; but not all Latin Americans live there, so some Latin Americans are Latin-speakers.

7. Carrot-eaters are health-food freaks, and no one who is crazy about health-food eats chocolate; so chocolate-freaks aren't carrot-eaters.

8. All rooms look their best if they are used by the people they belong to. Unless a room is arranged in a way that allows it to function comfortably, it will never be used. Therefore no room will look its best until it is comfortably arranged.
    —M. Hampton, *House and Garden*, March, 1987

(Exercises 9–11 are taken or adapted from *The Art of Thinking*, also called *Port-Royal Logic*, a seventeenth-century logic text designed by Antoine Arnauld to teach a young nobleman everything there was to know about logic in ten days.)

9. That which has no parts cannot perish by dissolution of its parts.
   The soul has no parts.
   _____
   The soul cannot perish by dissolution of its parts.

10. No virtue is offensive.
    Some zeal is not inoffensive.
    _____
    Some zeal is nonvirtuous.

11. All liars are unbelievable.
    Every upright person is believable.
    _____
    All liars are persons who are not upright.

VIII. RECONSTRUCTING ORDINARY-LANGUAGE ARGUMENTS AS SYLLOGISMS

Many arguments that are incompletely stated in English or that contain sentences not in categorical form can be reasonably reconstructed as categorical syllogisms.

Examples

(a)   Consider the following passage from Simone de Beauvoir's *The Ethics of Ambiguity*:

In *Plutarch Lied* Pierrefeu rightly says that in war there is no victory which can not be regarded as unsuccessful, for the objective which one aims at is the total annihilation of the enemy and this result is never attained.

This argument can be stated in syllogistic form:

All successful victories in war achieve total annihilation of the enemy.
No actual victories in war achieve total annihilation of the enemy.
_____
No actual victories in war are successful victories in war.

(b)   The following argument, from Chapter 12 of Leo Tolstoy's *What is Art?*, can also be recast as a syllogism:

Accustoming people to something resembling art disaccustoms them to the comprehension of real art. And that is how it comes about that none are more dull to art than those who have passed through the professional schools and have been most successful in them. Professional schools produce an hypocrisy of art.

Syllogistically, this argument can be expressed

All who have successfully passed through professional schools of art have been accustomed to something resembling art.

All who have been accustomed to something resembling art are persons most dull to real art.

All who have successfully passed through professional schools are persons most dull to real art.

(c)   The next argument is from St. Augustine's *Confessions*, Book X. When an unstated (but obviously intended) premiss is supplied, it can be viewed as a categorical syllogism:

> [A] happy life is not seen with the eye, because it is not a body.

In syllogistic form, this argument becomes

> No happy lives are bodies.
> All things that can be seen with the eye are bodies.
>
> ---
>
> No happy lives are things that can be seen with the eye.

(d)   The final example is taken from *The Mismeasure of Man* by Stephen Jay Gould:

> If I had any desire to lead a life of indolent ease, I would wish to be an identical twin, separated from my brother and raised in a different social class. We could hire ourselves out to a host of social scientists and practically name our fee. For we would be exceedingly rare representatives of the only really adequate natural experiment for separating genetic from environmental effects in humans—genetically identical individuals raised in disparate environments.

A syllogistic reconstruction of this argument is

All who are genetically identical individuals raised in disparate environments are representatives of the only adequate natural experiment for separating genetic from environmental effects in humans.
All representatives of the only adequate natural experiment for separating genetic from environmental effects in humans are persons who can command a sufficient fee from social scientists to lead a life of indolent ease.

All genetically identical individuals raised in disparate environments are persons who can command a sufficient fee from social scientists to lead a life of indolent ease.

IX. QUASI-SYLLOGISM AND SORITES

Quasi-Syllogism

A syllogism with a universal premiss, a premiss stating that a given individual is a member of the subject class, and a conclusion stating that the individual is a member of the predicate class, such as

All men are mortal.
Socrates is a man.

———————————

Socrates is mortal.

is called a *quasi-syllogism*. Although this is obviously an instance of a valid form of reasoning, it is not a categorical syllogism as it stands, because the sentences that mention a specific individual (called *singular* sentences) are not categorical. Some treatments of syllogistic logic cover this fundamental form of argument by interpreting singular sentences as disguised universal generalizations:

All members of the class in which the only member is Socrates are men.

If the singular sentences are interpreted in this way, the preceding quasi-syllogism above becomes an instance of the valid form:

All M are P.
All S are M.

———————————

All S are P.

Quasi-syllogisms can also occur with negative universal premisses:

No whales are fishes.
Shamu is a whale.

———————————

Shamu is not a fish.

The conclusion in this syllogism is interpreted as

No members of the class whose only member is Shamu are fishes.

Interpreting the singular premiss as in the other quasi-syllogism, this quasi-syllogism becomes an instance of the valid categorical form:

No M are P.
All S are M.

———————————

No S are P.

An alternative way of interpreting the quasi-syllogism will be discussed in Chapter 10.

Sorites

A *sorites* is an argument with more than two categorical sentences as premisses from which a final categorical conclusion may be drawn by performing a series of syllogistic inferences. In a sorites with three premisses, the intermediate syllogistic conclusion drawn from a pair of the stated premisses is used as an additional premiss and combined with the third premiss to yield the final conclusion of the argument.

In a sorites with more than three premisses, the process of drawing intermediate conclusions and using them as additional premisses is performed as often as may be required to reach the final conclusion. Lewis Carroll, the brilliant logician who is best known as the author of *Alice in Wonderland*, discusses this type of argument in his *Symbolic Logic*. All of the following examples are taken from this work. Solutions to the first two examples are given. The remaining sets of premisses are intended as exercises.

Examples

(a)   (i) No ducks waltz.
     (ii) No officers ever decline to waltz.
     (iii) All of my poultry are ducks.

Taking "ducks" as a middle term, the first and third premisses can be combined to yield the intermediate conclusion:

     (iv) No poultry of mine waltz.

"No officers ever decline to waltz" can be obverted to obtain "All officers waltz." This can then be combined with the intermediate conclusion (iv) to yield the final conclusion:

     (v) No officers are poultry of mine.

The conclusion "No poultry of mine are officers," which is equivalent to (v) could also be drawn from these premisses.

(b)   (i) No potatoes of mine that are new have been boiled.
     (ii) All my potatoes in this dish are fit to eat.
     (iii) No unboiled potatoes of mine are fit to eat.

Taking "things that are fit to eat" as a middle term, premisses (ii) and (iii) can be combined to provide an intermediate conclusion:

     (iv) No unboiled potatoes of mine are my potatoes in this dish.

Before this intermediate conclusion can be combined with (i), the number of terms must be reduced. Since "boiled" and "unboiled" are complementary, we will obvert (i), in which "boiled" occurs in the predicate position. Obverting (i) gives us

     (v) All potatoes of mine that are new are unboiled (potatoes of mine).

Combining (iv) and (v), we have the final conclusion:

No potatoes of mine that are new are my potatoes in this dish. (Or, less awkwardly, "None of my new potatoes are in this dish.")

Exercise

Show that the conclusion "All of my new potatoes are unfit to eat" follows from the three original premisses.

(c) (i) No one takes in the *Times* unless he is well educated.
  (ii) No hedge-hogs can read.
  (iii) Those who cannot read are not well educated.

(d) (i) Every one who is sane can do logic.
  (ii) No lunatics are fit to serve on a jury.
  (iii) None of your sons can do logic.

(e) (i) All hummingbirds are richly colored.
  (ii) No large birds live on honey.
  (iii) Birds that do not live on honey are dull in color.

(f) (i) No birds, except ostriches, are nine feet high.
  (ii) There are no birds in this aviary that belong to anyone but me.
  (iii) No ostrich lives on mince pies.
  (iv) I have no birds less than nine feet high.

X. REVIEW

We would expect a rather specialized terminology to have developed in connection with a subject that has been studied in classrooms for more than 2,000 years. Certainly, this has been the case with syllogistic logic. Although some of this terminology is used predominately in logic classes, much of it has found its way into the everyday vocabulary of educated people. A list of the important new terms used in this chapter, with brief definitions, follows.

Categorical Sentence: There are four standard forms of categorical sentences. Letting S represent the subject term and P represent the predicate term, these forms are:

1. Every S is P. (universal affirmative, or A sentence)
2. No S is P. (universal negative, or E sentence)
3. Some S is P. (particular affirmative, or I sentence)
4. Some S is not P. (Particular negative, or O sentence)

Categorical Syllogism: The following features characterize this type of argument:

1. Two premises, and a conclusion, each of which is a categorical sentence.

2. Only three terms occur in the argument. One of the terms occurs once in each premiss; the other two terms occur once in one of the premisses and once in the conclusion.

Complementary Terms: A pair of terms is complementary when one term of the pair refers to a class and the other term of the pair refers to its *complement* (the class consisting of all things that are not members of the original class).

Contradictory Sentences: When one sentence in a pair is the negation of the other sentence, the pair of sentences is contradictory. In a pair of contradictory sentences, one is true and the other is false. For categorical sentences with the same subjects and predicates, the *A* and *O* sentences are contradictory, as are the *E* and *I* sentences.

Contraposition: The *contrapositive* of an *A* or an *O* sentence is formed by exchanging the positions of the subject and predicate terms and replacing each with its complement. Contraposition preserves meaning for *A* and *O* sentences, but not for *I* and *E* sentences.

Contrary Sentences: When a pair of sentences is related in such a way that they could both be false but could not both be true, the sentences are contrary to one another. In the Aristotelian interpretation of categorical sentences, the *A* and *E* sentences are contraries.

Conversion: A categorical sentence is *converted* when the subject and predicate terms are interchanged. Converting *I* and *E* sentences yields sentences with the same meaning as the original sentences; converting *A* and *O* sentences does not.

Distribution of Terms: When a sentence refers to every member of a class, the term referring to that class is said to be *distributed*. In *universal* categorical sentences, the subject terms are distributed; in *negative* categorical sentences, the predicate terms are distributed.

Existential Import: When a sentence asserts the existence of some object, the sentence has existential import. Universal categorical sentences, when understood as material conditionals, lack existential import. Particular categorical sentences have existential import.

Fallacies of Distribution: Mistakes in reasoning that occur when a term that is used collectively in the premisses is interpreted distributively in the conclusion (*fallacy of division*) or when a term that is used distributively in the premisses is interpreted collectively in the conclusion (*fallacy of composition*).

Figure of a Syllogism: The "figure" refers to the arrangement of the end terms ("*S*" and "*P*") and the middle term ("*M*") in the premisses. There are four figures:

MP	*PM*	*MP*	*PM*
SM	*SM*	*MS*	*MS*
SP	*SP*	*SP*	*SP*

Obversion: A categorical sentence is *obverted* when the quality of the sentence is changed and the predicate term is replaced with its complement. The resulting sentence is a categorical sentence that is logically equivalent to the original sentence.

Quality of a Categorical Sentence: The quality of a categorical sentence refers to whether the sentence is negative or affirmative. The quality of *A* and *I* sentences is affirmative; the quality of *E* and *O* sentences is negative.

Quasi-Syllogism: A three-term syllogism with a universal premiss, a singular premiss, and a singular conclusion.

Sorites: An argument with more than two categorical sentences as premisses and with a categorical conclusion that is reached by drawing an *intermediate* syllogistic conclusion from two of the premisses and then using this conclusion in combination with another premiss to draw a further syllogistic conclusion. This pattern is repeated, using the remaining premisses, until the final conclusion is reached.

Subcontrary Sentences: When a pair of sentences is related in such a way that they could both be true but could not both be false, the sentences are subcontraries. Under the Aristotelian interpretation of categorical sentences, *I* and *O* sentences with the same subject and the same predicate terms are subcontraries.

Venn Diagrams: Sets of overlapping circles, which can be marked to indicate class membership, class exclusion, and class inclusion. These diagrams are used to exhibit the relations between classes in categorical sentences and to test for the validity of syllogisms.

XI. EXERCISES

1. For each of the following incomplete arguments, supply a premiss that will make the argument a valid categorical syllogism or quasi-syllogism. (Use the rules for valid syllogisms or Venn diagrams, if helpful.)

   a. Marijuana should not be legalized because it is potentially dangerous.

   b. Marijuana should be legalized because it is no more dangerous than alcohol, which is legal.

   c. Abernathy must be rich, since he never wears an overcoat.

   d. Female office workers work just as hard as male office workers and are just as productive. Therefore, female office workers should receive the same pay as male office workers in comparable positions.

   e. Since John gets sick only when he is nervous, he must have psychogenic illness.

   f. Not all socialists deserve to be persecuted, for some socialists are champions of human rights.

   g. Those who do not sin need not fear God, so you don't need to be afraid of God.

   h. Terry is a mathematician, so she must be musically talented.

   i. You had no right to take away his gun, because that gun was private property.

   j. If you failed, it's because you didn't try hard enough.

2. What syllogistic conclusion, if any, can be validly drawn from the following

pairs of premisses? (Use of the rules for valid syllogisms or Venn diagrams will prove helpful.)

    a. All beautiful things are expensive. Some beautiful things are made of inexpensive materials.

    b. Some sailors are adventurous. Some adventurous persons like long sea voyages.

    c. Whoever lives by the sword will perish by the sword. Some soldiers perish by the sword.

    d. Whatever goes up must come down. Stock prices are going up.

    e. Anything I say can be misinterpreted. Some misinterpretations are harmless.

    f. All grains are cereals. Some fruits are grains.

    g. No salt is an element. Some salts are soluble.

    h. All metals are fusible. Some conductors are nonmetals.

    i. All gondolas are boats. All gondolas have gondoliers.

    j. All children like candy. Some adults like candy.

    k. All first-basemen are athletes. No catchers are first-basemen.

3. Reconstruct each of the following arguments as a categorical syllogism, supplying plausible premisses when necessary. Test each syllogism for validity, using the rules for valid syllogisms or Venn diagrams.

    a. Some valid arguments have false conclusions, but not all syllogisms are valid; so some syllogisms have true conclusions.

    b. None but the rich can afford to be idle. Anyone who can afford to be idle is a threat to the Puritan work ethic, so some rich persons threaten the Puritan work ethic.

    c. Skillfully handcrafted items that are beautiful, enduring, and useful are never inexpensive, so Navajo rugs command a high price.

    d. A clever cook avoids making soufflés for dinner parties. No home economics major is not a clever cook. Therefore, no home economics major fails to avoid making soufflés for dinner parties.

    e. Some custards are soft, but no ices are soft; so some ices are not custards.

    f. Fallacious arguments are unconvincing. None of your arguments are fallacious. Therefore, all of your arguments are convincing.

    g. Some professors are ignorant. None who are ignorant are fit to teach college students. So some who are unfit to teach college students are professors.

    h. He who hesitates is lost, but the lost shall be found; so hesitators won't stay lost.

    i. All reporters are aggressive. None but reporters have daily deadlines. So no nonaggressive persons have deadlines.

    j. Syllogisms all have two premisses. Not all syllogisms are categorical. Some noncategorical syllogisms have two premisses.

    k. Decent newspapers cannot attain a wide circulation, for they do not emphasize sensational material. We all know that papers that emphasize sensational material attain a wide circulation.

Arguments in Which Validity Depends on Relations

C H A P T E R   1 0

I. INTRODUCTION

In preceding chapters, we analyzed two important types of arguments: truth-functional arguments and categorical syllogisms. For each type of argument, validity was shown to be a matter of *form*. The validity of truth-functional arguments is dependent on logical connections between the sentences that make up the argument, whereas the validity of categorical syllogisms is dependent on logical connections between the subject terms and the predicate terms within sentences. In our analysis of both truth-functional and syllogistic arguments, we ignored the *content* of the arguments. Simple sentences in truth-functional arguments and class terms in categorical syllogisms were represented by letters of the alphabet, allowing us to express the forms of these arguments in a general way. In the case of truth-functional arguments, further formalization was introduced by the use of symbols to represent the truth-functional connectives "and," "not," "or," "if . . . then," and "if and only if."

Logicians believe that *any* deductively valid argument is an instance of some valid *argument form*. Accordingly, the history of logic has been the history of an increasing awareness of the formal properties of arguments that are recognized intuitively as valid. Aristotle's theory of syllogisms was the first formal account of arguments. Shortly after Aristotle, the Stoic logicians developed a comprehensive theory of the forms of truth-functional arguments. Only much later did another important class of arguments receive formal treatment. The validity of these arguments depends on certain formal properties of *relations* mentioned in them. These *relational arguments* will be the subject of this chapter.

II. EXAMPLES OF RELATIONAL ARGUMENTS

The following arguments are obviously valid:

(1) New Maseratis are more expensive than new Cadillacs.
New Cadillacs are more expensive than new Fords.
———————————————————————————
New Maseratis are more expensive than new Fords.

(2) Jack is older than Jill.
————————————
Jill is not older than Jack.

(3) One British pint is equal to 570 milliliters.
————————————————————————
570 milliliters is equal to one British pint.

Using only the techniques of truth-functional logic and syllogistic logic, we cannot represent the forms by virtue of which any of these arguments are valid. In each case, the validity of the argument depends essentially on some property of the relations ("more expensive than," "older than," "equal to") referred to in the arguments, rather than simply on connections among the sentences in the argument or on how the subjects and predicates of the sentences are connected.

III. IMPORTANT PROPERTIES OF RELATIONS

Argument (1) is valid because if one thing is more expensive than a second, and the second is more expensive than a third, then the first is more expensive than the third. When a relation, such as "more expensive than" exhibits this feature, the relation is said to be *transitive*. Many ordinary relations are transitive. Some examples of transitive relations are: "older than," "younger than," "prettier than," "equal to," "greater than," "ancestor of," "descended from."

Not all relations are transitive. Some are *intransitive*. If the fact that one member is related to a second, and the second has the same relation to a third *rules out* the first member standing in that relation to the third, the relation is intransitive. The following argument is valid because the relation "mother of" is intransitive:

> Ruth is the mother of Betty.
> Betty is the mother of Claudia.
> _____
> Ruth is *not* the mother of Claudia.

Other examples of intransitive relations are "father of" and "twice as large as."

Some relations are neither transitive nor intransitive. ("Transitive" and "intransitive" are contrary terms, not contradictories.) These are called "*nontransitive relations*." If the first member is related by a nontransitive relation to a second and the second has that relation to a third, then the first member may or may not be related to the third in that way.

"Cousin of" is a nontransitive relation. If James is a cousin of Alice and Alice is a cousin of Richard, James may or may not be Richard's cousin. No conclusion can be drawn regarding the relation between the first and third members on the basis of a nontransitive relation between the first and second and the second and third. Some other nontransitive relations are "takes a class with," "likes some of the same foods as," "is a friend of," "loves," and "is in a carpool with."

All of the relations mentioned thus far are relations between things or individuals that are considered *two* at a time. These are called *binary relations*, or two-termed relations. The two things that are related by a binary relation are called the *terms* of the relation. Not all relations are binary. In "Clarissa bought her books from Edward," a relation connects three terms: Clarissa, her books, and Edward. The following sentence involves a four-term relation: "Tony gave money to Sally for the hospital fund-raiser." Although it becomes awkward to construct English sentences involving relations with more than four or five terms, theoretically any number of terms can be related. To avoid complexities, and to focus on some important properties of binary relations, our discussion in this chapter will be confined to binary relations that relate only two terms.

If we limit our consideration to binary relations, then the following sentence is true: Any relation whatsover falls into *exactly one* of the following categories: transitive, intransitive or nontransitive.

The relation mentioned in argument (2) in Section II ("older than") is a transitive relation. However, the validity of this argument does not depend on the transitivity of that relation but on another of its properties. "Older than" is an *asymmetric relation*. If the first member is related by an asymmetric relation to the second, then the second is *not* related to the first in that way. "Greater than," "less than," "weighs more than," and "mother of" are familiar examples of asymmetric relations.

If the fact that the first member has a relation to the second *implies* that the second has that same relation to the first, then the relation is said to be *symmetric*. "Equal to," "weighs the same as," "not identical with," and "sibling of" are all symmetric relations. The validity of argument (3) in Section II depends on the symmetry of "equal to."

There are also *nonsymmetric* relations in which the fact that the first member is related to the second *neither* implies *nor* rules out the second member having that relation to the first. "Brother of" is a nonsymmetric relation. Two individuals can be related in such a way that one is the brother of the other but the second is not brother of the first (when the second is female). Of course, in the case of two males, if the first is brother to the second, then the second is brother to the first. Since either situation is possible for two arbitrarily selected individuals, "brother of" is a nonsymmetric relation.

Every binary relation falls into *exactly one* of these three categories: symmetric, asymmetric, or nonsymmetric.

If an individual or a thing is related to itself by some relation, then that relation is said to be *reflexive*. Obviously, "identical with" is a reflexive relation; everything is identical with itself. Other examples of reflexive relations are "equal to" and "is the same color as."

When a relation is such that no individual or thing can have that relation to itself, then the relation is said to be *irreflexive*. Examples of irreflexive relations are "unequal to," "different from," "not the same as," and "greater than."

Some relations are *nonreflexive*. Individuals or things *may or may not* bear such relations to themselves. "Loves," for example, is nonreflexive; some persons love themselves, but others do not.

It may seem a bit odd to regard a relation as two-termed when the "two" things being related are one and the same. Nevertheless, it makes perfectly good sense to speak of a thing either having or failing to have some relation to itself. In general, the terms in any binary relation need not refer to distinct individuals.

Exercises

1. State whether each of the following relations is
    (1) Transitive, intransitive or nontransitive.
    (2) Symmetric, asymmetric, or nonsymmetric.
    (3) Reflexive, irreflexive, or nonreflexive.

    a. Loves   f. Is preferred to
    b. Cousin of   g. Plays better than
    c. Belongs to   h. Is taller than
    d. Looks like   i. Is identical with
    e. Less than   j. Is the same age as

2. Name ten different binary relations, and categorize each as transitive, symmetric, reflexive, and so on.

IV. USING QUANTIFIERS TO EXPRESS RELATIONS

Aristotle used *variables* (letters of the alphabet) to represent class terms when he formulated principles of reasoning. Using variables in this way simplifies the expression of principles and makes it easier to recognize the formal properties of arguments. The use of letters to represent sentences in truth-functional logic is a twentieth-century innovation. We can grasp some of the simplicity that we gain by applying this technique if we compare our formulation of *affirming the antecedent*:

$$p \rightarrow q$$
$$p$$
$$\underline{\qquad\qquad}$$
$$q$$

with the formulation of the ancient Stoic logicians:

> If the first, then the second.
> The first.
> _____
> Therefore, the second.*

When truth-functional argument forms involve numerous simple sentences, the use of sentence letters is even more attractive. (Try to express one of the dilemma forms of argument using expressions such as "the first," "the second," "the third," and so on.)

Twentieth-century developments in the symbolization of logic enable us to express the properties of relations in a compact way. The symbolic languages commonly used by modern logicians provide an adequate formulation of categorical syllogisms as well and, by employing symbols common to various types of arguments, serve to make apparent important logical similarities among truth-functional arguments, syllogistic arguments, and relational arguments.

In the following sections, we will speak of *translating* English expressions into artificial symbolic language. These translations are not intended to capture all of the nuances that could be expressed in the English language. Their purpose is to identify the features of arguments that are important for determining their validity. The symbols that you will be introduced to here are designed to capture only those features.

For any translation to be possible, the symbols of the artificial language must be *interpreted*. *Interpretations* specify the meanings of the symbols to the extent that truth conditions (the conditions under which sentences in the artificial language are true or false) are clearly specified. We have already done this (using truth tables) for the symbols used in truth-functional logic. Since the same connectives will be used here, the following summary is provided (remember, "p" and "q" are sentence letters):

---

*Benson Mates, *Elementary Logic*, p. 214.

1. "$\sim p$" is true if and only if p is false.
2. "$(p \vee q)$" is false only in cases when both "p" and "q" are false; otherwise, it is true.
3. "$(p \bullet q)$" is true only in cases when both "p" and "q" are true; otherwise, it is false.
4. "$(p \rightarrow q)$" is false whenever "p" is true and "q" is false; otherwise, it is true.
5. "$(p \leftrightarrow q)$" is true whenever "p" and "q" have the same truth value; otherwise, it is false.

Other features of interpretations will be discussed in context as they arise.

1. Symbolizing the Universal Quantifier

In the universal affirmative form "All S are P," "all" is called a *universal quantifier*. We have already discussed in Chapter 9 the logical structure and different ways of expressing these *universal affirmative sentences*. In the modern symbolic language, the universal affirmative is expressed as a kind of conditional:

If anything is an S then it is a P.

An alternative formulation is:

For any individual (person, place, or thing), if it is an S, then it is a P.

The universal quantifier is commonly symbolized by a lowercase letter from the end of the alphabet enclosed in parentheses. Examples are

(x) Read: "For any x"
(y) Read: "For any y"
(z) Read: "For any z"

In symbolizing the universal affirmative sentence, the same letter that is in the quantifier is used in place of pronouns such as "it" to refer to the same individuals. Thus, to symbolize "For any individual, if it is an S then it is a P," we write

$$(x) (Sx \rightarrow Px)$$

Parentheses enclose the expression following the quantifier to indicate that the xs in this expression are those referred to by the quantifier that precedes the expression. The letters used in this way are called *individual variables*; the uppercase letters used to represent *classes* of individuals are called *predicate letters*.

Now, suppose that we want to translate the English categorical sentence "All suffragettes are feminists" into a symbolic sentence that represents the meaning of the English sentence as closely as possible. The first step is to specify a *domain of interpretation*, or the *set of all individuals* that we will refer to in the artificial language. This domain may vary from interpretation to interpretation. In one situation we may be talking only about numbers and can choose the *set of all numbers* as our domain of interpretation. In another situation, we may be referring only to persons and can choose the *set of all persons* as our domain. The domain of interpretation can be any nonempty set of individuals. To simplify matters for all interpretations in this chapter, unless otherwise noted, we will select as our domain of interpretation the set of all individuals. (The members of this domain are all persons, things, numbers, and so on.)

Predicate letters will be interpreted as referring to *classes* (sets) of individuals in the domain. To translate our sentence, we need to interpret one predicate letter as referring to the class of suffragettes, and a second predicate letter as referring to the class of feminists. We will interpret *S* as the class of suffragettes, and *F* as the class of feminists. Then "All suffragettes are feminists" can be translated into

$$(x)(Sx \rightarrow Fx)$$

The universal negative sentence ("No *S* are *P*") has a structure similar to the universal affirmative and is written

$$(x)(Sx \rightarrow \sim Px)$$

("For any individual, if it is an *S*, then it is not a *P*").

To translate the sentence "No chihuahuas are guide-dogs," we interpret:

C: the class of chihuahuas
G: the class of guide-dogs

and write

$$(x)(Cx \rightarrow \sim Gx)$$

2. Symbolizing the Existential Quantifier

The quantifier "some" is called the *existential quantifier. Particular affirmative sentences* and *particular negative sentences* assert both that some individual *exists* and that the individual either *has* or *lacks* some property. These sentences are said to have *existential import.* Universal sentences lack existential import, since they do not assert the existence of anything.

The *I* and *O* sentences have a different structure from universal sentences. They resemble conjunctions rather than conditionals:

I: Some *S* are *P*.
There is some individual that is an *S and* also a *P*.

O: Some *S* are not *P*.
There is some individual that is an *S* and not a *P*.

The existential quantifier is symbolized by a backward "E" followed by an individual variable and enclosed in parentheses: $(\exists x)$.

To symbolize the existential, or particular, affirmative categorical sentence, we write

$$(\exists x)(Sx \cdot Px)$$

which can be read: "There is some *x* such that it is *S* and it is *P*."

To symbolize the existential (particular) negative categorical sentence, we write

$$(\exists x)(Sx \cdot {\sim}Px)$$

which can be read: "There is some *x* such that it is *S* and it is not *P*."

Exercises

Provide suitable interpretations for predicate letters, and translate the following sentences into the symbolic language:

1. Some dogs have fleas.

2. Some cats are not independent.

3. No dogs are vegetarians.

4. All cats are independent.   *For all x, if its a cat then its independent*

5. There are wild cats.

6. Cats are quadrupeds.

7. Not all dogs bark.

8. All dogs bark and all cats meow.

9. Some dogs bark, but some do not.

10. Dogs and cats are fine pets.

11. If some cats are wild, then some are tame.

12. If no dogs are cats, then no cats are dogs.

3. Symbolizing Relational Sentences

With a minor modification, the symbols used to represent categorical sentences can be adapted to express relations. The class terms that occur in categorical sentences can be thought of as *one-place predicates*. Using symbols, we indicate that an individual *x* is a member of a class *S* by writing a predicate letter followed by a single individual variable: *Sx*. In a similar manner, we can think of binary relations as *two-place predicates*. Using symbols, we indicate that an individual *x* stands in a relation *R* to an individual *y* by writing that predicate letter followed by the pair of variables, taken in the proper order: *Rxy*.

Two-place predicate letters are interpreted as referring to sets of *ordered pairs* of individuals who are related by the relation in question. For example, we could interpret the predicate letter "*L*" as referring to the set of all pairs of individuals such that the first member of the pair loves the second member of the pair. In specifying such interpretations, we use the following notation:

$$L: \underline{\qquad} \text{loves} \ldots$$

Using quantifiers, predicate letters, and individual variables, generalizations that involve relations can be expressed in symbols. For example, if we interpret "*L*" as above, we can translate "Everything loves everything" into symbols:

$$(x)(y)(Lxy)$$

If we want to translate the sentence "Everybody loves everybody," we need to use a predicate letter to represent the class of persons. If we interpret *P* in this way, then the sentence is translated:

$$(x)(y)((Px \bullet Py) \rightarrow Lxy)$$

which can be read: "Given any *x* and any *y*, if *x* is a person and *y* is a person then *x* loves *y*." Note that if we choose to limit our domain of interpretation to the set of all persons, then "Everybody loves everybody" is translated

$$(x)(y)(Lxy)$$

Given the same interpretation of "*L*," "Something loves something" is translated as

$$(\exists x)(\exists y)(Lxy)$$

Again, interpreting "*P*" as the class of persons, and "*L*" as loves, "Somebody loves somebody" is translated:

$$(\exists x)(\exists y)(Px \bullet Py \bullet Lxy)$$

In contrast to generalizations about relations, sentences such as "Ruth is the mother of Betty" state that some specific individual is related to another specific individual. In our symbolic language, lowercase letters from the earlier part of the alphabet (a–t) are interpreted as referring to individuals. These letters, called *individual constants* perform the same function in the symbolic language as proper names perform in ordinary language. For example, we could symbolize the sentence "Socrates is mortal" by interpreting "*s*" to refer to Socrates and "*M*" to refer to the class of mortals and writing

$$Ms$$

Socrates, one of the most important philosophers of all time, was married to Xanthippe. If we interpret "*H*" to refer to "_____ is husband of . . . ," "*s*" to refer to Socrates, and "*a*" to refer to Xanthippe, then

$$Hsa$$

is true, for it says that Socrates is the husband of Xanthippe. Given the same interpretations,

$$Has$$

is false, for it says that Xanthippe is the husband of Socrates. Obviously, "husband of" is an asymmetric relation.

Using quantifiers, individual variables, and two-place predicate letters, we can conveniently and precisely characterize important properties of binary relations. If R is some two-place relation, then we can symbolically express any of the following properties of R:

1. R is reflexive: $(x) Rxx$
   The symbolic formula can be read: "Given anything, it stands in relation R to itself."
2. R is irreflexive: $(x)(\sim Rxx)$
   "Given anything, it is not related by R to itself."
3. R is nonreflexive: $\sim(x)(Rxx) \bullet \sim(x)(\sim Rxx)$
   "It is not the case that R is reflexive, and it is not the case that R is irreflexive. (Or, "R is not reflexive, and R is not irreflexive.")
4. R is symmetric: $(x)(y)(Rxy \rightarrow Ryx)$
   "Given any x and any y (not necessarily distinct), if x bears relation R to y, then y bears relation R to x."
5. R is asymmetric: $(x)(y)(Rxy \rightarrow \sim Ryx)$
   "Given any x and any y (not necessarily distinct), if x bears relation R to y, then y does not bear relation R to x."
6. R is nonsymmetric:
   $\sim(x)(y)(Rxy \rightarrow Ryx) \bullet \sim(x)(y)(Rxy \rightarrow \sim Ryx)$
   "R is not symmetric, and R is not asymmetric."
7. R is transitive: $(x)(y)(z)((Rxy \bullet Ryz) \rightarrow Rxz)$
   "For any three individuals x, y, z (not necessarily distinct), if the first

bears relation R to the second and the second bears relation R to the third, then the first bears relation R to the third."

8. R is intransitive: $(x)(y)(z)((Rxy \cdot Ryz) \to \sim Rxz)$

"For any three individuals x, y, z (not necessarily distinct), if x bears relation R to y and y bears relation R to z, then x does not bear relation R to z."

Exercises

Express each of the following in symbols, providing interpretations for symbols when necessary. Be sure to specify the domain of interpretation.

1. R is nontransitive.

2. Mary loves someone.

3. John loves himself.

4. John loves himself and Mary.

5. Mary does not love John.

6. Someone loves Mary.

7. Everyone loves John.

8. No one loves John.

9. Mary loves no one.

10. Everyone loves John, or everyone loves Mary.

11. Not everyone loves himself.

12. Someone does not love himself.

4. Multiple Quantifiers

To symbolize most generalizations involving relations, we must use more than one quantifier. For example, to state the property of transitivity of a relation, three universal quantifiers are required. When multiple quantifiers are all of the same type (all universal or all existential), the order in which they are placed at the beginning of the symbolized expression is irrelevant. Assuming that R is interpreted the same way in each case, there is no difference in meaning among the following:

$$(x)(y)(z)((Rxy \cdot Ryz) \to Rxz)$$
$$(y)(x)(z)((Rxy \cdot Ryz) \to Rxz)$$
$$(z)(y)(x)((Rxy \cdot Ryz) \to Rxz)$$

Likewise, there is no difference in meaning between

$$(\exists x)(\exists y)(Rxy \bullet Ryx)$$

and

$$(\exists y)(\exists x)(Rxy \bullet Ryx)$$

However, when there are multiple quantifiers of both types in a single expression, care must be taken, for the meaning may not be preserved when quantifiers are reordered. Consider the sentence "Everybody has a mother." Let us limit our domain to the set of persons.

$$M: \underline{\hspace{1cm}} \text{ is the mother of } \ldots$$

The symbolic sentence is

$$(x)(\exists y)(Myx)$$

Based on the given interpretation for M, the symbolic sentence can be read

Given any x, there is some y such that y is the mother of x.

In other words, the sentence says that for any person, there is someone who is the mother of that person.

If the order of the quantifiers is reversed, the symbolic sentence becomes

$$(\exists y)(x)(Myx)$$

Based on the given interpretation for M, this sentence can be read

There is some y such that given any x, y is the mother of x.

In other words, someone is the mother of everyone! When "someone" occurs at the beginning of the expression, it means "some one person," and it is clearly false that some one person is the mother of everyone. When "someone" occurs in the position shown in the first translation, it means "someone or other," and it is true that every person has someone or other as a mother. Thus, although these two symbolic expressions differ only in the order in which the quantifiers are placed at the beginning of the expression, they have very different meanings.

Exercise

Using the set of persons as the domain of interpretation and interpreting "L" as "$\underline{\hspace{1cm}}$ loves . . . ," express each of the following in symbolic language.

1. Everyone loves someone (or other). $(x)(\exists y)(Lxy$

2. No one loves everyone. $\sim(\exists x)(y)(\sim Lxy)$

3. No one loves anyone.

4. Someone loves everyone.

5. There is someone whom no one loves.

5. The Fallacy of Every and All

It was—and is—widely believed that everything that happens does so as a result of some cause. In antiquity, the claim, "Everything that happens has a cause" was used as a premiss to infer that there is some "first cause" of everything. If this argument is valid, however, it must be an instance of some form other than the following:

$$(x)(\exists y)(Cyx)$$
$$\overline{(\exists y)(x)(Cyx)}$$

because this form is invalid. Based on the intended interpretation (*C:* ____ causes . . .), the symbolization provides a reasonable translation of the argument, as just stated above. However, it is possible to interpret *C* in such a way that the premiss is obviously true, but the conclusion is obviously false (*C:* ____ is mother of . . .). Since an instance of the argument form is invalid, namely (when the domain of interpretation is the set of all persons)

Everyone has a mother.
_____
Someone is everyone's mother.

the form itself is invalid. For an argument form to be valid, every interpretation of the nonlogical symbols (all symbols except the connectives and the quantifiers) must result in a valid argument.

This fallacious form of argument is called the *fallacy of every and all*. We must remember, however, that an argument that is an instance of some fallacious *argument form* may not be an invalid *argument*. The argument is invalid only if it is not an instance of any valid argument form. Nevertheless, as with truth-functional arguments, we should at least suspect invalidity when an argument is an instance of an invalid form and when no analysis of the argument is provided to show that it is an instance of some valid form.

Aristotle's argument for the existence of a first cause, or "prime mover," actually involved at least one further premiss: an infinite series of causes and effects is impossible. We might symbolize Aristotle's rejection of an infinite regress of causes—the claim that there must be some cause that is not the effect of any other cause—as

$$(\exists y)((\exists x)(Cyx) \bullet \sim(\exists z)(Czy))$$

Or, "There is a *y* such that *y* causes some *x* and no *z* causes *y*." Even the addition of this premiss does not allow us to conclude that there is just one first cause, however, for there may be more than one "uncaused cause." ("Some" means "at least one"; it does not mean "exactly one.")

Although it is difficult to analyze some of Aristotle's arguments because of problems with translating the ancient Greek language and because the early texts have been altered and are incomplete, many interpreters impute the fallacy of every and all to Aristotle in more than one context. In commenting on Aristotle's apparent use of the premiss that every action has a final end to support the conclusion that there is one and the same end to all actions, called the "Supreme Good," a contemporary philosopher has said in defense of the founder of logic:

> This is a type of reasoning [relational logic] that lies beyond the reach of his own formal logic. He may, for this reason, have been more easily deceived by this fallacy.*

V. SYMBOLIZING ARGUMENTS

One of the advantages of modern symbolic languages is their capacity to expose important similarities in structure among various types of arguments. Consider, for example, the following quasi-syllogism:

All princesses are beautiful.
Diana is a princess.
_____

Diana is beautiful.

based on the interpretation:

> P: the class of princesses
> B: the class of beautiful persons
> d: Diana

the argument can be translated

$$(x)(Px \rightarrow Bx)$$
$$Pd$$
$$\overline{}$$
$$Bd$$

This form is similar to the form of *affirming the antecedent*:

$$p \rightarrow q$$
$$p$$
$$\overline{}$$
$$q$$

* D. J. O'Connor, "Aristotle," in *A Critical History of Western Philosophy*, edited by D. J. O'Connor.

We can also consider the fact that a universal generalization is a sentence that says something about every individual in the domain of interpretation. If what the universal generalization says is true of every individual in the domain, then it is true of any *particular* individual in the domain. For example, based on the given interpretation, if

$$(x)(Px \rightarrow Bx)$$

is true, then so is

$$Pd \rightarrow Bd$$

If we replace the first premiss with a particular instance of the generalization ("$Pd \rightarrow Bd$"), then the argument becomes

$$Pd \rightarrow Bd$$
$$Pd$$
$$\overline{}$$
$$Bd$$

This is obviously the same form as affirming the antecedent and is therefore a valid argument form. Thus, the original quasi-syllogism is valid. This method of determining the validity of the argument form of quasi-syllogisms seems less arbitrary than the treatment suggested in Chapter 9. There, sentences like "Diana is a princess" were treated as a type of universal generalization: "All members of the class of which Diana is the only member are princesses." This method was somewhat artificial because universal generalizations lack existential import, but the sentence "Diana is a princess" ordinarily would be regarded as false if she did not exist.

A detailed discussion of the systems of logic that employ quantifiers is beyond the scope of this text. It is worth noting, however, that all these systems have a rule of inference that permits a move to be made from universally quantified sentences to their particular instances. Additional rules allow removing existential quantifiers and replacing both types of quantifiers after they have been removed in specified circumstances. With this in mind, consider the similarity between the following syllogistic form of argument and the truth-functional form of hypothetical syllogism:

$(x)(Sx \rightarrow Mx)$	$p \rightarrow q$
$(x)(Mx \rightarrow Px)$	$q \rightarrow r$
$\overline{(x)(Sx \rightarrow Px)}$	$\overline{p \rightarrow r}$

Similarities between syllogistic arguments, truth-functional arguments, and relational arguments also become apparent when we use this symbolic language. For example, the validity of the argument "Marcy ran faster than Sam, and Sam ran faster than Carrie; therefore, Marcy ran faster than Carrie," depends on the true, but unstated premiss that "ran faster than" is a transitive relation. The argument can be symbolized, using the following interpretation:

R: _____ ran faster than . . .

m: Marcy s: Sam c: Carrie

$(x)(y)(z)((Rxy \bullet Ryz) \to Rxz)$
$Rms \bullet Rsc$

_____

Rmc

Here, too, the symbolism shows the similarity between this form and *affirming the antecedent*.

The value of symbolic techniques in modern logic should not be underestimated. The use of appropriate symbols has allowed advances to be made in this field that are comparable to the advances in mathematics that resulted from the replacement of the system of Roman numerals with the system of Arabic numerals.

VI. REVIEW

In Chapter 10, you have been introduced to arguments in which validity depends on the properties of binary relations referred to in the arguments. You have also been introduced to some of the symbolic techniques used in modern logic to express the forms of these arguments, and have been shown how some of these forms resemble familiar truth-functional forms.

Every binary relation falls into exactly one of each of the following categories:

1. Transitive, intransitive, nontransitive.
2. Symmetric, asymmetric, nonsymmetric.
3. Reflexive, irreflexive, nonreflexive.

You should review the definitions presented in this chapter of these properties of relations, and be able to categorize examples of binary relations according to these properties.

In many arguments in which validity depends on some property of a relation referred to in the argument, the premisses do not include a statement of that property. You should be able to recognize such unstated premisses and to supply them when you reconstruct these arguments.

You should be able to translate categorical sentences and sentences involving relations from English into the logical symbolism that reveals their logical structure. To do this, you need to remember that universal sentences are to be treated as quantified conditional sentences and that existential (particular) sentences are to be treated as quantified conjunctions.

Finally, you should be able to recognize apparent instances in English of the *fallacy of every and all*. This fallacy occurs when sentences containing both universal and existential quantifiers are treated as if truth is always preserved when the order in which their quantifiers occur are exchanged. The ability to symbolize such English sentences helps us to avoid this fallacy.

VII. EXERCISES

1. For each of the following arguments, name the property of the relation that makes the argument valid:
   a. Horses can outrun greyhounds, and greyhounds exist. But greyhounds can outrun rabbits, so horses can outrun rabbits.
   b. Seven is greater than the square root of 48, so the square root of 48 is not greater than 7.
   c. John is married to Sarah, so Sarah is married to John.
   d. Marianne's hair is the same color as Caroline's, and Caroline is a blond, so Marianne is a blond.

2. Relations that are transitive, symmetric, and reflexive are called *equivalence relations*. Can you give three examples of equivalence relations?

3. Relations that are transitive, asymmetric, and irreflexive are called *ordering relations*. Can you give an example of an ordering relation?

4. When an individual *a* is related by a relation *R* to individual *b*, then *b* is said to be related to *a* by a relation called the *converse of R*. What is the converse of the following relations?
   a. Husband of
   b. Parent of
   c. Greater than
   d. Greater than or equal to
   e. Owned by

5. When a relation is symmetric, what can we say about its converse?

6. Provide a suitable interpretation and translate the following into the symbolic language developed in this chapter, using relational predicates when appropriate:
   a. Cats make better pets than dogs.
   b. Some cats are smarter than any dog.
   c. Every dog fears some cat.
   d. Some cat is feared by every dog.
   e. Christopher is Virginia's brother.
   f. Not everyone has a cousin.
   g. Cats and dogs are smarter than goldfish.
   h. Snakes eat mice.
   i. Every rich woman owns a piano.
   j. Some poor people own pianos.

    k. Christopher plays pianos.
    l. "Cousin of" is not a transitive relation.

7. Provide a suitable interpretation and symbolize all four of the arguments in Exercise 1 of this set. Be sure to symbolize the unstated premisses concerning the properties of the relations involved as well as the stated premisses.

8. G. E. M. Anscombe, in *An Introduction to Wittgenstein's Tractatus*, draws attention to the following argument. What is wrong with it?

> At all times there is a possibility of my abstaining from smoking. Therefore, there is a possibility of my abstaining from smoking at all times.

9. Construct (or find) an example of an argument in English that apparently commits the fallacy of every and all.

10. Give an example of a relation that is reflexive but not symmetric.

Paying Special Attention to the Language of Arguments: Definitions

---

C H A P T E R   1 1

I. AMBIGUITY AND VAGUENESS

Assessing the correctness of deductive or inductive arguments requires paying special attention to the language in which the arguments are cast. Before we can decide whether or not a conclusion of an argument follows from its premisses, we must understand what the premiss sentences and the conclusion sentence mean. This task can be complicated by the *vagueness* or the *ambiguity* of many English expressions. We have already adopted certain conventions to eliminate ambiguities in logical connectives, such as "or" and "if . . . then." These conventions help us to represent the formal structures of arguments so that we can test their validity. In this section, we will discuss how ambiguity and vagueness in expressions that are not logical connectives affect arguments.

1. Ambiguity

An expression is *ambiguous* if it has more than one distinct meaning. In English, the word "pen" is ambiguous. It can be used to refer to an instrument for writing, an enclosure for animals, or a penitentiary, and its intended meaning within the context of an expression may not be obvious. Frequently, the sentence in which the word occurs does make its meaning clear. Sometimes, a broader context— several sentences, or an account of the circumstances in which the sentence is uttered or written—is needed to resolve an ambiguity. For example, in the sentence "Mark's pen won't write," the meaning of "pen" is clear. However, more information than "Mark couldn't get out of the pen" is needed to know whether Mark was trapped in an animal pen or in a penitentiary.

When we evaluate syllogisms and quasi-syllogisms, we must see that expressions are used in the same sense each time they occur within a single argument. If an ambiguous expression is used in more than one way, there may be more than three terms in the argument, even though the same English expression is used for two of the terms. Consider the following argument:

Mad men should not be permitted to make important decisions concerning the lives of others.
My father is mad.

My father should not be permitted to make important decisions concerning the lives of others.

Suppose that this argument is offered in the following context: My father, whose mental competence is not in question, is mad (angry) at me because I took a curve at a reckless speed and rolled his car over. He has refused to let me drive his car in the future—a decision that significantly inconveniences me.

The first premiss is plausible only if the term "mad" is understood in the sense of "not mentally competent." But in the second premiss, the meaning of "mad" is different: here, "mad" means the same as "angry." So although the argument resembles a quasi-syllogism, it actually contains more than three terms and is not a valid argument.

When the persuasive force of an argument depends on shifts of meaning in ambiguous terms—called *"equivocations"*—the argument is said to commit the *fallacy of equivocation*. In the preceding example, the equivocation involves the single ambiguous word, "mad." In other cases, the equivocation may result from the ambiguity of a whole sentence or larger unit of language. Consider the following extract from the *Journal* of John Wesley (the founder of Methodism):

> 1751. London. I was carried to the Foundery and preached, kneeling (as I could not stand) on part of the Twenty-third Psalm.

Wesley had sprained his ankle and had preached in a kneeling position. His text was the Twenty-third Psalm. However, the sentence could be understood to mean that he knelt on a copy of the Psalm as he preached.

The type of ambiguity in Wesley's sentence, sometimes called *"amphiboly,"* is the result of ambiguous sentence structure instead of a single ambiguous term. Such ambiguities can occur when commas are omitted or improperly placed or when grammatical rules for the placement of modifiers are ignored. For example, "He has two grown sons and a daughter in the nunnery" is a puzzling sentence for it suggests that the sons as well as the daughter are in the nunnery. The ambiguity is resolved when a comma is placed after "sons." Another example is "The guards and prisoners who refused to join in the prison break were tied and left behind," which sounds as if there were guards who refused to break out of prison! There should be a comma following "guards" and a comma following "break." The sentence "They have brown and green eyes" is ambiguous; it could mean that the persons referred to have multicolored eyes, but it is probably an attempt to express "Some of them have brown eyes and some have green eyes."

Other ambiguities arise through the use of adjectives and adverbs that are *relative terms*. "Small" and "large" are examples of such terms. A large mouse is not a large animal. A small skyscraper is probably not a small building.

Ambiguity can also result from shifting the *accent* or emphasis on certain words when a passage is read or spoken. Boswell, in his *Journal*, criticized a fellow lawyer for inferring that it was all right to lie *for* his client on the grounds that the Ninth Commandment, which is usually interpreted as a prohibition of lying, actually says "Thou shalt not bear false witness *against* thy neighbor."

There are no recipes for avoiding and detecting fallacies of equivocation; but the recognition that many words do have more than one meaning, that grammatical constructions can be misleading, and that shifts in emphasis can change the meaning of a passage provides some defense against the most serious mistakes. In some situations, it may be necessary to ask for or to give a definition of an ambiguous term to prevent misunderstanding. (Techniques for definition will be discussed in Section II.)

When our primary purpose is to present or to evaluate evidence, it is advisable to resolve ambiguities and to make all claims as explicit and precise as possible. Nevertheless, conveying information to be used in arguments is only one use of language. Ambiguities play an important and valuable role in the expressive language of poetry, in which the use of words and expressions to evoke a number of different images and to convey several meanings is crucial. Puns and other forms of humor also depend on ambiguity. Our language would be terribly impoverished without such ambiguities.

Exercises

Discuss the ambiguities on which the following arguments depend:

1. Mary is a person who is a good dancer. Therefore, Mary is a good person.

2. Jumbo is a small elephant. Therefore, Jumbo is a small animal.

3. All women are not feminists. Betty Friedan is a woman. Therefore, she is not a feminist.

4. Camels are the ships of the desert. Ships, in order to move, must be propelled by motors, sails, or oars. Therefore, camels must be propelled by motors, sails, or oars.

5. *Lord Caversham:* Good evening, Lady Chiltern! Has my good-for-nothing young son been here?

   Mabel Chiltern: (coming up to Lord Caversham): Why do you call Lord Goring good-for-nothing?

   Lord Caversham: Because he leads such an idle life.

   Mabel Chiltern: How can you say such a thing? Why he rides in the Row at ten o'clock in the morning, goes to the Opera three times a week, changes his clothes at least five times a day, and dines out every night of the season. You don't call that leading an idle life, do you?
   —Oscar Wilde, "An Ideal Husband"

6. In antiquity, the oracle at Delphi was consulted for advice about important undertakings. Croesus the Rich, king of Lydia, asked the oracle if he would succeed in a war against Persia. "The only answer the Greek holy of holies gave him was that by going to war he would destroy a great empire. It happened to be his own, but, as the priestess pointed out, she was not responsible for his lack of wit."
   —Edith Hamilton, *The Greek Way*

(Discuss the ambiguity on which Croesus's inference depended.)

7. Arguments for the safety of nuclear power contend that since humans have lived with a certain amount of natural radiation with acceptable consequences, this is a normal condition, and that thus it is all right (moral) for nuclear plants to increase the amount of radiation by a "small" amount (a factor of two or less).

2. Vagueness

An expression is *vague* if "borderline cases" occur in which it is unclear whether or not the expression is applicable. Vagueness differs from ambiguity in that an ambiguous term is one that has at least two distinct, *nonoverlapping* meanings. Some English words, such as "kid," are both ambiguous and vague. "Kid" is ambiguous because it can refer to a young goat or a young child. In the first sense, "kid" is not vague, for goats stop being kids when they are one year old. However, there is no clear cutoff point at which a person is no longer a "kid." In this section, we will ignore possible ambiguities of the terms discussed so that we can concentrate on vagueness.

A standard example of a term that is vague in the sense that it has borderline cases of application is "bald." A person with no hair at all is bald; a person with a full head of hair is not bald. But there are cases in which it is unclear whether the term "bald" is applicable or not. Other examples of terms that are vague in this sense are "old," "happy," "rich," and "thin." Most color terms are also vague.

Vague terms, like ambiguous terms, can cause difficulties in arguments. For example, the argument that concludes a man is not religious on the grounds that he does not attend church regularly is defective because it fails to recognize that "religious" is a vague term. There are a number of distinct criteria for being religious, including—but not limited to—belief in a supernatural being; membership in an organized religion; adoption of an ethical code or set of altruistic values; performance of acts of devotion or piety; and a sense of reverence toward fellow humans, other living things, or even the entire universe. It is appropriate to call a person "religious" when all, or only some, of these criteria are applicable.

Since "religious" is a vague term, it is unclear just how many of these criteria must be met in order to apply the term "religious" to someone. If all of them are applicable to some person, that person is religious. If none of these criteria apply, the person is not religious. Evidence that someone does not attend church regularly appeals to only one of the criteria and is clearly not enough to support the conclusion that the person is not religious.

Vagueness is a pervasive, important, and useful feature of language, and it would be foolish—if not impossible—to try to eliminate all vague terms. Ordinary social conversation would be severely hampered without such comfortable but vague expressions as "See you soon," or "I'll call you sometime," or "How have you been?—Just fine." International diplomacy depends heavily on vague language. Threats can be communicated by using such expressions as "The government has warned that it will take strong measures if its territorial waters are violated" without giving away any secrets or risking loss of face.

In some circumstances, however, vague words should be given precise definitions. For example, although the vagueness of the term "religion" poses no problems in most ordinary contexts, some historical situations demand a precise definition of this term. For a long time in the United States, conscientious objectors to military service who were members of some religion were treated differently from conscientious objectors who were not religious. Religious objectors were assigned to alternate nonmilitary service. Nonreligious objectors went to jail.

Leaving aside the question of whether any religious test should be applied to conscientious objectors, obviously, when something as serious as a prison sentence is at stake, it is important to state precisely the conditions under which someone will be assigned to prison. What is needed in this particular situation is a definition of "religion" that will reduce its vagueness. In the next section, various techniques for defining terms, as well as several types and purposes of definition, including definitions to reduce vagueness, will be discussed.

II. DEFINITIONS

Many books have been written on various aspects of linguistic meaning. In this text, we will touch briefly on only a small part of this fascinating subject. Here, we will be concerned primarily with the meanings of words only insofar as their meanings affect the understanding and evaluation of arguments. A number of different ways of defining words (giving their meanings) are suitable for different purposes.

1. Ostensive Definition

Among the most primitive ways to define a term is to point to individuals, things, or events to which the term applies, or to display them, or to use some other nonverbal method of drawing attention to the objects being defined. Parents use this technique to introduce many words to their infants. They point to baby's eyes, nose, and ears, to dogs, cats, and birds, and to many other objects, while uttering the words that refer to the objects. This technique is called ostensive definition. It is fundamentally important because it establishes a link between words and objects in the world that are referred to by words.

There are, however, limits to the usefulness of ostensive definition. Sometimes attention is directed to the wrong object. A baby may notice the pointing finger rather than the nose when the word "nose" is uttered. Or the baby may suppose that the whole face or the whole person is meant by "nose." A general term, such as "eye," can be defined ostensively only by pointing to particular eyes, and there is always the danger that some special feature of the particular eyes, such as their color, will be mistakenly attached to the general term "eye."

Definition by ostension is further limited because there may be no objects in the vicinity of the type for which a definition is required. A New Yorker can offer ostensive definitions of skyscrapers in midtown Manhattan—but not in the New Guinea highlands, unless some appropriate pictures are available. Moreover, the technique of ostensive definition is not suitable for abstract objects, such as numbers, the gross national product, or the average worker. Abstract objects cannot be pointed to or displayed. Nevertheless, despite these limitations, ostensive definition is useful in many circumstances because it provides a crucial connection between language and nonlinguistic aspects of the world.

2. Verbal Extensional Definition

Ostensive definition is sometimes called *nonverbal extensional definition.* The *extension* of a term is the set of individuals, objects, or events to which the term can be correctly applied. The extension of "boat" is the set of all boats; the extension of "dog" is the set of all dogs; the extension of "prizefighter" is the set of all prizefighters. In ostensive definition, as we have seen, some member or members of the set to which the term applies are pointed to, pictured, or displayed in some way.

Verbal extensional definitions also select members of the set to which the term applies, but the selection is accomplished verbally by naming members of the set. For example, "prizefighter" might be defined by naming some prizefighters, such as Muhammad Ali, Joe Louis, and Sonny Liston; "president of the United States" might be defined by naming Washington, Adams, Jefferson, Lincoln, Roosevelt, Carter, and Reagan.

Verbal extensional definitions, like ostensive definitions, have limitations. Terms such as "prizefighter" refer not only to all present and past prizefighters but also to future prizefighters. In such cases, it is impossible to provide a complete verbal extensional definition that lists all members of the class. When only a partial listing is given, misunderstanding can occur because it is possible to focus on some property shared by all members of the list that is not the same as the term being defined. For example, Ali, Louis, and Liston are not only all prizefighters, they are also all heavyweights, all world champions, and all blacks.

Another limitation of the technique of verbal extensional definition is the difficulty of listing members of sets when the members have no names. Sometimes *subsets* (rather than *members*) of the set that is the extension of a term can be listed, and this may suffice to convey the meaning of the term. For example, we could define "marsupial" extensionally by naming various kinds of marsupials, such as opossums, kangaroos, and wallabies. But it would be very difficult to formulate a verbal extensional definition of "kangaroo." Individual kangaroos do not ordinarily have names, and various types of kangaroos are not known by familiar enough terms to convey their meaning to someone who does not know what a kangaroo is.

3. Intensional Definition

The *intension* of a term is the set of *all and only* those properties that a thing must possess for that term to apply to it. For example, a person must possess the property of being a professional boxer for the term "prizefighter" to be correctly applicable. When a term is given an *explicit* intensional definition, a phrase equivalent in meaning to the term is stated, as in

"Prizefighter" means "a professional boxer."

All intensional definitions are verbal. We can distinguish several types of explicit intensional definitions by recognizing that definitions have various purposes.

i. Definitions that Show How a Word Is Commonly Used

Most dictionary definitions, such as the intensional definition of "prizefighter" just given, are of this type. They are sometimes called *"lexical definitions."* To do its job properly, a lexical definition should be neither too narrow nor too broad. The definition should state the set of properties possessed by all things to which the term applies, and only to those things. For example, the following definition of "knife":

> "Knife" means "an instrument for cutting"

is too broad; some instruments for cutting, namely scissors, are not knives. The definition of "table"

> "Table" means "a piece of furniture consisting of a flat top set horizontally on four legs"

is too narrow; some tables have fewer and some tables have more than four legs.

A definition can be both too broad and too narrow. For example,

> "Cat" means "domestic animal"

is too *broad*, since "domestic animal" applies to livestock, dogs, and various other pets as well. The definition is also too *narrow*, since many wild animals belong to the cat family.

In addition to being neither too broad nor too narrow, lexical definitions should not be circular. A *circular definition* incorporates the term being defined, or some variant of that term, in the definition. For example

> "Full-time student" means "a person who is enrolled full time at his or her school"

is a circular definition. Such definitions are not helpful in conveying the meaning of a word. Sometimes, circularity is not as apparent as it is in this example, because there are several definitions in the circle. Consider the following set of definitions, taken from a recently published dictionary:

> "Grazing" means "feeding on growing grass."

> "Grass" means "any of various green plants that are eaten by grazing animals."

What we learn from these definitions is little more than that grazing animals feed on growing grass and grass is what is eaten by grazing animals. This pair of definitions comes quite close to being circular.

ii. Definitions that Introduce a New Word into the Language

Occasionally, when new situations arise or our interests shift to features not previously noted as important, it is useful to introduce a new word into the language. The definitions that introduce new words are called *"stipulative definitions."* For example, the term "astronaut" is a recent introduction to the language. At the time it was introduced, its meaning was stipulated:

"Astronaut" means "a person trained to make rocket flights to outer space."

Before the middle of this century, there were no rocket flights to outer space and no persons were trained to make these flights. Thus, there was no reason to have a special term to refer to such persons. New words can always be introduced into a language when salient features of the world make them applicable.

The *conventional* nature of language is most apparent in stipulative definitions. Expressions in a language do not acquire their meanings as a result of some *natural* connection between the words and the things in the world that the words denote. The connection between the word "thunder" and the meteorological phenomenon of thunder is *conventional*, unlike the *natural* connection between thunder and lightning. Words have the meanings they do as a result of the widespread acceptance of proposals to use them in a certain way. This is not to say that the first humans who used language stipulated the meanings of all of the original expressions in a manner similar to the stipulation of the meaning of "astronaut." Although the origins of language are a complete mystery, such a scenario seems highly unlikely. Nevertheless, given what we do know about the development of languages—the ways in which new words are added and words that are no longer useful are discarded—the conventional nature of language seems indisputable. Different human languages use different words to refer to many of the same features of the world (the development of different languages involved the adoption of different conventions) but no language is more correct or "true to the world" than another language.

Although new words can be introduced into language and their meanings can be stipulated by whoever introduces them, stipulative definitions must meet two requirements if they are to be acceptable:

1. *A term that is stipulatively defined should not already have a widely accepted standard meaning.* When Alice objects to Humpty Dumpty's claim that he is the master of words—words mean what he wants them to mean—she is complaining that he is stipulating new meanings for words with established senses that differ from their stipulated senses. Alice is justified in her complaint. Confusion obviously results from Humpty Dumpty's attitude toward words with established usage.

2. *A term that is stipulatively defined should be a useful addition to the language.* Making up new words and offering stipulative definitions for them may be an amusing pastime, but unless the new words serve some useful purpose, it is unlikely that the proposed definitions will be incorporated into the language. Special interests or studies often require the stipulation of a new vocabulary; space technology, which has prompted the introduction of many new terms besides "astronaut," is a case in point. There is, however, the danger that mere *jargon*—terminology that is incomprehensible to those outside a special-interest group—

may be substituted for ordinary language, even though the special interest requires no new concepts and could be expressed in terms with accepted standard meanings. Stipulative definitions of this type are unfortunate because they tend to result in the failure rather than the improvement of communication.

iii. Definitions that Reduce Vagueness

Sometimes, it is important to clarify the meaning of a vague term and make it more precise. Such definitions are called *precising definitions*. "Full-time university student" is a vague term in ordinary usage that means roughly "a person who devotes a major part of his or her energies to acquiring some type of knowledge or skill through university courses." However, the vagueness of the term poses a problem for universities that assign fees and benefits on the basis of whether students are full-time or part-time. Universities typically solve this problem by offering a precising definition of "full-time student" in their catalogs. One university lists the following definition of "full-time student":

> "Full-time student" means "student who is carrying a course load of at least twelve units a semester."

Note that this is not the same as a stipulative definition. No new term is being introduced, and a term already in use is not being given a completely different new meaning. In this precising definition, all borderline cases of the vague expression "full-time student" are simply eliminated by making a course load of at least twelve hours per semester the criterion for being a full-time student (at that university). This definition can be used to sort students at the university into two categories: those who are full-time and those who are not full-time.

Sometimes a word is given a special or technical meaning to be used in a particular context. We can classify this as a form of precising definition. In this text, we have already met many examples of such definitions introduced to aid our study of logic. "Valid," which is defined as "the term that applies to a deductive argument when it is impossible for the conclusion of that argument to be false if its premises are all true," is one example. "Argument," and "fallacy" are others. For musicians, "beat" and "tempo" are technical terms; their technical meanings are different from the senses they carry in ordinary contexts. All disciplines employ some technical vocabulary that those who want to understand the field must acquire.

Not all cases of reducing vagueness are as simple as the precising definitions mentioned so far. When a term, like "religion," is vague because there are a number of different criteria for applying the term, it can be very difficult to specify in a reasonable way just which criteria are most important or how many criteria must be met in order to apply the term. Recent debates concerning the definition of the "death of a person," and the "beginning of life of a person" make us aware of the complexity of the problem. Even when such definitions are proposed in judicial rulings that take into account public debates and studies by experts, they do not go unchallenged, for the definitions have grave and far-reaching social consequences. The definitions that are offered in these cases not only reduce vagueness but also involve a *theoretical* account of what it means to be a person. In such cases, definitions are appropriately classed as *theoretical*. Theoretical definitions differ from technical definitions, for whereas a technical definition specifies the meaning of a term as it is used in some area of study, a technical definition does not necessarily carry any commitment to the truth of some theory.

iv. Definitions for Theoretical Purposes

The term *theory* has several meanings, two of which will concern us here. In its first sense, "theory" refers to a general approach to, or belief about, some subject matter that is expressed in a set of interrelated statements concerning the nature of the subject. In this sense, we might speak of a theory of justice involving such statements as "Justice requires that all persons be treated similarly under similar circumstances," "Justice requires that individuals in a society be given equal opportunities and access to the good things in that society," "Justice demands that punishments should be tailored to the nature of the offense," and other such claims. The definition

"Death of a person" means "cessation of that person's brain functions"

involves a theory in this sense, that is, a set of interrelated claims concerning the special character of human life. This theory is committed to the view that the body that has totally and irreversibly lost the use of its brain but that may have its circulatory, respiratory, and other systems maintained by machine, is no longer a person. The term "vegetable" is sometimes applied in such situations to mark the transformation of the body from the time that it was the body of a person, capable of thought and feeling, to its passive state after loss of brain function. One who holds this theory of what it means for a person to die would, for example, probably agree that it is not immoral to remove a body that has lost all brain function from machines designed to maintain respiration. In addition, the theory supports the view that no harm is done to the *person* if vital organs from that body are removed for transplanting, provided proper permission was obtained from the person before he or she died or from relatives.

Another sense of "theory" refers to a set of general but precise claims about the nature of society or the physical world. Such theories often involve appeals to unobservable entities that form the basis for many other statements that can be confirmed or disconfirmed by observing the behavior of relevant features of the world. Theories in the physical sciences often assume this form. Examples from physics are: the theory of relativity, the theory of atomic physics, and the theory of classical mechanics.

Frequently, physicists take a term from ordinary language and redefine it for some theoretical purpose. For example, in classical mechanics, "work" is defined as "the product of force and distance" and "momentum" is defined as "the product of mass times velocity." In such a theory, many of the terms are defined explicitly by means of other terms in the theory.

However, some terms, such as "force," are not explicitly defined. No expression synonymous with "force" is presented in the theory of classical mechanics.

The meanings of such terms are given implicitly in the fundamental generalizations (or *laws*) of the theory. Newton's three laws of motion and his law of universal gravitation all say something about how forces behave (the effects of forces on bodies with respect to such other theoretical features as mass, acceleration, momentum, and distance). In a sense, we can say that the theory tells us what force is only insofar as it tells us how forces operate under various circumstances.

Theoretical definitions are similar to precising definitions in that both reduce vagueness. However, in addition to reducing vagueness, theoretical definitions connect the term being defined with other terms in the theory. A complete understanding of the theoretical meanings of both explicitly defined terms such as "work" and implicitly defined terms, such as "force," is gained only through an understanding of the entire theory.

v. Definitions Designed to Transfer Emotive Force

Definitions designed to transfer emotive force, such as feelings of approval or disapproval, are called *persuasive definitions.* Like other explicit intensional definitions, a persuasive definition should state the properties a thing must possess for the term to apply. However, persuasive definitions also convey an *attitude* toward what is being defined. For example, the definition

"Homosexual" means "one who has an *unnatural* desire for those of the same sex"

is designed to convey a negative or disapproving attitude toward homosexuals—through the use of the term "unnatural."

An attitude of approval—although it is a bit more subtle than the disapproving attitude in the definition of "homosexual"—is conveyed by the definition

"Democracy" means "the acceptance and practice of the principle of equality of rights, opportunities, and treatment; lack of snobbery."

An attitude of approval is present in this definition because most people are generally considered to approve such things as equality of rights and lack of snobbery. Perhaps, the emotive force of this definition of "democracy" can best be seen if we contrast it with the definition

"Democracy" means "rule by majority."

Most people would not regard this definition as persuasive. Its emotive force is probably quite neutral. "Rule by majority" does not engender the same degree of approval as appeals to equality of rights and lack of snobbery do.

If, however, there are some people who associate "rule by majority" with "mob rule," then the definition of "democracy" that equates it with "rule by majority" may convey negative emotive force to those persons.

As it so often happens, when more than one definition of the same term is offered, these two definitions of "democracy" differ in their statement of intension as well as in their emotive force. "Rule by majority" and "the acceptance and practice of the principle of equality of rights, opportunities, and treatment; lack of snobbery" do not refer to the same properties of a democracy.

Whether or not persuasive definitions are appropriate depends on the context in which a definition is offered. There is nothing intrinsically wrong with trying to persuade others to share our attitudes. Persuasive definitions are often presented in a humorous context. For example, "philosophy" has been defined as "a doubt which lives in one like a hookworm, causing pallor and lack of appetite." In this persuasive definition, as in many definitions proposed for humorous purposes, the intension of the term—the properties a thing must have if the term is to apply—is partially or completely ignored. When the purpose of a definition is entertainment, this can be perfectly acceptable. But if we are seeking the definition of an emotionally neutral term for the purpose of making its standard use known, then a persuasive definition is probably inappropriate and can be deceptive or misleading.

Familiarity with the technique of persuasive definitions increases our awareness that words that refer to the same objects may differ sharply in emotive force. It doesn't require much sensitivity to recognize the difference in attitudes carried or conveyed by the terms "woman" and "broad" or "black" and "nigger." Objectionable slang terms that are disrespectful to various ethnic, racial, and religious segments of the population are regrettably all too common.

Other expressions, however, can carry a similar negative emotive force in less obvious ways. Calling an airplane race in which the pilots are women a "powder-puff derby" conveys the attitude that such races are to be taken less seriously than races in which men are the pilots. Calling a woman who writes poetry a "poetess" suggests that she is really not quite up to the standards of a poet.

We should be especially sensitive to the emotive force of any expressions used in arguments, for emotively charged terms may lead us to accept or reject conclusions when this is not warranted by the evidence.

4. Contextual Definitions

Thus far, with the exception of implicit theoretical definitions, we have confined our discussion to defining terms by giving their intensions or extensions in an *explicit* manner. For the most part, the terms we have defined in this way have been common nouns and adjectives. Some words, however, such as prepositions, articles, and conjunctions, do *not* have an intension or an extension: they do not refer to things, events, persons, or activities, although they do have meanings and play an essential role in language.

These terms have primarily grammatical or *syntactic* meanings. Examples of such words are "and," "or," and "if ... then." Sometimes, these terms are defined explicitly, by presenting synonyms that have the same grammatical function ("and" means "also; in addition to; moreover; as well as"). More often, however, these terms are defined *implicitly*, by stating their grammatical functions, and then giving examples (contexts) in which the term occurs. Such definitions are called *contextual definitions*. For example, "or" can be defined as a *coordinating conjunction* that introduces an alternative, as in "I'll offer him beer or wine." "Or" may also be defined as a word that connects sentences in such a way that the compound sentence that is formed is true whenever either of the sentences it connects is true and which is false otherwise. Our truth-table definitions of the logical connectives are implicit definitions of this type.

Another kind of implicit contextual definition presents an expression (context) equivalent in meaning to an expression in which the term to be defined occurs. For example, "unless" is contextually defined in the following:

"We'll have a picnic unless it rains" means the same as "If it doesn't rain, then we'll have a picnic."

In this definition, no single expression *synonymous* with "unless" is explicitly presented. Instead, the defining expression is synonymous with the whole expression in which "unless" occurs, and it does not contain "unless."

Exercises

1. Classify each of the following definitions as to type:
   a. "Communism" means "an economic theory or system of ownership of all property by the community as a whole."
   b. "Communism" means "a form of government characterized by rigid state planning and control of the economy, ruthless suppression of all opposing political parties, suppression of individual liberties under a dictatorship, and expansion by military action and subversion."
   c. "Nucleus" means "the central part of an atom, the fundamental parts of which are the proton and the neutron. It carries a positive charge and constitutes all the mass of the atom. It is what remains after the orbital electrons have been stripped away."
   d. "The Big Ten" means "Indiana University, Ohio State, Michigan, Michigan State, Northwestern, Illinois, Wisconsin, Purdue, Minnesota, and Iowa."
   e. "Monotreme" means "platypuses and echidnas."
   f. "Monotreme" means "egg-laying mammal."
   g. "Naturalistic" means "glorifying all the meanness of human nature and the sordidness of human existence, emphasizing the disgusting, crude, animal part of human nature."
   h. "Overweight" means "exceeds the United States government's standard chart's recommended weight per height by at least 10 percent."
   i. In order to save space in the written reports of the curriculum committee, we will let "FLC" mean "first-year logic course."
   j. It's just as "I believe in God" often means "I prefer not to think," so does "I love you" often mean "I want to own you."
      —John Fowles, *Daniel Martin*

   k. "Water freezes *only if* it has a temperature of 32°F or lower" means "*If* water freezes *then* it has a temperature of 32°F or lower."

l. "Living ex-president of the United States of America" means "Richard Nixon, Gerald Ford, Jimmy Carter, and Ronald Reagan."

m. "Superfluous" means "unnecessary."

n. "The" is a definite article that is used to refer to a particular person, place, or thing.

o. "Lecturing" means "a boring way of teaching in which the teacher drones on for nearly an hour while the students try to stay awake."

p. "Properly dressed for dining at local restaurants" means "wearing shoes and a shirt."

q. "The best age of a person" means "the age at which the person is old enough to know what's what and not old enough to show it."

r. Some anthropologists define "culture" as "a set of attributes and products of human societies, and therewith of mankind, that are extrasomatic and transmissible by mechanisms other than biological heredity."

s. "State university" means "an institution of higher learning that grants advanced degrees and is supported by taxes."

t. "Abortion" means "the deliberate murder of a human fetus."

2. What is wrong with each of the following *lexical definitions*?

a. "Politically" means "in a politic manner."

b. "Hamster" means "a small animal."

c. "Fork" means "a utensil for eating foods."

d. "Whale" means "a mammal that swims."

e. "Overture" means "the orchestral opening to a symphony."

3. At most state universities, residents and nonresidents of the state are charged different tuition fees for the same educational programs. Suppose you are a state legislator assigned to a committee to define "resident" for the purpose of charging tuition fees. What type of definition is required here? What considerations would guide your attempt to define "resident"? What definition would you propose?

4. Provide an *implicit contextual definition* of "neither . . . nor."

5. Discuss the different *emotive force* (if any) for each of the following pairs of terms. If you ignore emotive force, do both members of each pair have the same intensional meaning (does each member of the pair refer to the same things)?

a. Fragile—weak

b. Public servant—bureaucrat

c. Mexican-American—Chicano

d. Sweat—perspiration

e. Chairman—chairperson

f. Cop—police officer

g. Usher—usherette

h. House—home

i. Footwear—shoes

j. Psychiatrist—shrink

5. Operational Definitions

In addititon to ostensive definition, another type of nonverbal definition has been of special importance to scientific studies. The technique of operational definition was first proposed by Nobel physicist P. W. Bridgman (*The Logic of Modern Physics*, 1927). Bridgman was aware of the different emotive and referential aspects of meaning and of the way words can mean different things to different persons as a result of varying associations and contexts of use. He wanted to establish the meanings of scientifically important terms in a way that guaranteed that any scientist who used these terms would employ them in exactly the same way. Bridgman proposed specifying public and repeatable *operations*, such as measurement, to serve as criteria for application of scientifically important terms.

Consider the following example of an operational definition:

"Each side of my table is three feet long" means that when a standard yardstick is lined up with a side of my table, the ends of the yardstick coincide with the ends of my table.

The technique of operational definition is not intended to apply to abstract terms, such as "length." Instead, a public and repeatable physical operation (such as measurement with a standard yardstick) is specified for determining whether or not a sentence containing expressions such as "is three feet long" can be applied correctly to a situation. Nothing is lost by refusing to consider "length" in the abstract, since scientists use the concept of length only in specific contexts. Once we understand how to use sentences in which expressions like "three feet long" occur, then we understand what such expressions mean. Since the operation of measuring with a standard yardstick is public and repeatable, this operational definition guarantees that scientists will all use the expression "three feet long" in exactly the same way.

With suitable instruments for measuring, many of the terms used by scientists can be defined in this way. For example, "This flame is blue" can be operationally defined as meaning that when subjected to analysis by a spectrometer, the flame registers between 4240 angstrom units and 4912 angstrom units. Operations other than measurement can also be used. For example, "The liquid in this jar is acid" means that when a piece of litmus paper is placed in this liquid, the litmus paper turns pink. All that is required is that there is a high degree of agreement among various observers as to the outcome of the operation and that it be repeatable.

The technique of operational definition is not without problematic features. For example, there may be several different types of operations for measuring a phenomenon such as temperature and no operation for coordinating the various results. In such cases, we can not, strictly speaking, refer to "the temperature" of a particular object, but only, for example, to "the mercury thermometer temperature." This introduces some awkwardness into scientific discourse. However, many scientists are willing to pay this price in order to specify the meanings of terms by tying them to observations and measurements.

Additional, more serious problems arise in trying to define some of the more highly theoretical terms used by scientists, such as "electron," that refer to things that are not directly observable. Attempts to *reduce* these terms to terms that can be operationally defined have not been very successful. At this point, this program of operational definition seems to offer little hope for providing such definitions for *all* of the important terms used by physical scientists. Nevertheless, this form of definition is regarded as important in standardizing meanings of some words by establishing operational criteria for the application of those words.

Even though operational definitions were first proposed for the physical sciences and despite the difficulties encountered there, many social scientists have become enthusiastic about the possibility of constructing operational definitions for the terms that occur in their own disciplines. Behavioral psychologists, for example, believe that operational definitions are the best way to handle so-called mental terms, such as "intelligence," "belief," "anxiety," and "fear." They have tried to specify publicly observable features of behavior or physiology in order to define particular concrete uses of such terms. Some examples are:

"John Jones is afraid of the dark" means that whenever Jones is in a dark place, he breaks out in a cold sweat and begins to tremble.

"Maria Garcia is very intelligent" means that Garcia scored above 135 on the Stanford-Binet (IQ) test.

Operationalistic attempts to define mental terms are highly controversial and have been dismissed as completely inadequate by many persons. There are two major types of objections. One has to do with the obvious difficulty of trying to handle concepts such as "intelligence" in a quantitative manner. Measuring someone's intelligence is much less straightforward than measuring that person's height. The tests that have been proposed as measurements have been criticized for being tied to specific cultural backgrounds and for measuring only some of the broad group of features that make up intelligence in a human being. Similarly, physiological manifestations of fear, anxiety, and other mental states vary from person to person and culture to culture, making the specification of publicly observable criteria for determining the presence of such states highly problematic.

The second objection cuts a bit deeper across the program of operational definition. An operational definition of a mental property is intended to equate that property with the outcome of some operation. However, many people claim that even if we devised satisfactory tests for measuring intelligence, what we would measure could not be the same thing as the score on the test. The test score, these objectors say, might be a good *indicator* of the degree of intelligence possessed by a person, but it would not be the *same thing* as intelligence. In other words, they hold that the meaning of someone's being in a particular mental state cannot be equated with techniques for measuring the presence of that mental state.

Despite these difficulties, some strong supporters of operational definition claim that a term is scientifically meaningful only if it is susceptible to operational definition. They hold that terms that cannot be defined operationally are of no use to science, or that only insofar as the terms are amenable to operational definition are the things they refer to suitable objects for scientific study. Others take the more moderate view that although operational definitions play an important role in any science, there are limits to their usefulness, and that it is inappropriate to try to define *every* term used in a discipline in this way.

III. REVIEW

If we want to be able to state our beliefs, opinions, and judgments clearly, so that others can understand us, and if we want to be able to assess ordinary-language arguments, we must recognize that there are many aspects of meaning—extensional, intensional, grammatical (also called "syntactical"), emotive, and operational. Various types of definitions are designed to capture these aspects of meaning, and it is important to know how to use definitions to achieve the type of clarity that is required in a given context. A review of the terminology introduced in this chapter follows.

Ambiguous An expression is *ambiguous* when it has several distinct, *non-overlapping* meanings. Words with more than one distinct meaning are ambiguous, and ambiguities can also arise in larger units of language as a result of their grammatical structure or of the possible changes in meaning due to changes in emphasis.

Contextual Definition: A form of implicit definition in which terms are defined by showing how they are used in a given situation or situations. *Truth tables* provide implicit contextual definitions of logical connectives. Other examples are implicit definitions of theoretical terms and definitions presenting an expression in which the defined term occurs, along with a synonymous expression in which it does not.

Equivocation: The use of an ambiguous expression in more than one of its senses in a single context. When an argument depends on equivocation to establish a conclusion, the *fallacy of equivocation* is committed.

Extension: The set of objects to which a term refers.

Intension: The set of *all and only* those properties a thing must possess for the term to apply to it.

Intensional Definition: Defining a term by stating the properties a thing must possess for the term to apply to it. All intensional definitions are verbal. Further distinctions can be made among intensional definitions by considering the purposes of definition:

Lexical Definition: To present the accepted standard use of a term.

Stipulative Definition: To introduce a new term into the language.

Precising Definition: To reduce the vagueness of a term.

Persuasive Definition: To express or evoke an attitude, such as approval or disapproval, toward things referred to by the term.

Theoretical Definition: To construct a theory. Theoretical definitions may be *explicit*, in which case terms are defined by giving *synonymous expressions* formulated in the vocabulary of the theory or *implicit* (or *contextual*), in which case terms are defined according to their use in the laws or generalizations of the theory.

Operational Definition: Defining an expression by describing a publicly observable and repeatable operation that can be performed to determine whether or not a sentence containing the expression is correctly applicable to a given situation.

Ostensive Definition (*nonverbal extensional definition*): A nonverbal form of definition in which pointing or some other way of indicating the extension of a term is used to give the meaning of the term.

Syntactic Definition (*grammatical definition*): Terms that have no intension or extension are sometimes defined by indicating their *syntactic* or *grammatical* role in a language. These definitions are often supplemented by presenting a context in which the term occurs. (*Example*: "A" is an indefinite article, used in such expressions as "A dog ran out in the road.")

Vague: A term is *vague* if there are borderline areas in which it is unclear whether or not the term applies. *Vagueness* is a useful feature of language, but definitions that reduce vagueness are required in some circumstances.

Verbal Extensional Definition: Defining a term by listing or naming members of its extension.

IV. EXERCISES

1. Try to formulate *operational definitions* for each of the following:
    a. The term "sour" in "This lemon tastes sour."
    b. The expression "weighs 120 pounds" in "Joan weighs 120 pounds."
    c. The expression "believes that he will win a scholarship next year" in "Frank believes that he (Frank) will win a scholarship next year."

2. Social scientists often use questionnaires to formulate operational definitions. For example, they might be interested in arriving at an operational definition for the term "alcoholic" if they wanted to correlate alcoholism with some other social phenomenon, such as working in a particular profession or being subjected to the stresses of student life. Try to formulate a questionnaire that would operationally define whether or not the person who answers the questionnaire is an alcoholic. Mention any difficulties involved in devising such a questionnaire.

Proof Method for Truth-Functional Logic

A P P E N D I X 1

I. INTRODUCTION

Truth tables may be used to demonstrate the validity or the invalidity of any truth-functional argument form. However, these tables become unwieldy when an argument form contains more than four distinct sentence letters. An argument form with five distinct letters requires a truth table with 32 rows to show all of the possible combinations of truth values. Six sentence letters require a 64-row truth table, and adding just one more sentence letter requires an additional 64 rows. The chief advantage of applying other *proof methods* to truth-functional logic is their brevity compared to truth tables. The proof method presented here is a *tree method,* modeled on a simplified version of proof methods developed by Gerhard Gentzen.*

We will use the logical symbols already introduced for negation ($\sim$), conjunction ($\bullet$), disjunction (v), material conditional ($\rightarrow$), and material biconditional ($\leftrightarrow$). In addition, we will use the gate symbol ($\vdash$) to indicate the relationship of *logical consequence,* or *following from.* The conclusion in a deductively valid argument is a logical consequence of, or follows from, the premises of that argument. Instead of writing an argument form, such as *modus ponens,* in the standard form

$$p \rightarrow q$$
$$\underline{p}$$
$$q$$

we have used thus far, we will now write argument forms in the following way:

$$p \rightarrow q, p \vdash q$$

Premises, separated from one another by commas, are written to the left of the gate; the conclusion is written to the right of the gate. The preceding expression, which is called a *sequent,* may be read "q follows from the premises $p \rightarrow q$ and p."

The strings of sentence forms on the left and the right sides of the gate in a sequent are called *sequences.* In our example, the sequence on the left has two members ($p \rightarrow q$ and p); it is a sequence of "length two." The sequence on the right has one member (q); it is a sequence of "length one." Sequences may be of "length zero," in which case they are called *empty sequences,* or their length may be equal to any positive integer. All sequences are finite in length.

We have seen that when the length of a sequence on the left side of the gate is greater than one, the members of the sequence are separated by commas and each comma on the left is read as "and." When more than one member of the sequence appears on the right side of the gate, these members are also separated

---

*See Stig Kanger, "A Simplified Proof Method for Elementary Logic," in *Computer Programming and Formal Systems,* edited by P. Braffort & D. Hirschberg.

by commas, but each comma on the right is read as "or." For example, we may read the sequent

$$p \vee q, p \rightarrow r, p \rightarrow s, \sim q \vdash r \cdot s, t \rightarrow p$$

as "Either $r \cdot s$ or $t \rightarrow p$ follows from the premisses $p \vee q$, and $p \rightarrow$ r, and $p \rightarrow$ s, and $\sim q$."

An empty sequence to the left of the gate indicates a true (although unspecified) premiss. An empty sequence to the right of the gate indicates a true conclusion.

Examples

(a)   Read the sequent

$$\vdash p \rightarrow (q \vee \sim q)$$

as "$p \rightarrow (q \vee \sim q)$ follows from any true premiss."

(b)   Read the sequent

$$p, p \rightarrow q, \sim p \vdash$$

as "Any true conclusion follows from p, and $p \rightarrow q$, and $\sim p$."

If a sentence form follows from any true premiss, then that sentence form must itself always be true. A sentence form that follows from any true premiss whatsoever is a *tautology*. Similarly, if a set of premisses deductively yields any true conclusion whatsoever, that set of premisses must be *contradictory*.

II. THE PROOF METHOD

In the following discussion, we will use the Roman capital letters "A" and "B" to refer to sentence forms. The sentence forms thus denoted may be either simple or complex. We will use the script capital letters "$\mathcal{D}$," "$\mathcal{E}$," "$\mathcal{F}$," and "$\mathcal{G}$" to denote finite and possibly empty sequences of sentence forms.

The proof method employs eleven postulates, which include one axiom and ten rules of inference. Postulates P.1–P.11 are presented schematically here, with brief comments.

P.1 $\mathcal{D}, A, \mathcal{E} \vdash \mathcal{F}, A, \mathcal{G}$ (axiom)

In this sequent, the same *sentence form* (A) occurs both to the left and to the right of the gate; on both sides, it is separated from the other *sequences of sentence forms* ($\mathcal{D}, \mathcal{E}, \mathcal{F}, \mathcal{G}$) by commas. This means that a *disjunction* that contains A is said to follow from a set of premisses that includes A. Such a disjunction could not fail to follow, for if A is a true premiss, then the disjunction contains a true disjunct and the disjunction is true also. Thus, all the premisses cannot be true while the conclusion is false. In our proof method, this instance of the *consequence relationship* is considered to be a fundamentally valid argument form (an *axiom scheme*).

The rules of inference in this proof method are used to eliminate connectives, with the goal of "reducing" the original argument form to a series of simpler forms that are instances of the axiom. Each of the rules of inference (P.2–P.11) allows us to eliminate a main connective in a sentence form on either the left or the right hand of the gate.

P.2
$$\frac{\mathcal{D} \vdash \mathcal{F},\ \sim A,\ \mathcal{G}}{A,\ \mathcal{D} \vdash \mathcal{F},\ \mathcal{G}}$$
(eliminates $\sim$ on right)

P.3
$$\frac{\mathcal{D},\ \sim A,\ \mathcal{E} \vdash \mathcal{F}}{\mathcal{D},\ \mathcal{E} \vdash A,\ \mathcal{F}}$$
(eliminates $\sim$ on left)

P.4
$$\frac{\mathcal{D} \vdash \mathcal{F},\ A \cdot B,\ \mathcal{G}}{\mathcal{D} \vdash \mathcal{F},\ A,\ \mathcal{G} \qquad \mathcal{D} \vdash \mathcal{F},\ B,\ \mathcal{G}}$$
(eliminates $\cdot$ on right)

P.5
$$\frac{\mathcal{D},\ A \cdot B,\ \mathcal{E} \vdash \mathcal{F}}{\mathcal{D},\ A,\ B,\ \mathcal{E} \vdash \mathcal{F}}$$
(eliminates $\cdot$ on left)

P.6
$$\frac{\mathcal{D} \vdash \mathcal{F},\ A \vee B,\ \mathcal{G}}{\mathcal{D} \vdash \mathcal{F},\ A,\ B,\ \mathcal{G}}$$
(eliminates $\vee$ on right)

P.7
$$\frac{\mathcal{D},\ A \vee B,\ \mathcal{E} \vdash \mathcal{F}}{\mathcal{D},\ A,\ \mathcal{E} \vdash \mathcal{F} \qquad \mathcal{D},\ B,\ \mathcal{E} \vdash \mathcal{F}}$$
(eliminates $\vee$ on left)

P.8
$$\frac{\mathcal{D} \vdash \mathcal{F},\ A \rightarrow B,\ \mathcal{G}}{A,\ \mathcal{D} \vdash \mathcal{F},\ B,\ \mathcal{G}}$$
(eliminates $\rightarrow$ on right)

P.9
$$\frac{\mathcal{D},\ A \rightarrow B,\ \mathcal{E} \vdash \mathcal{F}}{\mathcal{D},\ \mathcal{E} \vdash A,\ \mathcal{F} \qquad \mathcal{D},\ B,\ \mathcal{E} \vdash \mathcal{F}}$$
(eliminates $\rightarrow$ on left)

P.10
$$\frac{\mathcal{D} \vdash \mathcal{F},\ A \leftrightarrow B,\ \mathcal{G}}{A,\ \mathcal{D} \vdash \mathcal{F},\ B,\ \mathcal{G} \qquad B,\ \mathcal{D} \vdash \mathcal{F},\ A,\ \mathcal{G}}$$
(eliminates $\leftrightarrow$ on right)

P.11
$$\frac{\mathcal{D},\ A \leftrightarrow B,\ \mathcal{E} \vdash \mathcal{F}}{\mathcal{D},\ \mathcal{E} \vdash A,\ B,\ \mathcal{F} \qquad A,\ B,\ \mathcal{D},\ \mathcal{E} \vdash \mathcal{F}}$$
(eliminates $\leftrightarrow$ on left)

When we want to show that one sequence follows from another, we write the premiss sequence, followed by a gate, followed by the conclusion. Then we draw a line below that sequent and construct a "tree" of sequents below it, using the rules of inference (P.2–P.11). If we are able to construct a tree with an instance of P.1 (the axiom) at the bottom of every branch, the proof has succeeded. If the sequence on the right is a logical consequence of the sequence on the left, we will always be able to construct such a tree.

In addition to the axiom and rules of inference of the proof method, one strategic rule for constructing proofs should be noted. Frequently, we may be able to continue a branch of the tree in more than one way, since we have more than one main connective to eliminate. When this happens, we always prefer applications of P.2, P.3, P.5, P.6, and P.8 to applications of the other rules. Our preference for these rules will minimize tree branching, because these rules themselves do not branch. Before we focus on considering the justification of inference rules, we will consider some examples of proofs.

Examples

(a) To show that $p \lor q$ follows from p, we construct the following tree:

$$\frac{p \vdash p \lor q \quad \text{(apply P.6)}}{p \vdash p, q \quad \text{(axiom)}}$$

Here, only one main connective (the $\lor$ on the right) can be eliminated. Thus, P.6 is the appropriate rule. In applying P.6 to the sequent on the top line, A represents p, the sentence form to the left of the connective, and B represents q, the sentence form to the right of the connective. $\mathcal{D}$ represents the sequence that is left of the gate (p). $\mathcal{F}$ and $\mathcal{G}$ are the sequences to the right and the left of the sentence form A $\lor$ B, respectively; in this example, $\mathcal{F}$ and $\mathcal{G}$ are empty sequences. In the sequent below the line, the same sequence $\mathcal{D}$ (p) is to the left of the gate. On the right of the gate, the $\lor$ has been eliminated and replaced by a comma. The sequent below the line is an instance of the axiom, for the same sentence form (namely, p) occurs, separated from other sentence forms by commas, on the right of the gate, and also on the left. Thus, we have shown that $p \lor q$ follows deductively from p.

(b) To show that q follows from $p \to q$, $\sim p \to r$, and $\sim q \to \sim r$, we construct the following tree:

(1)
$$\frac{p \to q, \sim p \to r, \sim q \to \sim r \vdash q}{}$$

(2)
$$\frac{\sim p \to r, \sim q \to \sim r \vdash p, q \qquad q, \sim p \to r, \sim q \to \sim r \vdash q^*}{}$$

(3)
$$\frac{\sim q \to \sim r \vdash \sim p, p, q \qquad r, \sim q \to \sim r \vdash p, q}{}$$

(4)
$$\frac{p, \sim q \to \sim r \vdash p, q^* \qquad r \vdash \sim q, p, q \qquad r, \sim r \vdash p, q}{}$$

(5)
$$q, r \vdash p, q^* \qquad r \vdash r, p, q^*$$

Line (1) contains the sequent, with the premises on the left and the conclusion on the right of the gate. The only main connectives are $\to$s to the left of the gate, so the only applicable rule is a branching one, P.9, which could be applied to any of the three sentence forms that make up the sequence on the left.

In this proof, P.9 is applied to the first conditional, $p \to q$. Thus, A is p, and B is q. $\mathcal{D}$, which refers to any sequence to the left of A $\to$ B, is empty, and $\mathcal{E}$ denotes the sequence $\sim p \to r$, $\sim q \to \sim r$. $\mathcal{F}$ refers to everything to the right of the gate (in this case, q).

Line (2) is the result of applying P.9 to $p \to q$ in line (1). The right-hand branch ends in an axiom (indicated by the *), with an occurrence of the sentence form q on both the right and the left sides of the gate. That branch is now complete. The left branch is not an instance of the axiom but contains further connectives that may be removed. Again, the only main connectives are the $\to$s on the left, so P.9 is applicable.

Line (3) is the result of applying P.9 to $\sim p \to r$ in line (2). Here, A is $\sim p$ and B is r. $\mathcal{D}$ is empty, $\mathcal{E}$ is $\sim q \to \sim r$, and $\mathcal{F}$ is the sequence p, q. Neither of these branches is an instance of the axiom, but connectives remain, so each branch is continued.

In the left branch of the tree, a main connective on the right is a negation sign. Our strategy rule tells us to prefer the application of P.2 over any of the branching rules. Applying P.2 gives us p as A and $\sim q \to \sim r$ as $\mathcal{D}$. $\mathcal{F}$ is empty, and $\mathcal{G}$ is the sequence p, q to the right of $\sim$ A. After applying P.2, this branch ends in an instance of the axiom on the left branch of line (4).

In the right branch of the tree, the only main connective is once more a $\to$ on the left side of the gate, so that P.9 is applicable. Line (4), on the right gives the result of applying this branching rule. Neither branch ends in an axiom at this stage, so both branches continue.

In the left branch, a negation on the right is eliminated by applying P.2, which results in the branch ending in an axiom on line (5). In the right branch, there is a negation on the left, which is eliminated by applying P.3; that branch also ends in an axiom on line (5).

Thus, each branch of the tree ends in an axiom, and we have succeeded in proving that q is a consequence of $p \to q$, $\sim p \to r$, and $\sim q \to \sim r$.

(c) To show that $\sim q$ is not a consequence of $p \to q$ and $\sim p$, we construct the following tree:

(1) $\quad \underline{p \to q, \sim p \vdash \sim q}$ $\quad$ (P.3 applied to $\sim p$)

(2) $\quad \underline{p \to q \vdash p, \sim q}$ $\quad$ (P.2 applied to $\sim q$)

(3) $\quad \underline{q, p \to q \vdash p}$ $\quad$ (P.9 applied to $p \to q$)

(4) $\quad q \vdash p, p \qquad q, q \vdash p$

In this case, we see two branches on line (4) that do not end in axioms. Whenever at least one branch does not end in an axiom and cannot be extended because no more connectives can be removed, we have a proof that the alleged conclusion does not follow from these premises—that the argument form is invalid.

(d) To show that $\sim(p \bullet q) \leftrightarrow (\sim pv \sim q)$ is a tautology, we construct the following tree:

(1) $\qquad \vdash \sim(p \bullet q) \leftrightarrow (\sim p \lor \sim q)$ (P.10)

(2) $\dfrac{\sim(p \bullet q) \vdash \sim p \lor \sim q}{}$ (P.3) $\qquad \dfrac{\sim p \lor \sim q \vdash \sim(p \bullet q)}{}$ (P.2)

(3) $\dfrac{\vdash p \bullet q, \sim p \lor \sim q}{}$ (P.6) $\qquad \dfrac{p \bullet q, \sim p \lor \sim q \vdash}{}$ (P.5)

(4) $\dfrac{\vdash p \bullet q, \sim p, \sim q}{}$ (P.2) $\qquad \dfrac{p, q, \sim p \lor \sim q \vdash}{}$ (P.7)

(5) $\dfrac{p \vdash p \bullet q, \sim q}{}$ (P.2) $\dfrac{p, q, \sim p \vdash}{}$ (P.3) $\dfrac{p, q, \sim q \vdash}{}$ (P.3)

(6) $\dfrac{q, p \vdash p \bullet q}{}$ (P.7) $p, q \vdash p^*$ $p, q \vdash q^*$

(7) $p, q \vdash p^* \quad p, q \vdash q^*$

Note that each branch of this tree ends in an axiom. To prove that a sentence form is a tautology, it is sufficient to show that the sentence form follows from any true premiss. Thus, we set up the proof by placing an empty sequence to the left of the gate and the supposed tautology to the right of the gate. If every branch does end in an axiom, we have shown that the sentence follows from any true premiss and that it must itself be true. If some branch fails to end in an axiom and cannot be continued, then the sentence form is not a tautology.

Exercises

1. Use the proof method to determine the validity or the invalidity of each of the following argument forms:

a. $\dfrac{p \to q}{p \to (p \bullet q)}$

b. $\dfrac{p \lor q}{\sim p \lor \sim q}$

c. $\dfrac{p \to (q \to r)}{(p \to q) \to r}$

d. $\dfrac{p \to (q \to r)}{(p \bullet q) \to r}$

e. $\dfrac{\begin{array}{c} p \to (q \to r) \\ (q \to r) \to s \end{array}}{p \to s}$

f. $\dfrac{\begin{array}{c} p \to (q \to r) \\ q \to (r \to s) \end{array}}{p \to s}$

g. $\dfrac{\begin{array}{c} (p \lor q) \to (p \bullet q) \\ p \bullet q \end{array}}{p \lor q}$

2. Use the proof method to determine whether or not the following sentence form is *tautologous:*

$$(p \rightarrow (q \rightarrow r)) \rightarrow ((p \rightarrow q) \rightarrow (p \rightarrow r))$$

How many rows would a truth table require to show this? How many lines would it take you to construct a truth table for this sentence form?

3. Use the proof method to show whether or not the following sentence form is a *self-contradiction:*

$$(p \rightarrow q) \bullet (q \rightarrow r) \bullet p \bullet \sim r$$

III. JUSTIFYING THE RULES OF INFERENCE

A deductive rule of inference is *justified* when it can be shown that the use of the rule will never lead from true premisses to a false conclusion—or, in other words, when it can be shown that the rule is *truth-preserving.*

When we remove connectives by using the rules of inference in this proof method, we reduce a complicated sequent (argument form) to a series of *less complicated* sequents, in the sense that each of the sequents below the lines has fewer truth-functional connectives than the sequents above the lines. What we want to show is that the use of any of the rules P.2–P.11 for eliminating connectives will result in sequents below the line with right-hand sequences that are the logical consequences of their left-hand sequences if and only if the right-hand sequence above the line is a logical consequence of its left-hand sequence.

The rules of inference used in this proof method depend for their justification on:

1. The definition of *logical consequence,* which states that a sentence (or sentence form) A is a logical consequence of a set of sentences (or sentence forms) $\mathcal{D}$ if it is impossible for all of the sentences (sentence forms) in the set $\mathcal{D}$ to be true while the sentence (sentence form) A is false.
2. The definitions of the *truth-functional connectives* ($\sim$, v, $\bullet$, $\rightarrow$, $\leftrightarrow$).
3. The understanding that commas to the left of the gate represent "and" and that commas to the right of the gate represent "or."

In each rule, we note that the sequences $\mathcal{D}$, $\mathcal{E}$, $\mathcal{F}$, and $\mathcal{G}$ simply reappear unchanged in sequents below the line. They are never dropped or modified in any way. For this reason, we can ignore their content in justifying rules P.2–P.11. In other words, we can simply regard these sequences as *empty sequences* and focus on how the removal of the connectives that relate A and B affects the consequence relationship.

Justification of P.2

P.2
$$\frac{\mathcal{D} \vdash \mathcal{F}, {\sim}A, \mathcal{G}}{A, \mathcal{D} \vdash \mathcal{F}, \mathcal{G}} \quad \text{(eliminates} \sim \text{on right)}$$

If we regard the sequences $\mathcal{D}$, $\mathcal{F}$, and $\mathcal{G}$ as empty, then the sequent above the line says that ~A is a consequence of an empty sequence. This means that ~A must be a tautology. Then A itself must be a self-contradiction, since A is equivalent to the denial of ~A, and the denial of a sentence form that must be true is a sentence form that must be false. But if A is a self-contradiction, then any conclusion, including an empty sequence, follows from it. The sequent below the line says that an empty sequence follows from A, and this is so if and only if ~A follows from an empty sequence.

Justification of P.3

P.3
$$\frac{\mathcal{D}, {\sim}A, \mathcal{E} \vdash \mathcal{F}}{\mathcal{D}, \mathcal{E} \vdash A, \mathcal{F}} \quad \text{(eliminates} \sim \text{on left)}$$

Again, we assume that $\mathcal{D}$, $\mathcal{E}$, and $\mathcal{F}$ are empty. Then the sequent above the line in P.3 says that an empty sequence follows from ~A. Thus, ~A is a self-contradiction. But this means that A is a tautology, and a tautology follows from an empty sequence. So the consequence relationship holds in the sequent below the line in P.3 if and only if it holds in the sequent above the line.

Justification of P.4

P.4
$$\frac{\mathcal{D} \vdash \mathcal{F}, A \cdot B, \mathcal{G}}{\mathcal{D} \vdash \mathcal{F}, A, \mathcal{G} \qquad \mathcal{D} \vdash \mathcal{F}, B, \mathcal{G}} \quad \text{(eliminates} \cdot \text{on right)}$$

P.4 allows us to eliminate a conjunction ($\cdot$) on the right side of the gate. If a conjunction follows from any premisses—including the *empty set* of premisses—then each of the conjuncts separately follows from those same premisses. Thus, there are two sequents below the line, and each of these sequents contains one conjunct on the right side of the gate. Conversely, if each of two sentence forms follows from identical sets of premisses, then their conjunction follows from that set of premisses.

Justification of P.5

P.5
$$\frac{\mathcal{D}, A \cdot B, \mathcal{E} \vdash \mathcal{F}}{\mathcal{D}, A, B, \mathcal{E} \vdash \mathcal{F}} \quad \text{(eliminates} \cdot \text{on left)}$$

P.5 allows us to eliminate a conjunction ($\cdot$) on the left side of the gate. Consider an argument form with a conjunction with two members (A and B) as its only premiss. A conjunction is true if and only if both of its conjuncts are

true. If the conclusion follows from this premiss, then the conclusion clearly
follows from the two premisses A and B. If the conclusion does not follow from
A • B, then it will not follow from the two separate premisses A and B. In P.5, a
conjunctive premiss above the line is simply split into two separate premisses
below the line. (Remember that the comma on the left side of the gate is read
as "and.") All other sequences ($\mathcal{D}$, $\mathcal{E}$, and $\mathcal{F}$) are simply carried along without
alteration.

Justification of P.6

P.6
$$\frac{\mathcal{D} \vdash \mathcal{F}, A \vee B, \mathcal{G}}{\mathcal{D} \vdash \mathcal{F}, A, B, \mathcal{G}} \quad \text{(eliminates v on right)}$$

The justification of P.6 is quite obvious if we consider that commas on the
right side of the gate are read as "or." To apply P.6, a wedge (v) on the right side
of the gate is replaced by a comma. If the disjunction A v B follows from the
premisses on the left, then either A follows from those premisses or B does. If
the disjunction does not follow, then it is not true that either A or B follows from
the premisses.

Justification of P.7

P.7
$$\frac{\mathcal{D}, A \vee B, \mathcal{E} \vdash \mathcal{F}}{\mathcal{D}, A, \mathcal{E} \vdash \mathcal{F} \quad \mathcal{D}, B, \mathcal{E} \vdash \mathcal{F}} \quad \text{(eliminates v on left)}$$

To apply P.7, a wedge on the left side of the gate is replaced with a comma.
If a conclusion follows from a disjunction (A v B), the conclusion must be true
if either A is true or B is true. However, this is equivalent to saying that the
conclusion follows from A and also from B. Thus, there are two sequents below
the line, and each sequent contains one disjunct as a premiss. Also, if a conclusion
follows from either of two premisses considered separately, then it clearly follows from the disjunction of those same premisses.

Justification of P.8

P.8
$$\frac{\mathcal{D} \vdash \mathcal{F}, A \rightarrow B, \mathcal{G}}{A, \mathcal{D} \vdash \mathcal{F}, B, \mathcal{G}} \quad \text{(eliminates} \rightarrow \text{on right)}$$

If a material conditional follows from some premisses, this means that if all
of the premisses are true, then the conditional is also true. But if the conditional
is true, then it cannot be the case that its antecedent is true and its consequent
is false. Thus, if the antecedent of the conditional is added to the premisses, then
the consequent must follow from those premisses supplemented by its antecedent. Similarly, if B follows from premisses that include A, then the sentence form
A → B will be true if those premisses (excluding A) are all true. This justifies
the application of P.8.

Justification of P.9

P.9
$$\frac{\mathcal{D}, A \rightarrow B, \mathcal{E} \vdash \mathcal{F}}{\mathcal{D}, \mathcal{E} \vdash A, \mathcal{F} \quad \mathcal{D}, B, \mathcal{E} \vdash \mathcal{F}}$$
(eliminates → on left)

Consider that A → B is logically equivalent to ~A v B. If we apply P.7 to the sequent $\mathcal{D}$, ~A v B, $\mathcal{E} \vdash \mathcal{F}$, we obtain sequents $\mathcal{D}$, ~A, $\mathcal{E} \vdash \mathcal{F}$ and $\mathcal{D}$, B, $\mathcal{E} \vdash \mathcal{F}$ below the line. If we then apply P.3 to $\mathcal{D}$, ~A, $\mathcal{E} \vdash \mathcal{F}$, we obtain $\mathcal{D}$, $\mathcal{E} \vdash A$, $\mathcal{F}$. This sequent and the sequent $\mathcal{D}$, B, $\mathcal{E} \vdash \mathcal{F}$ occur below the line in the application of P.9.

Justifications of P.10 and P.11

P.10
$$\frac{\mathcal{D} \vdash \mathcal{F}, A \leftrightarrow B, \mathcal{G}}{A, \mathcal{D} \vdash \mathcal{F}, B, \mathcal{G} \quad B, \mathcal{D} \vdash \mathcal{F}, A, \mathcal{G}}$$
(eliminates ↔ on right)

P.11
$$\frac{\mathcal{D}, A \leftrightarrow B, \mathcal{E} \vdash \mathcal{F}}{\mathcal{D}, \mathcal{E} \vdash A, B, \mathcal{F} \quad A, B, \mathcal{D}, \mathcal{E} \vdash \mathcal{F}}$$
(eliminates ↔ on left)

These justifications are left as exercises. In each case, consider that A ↔ B is logically equivalent to (A → B) • (B → A).

It is interesting to note that this proof method may be used effectively even when the user does not understand the justifications of the rules of inference or why they work. The rules work in such a way that machines may be designed to test the validity of argument forms as well as to test whether sentence forms are tautologous or self-contradictory. If you have some computer experience, you might try to write a program for generating proofs using this proof method.

IV. EXERCISES

1. Use the proof method to decide whether the last sentence form is a logical consequence of the remaining sentence forms:

a. $p \rightarrow q$
  $\sim p \rightarrow r$
  $\sim q \rightarrow r$
  $\sim q$

b. $p \rightarrow q$
  $r \rightarrow \sim s$
  $q \rightarrow r$
  $p \rightarrow \sim s$

c. $(p • q) \rightarrow (r • s)$
  $\sim (q \text{ v } s)$
  $t \rightarrow (\sim q \rightarrow (p • r))$
  $\sim t$

d. $p \rightarrow q$
  $r \rightarrow s$
  $\sim s \rightarrow p$
  $q \rightarrow r$
  $\sim s \rightarrow t$

e. $(p \rightarrow q) \text{ v } (r \rightarrow s)$
  $(p \rightarrow s) \text{ v } (r \rightarrow q)$

f. $(p \leftrightarrow q) \rightarrow r$
  $\sim r$
  $\sim p • q$
  s

2. Use the proof method to determine which of the following are tautologies. Take care to identify the main connectives correctly.

    a. $(p \rightarrow q) \vee (\sim p \rightarrow q)$

    b. $(p \rightarrow q) \rightarrow ((r \rightarrow (q \rightarrow s)) \rightarrow (r \rightarrow (p \rightarrow s)))$

    c. $((p \rightarrow q) \rightarrow (q \rightarrow r)) \leftrightarrow (q \rightarrow r)$

    d. $((p \rightarrow q) \rightarrow r) \rightarrow ((p \rightarrow r) \rightarrow r)$

    e. $(\sim p \rightarrow r) \rightarrow ((q \rightarrow r) \rightarrow ((p \rightarrow q) \rightarrow r))$

    f. $\sim(p \rightarrow q) \leftrightarrow (p \rightarrow \sim q)$

3. Using sentence letters to represent simple sentences, translate each of the following English arguments into argument forms. Then use the proof method to determine the validity or the invalidity of each argument form.

    a. Either the economy will improve or the stock market will crash. If the stock market crashes, banks will fail. But banks will not fail. So it is not the case that if the economy improves, the banks will fail.

    b. The president is happy if and only if his favorite bills are passed by Congress. If the president is happy, his staff feels good. But if the staff members feel good, they are in no condition to work for the bills, and if that is the case, the President's favorite bills will not be passed by Congress. Therefore, the President is unhappy.

    c. If the Republicans choose a good candidate, they will win the election unless there is a split in the party. It is not true that if the Republicans meet in Chicago, there will be a split in the party. But if they meet in Chicago, they will choose a good candidate. So they will choose a good candidate, and they will win the election.

    d. If some archaeologists are correct, then the first humans entered North America across the Bering Strait 30,000 years ago. If they crossed the Bering Strait 30,000 years ago, they must have spent time in what is now Alaska. If they spent time in what is now Alaska, they must have left artifacts with radiocarbon dates of about 30,000 years old. If such artifacts are there, they will be uncovered if the archaeologists excavate. So if the archaeologists excavate and if some archaeologists are correct, then they will uncover 30,000 year-old artifacts in Alaska.

Index of Fallacies

Ad Baculum: (*See* **Appeal to Force**)

Ad Hoc Reasoning: (Chap. 7, p. 211) Hypotheses are tested by deriving predictions from them and observing whether or not the predictions are true. Usually, however, predictions cannot be derived simply from the hypothesis to be tested. Additional assumptions (auxiliary hypotheses) are required to connect the predictions with the hypothesis that is tested. When the auxiliary hypotheses have no independent justification, and are brought in (or rejected) for no other reason than to save (or refute) a favored hypothesis, they are called *ad hoc* assumptions. To invoke such assumptions is to be guilty of *ad hoc* reasoning.

Ad Hominem: (*See* **Argument Against the Person**)

Ad Misericordium: (*See* **Appeal to Pity**)

Affirming the Consequent: (Chap. 6, p. 187) This is a fallacious form of argument that resembles the valid form of *denying the consequent.* Its structure involves a conditional premiss ("If *p* then *q*"), an additional premiss that affirms the consequent ("*q*"), and a conclusion that affirms the antecedent ("*p*"). It is possible for an argument in this form to have true premisses and a false conclusion.

Appeal to Force: (Chap. 2, p. 56) This fallacy occurs when a threat of force is somehow put forth as evidence for a conclusion.

Appeal to Pity: (Chap. 2, p. 56) This fallacy occurs when sympathy or pity for the circumstances of some person or persons is somehow put forth as evidence for a conclusion.

Appeal to Consensus: (Chap. 3, p. 76) Arguments that offer majority opinion as a reason to believe some claim are fallacious unless there is a good reason to believe that the majority opinion is correct. The mere fact that many people or even most people believe a claim is not good evidence for it.

Argument Against the Person: (Chap. 3, p. 74) An argument that concludes that a claim is false because it was made by a particular person is fallacious unless there are good reasons to believe that most of what that person says about the subject matter of the conclusion is false. Sometimes the character of the person is attacked (**Abusive ad Hominem**), sometimes the person's circumstances are attacked (**Circumstantial ad Hominem**), and sometimes the person is attacked for somehow being associated with the position criticized in the argument (**Tu Quoque**).

Argument from Authority: (Chap. 3, p. 72) An argument that concludes that some claim is true because some authority believes the claim is fallacious unless (1) the so-called authority is a genuine authority, (2) the authority is speaking in his or her area of expertise, and (3) there is no substantial disagreement among authorities in the subject area of the conclusion. To argue that a conclusion is correct merely because some authority figure accepts it is fallacious.

Biased Statistics: (Chap. 3, p. 93) An inductive argument that is based on a sample is fallacious if the sample is constructed in such a way that it cannot be expected to capture the relevant variety in the population.

Black-and-White Thinking: (Chap. 8, p. 236) When we ignore a whole range of alternative possibilities and focus only on the extremes (for example, best-worst, priceless-worthless, friend-foe), and frame an argument, such as a disjunctive syllogism or dilemma, in terms of the extremes, we commit the fallacy of **Black-and-White Thinking.**

Circular Reasoning: (Chap. 3, p. 99) This fallacy occurs when the truth of the conclusion is already assumed in the premises offered in support of the conclusion. If the conclusion of such an argument is in doubt, then premises that are equally dubious cannot offer convincing support for the conclusion.

Composition: (Chap. 9, p. 288) This fallacy occurs when a term that is used distributively (referring to each member of a class or each part of a whole) in the premises is interpreted collectively (referring to the class or the whole) in the conclusion. In such cases, the term is used ambiguously; its meaning in the premiss is not the same as its meaning in the conclusion.

Confusing Cause and Effect: (Chap. 4, p. 136) This mistake occurs when an event or type of event that is directly causally connected with another is mis-identified as the cause when it is the effect or *vice versa*. Since it is widely understood that effects cannot precede their causes, most instances of this fallacy result from difficulty in sorting out which event is temporally prior to the other.

Confusing Coincidental Relationships with Causal Relationships (Post Hoc): (Chap. 4, p. 134) The name of the fallacy describes it. Temporal succession of events is not adequate evidence of a causal relationship between them. But if an event is unusually interesting or important, we look for its cause, and sometimes (fallaciously) identify some pertinent *preceding* event as "the cause" on grounds of precedence alone.

Confusing the Harm or Benefits That Result from Holding a Belief with Evidence for It: (Chap. 4, p. 139) The name of the fallacy describes it. We are in danger of committing this fallacy when our desire to achieve the perceived benefits or avoid the perceived harms clouds our ability to assess evidence for a claim.

Denying the Antecedent: (Chap. 6, p. 187) This fallacy occurs when we offer or accept as valid the following form of argument:

If *p* then *q,* but not *p*, therefore not *q*.

This invalid form resembles the valid form of *denying the consequent*.

Division: (Chap. 9, p. 288) This fallacy occurs when a term that is used collectively in the premises is interpreted distributively in the conclusion.

Equivocation: (Chap. 11, p. 325) If the conclusion of an argument depends on a shift in meaning of an ambiguous term, phrase, or grammatical construction in the context of that argument, the fallacy of equivocation is committed.

Every and All: (Chap. 10, p. 317) Sentences that contain both universal and existential quantifiers (every, all, some) can change meaning when the order of the quantifiers is reversed, and so after reversal, the two sentences may not follow from one another. For example, "someone" in "Everyone loves someone" means "someone or other" whereas "someone" in "Someone is loved by everyone" means "some one person." The first sentence follows from the second, but the second does not follow from the first. If the conclusion of an argument depends on failure to recognize such a shift in meaning, the fallacy of every and all is committed.

Fallacies of Distribution (*See* **Composition** and **Division**)

False Analogy: (Chap. 3, p. 83) This fallacy occurs when the relevant dissimilarities between the types of objects mentioned in the premises of an analogical argument are ignored.

False Dilemma: (*See* **Black-and-White Thinking**)

Gamblers Fallacy: (Chap. 5, p. 169) This fallacy occurs if we interpret what happens "on average" or "in the long run" in such a way as to suppose that departures from what is average will be corrected in the short run.

Genetic Fallacy: (Chap. 4, p. 138) This fallacy occurs whenever some nonevidential feature connected with the origin of a claim (such as who said it or how it first came to be believed) is taken as evidence for or against it.

Hasty Generalization: (Chap. 3, p. 93) This fallacy occurs in inductive reasoning when a conclusion is drawn from a sample that is too small.

Ignoring a Common Cause: (Chap. 4, p. 136) When we attribute a direct causal relationship between two events that are only indirectly related to one another through a common underlying cause of both, we commit this fallacy. The fallacy would occur, for example, if we were to argue that red spots cause a child to have a fever, when both features are *symptoms* of some underlying cause, such as measles.

Incomplete Evidence: (Chap. 3, p. 69) When we construct or evaluate an inductive argument, we must take account of all available relevant evidence that would affect the truth of the conclusion. If we deliberately ignore or carelessly fail to obtain such evidence, we commit this fallacy.

Misleading Vividness: Chap. 3, p. 94) This fallacy occurs when some particularly vivid information is weighted disproportionately so that a substantial amount of statistical support for a conclusion is deemed less important than it really is.

Post Hoc (*See* **Confusing Coincidental Relationships with Causal Relationships**)

Tu Quoque (*See* **Argument Against the Person**)

Bibliography

Allen, Gary. *None Dare Call It Conspiracy,* 1972, Council Press, Rossmoor, California.

Anscombe, G. E. M. *An Introduction to Wittgenstein's Tractatus,* 2nd ed., 1959, Harper and Row, New York.

Aristotle. *The Works of Aristotle,* ed. W. D. Ross, 1921, Oxford University Press, Oxford.

Arnauld, Antoine. *The Art of Thinking,* trans. J. Dickoff and P. James, 1964, Bobbs-Merrill Co., Indianapolis.

Asimov, Isaac. *The Intelligent Man's Guide to the Biological Sciences,* 1960, Basic Books, New York.

Asimov, Isaac. *The Intelligent Man's Guide to the Physical Sciences,* 1960, Basic Books, New York.

Augustine, Saint. *The Confessions of St. Augustine,* trans. E. B. Pusey, 1951, Pocket Books, New York.

Binford, Lewis. *Bones,* 1981, Academic Press, New York.

Bloom, Alan. *The Closing of the American Mind,* 1987, Simon and Schuster, New York.

Bok, Sissela. *Secrets,* 1984, Oxford University Press, Oxford.

Boorstin, Daniel J. *The Discoverers,* 1983, Random House, New York.

Boswell, James. *Boswell for the Defense,* ed. W. K. Wimsatt, Jr. and F. A. Pottle. 1959, McGraw-Hill, New York.

Boswell, James. *Boswell on the Grand Tour,* ed. F. Brady and F. A. Pottle, 1955, McGraw-Hill, New York.

Boswell, James. *In Search of a Wife,* ed. F. Brady and F. A. Pottle, McGraw-Hill, New York, 1956.

Boswell, James. *Life of Johnson,* ed. C. G. Osgood, 1917, Charles Scribner's Sons, New York.

Boswell, James. *The Ominous Years,* ed. C. Ryekamp and F. A. Pottle, 1963, McGraw-Hill, New York.

Braffort, P. and D. Herschberg. *Computer Programming and Formal Systems,* 1967, North Holland, Amsterdam.

Bridgman, P. W. *The Logic of Modern Physics,* 1927, Macmillan, New York.

Campbell, Keith. *Body and Mind,* 1970, Doubleday, Garden City, New York.

Carroll, Lewis. *Alice's Adventures in Wonderland,* 1962, Macmillan Co., New York.

Carroll, Lewis. *Symbolic Logic,* 1958, Dover Publications, New York.

Chesterfield, Lord (Philip Dormer Stanhope). *Lord Chesterfield's Letters,* A. L. Burt Co., New York.

Chesterton, G. K. *The Father Brown Omnibus,* 1951, Dodd, Mead and Co., New York.

Culbertson, James T. *Mathematics and Logic for Digital Devices, 1958, D. Van Nostrand Co., New York.*

Darwin, Charles. *The Origin of Species,* 1903, Hurst And Co., New York.

De Beauvoir, Simone. *The Ethics of Ambiguity,* trans. B. Frechtman, 1964, Citadel Press, New York.

Deetz, James. *Invitation to Archaeology,* 1967, Natural History Press, Garden City, New York.

Descartes, René. *Discourse on Method and Meditations on First Philosophy,* trans. Donald A. Cress, 1980, Hackett Publishing Co., Indianapolis.

Devlin, Patrick Lord. *The Enforcement of Morals,* 1965, Oxford University Press, London, Oxford, New York.

Dickens, Charles. *Our Mutual Friend,* 1894, Houghton Mifflin, Boston.

Doyle, Sir Arthur Conan. *The Annotated Sherlock Holmes,* ed. W. S. Baring-Gould, 1967, Clarkson N. Potter, New York.

Dunn, L. C. and T. H. Dobshansky *Heredity, Race, and Society,* 1946, Penguin Books, New York.

Durrell, Lawrence. *Prospero's Cell and Reflections on a Marine Venus,* 1960, Dutton, New York.

Eliot, George. *Felix Holt,* John W. Lovell Co., New York.

Eliot, George. *Middlemarch,* John W. Lovell Co., New York.

Ehrlich, Paul. *The Population Bomb,* 1968, Ballantine Books, New York.

Firestone, Shulamith. *The Dialectic of Sex,* 1971, Jonathan Cape, New York.

Fowles, John. *Daniel Martin,* 1977, Little, Brown Co., Boston.

Frankfurt, Harry. *Demons, Dreamers, and Madmen,* 1970, Bobbs-Merrill Co., Indianapolis.

Freud, Sigmund. *The Basic Writings of Sigmund Freud,* trans. and ed. A. A. Brill, Modern Library, New York.

Fussell, Paul. *Class,* 1983, Summit Books, New York.

Galbraith, J. K. *The Affluent Society,* 1976, Houghton Mifflin, Boston.

Gissing, George. *The Odd Woman,* 1971, W. W. Norton, New York.

Glob, P. V. *The Bog People,* 1971, Ballantine Books, New York.

Goodman, Nelson. *Ways of Worldmaking,* 1987, Hackett Publishing Co., Indianapolis.

Gould, R. A. *Living Archaeology,* 1980, Cambridge University Press, Cambridge.

Gould, Stephen J. *The Flamingo's Smile,* 1985, W. W. Norton, New York.

Gould, Stephen J. *The Mismeasure of Man,* 1981, W. W. Norton, New York.

Greene, T. M. *The Arts and the Art of Criticism,* 1973, Gordian Press, New York.

Guthrie, W. K. C. *The Greeks and their Gods,* 1955, Beacon Press, Boston.

Harris, Marvin. *The Rise of Anthropological Theory,* 1968, Thomas Y. Crowell Co., New York.

Hume, David. *Dialogues Concerning Natural Religion,* ed. N. Pike, 1970, Bobbs-Merrill Co., Indianapolis.

Hume, David. *A Treatise of Human Nature,* ed. L. A. Selby-Bigge, 1888, Oxford University Press, London.

Huxley, Julian. *New Bottles for Old Wine,* 1957, Harper and Brothers, New York.

Irving, Washington. *Bracebridge Hall,* H. M. Caldwell Co., New York.

Jochim, M. A. *Strategies for Survival,* 1981, Academic Press, New York.

Jolly, C. and F. Plog. *Physical Anthropology and Archaeology,* 2nd ed., 1979, Alfred A. Knopf, New York.

Kitcher, Philip. *Abusing Science,* 1982, MIT Press, Cambridge, Massachusetts.

Koestler, Arthur. *The Invisible Writing,* 1954, Macmillan Co., New York.

Laclos, C. de. *Les Liaisons Dangereuses,* trans. P. W. K. Stone, 1961, Penguin Books, Baltimore.

Lenin, V. I. *Collected Works* Vol. 14, 1927, V. I. Lenin Institute, Moscow.

Levi, E. H. *An Introduction to Legal Reasoning,* 1970, University of Chicago Press, Chicago.

Lucretius. *On the Nature of the Universe,* trans. E. E. Latham, 1951, Penguin Books, Baltimore.

Maalfjit, A. de W. *Images of Man,* 1974, Alfred A. Knopf, New York.

MacMahon, B. and T. F. Pugh. *Epidemiology,* 1978, Little Brown Co., Boston.

MacMahon, B., T. F. Pugh and J. Ipsen. *Epidemiologic Methods,* 1960, Little, Brown Co., Boston.

Malone, Michael. *Handling Sin,* 1986, Little, Brown Co., Boston.

Mates, Benson. *Elementary Logic,* 2nd ed., 1972, Oxford University Press, New York.

Mill, John Stuart. *A System of Logic,* 8th ed., 1874, Harper and Bros., New York.

Millett, Kate. *Sexual Politics,* 1970, Doubleday Co., Garden City, New York.

Morris, H. M. *Introducing Creationism in the Public Schools,* 1975, Creation Life Publishers, San Diego.

Morris, Herbert. *On Guilt and Innocence,* 1976, University of California Press, Berkeley.

Mumford, Lewis. *Technics and Human Development,* 1966, Harcourt Brace, New York.

Murphy, J. G. *Civil Disobedience and Violence,* 1971, Wadsworth Publishing Co., Belmont, California.

Murray, Gilbert. *The Literature of Ancient Greece,* 1956, University of Chicago Press, Chicago.

Newman, J. R. *The World of Mathematics,* 1956, Simon and Schuster, New York.

Nisbett, R. and L. Ross. *Human Inference: Strategies and Shortcomings of Social Judgment,* 1980, Prentice-Hall, Englewood Cliffs, New Jersey.

Nietzsche, Friedrich. *The Philosophy of Nietzsche,* Modern Library, New York.

O'Connor, D. J., ed. *A Critical History of Western Philosophy,* 1964, Free Press, New York.

Pliny the Elder. *The Natural History of Pliny,* trans. John Bostock, 1855, H. G. Bohn, London.

Reid, Thomas. *Works,* 6th ed., ed. W. Hamilton, 1863, Edinburgh.

Rousseau, Jean-Jacques. *The Social Contract,* ed. C. M. Sherover, 1974, New American Library, New York.

Routley, R. and V. "Nuclear power," In *And Justice for All,* edited by T. Regan and D. Van De Veer, 1982, Rowman and Allanheld, Totowa, New Jersey.

Russell, Bertrand. *My Philosophical Development,* 1959, Simon and Schuster, New York.

Russell, Bertrand. *Religion and Science,* 1961, Oxford University Press, New York.

Russell, Bertrand. *Skeptical Essays,* 1928, W. W. Norton, New York.

Salmon, W. C. *Logic,* 3rd ed., 1983, Prentice-Hall, Englewood Cliffs, New Jersey.

Salmon, W. C. *The Foundations of Scientific Inference,* 1967, University of Pittsburgh Press, Pittsburgh.

Shakespeare, William. *Merchant of Venice,* 1965, Airmont Publishing Co., New York.

Shakespeare, William. *King Lear,* 1966, Airmont Publishing Co., New York.

Shrader-Frechette, K. S. *Nuclear Power and Public Policy,* 1980, D. Reidel, Dordrecht, Holland.

Smith, Adam. *The Wealth of Nations,* 1863, Adam and Charles Black, Edinburgh.

Smith, A. H. *The Mushroom Hunter's Field Guide,* 1958, University of Michigan Press, Ann Arbor.

Storr, Anthony. *The Psychodynamics of Creativity,* 1977, Geigy Pharmaceuticals, Ardsley, New York.

Strong, R. *Henry, Prince of Wales, and England's Renaissance,* 1986, Thames and Hudson, New York.

Suppes, Patrick. *A Probabilistic Theory of Causality,* 1970, North-Holland, Amsterdam.

Swartz, Robert J. *Perceiving, Sensing and Knowing,* 1965, Anchor Books, Garden City, New York.

Thompson, J. Eric S. *Maya Archaeologist,* 1963, University of Oklahoma Press, Norman.

Tolstoy, Leo. *The Death of Ivan Ilych and Other Stories,* 1960, New American Library, New York.

Tolstoy, Leo. *What Is Art?,* 1960, Liberal Arts Press, Indianapolis.

Twain, Mark. *The Writings of Mark Twain, 1899–1922,* F. Collier and Sons Co., New York.

Wesley, John. *The Journal of John Wesley,* ed. P. L. Parker, 1974, Moody, Northbrook, Illinois.

Westfall, Richard S. *The Construction of Modern Science: Mechanisms and Mechanics,* 1971, Cambridge University Press, Cambridge, United Kingdom.

Wharton, Edith. *The Custom of the Country,* 1913, Charles Scribner's Sons, New York.

White, Antonia. *Frost in May,* 1981, Penguin Books, London.

Wilde, Oscar. *The Plays of Oscar Wilde,* Modern Library, New York.

Wootton, Barbara. *Crime and the Criminal Law,* 1963, Stevens, London.

Young, Agatha. *The Men Who Made Surgery,* 1961, Hillman Books, New York.

Zinsser. *On Writing Well,* 2nd ed. 1980, Harper and Row, New York.

Answers to Selected Exercises

Chapter 1

Pages 5–10

1. You could accept your friend's word in this case without seeking further evidence because if she is correct you may find a bargain, and even if she is mistaken you would not lose much.

3.a. Dr. Smith asserts that the *Amanita verna* is deadly poisonous. He also asserts that the symptoms are delayed and that applications of first aid are almost useless.

3.b. "Never eat a white *Amanita*" is a warning or command, not an assertion.

3.c. It is wise to take the advice of the expert with no need to seek more evidence. Too much is at stake to go against this advice just to taste a pretty mushroom.

5.a. The advertiser asserts that the management consultant firm can solve any problem you have. It also asserts that over two thousand men and women . . . have invested the time, money, and effort to create a breakthrough in business, career, social life. (The ad suggests, but does not actually assert, that the time, money, and effort were invested in this firm!)

5.b. No evidence is offered for these grand claims. The assertions are so over-blown that they should make us suspicious. Certainly evidence should be sought before turning over any money to the firm. One way to acquire evidence would be to ask the firm for references from satisfied customers and to speak with them yourself.

Pages 17–20

A.1. In England under the blasphemy laws it is illegal to express disbelief in the Christian religion.[1] It is also illegal to teach what Christ taught on the subject of non-resistance.[2] Therefore, (whoever wishes to avoid being a criminal must profess to agree with Christ's teachings but must avoid saying what that teaching was).

A.3. All 70 students who ate dinner at the fraternity house on Friday became ill during the night.[1] None of the students who live at the house but who didn't dine there that night became ill,[2] so (the illness must have been food poisoning caused by something served for dinner at the house on Friday).

A.5. We can suspect that (the inventor [of eyeglasses] was not an academic), for professors delight in boasting of their inventions[1] and before the thirteenth century we have no record by any such self-styled inventor.[2]

B.1. Women tend to do better on essay tests than on timed, multiple-choice tests.[1] Men tend to do better on timed, multiple-choice tests than on essay tests.[2] SAT tests are timed, multiple-choice tests.[3] [Therefore] (SAT tests are biased in favor of men).

B.3. [Since] [E]ven if there is a non-negligible probability of a [nuclear] reactor accident,[1] still (that is acceptable), being of no greater order than the risks of accidents that are already socially acceptable.[2]

C.1. In this example, "because" is not used to introduce a premiss. It is used to introduce the causes of the parents' objections. This is not an argument.

C.3. In this example, "Since" is used to indicate passage of time. This is not an argument.

C.5. In this example, "Thus" is used to introduce some examples. This is not an argument.

Pages 22–23

1. Because publishers are aiming at a national market,[1a] (the number one criterion for any textbook is avoidance of controversy).[a] Since they must respond to a variety of specific criteria from their buyers,[1b] (this has resulted in what has been called the "dumbing down" of textbooks).[b]

Pages 27–28

A.1. Statistical generalization.

A.3. Universal generalization.

B.1. Women office workers work just as hard as men office workers and are just as productive.[1] Therefore (women office workers should receive the same pay as men in comparable positions).
   Missing premiss: All who do comparable work should receive comparable pay. (Plausible)

B.3. (Marijuana should be legalized) because it is no more dangerous than alcohol, which is already legal.[1]
   Missing premiss: Any substance that is not more dangerous than a substance that is already legal should be legalized. (The plausibility of such a premiss is questionable.)

B.5. (Marijuana should not be legalized) because it leads to the use of harder drugs, such as heroin.[1]

Missing premiss: Anything which leads to the use of hard drugs should not be legalized. (Plausibility of this can be questioned.)

Pages 31–33

1. Conclusion 1: The human-life bill would cost taxpayers 40 billion dollars each year.
Premisses 1: If the bill is passed and abortions are made illegal, at least another 700,000 babies will be born next year. About two-thirds of the mothers will collect welfare. Instead of a single cost of $125 for an abortion, we will pay $1,000 to $1,500 for a delivery, and at least $100,000 to support these welfare children until they reach maturity.
Conclusion 2: 400,000 additional welfare babies will be born each year.
Premisses 2: 1.4 million abortions per year are now being performed. If abortion is made illegal, half of those women will have babies. Two-thirds of those who have babies that would have otherwise been aborted are on welfare.
Additional material: The proponent of the argument, Dr. George Ryan, claims that the bill will leave government on our backs and put government in our bedrooms. He also claims that half of the women who want abortions will get them illegally or go out of the country for the abortions. This material plays the role of encouraging a negative attitude towards the bill.

3. Conclusion: Who says that chauvinists are chivalrous? (This is stated as a rhetorical question, with the intended meaning of an assertion: chauvinists are not chivalrous.)
Premisses: Last year the Jaycees voted to kick out the women members they had previously recruited. They even voted to kick out the chapters who wouldn't kick out the women they had previously invited.
Additional material: The final paragraph reports the ruling of Minnesota courts forbidding such discrimination and explains why the courts so ruled. (The author is not *arguing* that the courts ruled this way.) The courts' argument could be reconstructed thus: Conclusion: The Jaycees cannot refuse membership to women.
Additional Premisses: The Jaycees operate as a public business. No duly designated public business can refuse to admit women.

Pages 35–38

1. Conclusion: It is just and right that woman accept as lord and master him whom she led to sin.
Premiss: Adam was led to sin by Eve and not Eve by Adam.
Missing Premiss: *Wildly implausible.* If the first woman led the first man to sin, then every woman should accept her man as her lord and master.

3. Scanlon's conclusion: The $91 million lost aid was worth it as a matter of principle.
His premiss: The federal government has no right to force a state legislature to spend money for anything.

Additional material: Background information about the federal requirement for an emission-inspection program and the legislators' refusal to enact it.

5. Conclusion 1: Hair analysis is a good way to screen large groups of people for exposure to toxic trace materials.

Premises 1: Concentrations of lead, cadmium, arsenic, and mercury in hair have provided a good record of exposure, according to studies. Analysis of lengthwise hair sections can show the approximate time when a short, intense exposure occurred.

Conclusion 2: Analysis of lengthwise sections of hair can show the approximate time when a short, intense exposure occurred.

Premiss 2: The metal grows out with the hair.

Conclusion 3: It may be that measurements of chromium in hair will be useful in identifying people with diabetes and in monitoring the course of the disease.

Premiss 3: Chromium is essential for the hormone insulin to work properly. (An implicit premiss connecting insulin deficiency with diabetes is involved.)

7. Conclusion: The Air Force does not spend $12.6 million per year for private pet service by veterinarians.

Premises: The money paid to veterinarians is for inspection of meat used at military facilities. All services performed on privately owned animals is paid for by owners.

Additional material: The proponent states qualifications (23 years in the armed forces) for knowing how the money is spent, and also states approval of this expenditure.

Chapter 2

Pages 47–48

2.a. T

2.c T

3.a. Deductive.

3.e. This is not a correct deductive argument.

Pages 53–56

2.a. Premiss: The introduction of cooperative marketing into Europe greatly increased the prosperity of the farmers.

Conclusion: A similar system [of cooperative marketing] will greatly increase the prosperity of United States farmers.

This argument can be understood as an inductive argument based on the (unstated) similarities between the situation of farmers in the United States and farmers in Europe. If the unstated premises about alleged similarities were stated we could say something about how plausible they are; or, if we know something about the situation of farmers, we might be able to supply the missing premises. Without special knowledge though, it is difficult to supply or evaluate such premises.

2.d. Premiss: The *Farmers' Almanac*, which has an excellent record on such matters, predicts that we are in for a hard winter this year.
     Conclusion: There is going to be a tough winter ahead.
     This can be understood as an inductive argument in which the conclusion is based on what happens usually (correct predictions in the *Farmers Almanac*).

2.g. Premisses: (1) That looking black is not in our culture a necessary condition for being black can be seen from the phenomenon of passing. (2) That it is not a sufficient condtion can be seen from the book *Black Like Me*, by John Howard Griffin, where "looking black" is easily understood by the reader to be different from being black.
     Conclusion: Skin hue is neither a necessary nor a sufficient condition for being classified as black in our culture.
     This argument is deductive.

Pages 59–63

1. A group of houseplants exposed to four hours of flourescent light in addition to normal daylight grew more quickly than others that were not exposed to the additional lighting.
They were also generally greener and healthier looking.

Fluorescent light is good for houseplants.

    Inductive. Generalization based on a sample.

3. Any individual dependence (loss of liberty) is so much force denied to the body of the state.
Liberty cannot exist without equality.

The greatest good of all, which ought to be the aim of every system of legislation, can be summed up in two principal objects, liberty and equality.

    Intended to be deductive. A premiss is needed to connect force denied to the body of the state with the greatest good of all.

5. The results cited in the sample of treatments with carbolic acid represent a mortality of 15 percent as against the general record of more than 30 percent.

Carbolic acid is effective in fighting hospital diseases.

    Inductive. Reasoning based on a sample.

6. The vandals had to bring paint to mutilate the temple in the way described.

The attack was planned.

Probably intended to be deductive. Missing premiss: If supplies used in vandalizing are brought along, the attack of vandalism is a planned attack.

Chapter 3

Pages 68–69

1.a. Reference class: professional hair dyes
 Attribute class: peroxide dyes
This is a strong argument, based on the high percentage.

2.a. Most wild mushrooms cause illness if ingested.
 This is a wild mushroom.

This will cause illness if ingested.

Page 71

1. The person who is chosen to be Russian ambassador to the United Nations is an experienced diplomat. Most diplomats are well trained in languages and diplomacy, and most of them know English.

Pages 78–80

1. [Charles Colson was convicted of perjury in connection with the Watergate break in.]
 Colson says that the CIA knew about the Watergate break in in advance. Most of what Colson says about Watergate is false. Therefore the CIA did not know about the Watergate break in in advance.
 This is an argument against the person (abusive *ad hominem*), and is legitimate given the background evidence of perjury in the case.

3. Many prisoners have complained that conditions in the county jail are unsanitary. Most of what the prisoners say about conditions in the jail is false. Therefore, conditions in the jail are not unsanitary.
 This is an argument against the person (circumstantial *ad hominem*), but is fallacious because we have no reason to believe that prisoners (in jail for a variety of reasons) are very likely to be dishonest about their living conditions in the jail. The second premiss in the reconstructed argument is unsupported.

5. This argument is in standard form, but it is a fallacious argument from consensus. The opinion of "most people" about the effects of smoking marijuana does not carry any special weight.

Pages 85–88

1. Conclusion: Cigarette smoking causes lung cancer in humans.

   Premiss: Tar, extracted from cigarette smoke, when smeared on the skin of mice in laboratories causes skin cancers.

   Unstated premisses: Mice are physiologically similar to humans in relevant ways. The causes of skin cancer are relevantly similar to the causes of lung cancer.

   There are too many disanalogies for this argument to be very persuasive. Also, we need to know about the amounts of tar, and the methods used to induce skin cancer in mice. We need to know about any relevant similarities between human lungs and mice skin, and so on.

3. Conclusion: Perfect thoughts cannot come from imperfect people.

   Premiss: Heat can't come from something cold.

   It would be difficult to make a case for this as an argument from analogy, since it is difficult to state the ways in which cold things and imperfect people are similar.

9. Conclusion: The chemist who compounded the hair wash was liable to the wife of the purchaser for injuries caused by the wash.

   Premiss: The imperfect hair wash was like the imperfect gun in the *Langridge* case. Recovery by the plaintiff was allowed in the *Langridge* case. "Fraud" and "negligence" are relevantly similar where such suits are concerned.

   Although one could question the relevant similarity between fraud and negligence, if they are similar the analogy is strong.

Pages 97–98

1. Conclusion: 2,567° Celsius is the boiling point for copper.

   Premiss: Two samples of very pure copper had a boiling point of 2,567° Celsius.

   This argument is good. The sample is small, but the population of bits of pure copper is uniform with respect to the property of boiling point.

3. Conclusion: 70 percent of all marijuana users will go on to try heroin.

   Premiss: 70 percent of a large sample of heroin users started their drug careers on marijuana.

   Fallacious argument. The sample is biased.

Pages 102–106

1. Statistical syllogism:

   80 percent to 90 percent of those who follow the special diet produce the boy or girl babies they want.

   This woman who wants a boy (girl) will follow the special diet for a boy (girl).

   This woman who wants a boy (girl) will produce a boy (girl).

Inductive generalization:

In a study of 47 French couples from 1970 to 1980, 39 (83 percent) produced a child of the sex they wanted.

In Canada, a study of 224 couples on special diets revealed an 80 percent success rate.

In five health centers in Paris and five outside the city, the success rate is approximately 90 percent.

Between 80 percent and 90 percent of all couples who follow the special diet will produce a child of the sex they want.

3. Johnson uses an analogy between military service— where beatings by superior officers are permitted—and schools. The argument is weak because of strong dissimilarities between the two cases. For example, the purpose of the military is to provide defense for the country. Instant and unquestioning obedience has its value here, but the purpose of schools is to train young minds, to develop responsible citizens who can think for themselves. Pufendorf is a legal scholar. What he says about the legality of beatings does not necessarily extend to the moral justification of the practice, which is what seems to be in question here.

5. The argument is based on (unstated) analogies between humans and experimental animals. Premisses state the effects of the drug on those animals.

Chapter 4

Page 111

1. Some area of the road leading to the place of work might have had nails or other sharp objects on it.

3. An insect such as the gypsy moth may be attacking the trees, or a drought could be responsible.

Page 113

1. One of the plants could have been a weakling; one could be planted in a more sunny spot than the other; one could have been attacked by disease or insects.

Pages 118–21

1. (1) The decreased rate of mortality in one group of encephalitis patients.
   (2) Members of one group were given ara-A. Members of the other group were given an inert substance.
   (3) Joint method of agreement and difference.
   (4) The drug ara-A causes a decrease in the rate of mortality among patients with encephalitis.

7. (1) Higher than normal rate of malignant skin cancer among members of the Washington, D.C., Police Department.
   (2) All twelve policemen afflicted with skin cancer had used tear gas to quell riots and demonstrations between 1968 and 1971.
   (3) Method of agreement.
   (4) One chemical component of tear gas apparently causes cancer.

10. (1) Increased rate of development of caries.
    (2) Patients (436) on a nutritionally adequate diet had a slow rate of caries development over a period of several years. Subsequently, they were divided into nine groups, and sucrose was introduced into the diet in various forms and with varying degrees of frequency of intake. Caries increased significantly, particularly when the ingestion of sucrose was frequent and when the form of sucrose was sticky or adhesive. After two years on the test diets, the control diet was resumed, and the caries activity returned to the slow rate.
    (3) Method of concomitant variation.
    (4) Rise and fall of rate of caries development is directly related to rise and fall in amount, frequency, and form of sucrose consumption.

Pages 125–26

1. In Exercise 1, a control group of patients with the disease receive an inert substance, and an experimental group of patients receive ara-A. Randomized experimental design.

In Exercise 2, an experimental group of former Alzheimer's patients show loss of neurons, and a control group of those without the disease do not show loss of neurons. Retrospective study.

In Exercise 3, an experimental group of junior high students is given anti-smoking propaganda; no propaganda is given to the control group of students. Randomized experimental design.

(Other exercises in the previous section also exemplify controlled experiments.)

Pages 130–31

Note: In many of these exercises, "probabilistic cause" would be a reasonable answer, depending on available background information, when "against a background of accepted, stable, necessary conditions" is given as the answer. Lack of context in these exercises is a source of ambiguity, but such ambiguity is present in real-life situations and is worth discussing.

1. Against a background of accepted, stable, necessary conditions, not having enough time to finish the exam is a sufficient condition for failing the exam.

3. Jean is the agent causally responsible for William's appearance at the party. Viewed another way, Jean's invitation might be a sufficient condition against a background of acceptable, stable, necessary conditions for William to attend.

5. Here there is an implicit reference to an agent who stored the rags. Also the stored oily rags can be considered a sufficient condition against a background of accepted, stable, necessary conditions.

Pages 141–44

1. Ignoring a common cause.

2.a. This is a possible *post hoc.* Persons who are 89 years old are susceptible to death from many different causes.

2.f. Confusion of cause and effect. The riots were not started to obtain television sets. The thefts were a result of the conditions of disorder that prevailed during the riots.

2.g. Genetic fallacy. A causal explanation of Tom's paranoia is not a justification for it.

3.a. Ignoring a common cause. The slow metabolism of Cornaro was a cause both of his slender diet and of his long life.

Chapter 5

Pages 156–57

1. $4/52 + 4/52 = 8/52 = 2/13$ (Rule 3)

4. $1 - Pr(3 \text{ heads}) = 1 - 1/8 = 7/8$ (Rule 4 and Theorem)

6. Drawing an ace and a king on two draws can occur in either of two mutually exclusive ways: ace on the first and king on the second, or king on the first and ace on the second. Using Rule 4, the probability of the first component of the disjunction is $4/52 \times 4/51 = 16/2652$; the probability of the second disjunction is also $4/52 \times 4/51 = 16/2652$. Using Rule 3, and adding these probabilities, we find the probability of drawing an ace and a king on two draws without replacement is $32/2652$ or $4/663$.

7.a.i. $16/100$ $(4/25)$

7.a iv. $50/100 \times 16/100 = 8/100$ $(2/25)$

9. Ignoring leap years, $1/365$.

Pages 172–74

1.a. $(1/1{,}000 \times \$500) - \$1 = -\$.50$

1.b. $(1/1{,}000 \times \$1{,}500) - \$3 = -\$1.50$

1.c. $(1/1,000 \times \$500) + (1,000 \times \$500) + (1/1,000 \times \$500) - \$3 = -\$1.50$

3.a. Decision under uncertainty.

3.b. Yes, since the sole purpose of the charity dinner is to raise money.

3.c,d.

	Rain	No Rain
Indoors	$440	$170
Outdoors	$80	$500

There is no best action. If there is a satisfactory action, it is to have an indoor buffet supper.

   If there is no satisfactory action, the gambler would choose the outdoor picnic, the cautious player would choose the indoor picnic. The calculator would see that the average utility of the indoor supper is $305, the average utility outdoor picnic is $290, and would choose the indoor supper.

Chapter 6

Page 182

1.a. If you do not keep up with the assignments, then you cannot do well in math and logic classes.

1.c. If you want something very much, then you work hard to achieve it.

2.a. If *q*, then *p*.   True.

2.c. If *q*, then *q*.   True.

Pages 190–91

I.3. If the Steelers beat the Oilers, then the Steelers go to the playoffs.
The Steelers beat the Oilers.
_____

The Steelers go to the playoffs.

Affirming the Antecedent.

I.6. If primitive peoples did not cross the Pacific Ocean, then there would not be a strong resemblance between Polynesian artifacts and South American artifacts.
It is not the case that there is not a strong resemblance between these artifacts.
_____

It is not the case that primitive peoples did not cross the Pacific Ocean.

Denying the Consequent.

I.7.   If there are moths in the house, then they make holes in the carpet.
There are holes in the carpet.

There are moths in the house.

Affirming the Consequent.

II.1.a. Sally won the marathon. The compound is not truth-functional because the truth of the sentence "Jake believes that Sally won the marathon" does not depend solely on the truth of "Sally won the marathon."

Chapter 7

Pages 205–207

1. (1) The high-cholesterol diet is the cause of the high incidence of heart attacks.
(2) Observable prediction: A reduction in cholesterol in the diets of people in this area will yield a reduction in the incidence of heart attacks.
Auxiliary hypothesis: Cholesterol (rather than some other ingredient in the diet) is related to heart attacks.
(3) Alternative hypothesis: The hard work that the men do is the cause of the high incidence of heart attacks.
(4) Current medical theory gives the original hypothesis a high prior probability.

3. (1) Intellectual achievements of Jews are (partly) caused by inherited myopia.
(2) Observable prediction: A random sample of near-sighted non-Jews will contain a higher proportion of intellectuals than a comparable sample of non-Jews who are not nearsighted.
Auxiliary hypothesis: Those who are unfit for sports turn to intellectual pursuits.
(3) Alternative hypothesis: Intellectual achievements are the result of greater-than-average intellectual abilities and the placement of a high value on intellectual achievement.
(4) The original hypothesis has a low prior probability. Burt's theories on this topic border on "crank," and no other evidence supports his view.

Page 209

1.a. Hypothesis: Colds can be cured by treatments that consist of shining infrared light on the feet for ten-minute periods.

Pages 214–17

1. Hypothesis: The student missed the test to deal with a family crisis. (Plausible,

on the basis of the student's story and auxiliary hypotheses about truth-telling as a norm of human communication.)

Disconfirming observation: The student was seen at the Student Union.

Alternative hypothesis: The student was unprepared to take the test.

3. Hypothesis: Oxygen in the air was the cause of the failure of cauterization to cure gangrene. (Vaguely plausible, since oxygen was present in cases in which gangrene appeared after treatment.)

Disconfirming observation: Oxygen was always present, but sometimes gangrene was cured and sometimes it was not cured.

Alternative hypothesis: Something other than oxygen caused gangrene to reappear.

Pages 219–20

1.a.i. $100/300 \times 50/100 = 1/6$

  ii. $200/300 \times 150/200 = 1/2$

b.i.
$$\frac{1/3 \times 1/2}{(1/3 \times 1/2) + (2/3 \times 1/4)} = \frac{1/6}{1/6 + 1/6} = \frac{1}{2}$$

3.f.
$$\frac{1/6 \times 1/4}{(1/6 \times 1/4) + (5/6 \times 3/4)} = \frac{1/24}{1/24 + 15/24} = \frac{1}{16}$$

Pages 223–24

1.a. 0.05

b.
$$\frac{0.05 \times 0.80}{(0.05 \times 0.80) + (0.95 \times 0.20)} = \frac{0.04}{0.23} = 0.17$$

2.a. $(0.8 \times 0.5) + (0.2 \times 0.9) = 0.58$

b.
$$\frac{(0.8 \times 0.5)}{(0.8 \times 0.5) + (0.2 \times 0.9)} = \frac{0.4}{0.58} = 0.69$$

Chapter 8

Pages 236–37

1. Hypothetical Syllogism

3. Disjunctive Syllogism

Page 242

1.a. q • ~p

1.c. q → r

1.d. p • (r → q)

2.a. Logic is easy and symbols cannot be used.

2.c. Logic is not fun and symbols cannot be used.

4.b.

p	q	p → q	~q	p → ~q	~(p → q)
T	T	T	F	F	F
T	F	F	T	T	T
F	T	T	F	T	F
F	F	T	T	T	F

Not logically equivalent.

Pages 243–44

1. T   3. T   6. F

Pages 249–52

1.a.

p	q	~p	~q	~p v ~q	p • q
T	T	F	F	F	T
T	F	F	T	T	F
F	T	T	F	T	F
F	F	T	T	T	F

Valid.

1.g.

p	q	r	s	q→r	r→s	p→(q→r)	q→(r→s)	p→s
T	T	T	T	T	T	T	T	T
T	T	T	F	T	F	T	F	F
T	T	F	T	F	T	F	T	T
T	T	F	F	F	T	F	T	F
T	F	T	T	T	T	T	T	T
T	F	T	F	T	F	T	T	F
T	F	F	T	T	T	T	T	T
T	F	F	F	T	T	T	T	F
F	T	T	T	T	T	T	T	T
F	T	T	F	T	F	T	F	T
F	T	F	T	F	T	T	T	T
F	T	F	F	F	T	T	T	T
F	F	T	T	T	T	T	T	T
F	F	T	F	T	F	T	T	T
F	F	F	T	T	T	T	T	T
F	F	F	F	T	T	T	T	T

Not valid.

2.a.   p: The game has been sold out.
       q: The game has been cancelled.
       r: I won't be able to see the game.

$$p \vee q$$
$$\underline{(p \rightarrow r) \bullet (q \rightarrow r)}$$
$$r$$

3.   p: I let my brother remain unburied.
     q: I could not bear the pain.

$$q \rightarrow p$$
$$\underline{\sim p} \qquad \text{Valid instance of denying the consequent.}$$
$$\sim q$$

Pages 254–55

1. If the conclusion is a tautology, then it cannot be false. Thus, the argument cannot have all true premises and a false conclusion.

5.a. $((p \vee q) \bullet p) \rightarrow \sim q$

6.a.

p	q	$p \rightarrow q$	$q \rightarrow p$	$(p \rightarrow q) \rightarrow (q \rightarrow p)$
T	T	T	T	T
T	F	F	T	T
F	T	T	F	F
F	F	T	T	T

Contingent.

7.a.　p:　You can't win.
q:　You don't try.
$p \rightarrow q$ Contingent.

Page 262

1.a. $(p \bullet q) \vee (\sim p \bullet q) \vee (\sim p \bullet \sim q)$

2.a. $(p|q)|(p|q)$

4. An *exclusive or* switch.

Chapter 9

Pages 271–72

1.a. Some fiddlers are not bass fiddlers.

1.c. No politicians are statesmen.

2.a. It always rains in southern California.

2.c. He has a cat for a pet.

3.a. Peas are usually eaten with a knife.

3.b. Carrots are not orange.

3.c. Baseball is not less interesting than football.

Page 280

1. All persons who could love him are persons who are mothers. See Figure 9-5, p. 276.

6. Some apples are not red. See Figure 9-8, p. 280.

13. No times are times when it rains in southern California. See Figure 9-6, p. 278.

Pages 285–86

1.a. *S:* animals   *P:* things that are able to think   *M:* things that feel pain   See Figure 9-1a below. Valid.

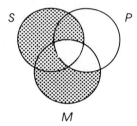

1.c. *S:* children   *P:* good persons   *M:* persons who are cruel to animals   See Figure 9-3a below. Valid.

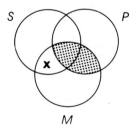

2.a. No conclusion   See Figure 9-11a below.

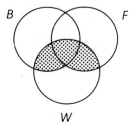

2.c. Some professors are not students.   See Figure 9-13a below.

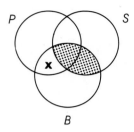

Page 288

1. Fallacy of composition.

Pages 293–94

1.a. All ostriches are birds.
      All ~~birds~~ ^{ostriches} are nonflyers.
      _____

      Some birds are nonflyers.

      Invalid. End term (birds) distributed exactly once.

1.c. Some generals are not warmongers.
      Some admirals are warmongers.
      _____

      No admirals are generals.

      Invalid. End terms distributed in conclusion, but not in premisses.

Pages 296–97

1. All sexists are persons who oppose equal rights for women.
    Some men are persons who oppose equal rights for women.
    _____

    Some men are not sexists.   ⟨don't⟩

    Invalid. (Undistributed middle term.)

3. All modern-style architecture is stark.
    Some new buildings are not stark.
    _____

    Some new buildings are not modern-style architecture.

    Valid.

Page 301

c. From (ii) and (iii), (iv) No hedgehogs are well educated. From (iv) and (i), No hedgehogs take in the *Times*.

f. From (i) and (iv), (v) All my birds are ostriches. From (v) and (iii), (vi) None of my birds live on mince pies. From (vi) and (ii), No birds in this aviary live on mince pies.

Pages 303–304

1.a. No potentially dangerous things are things that should be legalized.

1.c. All persons who do not wear overcoats are rich.

2.a. Some expensive things are made of inexpensive materials.

2.b. No conclusion.

3.a. Some valid arguments are arguments with false conclusions.
Some syllogisms are not valid arguments.
_____

Some syllogisms are not arguments with false conclusions.

Invalid.

3.c. All skillfully handcrafted items that are beautiful, enduring, and useful are expensive.
All Navajo rugs are skillfully handcrafted items that are beautiful, enduring, and useful.
_____

All Navajo rugs are expensive.

Valid.

Chapter 10

Page 308

1.a. Nontransitive, nonsymmetric, nonreflexive

1.c. Nontransitive, nonsymmetric, nonreflexive

Page 312

Interpretation: D: the class of dogs; F: the class of fleas; C: the class of cats, and so on.

1. $(\exists x)(Dx \bullet Fx)$

3. $(x)(Dx \to {\sim}Vx)$

Page 315

Domain of interpretation: everything
m: Mary j: John L: . . . loves _____

1. $\sim(x)(y)(z)((Rxy \bullet Ryz) \to Rxz) \bullet \sim(x)(y)(z)((Rxy \bullet Ryz) \to {\sim}Rxz))$

3. Ljj

9. $(x){\sim}Lmx$

Pages 316–17

1. $(x)(\exists y)Lxy$

5. $(\exists x)(y){\sim}Lyx$

Pages 321–22

1.a. "Can outrun" is transitive.

2. (1) weighs the same as

4.a. wife of

6. Domain of interpretation: everything

C: cat	B: . . . makes a better pet than _____
D: dog	W: . . . is smarter than _____
S: snake	F: . . . fears _____
M: mouse	A: . . . is brother of _____
G: goldfish	J: . . . owns _____
R: rich woman	H: . . . is cousin of _____
M: piano	E: . . . eats _____
P: person	a: Virginia
O: poor	c: Christopher

a. $(x)(y)((Cx \bullet Dy) \to Bxy)$

c. $(x)(Dx \to (\exists y)(Cy \bullet Fxy))$

10. Greater than or equal to

Chapter 11

Page 326

1. "Good," when applied to a skill such as dancing, refers to a level of technical expertise. When applied to a person, "good" refers to moral qualities.

5. Lord Caversham uses "idle" to mean "not doing any work." Lady Chiltern uses "idle" to mean "inactive."

Pages 336–37

1.a. Lexical

1.c. Theoretical.

1.e. Verbal extensional.

1.g. Precising.

2.b. Too broad and too narrow.

5. (Suggested answers—others may be equally good.)

5.a. "Fragile" connotes delicacy, fineness. "Weak" has a negative connotation of being not strong enough for some purpose.

5.d. Some people believe that "perspiration" is a more genteel term—"Horses sweat; people perspire."

Page 341

1. (Other correct answers are possible.)

1.a. When I taste this lemon, it puckers my mouth.

Appendix 1

Pages 348–49

1.a.

$$\cfrac{\cfrac{p \to q \vdash p \to (p \bullet q)}{p, p \to q \qquad \vdash p \bullet q}}{{}^{*}\,p, p \to q \vdash p \qquad \cfrac{p, p \to q \vdash q}{{}^{*}\,p \vdash p, q \;\;{}^{*}\,p, q \vdash q}}$$

Valid.

1.c.

$$\underline{p \rightarrow (q \rightarrow r) \vdash (p \rightarrow q) \rightarrow r}$$

$$\underline{p \rightarrow q, p \rightarrow (q \rightarrow r) \vdash r}$$

$$\underline{p \rightarrow (q \rightarrow r) \vdash p, r} \qquad\qquad q, p \rightarrow (q \rightarrow r) \vdash r$$

$$\vdash p, p, r \qquad q \rightarrow r \vdash p, r$$

There is need to continue the tree, since there is a branch that does not terminate in an axiom. Invalid.

3.

$$\underline{(p \rightarrow q) \bullet (q \rightarrow r) \bullet p \bullet \sim r \vdash}$$

$$p \rightarrow q, q \rightarrow r, p, \sim r \vdash$$

$$p \rightarrow q, q \rightarrow s r, p \vdash r$$

$$\underline{{}^* q \rightarrow r, p \vdash p, r} \qquad \underline{q, q \rightarrow r, p \vdash r}$$

$$\qquad\qquad\qquad {}^* q, p \vdash q, r \; {}^* q, r, p \vdash r$$

Self-contradiction.

Pages 352–53

1.a.

$$\underline{p \rightarrow q, \sim p \rightarrow r, \sim q \rightarrow r \vdash \sim q}$$

$$\underline{q, p \rightarrow q, \sim p \rightarrow r, \sim q \rightarrow r \vdash}$$

$$\underline{q, \sim p \rightarrow r, \sim q \rightarrow r \vdash p} \qquad\qquad q, q, \sim p \rightarrow r, \sim q \rightarrow r \vdash$$

$$\underline{q, \sim q \rightarrow r \vdash \sim p} \qquad q, r, {}^\backprime q \rightarrow r \vdash p$$

$$\underline{q \vdash \sim q, \sim p} \qquad q, r \vdash \sim p$$

$$\underline{q, q \vdash \sim p}$$

$$p, q, q \vdash$$

This branch does not terminate in an axiom. The last sentence form ($\sim q$) is not a consequence of the others.

2.a.

$$\underline{\vdash (p \rightarrow q) \vee (\sim p \rightarrow q)}$$

$$\underline{\vdash p \rightarrow q, \sim p \rightarrow q}$$

$$\underline{p \vdash q, \sim p \rightarrow q}$$

$$\underline{\sim p, p \vdash q, q}$$

$$p \vdash p, q, q$$

Tautology.

2.f. ⊢ ~(p → q) ↔ (p → ~q)

~(p → q) ⊢ p → ~q	p → 'q ⊢ ~(p → q)
p, ~(p → q) ⊢ ~q	p → q, p → ~q ⊢

p ⊢ p → q, ~q	p → ~q ⊢ p q, p → ~q ⊢
p, q ⊢ p → q	⊢ p, p ~q ⊢ p

*p, p, q ⊢ q

Not a tautology.

3.a. (Translation only)
p: The economy will improve.   q: The stock market will crash.   r: Banks will fail.

(p v q), (q → r), ~r ⊢ ~(p → r)

Index